Integrating Schools in a Changing Society

Integrating Schools in a Changing Society

New Policies and Legal Options for a Multiracial Generation

Edited by

ERICA FRANKENBERG

and

ELIZABETH DEBRAY

THE UNIVERSITY OF

NORTH CAROLINA PRESS

Chapel Hill

KH

This book was published with the assistance of the z. smith reynolds fund *of the University of North Carolina Press.*

Set in Minion and Meta types
by Tseng Information Systems, Inc.

The paper in this book meets the guidelines for permanence and durability of the Committee on Production Guidelines for Book Longevity of the Council on Library Resources.

The University of North Carolina Press has been a member of the Green Press Initiative since 2003.

Library of Congress Cataloging-in-Publication Data
Integrating schools in a changing society : new policies and legal options for a multiracial generation / [edited by] Erica Frankenberg, Elizabeth DeBray.
p. cm.
Includes bibliographical references and index.
ISBN 978-0-8078-3512-8 (hardback)
1. School integration — United States. 2. Discrimination in education — United States. 3. Multicultural education — United States. 4. Educational equalization — United States. 5. Education and state — United States. 6. Educational law and legislation — United States. I. Frankenberg, Erica. II. DeBray, Elizabeth.
LC214.2.I68 2011
370.1170973 — dc23   2011017790

15 14 13 12 11   5 4 3 2 1

2/28/12

In memory of Ashley Osment,

a tireless advocate for civil rights

and educational opportunity

Contents

Acknowledgments

The beginnings of this volume arose from a deeply enriching, collaborative planning process culminating in a conference in Chapel Hill, North Carolina, in April 2009. Although far too many helped with that conference for us to fully acknowledge everyone, we want to particularly recognize the sponsors and involved individuals: at the University of North Carolina Law School and Center for Civil Rights, Julius Chambers, Dean Jack Boger, Leah Aden, Adrienne Davis, Ashley Osment, Catherine Ringo Pearce, and Benita Jones; at the University of Georgia, Allen Cohen, interim director of the Georgia Education Policy and Evaluation Center, and Dean Andy Horne; and at the Civil Rights Project/Proyecto Derechos Civiles at the University of California at Los Angeles, Gary Orfield, Genevieve Siegel-Hawley, Laurie Russman, and Patricia Gándara. Conference proposal reviewers included Andrew Grant-Thomas, Jennifer Jellison Holme, Roslyn Mickelson, Gary Orfield, Charles Daye, and James Ryan. Funding for this event included contributions from the Open Society Initiative; the Ford Foundation; the Office of the Vice Chancellor for Research and Economic Development at UNC; the UNC School of Law; North Carolina Advocates for Justice; the University of Georgia College of Education; Brooks, Pierce, McLendon, Humphrey, and Leonard, LLP; Patterson Harkavy, LLP; and Epting and Hackney.

At UNC Press, Mark Simpson-Vos ably shepherded us through the review process. Leah Aden and Genevieve Siegel-Hawley were particularly helpful as we shaped this volume. We are appreciative of the comments from anonymous reviewers that strengthened the final volume. We also had the able technical support of Meca Mohammed, Wendy Dubner, and Kyra Young in preparing the manuscript. The audience and discussants at both the North Carolina conference and the Washington, D.C., briefing in 2009 were helpful in shaping some of these individual essays as well as the overall volume.

Elizabeth DeBray thanks her family for love and support, and particularly hopes for an integrated future for Bishop. She thanks both Eric Houck and Sheneka Williams for their colleagueship and encouragement during the project. Erica Frankenberg is fortunate to have the enthusiastic support and love of Mark Kissling. We both thank Gary Orfield for his mentorship over the past decade, at Harvard and beyond. You brought us together a decade ago as two young women from the South to study issues of resegregation in that region and continue to inspire and challenge us.

We have dedicated the book to Ashley Osment, who was our deeply inspirational friend and colleague. As the education attorney at the UNC Civil Rights Center, she was part of our initial team envisioning the 2009 conference, recruiting and commissioning papers, and helping with other aspects of the event. She embodied to all who knew her passion and commitment to equality of educational opportunity, and to human and civil rights.

ERICA FRANKENBERG & ELIZABETH DEBRAY

Introduction
Looking to the Future

Some social commentators and scholars have recently posited that policy makers' lack of attention to furthering integration—outside of a paean to *Brown v. Board of Education* on anniversaries of that milestone decision—demonstrates that desegregation's time has passed. Other writers, including distinguished legal scholar Derrick Bell, have argued that while school desegregation is a worthy goal, it has become politically unfeasible, particularly in light of demographic realities and legal rulings, the most recent being the U.S. Supreme Court's decision in *Parents Involved in Community Schools v. Seattle School District No. 1* (*PICS*, 2007) striking down two districts' voluntary integration policies.[1] Still others contend that the public wants good schools regardless of the racial composition of schools or classrooms.

We disagree. Though we are conscious of the political challenges facing integration, we do not believe that desegregation's time has necessarily passed. The goals of public schools, broadly to prepare children for their duties as citizens and contributors to our society and economy as adults and more specifically to improve the achievement and attainment of all students, we believe, are best achieved through the pursuit of integrated, equitable schools. While segregation continues to rise, as it has for the past two decades for black and Latino students, we know much more than we did before *Brown* about *why* segregation is harmful and *how* we might construct policies that promote integrated schools. Millions of students, teachers, and community members across the racial spectrum who experienced racial integration and emerged more supportive of integration efforts provide a human face to these facts. What's more, as Gary Orfield reminds us in the conclusion to this book, despite the political and legal civil rights setbacks, today's climate is much more receptive to contemporary legal and social science arguments than the environment of the first half of the 20th century. Though the obstacles to integration are significant, this moment in time has advantages unavailable to the *Brown* lawyers and their brave plaintiffs in the South decades ago. Further, unlike desegregation efforts of the 20th century that largely focused on the

1

South, issues of resegregation are not limited to the South—until recently, in fact, black students were *least* segregated in that region. Contemporary segregation is national, multiracial, and complex, and this collection of essays will reflect these new dimensions.

Why this moment, politically and legally, for a reexamination of the prospects of integration? After all, the Supreme Court's long march away from enforcing the principles of *Brown* and the impact of this judicial retreat on school districts, particularly those in the South, have been discussed elsewhere.[2] While Supreme Court decisions in the 1990s focused on the end of court-supervised desegregation plans, in part to return student assignment decisions to locally elected school boards, and some lower federal courts restricted the use of race in magnet school or other specialized school assignments, voluntarily adopted integration policies were unaffected by these decisions.

However, in *PICS*, the Court limited integration efforts that had been voluntarily implemented by Louisville and Seattle, finding that the districts' use of a student's race to determine whether school choices or transfers were granted violated the 14th Amendment of the U.S. Constitution. At the same time a majority of justices agreed with the districts' arguments that preventing racial isolation and creating diverse schools were compelling governmental issues. School districts, educators, advocates, and civil rights community tried to make sense of the contradictory messages: while the Court affirmed the goals of integration, it suddenly made unavailable one of the most popular tools to promote systemwide integration and left it unclear what *would* pass constitutional muster.

This collection explores the meaning of *PICS* and what is possible in its aftermath and in our current policy context. These questions are critically important to consider, since this country's demographic changes are particularly noticeable in its public schools, which soon will have a majority of students of color—a reality that already exists in the West and the South. This diversity is spreading throughout suburban districts that may have had little experience with heterogeneous enrollments. At the same time, the stakes for students and society are higher than ever, given the increased need for a high school diploma and beyond in today's economy. This book then more broadly aims to set an agenda for public schools for a multiracial generation of children who are entering and projected to enter our public schools in the coming decades.

In essence, the argument of these essays is that the basic lesson of *Brown* was (and is) correct, but that it is not being applied for many reasons, including recent court decisions. This book is a way to restart and reinvigorate the process of attaining an equitable and integrated multiracial society—building on what we have learned and applying it to our society's new, multidimensional racial and socioeconomic inequality. Schools in the early 20th century were viewed as the means of challenging racial segregation and inequality. We strongly believe that, at the beginning of the 21st century, schools remain a powerful tool for attaining individual opportunity and a thriving multiracial democratic society.

This book was designed to show what new evidence exists about integrated education and its relationship to equality of educational opportunity; what the political prospects are; what we know about new policy alternatives, including using socioeconomic status; and what the federal role could be in encouraging such options. As Gary Orfield writes later in this book, "We are a society in which legal strategies and powerful legal reasoning matter greatly. We need thinking with the boldness and intensity of that which brought down the apartheid system of the South." Yet this need for new legal and policy solutions has arrived at the same moment as severe economic retrenchment, which in many communities can be politically translated into rationales for enacting policies that move backward, not forward.

PICS is the latest of a long string of judicial decisions that first lessened what was required of school districts to comply with *Brown* and then limited what could be done voluntarily to pursue the ideals of the decision. Legally, what is now needed is nothing short of a new strategy like that of Charles Hamilton Houston, who devised the approach implemented by NAACP lawyers including Thurgood Marshall to challenge state-imposed segregation. Their legal effort, culminating in *Brown*, was novel in its use of social science to illustrate findings of fact that later led to legal conclusions overturning an entire way of life in southern schools. Today's effort will have to be multidisciplinary as well. As such, this book seeks to begin anew what has been called elsewhere "the ongoing nation-building task of implementing *Brown*'s goal of high-quality, integrated education."[3] Certainly PICS is a legal hurdle, but above all it is the most recent in a long series of political obstacles that confuse the issue of integration. This book focuses mainly on the policies (and politics) of integration since there has been a vacuum on this topic for decades.

In the immediate aftermath of PICS, some scholars argued that its impact might be limited, because relatively few districts had been utilizing voluntary integration plans.[4] Indeed, many of the barriers to contemporary integration existed well before PICS,[5] yet the decision did strike down one of the most commonly used voluntary integration methods, controlled choice. Moreover, just as "freedom of choice" plans used in the South during the 1960s as a means of compliance with *Brown* placed the entire burden of desegregation on black students choosing to attend what were often hostile, almost all-white institutions, if integration is to occur today, current jurisprudence and policy impose on school boards considerable legal and political risk if they seek to implement student assignment plans that are both effective and likely to withstand opaque, changing legal standards. Such efforts may require significant time to devise plans specific to the district's particular context and goals as well as to educate the public about the plan and the rationale for its adoption. As Erica Frankenberg's essay explains, Justice Anthony Kennedy's opinion clearly leaves legal latitude for a variety of governmental options to support desegregation. Our own recent research about the response to PICS suggests that while the ruling has been drawn on by a handful of federal judges—such as in the Tucson, Arizona, case—to justify a push for unitary status (that is, when a court determines that a district has eliminated the "dual" system of segregation and ends judicial oversight), some local communities, both those under court order and those not under court order, have pushed to preserve magnet schools and other means of creating diverse schools. In San Diego, magnet schools have been strengthened even amid the budget crisis. In Nashville, a school board plan to return to neighborhood schools, which research in other districts where residential segregation remains stubbornly high demonstrates often results in segregated schools, has been challenged in federal district court by parents alleging that their children are being relegated to inferior schools. Interdistrict transfer plans that seek to overcome the segregation between districts have also survived scrutiny, often because of long-standing local political capital.[6] Indeed, the political will to pursue diversity in a changing context is a recurring theme of these essays.

Part 1 of this book, "Where We Have Been and Where We Are Now," assesses the current moment in light of the past. John Boger's description of the decades of collaborative effort by lawyers, social scientists, and community members to pursue integration is a sobering reminder of how short-lived the victories of the civil rights movement can be, and how difficult educational reform can be to sustain. Describing the innovative *Sheff v. O'Neill* case and the developments ending the long-standing voluntary integration policy in Wake County, North Carolina, he notes the particular political and legal fragility of voluntary integration efforts. He nonetheless urges a renewed commitment, arguing that no other policy efforts at integration have successfully provided equitable education for all students. Janelle Scott's essay reminds us that policy is often marked by periods of action and inaction. The focus on "choice as a civil right" carries the cost of a declining focus on the importance of achieving integration. She ends on a hopeful note of describing how different public and private, urban and suburban actors can form coalitions to support choice as a means to further integration. In this changing legal and policy environment, Erica Frankenberg reviews what is known from earlier efforts at integration, and contemplates how such policies might fare in a post-*PICS* era. She also assesses the relative strengths of various approaches. Chinh Le traces the history of civil rights enforcement, noting particularly the politicization that occurred under the administration of George W. Bush in the Office of Civil Rights (OCR) and the Civil Rights Division of the Justice Department, and the subsequent damage to the civil rights agenda. While the OCR has put in place some important initiatives, including strategic action plans to address disparate impact, and has announced plans to initiate three dozen wide-ranging civil rights investigations of school districts, Le describes what more can be done to reverse the chilling effect of the communications that were sent to local districts by the prior administration about voluntary integration in the aftermath of *PICS*.

Insofar as the recent goal of federal education policy has been to narrow the achievement gap, we think it is worth contemplating that the largest ever narrowing of scores between whites and blacks on the National Assessment of Educational Progress (NAEP) took place in the mid-1970s through the early 1980s,[7] a period of not only continuously increasing federal investment in compensatory education but also the desegregation of many large southern school systems. While scholars cannot directly attribute the narrowing of NAEP test scores to court-ordered desegregation, it is evident that the narrowing occurred while hundreds of thousands of African American students in the South and elsewhere gained access to schools outside their neighborhoods via metropolitan desegregation.[8] Likewise, a National Academy of Education panel concluded in 2007 that decades of research support the conclusion that the achievement of black students is higher in desegregated settings.[9]

Part 2, "The Case for Integration," includes two essays about different ends of the K–12 education system—one on kindergarten and first-grade gains by Douglas Ready and Megan Silander, and one on interdistrict magnet middle and high schools by Robert Bifulco, Casey Cobb, and Courtney Bell. Both find academic gains for students whose education occurs in integrated settings. Ready and Silander describe how resource inequalities in and out of schools for our youngest schoolchildren widen gaps in academic achievement. Bifulco, Cobb, and Bell similarly conclude that interdistrict choice offerings in metropolitan Hartford give urban and suburban students alike both cross-racial learning opportunities and access to high-quality learning environments.

Taken together, these essays reinforce the enduring premise of *Brown*: that segregation remains inherently unequal for students attending heavily minority schools.

Despite the growing empirical evidence that integration can help districts accomplish improved student achievement, it is just as clear—as some of the judicial opinions in the PICS decision demonstrate—that this "case" has not yet been firmly made in larger discussions about education. Louisville, Kentucky, and Wake County, North Carolina, at present demonstrate the political vulnerability of even long-standing student assignment plans and remind us that making a case for more diverse schools is a political challenge that must be approached in the context of the history of desegregation in each community. Thus, this section includes essays that cause us to think about questions of local political will—the importance of continually communicating the strong evidence to make the case for pursuing integration. Amy Stuart Wells, Jacquelyn Duran, and Terrenda White describe the powerful experiences of graduates of integrated high schools and why they believe these experiences change them. Jennifer Jellison Holme, Sarah Diem, and Katherine Cumings Mansfield examine the development of a regional integration plan in Omaha, Nebraska, particularly the political challenges of defining integration as a shared interest beyond individual district lines.

Student assignment policies, of course, have been the technical work whose effectiveness and constitutionality Supreme Court decisions from *Green* to PICS have evaluated. Justice Kennedy's opinion in PICS left the door open to pursuing integration even as a majority of the justices struck down some of the most popular ways of achieving integration, leaving many district officials bewildered as to what was still permissible. In part 3, "Student Assignment: Policy Choices and Evidence," three essays contemplate the variety of types of plans utilizing socioeconomic status and the evidence of their effectiveness. These plans were touted as effective alternatives to policies using race by the Bush administration, among others, as the Supreme Court considered the Louisville and Seattle cases. Taken together, essays by Richard Kahlenberg, Sean Reardon and Lori Rhodes, and Genevieve Siegel-Hawley illustrate the complexity with which these plans have been implemented and their mixed record of success thus far. Although socioeconomic plans have gotten the most attention, part 3 also describes other assignment policies that districts have implemented. Sheneka Williams and Erica Frankenberg examine districts' use of "small-scale geography" to promote integration—an effort growing in popularity—while Claire Smrekar and Ellen Goldring describe contemporary uses of magnet schools and suggest how federal policy, including one of the longest-running federal programs to support integration, the Magnet Schools Assistance Program, could support these efforts. This section does not provide a one-size-fits-all approach to achieving integrated schools, but it does provide important new evidence about the various approaches local school districts are implementing.

The pursuit of school-level diversity has long been recognized as only one—albeit essential—part of the overall policy effort to provide high-quality, integrated education for students.[10] Part 4, "The Pursuit of School-Level Equity," examines strategies that help to pursue equity within schools. Eric Houck's piece discusses why resources matter in the post–unitary status era and shows that policymakers have choices about how and where to advocate for resources that will matter most to economically disadvantaged students. Where policymakers are unable to move students, for example, Houck suggests that district leaders should consider reallocating teachers to ensure equitable access to high-quality teachers for all students. Willis Hawley and Jacqueline Jordan Irvine outline what is needed to ensure that teachers within diverse schools are able to educate diverse groups of students, significant to consider given the persistently white nature of the teaching force and even many teacher-training institutions. Patricia Gándara's essay suggests how creating dual-language schools could provide enriching, equal-status integrated schooling experiences that would benefit students of all races. This suggestion is particularly important to consider due to the large percentage of Latino students in many regions of the country and their high levels of racial and linguistic segregation.

In both the earlier era of mandatory desegregation and today as integration efforts are more voluntary, we have often expected schools to be the agent of social change in our society. And while school integration has been among the most successful educational reforms in terms of equalizing access to opportunity and improving the life chances for poor and minority students as well as helping to improve racial attitudes and interracial comfort by creating opportunities for students of all racial backgrounds to get to know one another, schools cannot sustain integration without addressing inequality and segregation in other parts of society. Indeed, a hope of school desegregation efforts was that, as Justice Sandra Day O'Connor noted wistfully in *Grutter* about higher education's affirmative action policies, they would eventually not be needed if a residentially integrated, equitable society existed. Part 5, "Integrated Means toward Integrated Ends: Broadening Social Policies," brings a renewed focus on attempts at school integration as part of a larger, coordinated effort. Elizabeth DeBray and Erica Frankenberg, drawing on research about the *Gautreaux* and Moving to Opportunity programs, consider how federal legislation supporting a pilot program for housing and educational opportunity in metropolitan areas might be designed, even with a modest redirection of existing Section 8 housing voucher program. Myron Orfield reviews the history of cases supporting housing integration and urges a renewed focus on legal strategies.

In the conclusion, Gary Orfield reviews the failed policy alternatives to desegregation and argues that the current policy focus is making "bad conditions even worse" by punishing schools for the outcomes related to segregation. Hopefully, however, he suggests how the research in this book begins to move our discussion forward so that we can articulate the potential policy options and the vitally important reasons for pursuing them. He also describes roles that a variety of actors could play in developing a new social movement to expand opportunity for our diversifying public school enrollment.

The Political Prospects for Change

We believe that with all the hopes placed in the Obama administration, Congress is too often overlooked as a vehicle to support promising programs. In an environment of limited federal budgets, the incremental approach — instituting pilot programs (as was the case with Moving to Opportunity), planning good evaluations, and studying the results — is the most viable. Many of the novel efforts described in this collection of essays might be good candidates for wider piloting and evaluation. Congress has already taken one such small step by authorizing a small program to support local communities' efforts to maintain school diversity. At the encouragement of the NAACP Legal Defense and Education Fund and the Council of Great City Schools, the Technical Assistance for Student Assignment Plans (TASAP) competitive grant program was passed in 2009 to support voluntary integration initiatives in 10 districts.[11] Congress can also pass measures that would heighten civil rights enforcement. Chinh Le suggests, for instance, that the current administration revive debate on the provisions of the now lapsed Civil Rights Act of 2008, which aimed to undo the ban on private enforcement of disparate impact discrimination set by the Supreme Court in its 2001 *Sandoval* decision. Gary Orfield also notes that Congress could revive its assistance program to help schools better prepare for the changing demography, as it did during the 1970s.

The Obama administration has offered small grants to nearly a dozen school districts to provide technical assistance for designing legally viable integration policies, but such efforts could be greatly expanded and are dwarfed by other federal education initiatives. Further, federal incentives supporting the growth of charter schools persist despite evidence showing high levels of segregation in the charter school sector and questions about access for low-income and English Language Learner students.

There has been much discussion, during the 2008 presidential campaign and beyond, about the potential for a more aggressive equity agenda and progress in civil rights enforcement. This book points out that while the White House can certainly create a window for leadership and new policies, numerous institutions must continuously tackle a problem of the magnitude of resegregation. In 2009, a coalition of civil rights groups joined together to create the National Coalition on School Diversity, which hosted a conference to demonstrate support for desegregation as part of federal education policy and has released a series of issue briefs suggesting how federal policies (e.g., the Elementary and Secondary Education Act) and funding (e.g., charter schools, Race to the Top, 13 grants) could be modified to be more supportive of creating and sustaining racially diverse schools.[12] This coalition seeks to overcome the anemic support of desegregation efforts that has reigned even when Democrats control the White House and both houses of Congress. One early effort to summarize the benefits of magnet schools may have already borne fruit in March 2010, when a proposal to increase MSAP funding was made for the first time in years. This increase was coupled with new eligibility requirements for grants that gave more weight to districts that sought to eliminate racial isolation through magnet schools. The efforts of the National Coalition on School Diversity are parallel to those of civil rights and community groups in districts like Wake County or Boston that will not quietly allow districts to end their commitment to racial equity and integration.

NOTES

1. See, for example, Derrick Bell, "Opinion: School Diversity Another Way," *Chronicle of Higher Education*, 2 July 2007.

2. See Gary Orfield and Susan Eaton, eds., *Dismantling Desegregation* (New York: New Press, 1996); John C. Boger and Gary Orfield, eds., *School Resegregation: Must the South Turn Back?* (Chapel Hill: University of North Carolina Press, 2005).

3. Erica Frankenberg, Leah Aden, and Charles Daye, "The Future Is Now: Legal and Policy Options for Racially Integrated Education," *North Carolina Law Review* 88, no. 3 (2010): 713–24; quotation on 714.

4. James Ryan, "The Supreme Court and Voluntary Integration," *Harvard Law Review* 121 (2007): 131–57.

5. Erica Frankenberg and Chinh Le, "The Post-*Seattle/Louisville* Challenge: Extra-legal Obstacles to Integration," *Ohio State Law Journal* 69, no. 5 (2009): 1015–72.

6. Elizabeth DeBray, Erica Frankenberg, and Kathryn McDermott, "How Does *Parents Involved in Community Schools* Matter? Developing a Typology of Response," paper presented at American Educational Research Association Annual Meeting, Denver, April 2010.

7. Christopher Jencks and Meredith Phillips, eds., *The Black-White Test Score Gap* (Washington, DC: Brookings Institution Press, 1998); Jaekyung Lee, "Can Reducing School Segregation Close the Achievement Gap?," in *Lessons in Integration: Realizing the Promise of Racially Integrated Schools*, edited by Erica Frankenberg and Gary Orfield (Charlottesville: University of Virginia Press, 2007).

8. In 1990, more than 1 million students attended schools in 11 districts with metropolitan desegregation, many of which had such plans in place for at least two decades. See Gary Orfield, "Metropolitan School Desegregation," in *In Pursuit of a Dream Deferred: Linking Housing and Education Policy*, edited by john a. powell, Gavin Kearney, and Vina Kay (New York: Peter Lang, 2001), 121–57.

9. Robert Linn and Kevin Welner, eds., *Race-Conscious Policies for Assigning Students to Schools: Social Science Research and the Supreme Court Cases* (Washington, DC: National Academy of Education, 2007).

10. Willis Hawley et al., *Strategies for Effective School Desegregation* (Lexington, MA: Lexington, 1983); Erica Frankenberg and Gary Orfield, eds., *Lessons in Integration: Realizing the Promise of Racial Diversity in Our Nation's Public Schools* (Charlottesville: University of Virginia Press, 2007).

11. DeBray, Frankenberg, and McDermott, "How Does *Parents Involved in Community Schools* Matter?"

12. For more information, see Poverty and Race Research Action Council, "National Coalition on School Diversity: Reaffirming the Role of School Integration in K–12 Education Policy," http://prrac.org/full_text.php?text_id=1225&item_id=11691&newsletter_id=0&header=Current%20Projects.

PART I

Where Have We Been and

Where Are We Now?

Standing at a Crossroads
The Future of Integrated Public Schooling in America

Thirty-five years ago, Justice Thurgood Marshall wrote a profound dissenting opinion in the Detroit school desegregation case, *Milliken v. Bradley*, cautioning that "in the short run, it may seem to be the easier course to allow our great metropolitan areas to be divided up each into two cities—one white, the other black—but it is a course, I predict, our people will ultimately regret."[1]

Justice Marshall's perceptive and moving words brought to the American people his gravest of warnings—that the metropolitan regions of the Northeast and North Central states would one day regret turning back on the educational promises of *Brown v. Board of Education*[2] and decades of racial progress. Today we stand at an important crossroads: whether the nation will drift perilously toward the educational dystopia against which Marshall cautioned or follow a path that moves us closer to full educational equality and integration.

For more than 55 years, the United States has taken great pride in the racial progress achieved through the *Brown* decision, especially in the South. Yet the Court's 1954 decision has recently become more significant as history than as present-day reality for many of America's public school children. In this post-*Brown* era, millions of American children in all regions are again attending schools that are overwhelmingly one-race. Moreover, the cause of integration is no longer aided by the legal and political sanctions that brought down the walls of de jure segregation. The lawyers and advocates who courageously and successfully litigated *Brown* and its progeny asserted a broad reading of the original purposes of the 14th Amendment's equal protection clause as the basis for their challenge to the cramped separate-but-equal doctrine of *Plessy*,[3] and their efforts were eventually supported—and indeed required—by the legislative and executive branches.

Yet now in 2011, the full realization of *Brown* seems increasingly beyond our nation's collective grasp. Supreme Court jurisprudence has grown increasingly hostile toward efforts to assure integrated public schooling, which is decried by some as "social engineering." All race-conscious policies find themselves under a judicial cloud, whether they constitute bad faith maintenance of racial segregation or good faith efforts to bring children together across racial lines. School districts that operated blatantly separate and unequal black and white schools only two generations ago now find they can be released from any duty to foster desegregation so long as they pledge a "good faith" attempt to eliminate vestiges of this dual system and prove that "the vestiges of past discrimination have been eliminated to the extent practicable,"[4] even if the practical outcomes of their new "race neutral" student assignment policies veer sharply, in actual fact, toward resegregation. Moreover, litigants who might want to pursue constitutional legal challenges to these resegregating public schools are put to the stringent *Washington v. Davis*[5] test, which has required, since 1976, proof of official *motive* to discriminate, not mere adverse *impact* on minorities. This difficult constitutional standard, taken together with the Court's 2001 *Alexander v. Sandoval*[6] decision (which read this "intent" requirement into the Civil Rights Act of 1964), has together rendered it nearly impossible for nonwhite plaintiffs to prevail when they object in today's federal courts to the new generation of resegregative student assignment policies. Indeed, in 2007, a plurality of justices, led by Chief Justice John Roberts, shied away from acknowledging that achieving racial diversity might ever be a "compelling interest" for K–12 public schooling.[7]

Ironically, even as federal courts diminish their commitment to the preservation of racial integration, mounting social science evidence has deepened our understanding of the many ways decades of integration have actually improved the nation's public schools and communities, and the lives of the children in them. The power of such research has prompted numerous school systems around the country to embrace voluntary integration efforts to improve the overall quality of schools for their students — efforts like those implemented in Wake County, North Carolina; Berkeley, California; and Jefferson County, Kentucky, and other policy options to be discussed more fully in the essays of this book. Yet these voluntary efforts are extremely fragile politically and legally, and they remind us just how difficult it is in the present climate to maintain support for integration and meaningful educational reform.

Developing a New Legal Theory for Educational Reform
The Case of *Sheff v. O'Neill*

The plight of Hartford, Connecticut, in the mid-1980s speaks volumes about the prospect, and the limits, of educational reform in our time.

It was in the mid-1980s, under the indefatigable leadership of Director-Counsel Julius Chambers, that the NAACP Legal Defense Fund (LDF) sought to open a new legal front to address the unmet educational needs of families whom we then called "the minority poor." I was fortunate to be working with Chambers and the LDF at the time, and we looked to Connecticut for a number of reasons: it was among the very richest states in the country, yet with some of the nation's poorest cities. Those cities—New Haven, Hartford, Bridgeport, and Waterbury—were once home to some of the nation's leading industries—and still housed some of the nation's finest institutions of higher education. Yet by the 1980s, the public schools of these Connecticut cities were "mis-educating" tens of thousands of students who were overwhelmingly poor and black or Latino.

Despite its challenges, Connecticut offered some remarkably positive prospects. Its legislature had enacted educational statutes, under the leadership of a young chief education officer, Gerald Tirozzi, that had created "Connecticut Mastery Tests" (CMTS)—among the nation's first statewide achievement tests—to measure the performance of all Connecticut students in key subjects.[8] Nearly 17 years before No Child Left Behind, these new state tests appeared to offer reliable data on sharp racial and socioeconomic differences in student performance—data, LDF attorneys hoped, that would allow them to demand educational equity in all of Connecticut's public schools.

A legal coalition subsequently developed around this cause, about which Susan Eaton has since written so well,[9] proved unusually broad. Lawyers from the national American Civil Liberties Union (ACLU), the Puerto Rican Legal Defense Fund, and the NAACP Legal Defense Fund worked with leading civil rights groups in Connecticut, with added support from a prominent Hartford private attorney and a leading Connecticut law professor; they all were rallied by a strong, openhearted, and triracial coalition of parents.[10]

Beyond its early adoption of statewide testing, the state of Connecticut was doing something that very few states had ever done or have done since. It was driving dollars to school districts based not only on the number of children present in their schools but also on the number of students whose educational performances were low or whose families were in poverty.[11] Thus for every state dollar sent to a suburban school where a middle-class child was doing well, Connecticut sent 50 percent more toward schools that were educating low-performing, lower-income children.[12] In addition, the Connecticut legislature had adopted many special grant programs—remedial assistance, dropout prevention, health services—that strongly favored either low-wealth districts or districts with poorer and low-achieving students, or both.[13] Under these combined state aid programs, the Hartford school district regularly received nearly three times as much state funding, per pupil, as did suburban districts.[14]

Only one problem remained: none of this was improving the educational performance of lower-income and nonwhite children in Connecticut's largest urban districts.[15]

As in most states throughout the Northeast and North Central regions, school districts throughout Connecticut were geographically very small. The Hartford metropolitan area alone claimed 22 separate school districts, most of them only a few minutes apart by bus or car.[16] Yet demographic differences among the 22 districts were sharp: the Hartford district was 92 percent black and Latino in student population by the late 1980s,[17] and 63 percent of its students were on free and reduced-price lunches.[18] In contrast, nearby districts such as Avon, Simsbury, and West Hartford were 96 percent white,[19] with 5 percent or fewer students on free and reduced-price lunches.[20] These demographic differences, in turn, mirrored dramatic gaps in students' test scores between city and suburban districts. In suburban Avon and Simsbury, 9 percent of fourth-grade students were performing below remedial standards in mathematics; in Hartford, eight times as many students—70 percent—performed below minimal adequacy.[21]

The coalition's immediate impulse was to pull out its traditional legal "big guns": to assert claims based on the equal protection clause or Title VI in federal court.[22] Yet the traditional constitutional and statutory tools of the previous era were of no use.[23] In 1974, the Supreme Court had decreed in *Milliken v. Bradley* (the very case in which Marshall had issued his sharp warning) that federal courts lacked authority to order students bused across school district lines to achieve racial desegregation unless those lines had been drawn or maintained for racially discriminatory purposes.[24] *Milliken* effectively foreclosed a federal challenge in Connecticut: in the Hartford area, for example, most town lines were 200 years old, drawn long before the state began to offer public schooling to anyone.[25] Though radically different educational circumstances characterized poor, central-city Hartford from its wealthy suburban neighbors, legally cognizable, intentional racial discrimination was hard to find; even vast difference in educational performance did not suffice to demonstrate the malign racial intent required by the Court's *Milliken* and *Washington v. Davis* standards.[26]

The coalition thought briefly of turning to school finance litigation—that remarkably fertile, alternative source of so much educational change in the 1980s and 1990s.[27] The catch in Connecticut, however, was that the Connecticut Supreme Court had already ordered substantial school finance relief in 1977, and the state legislature, as noted above, had subsequently provided very real, substantial financial preferences for lower-income districts.[28] The only deficiency: none of these extra funds led to real educational progress.

Moreover, this was not a classic 1960s Mississippi situation of ruthless white domination; a Puerto Rican superintendent presided over Hartford public schools.[29] He and other dedicated black and Latino teachers and administrators had access to extraordinary sources of assistance.[30] In short, Connecticut's educational programs represent the legislative future toward which many other states and school districts still strive today. Yet the financially massive and politically difficult educational reforms that Connecticut had embraced so completely had not succeeded in improving student performance in its crowded, low-performing city schools; instead, Hartford and other overwhelmingly poor and minority urban school systems in Connecticut still faced massive educational failure.[31]

In what became central to the *Sheff v. O'Neill* litigation, the Connecticut coalition drew on sociologist James Coleman's finding from the 1966 congressionally mandated report: the educational performance of students appeared to depend, not alone on the wealth or poverty of a student's parents, but on the socioeconomic mix of his or her fellow students.[32]

This then novel "school composition" claim supported the very constitutional provisions that Connecticut had interpreted to require fair *funding* to all school districts. Coalition advocates argued that these exact provisions should also be read to guarantee fair *student assignment policies* to all, since the evidence was reliably mounting that to concentrate poor students in high-poverty schools would cause irreparable educational injury to them and their peers.[33] In other words, since the opportunity to learn among students from diverse socioeconomic backgrounds was likely a more important state enabler of student achievement than dollars alone, state policies that consciously maldistributed these crucial public resources should not be constitutionally tolerated. The coalition argued, in effect, that ending high-poverty schooling was a state constitutional imperative.

At the time of the *Sheff* litigation, it seemed that any broader reliance on this campaign would largely be limited to Northeastern and North Central states. Decades of school desegregation under *Brown*, *Green*,[34] *Swann*,[35] and cases that followed appeared to have moved most southern school districts far beyond the objectives of *Sheff*. Thanks to nearly twenty years of racial desegregation ordered by federal courts and implemented by courageous local school officials, racial and socioeconomically integrated public education had become a reality for a new generation of southern children. These educational changes, I remember thinking, would spare most southern children, black and white, the dismal educational fate that seemed all but inevitable for the poor and nonwhite children of Hartford and many other urban, Northern districts—should the *Sheff* litigation fail.[36]

A Major Ideological Shift
Greater Freedom, Less Governmental Interference

My expectations were terribly naïve. The federal courts, from the Supreme Court to local district courts, were, in time, to witness, and certainly now have undergone, massive ideological changes. In a triumvirate of Rehnquist cases decided in the early 1990s,[37] Chief Justice William Rehnquist, joined by Justices Antonin Scalia, Clarence Thomas, and Anthony Kennedy sent unmistakable signals that the era of federal judicial oversight of school desegregation efforts should rapidly draw to a close. "Out with *Brown* and *Green* and federal judicial supervision," they decreed in effect; "in with local school board prerogative, and local control."[38] And at almost the same time, the whole underlying national ideological landscape was beginning to change.[39] Somehow, school choice, by parents and their children, began to be seen as a civil right.[40]

Why such a radical shift in such a relatively short time? I have previously suggested, in a 2005 article in the book *School Resegregation: Must the South Turn Back?*, coedited with Gary Orfield, that American ideals fluctuate between two core values—equality and liberty.[41] *Brown* heralded a political era that focused on equality in American life, as a unanimous Supreme Court insisted that all children should receive equal educational opportunity. This concern for equality subsequently energized much of public life during the two decades that followed, not only among those supporting civil rights for black and brown citizens but also among those concerned with women's rights, disability rights, gay rights, and related campaigns, which won wide and deep popular support. Yet during the Reagan era, the American public was invited to, and did, shift its principal concern away from equality toward the "liberty" end of the spectrum, embracing the values of individual autonomy, free markets, deregulation, and a deep skepticism of governmental authority and intervention.

This growing new public emphasis colored not only economic preferences but nearly every aspect of political and social life. Presidents promised to appoint Supreme Court nominees who would be "strict constructionists" favoring local and state autonomy over federal authority. The Court itself became more responsive to and sympathetic of arguments grounded in individual liberty and highly suspicious of group categorization. If school integration had been, in effect, a project largely grounded in the nation's concern for equality — for other-regarding, socially responsive citizenship — the public opinion shift toward liberty led to a demand for school choice, charter schooling, and individual options — of the right to make educational choices for oneself, individually, or for one's children, without principal concern for social consequences or the impact on others. To this extent, many courts have gravitated, along with the larger public, toward a reduced federal role and legislatively chosen policies, rather than judicially enforced ones.[42] In reconsidering student assignment, parents began to declare that there was, or should be, an inherent right for families to decide where their own children would attend school, without regard for broader school board objectives or the cumulative impact of their individual choices. These claims have received favorable hearings from many courts and local school boards. Despite the knowledge of the benefits of desegregated schools — of the fruits of equality — in legislative chambers and courtrooms around the country, the demand for choice — liberty — has widely prevailed.

Our increasingly flexible global economy, moreover, implicitly strengthened this popular preference for liberty over equality. Despite globalism's potential to illuminate commonalities and interdependence, our increasing freedom to "get things when we want them," to "have it our way," to "participate in the retail market 24 hours a day," has led to a growing popular impatience with services of any kind that do not immediately meet our individual demands. Americans have allowed consumerist attitudes to creep ever deeper into aspects of life that have long been considered socially shared responsibilities, such as preparing the nation's most precious resources — its public school students. The Court's recent jurisprudence has come to reflect this ideology.

Even by liberty standards, however, the Roberts Court's plurality reading of *Brown* and the equal protection clause in the 2007 Louisville and Seattle cases seems stunningly perverse in its transformation, not only of Chief Justice Earl Warren's call in *Brown* for educational equality, but of Chief Justice Rehnquist's 1995 call to curb *Brown* in the name of local school board control, free of federal judicial intervention. A Supreme Court that in 1954 judicially ordered public schools to desegregate, and that in 1995 urged the withdrawal of further judicial oversight — elevating local school board choice as a paramount virtue, almost a constitutional necessity—found not a trace of irony in 2007 in forbidding local school boards to honor *Brown* by choosing voluntarily to bring children together across racial lines, to learn from each other.

The Supreme Court jurisprudence of *Brown* now hangs by a thread, with Justice Anthony Kennedy's enigmatic concurring opinion in the Seattle and Louisville cases the only remaining judicial impediment to a wholesale revocation of race-conscious student assignment. This seems clearly the consequence of a generation of relentless refashioning of equal protection doctrine by judges and advocates who have been constitutionally suspicious of any race-conscious governmental policies and indifferent to the reemergence of racial resegregation in schools.

Yet history rarely proceeds in an unbroken path, and today offers the prospect, in the wake of the nation's election in 2008 of its first African American president, that the course of the equal protection doctrine, and of public school policy, might once again see change. Some believe that the president's nominations to the Supreme Court of Justice Sonia Sotomayor, its first nonwhite female, a woman herself reared in poverty with a history of concern for social justice issues, and Justice Elena Kagan, a woman reared on the Upper West Side of New York City by a progressive family, might together reset the tone of the High Court in future days and years. President Obama might very well have additional opportunities to name judges to the nation's lower federal courts, but in the meantime the 5-4 split on the Supreme Court remains, and any possible change will have to come from the majority wing of the High Court. Some hoped that under Attorney General Eric Holder the nation could remake and rebuild a tattered Civil Rights Division that under the former administration had taken a 180-degree turn away from its historic roots, but no decisive transformation on issues of racial justice has emerged by 2011. In sum, while President Obama's future administrative and judicial choices, if made carefully and deliberately, might one day reestablish a basis for the pursuit of integrated public schools in America, that future is uncertain.

Yet in the meantime, at first gradually, then with increasing speed, the conservative tide of Rehnquist, Roberts, Scalia, and Thomas jurisprudence has come to predominate in local educational settings, and the educational fabric woven in *Swann* and *Green* has begun to unravel in many of the South's public schools. Racially identifiable public schooling, so long a feature of Northeastern and Midwestern states, has returned to much of the South, even as the wealth gap between whites and nonwhites has continued to widen, bringing a return of both racially segregated and high-poverty public schools, especially in the South's growing metro areas.[43] This is especially troubling, since after the 1970s the South stood proudly for a generation as an example to the rest of the country of the rich educational fruits of *Brown*, *Swann*, and *Green*.[44]

Alternatives to Race-Based Policies
The Case of Wake County, North Carolina

Some southern school districts, like that of Wake County, North Carolina, as noted at the outset, managed to avoid the growing federal disapproval of race-based student assignments in the 1990s. As student assignments on racial grounds began to face greater federal judicial scrutiny, some districts began to experiment with alternative ways to achieve heterogeneous public school classrooms. Rather than continuing to employ racial criteria and face possible "strict judicial scrutiny" of their actions, these school boards drew on the educational insights of Coleman, Christopher Jencks, and other researchers by assigning children to schools with an eye to their overall socioeconomic composition—to wit, family wealth or poverty (measured by the National School Lunch Program)[45]—and/or to relative student performance (measured by the percentage of students scoring at or above grade level in a given school). Wake County's strategy, for example, promised that all children throughout the district would be assigned to public schools that were relatively heterogeneous— none with more than 40 percent lower-income students and none with more than 25 percent low-performing students.[46] These student assignment plans had the legal virtue of being racially neutral, hence avoiding judicial challenge, while having the indirect effect of racially diversifying the schools since, as Richard Kahlenberg points out in his essay in this book, nonwhites on average remain more likely to be lower-income than do whites, and thus poverty and race are intricately connected.[47]

Now, however, after a decade of observing the largely positive educational consequences of the vast Wake County plan, the nation will see what transpires when this district's assignment policies are turned on their proverbial heads, not by judicial authority, but by political fiat. Voters in the November 2009 school board elections in Wake elected four new local school board members, and a majority now opposes the district's present student assignment plan and diversity policy goals. These electoral developments, in a large (139,000+ students) metropolitan school district that has seen continuing strong educational performance over the past decade, demonstrate just how politically fragile and unstable are racial or socioeconomic diversity policies that depend on continued popular support for their survival.

Why this electoral backlash? First, the new school board members employed powerful rhetoric to promote their cause during the fall 2009 electoral campaign. The values of diversity, socioeconomic balance, and student assignment became synonymous with busing, social engineering, and perpetual instability. Secondly, the candidates argued that Wake County's reassignment of thousands of students annually was almost exclusively the product of its commitment to diversity objectives. Although such shifting of students' schools (and a recent resort to mandatory year-round schooling) in fact grew principally from the school board's need to find space to house 5,000 to 7,000 new students who were arriving each year during the 2001–9 period, the school board challengers mobilized widespread parental exasperation with these annual dislocations necessitated by growth and scarce schoolroom space. In sum, many Wake parents were led to conclude that Wake's current student assignment policies were interfering too greatly with family autonomy in the name of abstract policy ends.

Moreover, many new citizens who were arriving in Wake County had no firsthand experience of the bitter, multidecade struggle for racial desegregation that had eventually led so many native North Carolinians of all races to craft, support, and deeply believe in the district's diversity policies. The new in-migrants rarely appreciated either the history behind, or the relative benefits that had flowed from, the Wake County approach, nor had they shared a full sense of the near-tragic experience of those southern districts that resisted these crucial goals. Finally, it would be a mistake not to add that well-organized, well-funded, and unapologetically partisan political forces were at work to unseat incumbents and place a majority of politically aligned, anti–diversity policy members on the school board.

Whatever the full explanation, after nearly a decade of voluntary socioeconomic integration, the newly elected Wake school board majority has already acted to end the district's most distinctive public policy.[48] A coalition of advocates has now emerged to protest these changes, and eyes across the nation are focused on Wake. This new pro-integration coalition has been animated by deep concern that Wake public schools will no longer benefit from the educational and social gains that came during a decade under the district's present student assignment scheme.

Other school districts, like Charlotte-Mecklenburg, North Carolina, opted much earlier in the first decade of the 21st century to pursue an about-face from their racially integrated pasts. Charlotte, which had become a national flagship for school desegregation in the three decades following the *Swann* decision in 1971, saw an end to federal judicial oversight of its schools in 2000. It swiftly moved to adopt a new "home school guarantee" plan that allowed parents to choose neighborhood schools for their children, despite the anticipated consequence that high-poverty, racially identifiable schools would quickly reemerge.[49]

The leaders of this new student assignment approach assured both themselves and all who raised doubts about their chosen course that additional funding would be supplied to the unfortunate children remitted to high-poverty schools.[50] "Have no fear," these educational advocates contended; "additional dollars driven to these schools will assure all students a 'sound basic education' in compliance with the state's long-running *Leandro* litigation."[51] Most Charlotte school leaders have since tried, in apparent good faith, to replicate the Hartford model, without full appreciation of how that story ended. Although some test scores in some of the most racially isolated Charlotte schools have since responded to infusions of new dollars and human resources, many Charlotteans, especially nonwhites, lament the continuing stark educational deficiencies in Charlotte's high-poverty and overwhelmingly black and Latino, central city schools, despite these additional resources.

Moreover, the delivery of new resources in Charlotte, even insofar as it has yielded temporary (though insufficient) educational gains, seems based on a precarious and unenforceable political promise. To continue to drive precious educational resources, on a two-to-one, or three-to-one basis, toward the neediest schools and children, may in fact be educationally indispensable—the quid pro quo in the devil's bargain accepting the reemergence of one-race and high-poverty education. Yet it is almost certainly politically unsustainable. However plausible in principle, it is unthinkable that popularly elected local officials will continue, in good times and bad, to direct a disproportionate fraction of their state and local dollars, as well as their most talented teachers and principals, to schools attended by the poorest and least politically well-connected children in Charlotte, rather than to schools attended by children from white and middle-income families who constitute their most politically powerful constituents. It is even more unlikely that federal or state courts would order such perpetually asymmetric funding as a constitutional necessity.

The subsequent history in *Sheff* indeed offers little consolation that a modified school finance theory will command necessary support from state courts. Although *Sheff* plaintiffs eventually prevailed in the Connecticut Supreme Court, it was on another, idiosyncratic state constitutional provision, and relief in Hartford schools since that 1996 decision has been long on promises but lamentably short on real change. North Carolina's principal school-finance case, *Leandro v. State of North Carolina*, has followed a similar course. In its unanimous decision in *Leandro* in 1997 and a subsequent 2004 North Carolina decision on the first phase of an implementation plan, the North Carolina Supreme Court made deep and moving promises doctrinally at the "liability" phase. Yet there have since been only modest changes in implementation of state school-equity policy, and virtually no traction to interject race directly into the school-finance debate. In 2005, the University of North Carolina Center for Civil Rights moved to intervene in the *Leandro* case, arguing that Charlotte's deliberate maintenance of high-poverty, racially isolated schools denied those students the constitutional right to a "sound basic education." The lower court, exercising its procedural discretion, refused to entertain this challenge, perhaps aware that requiring unwelcome changes in local student assignment policies—however clear the evidence that these policies were likely impairing the educational opportunities of lower-income and nonwhite children—was highly unlikely to be sustained on appeal. Although the *Sheff* and *Leandro* models have not yet led to substantial remedial changes, they remain conceptually available as legal bases for identifying violations of state education clauses where public schools are segregated by socioeconomic status. A new judicial era might one day view these theories as levers for meaningful change.

In the meanwhile, however, many voices continue to argue, in clear good faith, that all students everywhere can learn in any educational setting, irrespective of the social circumstances of their fellow students, if only their teachers and principals are provided the necessary resources and support systems. Indeed, the Obama administration seems to have embraced the notion that one-race schools in high-poverty settings do not necessarily doom students to failure. This view has the advantage of turning necessity into virtue: in many of the nation's largest metropolitan centers, especially outside the South, the populations of urban school districts are overwhelmingly nonwhite and poor. There is no meaningful judicial or local school board option in these districts to shift students to socioeconomically diverse schools, which lack white and/ or middle-income families, especially since, in *Milliken*, the Supreme Court foreclosed the legal option to order integration of central city students with those in outlying, wealthier suburban areas.

Yet while the Obama administration and other proponents of the Race to the Top program[52] can point to isolated examples of schoolwide successes in teaching students in high-poverty, racially isolated school settings, this is not a sustainable educational strategy. I know of no evidence anywhere, in any state, of a successful program of public elementary or secondary remediation in such schools, or of charter schooling—even if well funded—that has been brought to scale and has continued to provide a "minimally adequate" education to most children, much less offered "excellent" public education to large percentages of poor children assigned to the same schools throughout a district. There are occasional triumphs over the odds—achieved by an especially inspired teacher, or a gifted principal, or a brilliant superintendent, for short periods of time—educational flashes of achievement that, over and over and over again, have faded and been lost. Yet the absence of large-scale or continuing success anywhere in the United States, even in times of national and regional prosperity, should serve as the soberest caution and the gravest future warning about the viability of warehousing this generation's poorest nonwhite students in public schools far from the nation's more prosperous and well-favored children.

As communities like Wake County face the real and immediate prospect of a rapid return to resegregation, as public school integration itself remains a perilously contested notion nationwide, indeed, as federal courts ponder whether school board officials should be forbidden deliberately to build the very racially integrated school systems celebrated in *Brown*, progressive advocates everywhere must work tirelessly to reverse this tide of current opinion. Systematic decisions to forego "common schooling" for children of all races and backgrounds will almost certainly, in my view, bring devastating, life-constraining consequences to millions of young children from the nation's most racially and economically isolated families.

Where Should We Go from Here?
Our Obligation to the Future

Public school integration, as I by now clearly have revealed, seems an educational mission worthy of the full talents of the authors of this crucial collection of essays, of dedicated educators and policy makers, and indeed of every reader of this book. Others may opt to search for the Holy Grail of replicable educational strategies among the nation's high-poverty schools, and I wish them well. But until and unless these remedies are found, this book's unsettling message to its readership, and to the American public at large, is one many resolutely do not want to hear at present: that consigning some children to high-poverty schooling today cruelly destroys their educational and personal futures tomorrow—thousands, and tens of thousands of nonwhite and low-income children on whom our national future increasingly depends.

One additional educational consideration is obvious but needs restatement.

Although it is important to examine small or large cognitive gains in "test score results" from different educational settings, there is a more fundamental objective of school integration that test scores do not and cannot plumb. The broader and deeper purpose of public education is not merely to increase mathematical acuity or reading proficiency in individual students. Education is our society's most fundamental effort to "re-form itself" to re-create itself, in every new generation. As Chief Justice Earl Warren so rightly observed in *Brown*, "Education is perhaps the most important function of state and local governments. . . . It is the very foundation of good citizenship. Today it is a principal instrument in awakening the child to cultural values, in preparing him for later professional training, and in helping him to adjust normally to his environment."[53]

Schools are the chief setting in which the next generation's political values, its moral understanding, and its future democratic leadership are nourished and cultivated.[54] Scholars like Jomills Braddock at the University of Miami have contended for years that the greatest benefits of school desegregation come less from immediate improvement in students' educational performance than from the socialization of our youth for comfortable membership in our increasingly multiracial society.[55] Schools have an unparalleled capacity to offer daily experiences in racial and socioeconomic cooperation.

America's future workforce and political leadership are sure to be majority nonwhite within 50 years. Young Latino, Asian American, and African American students will certainly become, before their old age, this nation's new numerical majority. The racially heterogeneous children of this new century, all of them, need an education in working and living alongside each other. If we allow the fundamental debate over school assignment policies to turn on decimal point differences in student achievement and ignore what it means to educate a generation of children isolated from each other by race and class, I fear a day of national judgment will one day come on our divided educational system — as it has recently come to our nation's financial system, after decades of unheeded warnings about the need for greater regulation and investment sanity — and the nation will collectively look back then, too late, on its present educational folly.

The nation desperately needs, then, to weigh legal and policy options for racially integrated education — the very focus and topic of this book. May each American commit to work for a brighter educational future, striving earnestly against Justice Marshall's educational dystopia — a divided America we would all one day come to regret.

NOTES

This essay has been adapted from remarks made at a 2 April 2009 conference coconvened by the Center for Civil Rights at the University of North Carolina School of Law titled "Legal and Policy Options for Racially Integrated Education in the South and the Nation." I am deeply indebted to Catherine Pierce, Benita Jones, Stephanie Horton, and Erica Frankenberg for much of that adaptation and for many additional substantive and stylistic suggestions.

1. *Milliken v. Bradley*, 418 U.S. 717, 814–15 (1974).

2. *Brown v. Board of Education*, 347 U.S. 483 (1954), holding that the "separate but equal" doctrine in public education violated the equal protection clause of the 14th Amendment.

3. *Plessy v. Ferguson*, 163 U.S. 537 (1896), holding that separate facilities for blacks and whites did not violate the 14th Amendment so long as the facilities were equal.

4. *Board of Education of Oklahoma City Public Schools v. Dowell*, 498 U.S. 237, 89-1080 (1991); *Freeman v. Pitts*, 503 U.S. 467, 89-1290 (1992); *Missouri v. Jenkins*, 515 U.S. 70, 93-1823 (1995).

5. *Washington v. Davis*, 426 U.S. 229, 240 (1976). ("The invidious quality of a law claimed to be racially discriminatory must ultimately be traced to a racially discriminatory purpose.")

6. *Alexander v. Sandoval*, 532 U.S. 275, 287–88 (2001), providing that, "like substantive federal law itself, private rights of action to enforce federal law must be created by Congress. The judicial task is to interpret the statute Congress has passed to determine whether it displays an intent to create not just a private right but also a private remedy. Statutory intent on this latter point is determinative. Without it, a cause of action does not exist and courts may not create one, no matter how desirable that might be as a policy matter, or how compatible with the statute. Raising up causes of action where a statute has not created them may be a proper function for common-law courts, but not for federal tribunals." (Internal citations omitted.)

7. *Parents Involved in Community Schools v. Seattle School District No. 1*, 551 U.S. 724–25 (2007).

8. The CMT has been administered since 1985 and tests students' mastery of reading, writing, math, and science subject areas. Connecticut State Board of Education, Division of Assessment and Accountability, "The Connecticut Mastery Test: What Every Parent/Guardian Should Know about the CMT for Grades 3 through 8" (2008), http://www.csde.state.ct.us/public/cedar/assessment/cmt/resources/misc_cmt/standard_parent_brochure_english_2-6-08.pdf (accessed 12 January 2010).

9. See S. Eaton, *The Children in Room E-4: American Education on Trial* (Chapel Hill, NC: Algonquin, 2006), which provides a poignant look at the hardships faced by racially and socioeconomically isolated students in a poor, all-minority elementary school in Hartford, Connecticut.

10. Ibid., 81–111.

11. In 1977, the Connecticut Supreme Court invalidated a state school financing system based on property taxes, citing disparity in the ability of local communities to finance local

education and the legislature's failure to consider "the financial capability of [each] municipality." See *Sheff v. O'Neill*, 238 Conn. 1 678 A.2d 1277 (1996) (quoting *Horton v. Meskill*, 172 Conn. 648 [1977] [Horton I]). Prior to Horton, school financing was based almost exclusively on local property taxes, without the often equalizing addition of state financial support, thus causing tremendous disparities in funding between property-rich and poor districts. School finance reform—post–Horton I—attempted to account for these disparities by adjusting for such factors as district wealth, student wealth, student population, student performance, and school-year duration. These factors help to determine the Education Cost Sharing (ECS) grant each district will receive. "The basic ECS formula is simple. The number of students in each school district (weighted for educational need) is multiplied by the amount the state has determined a district should spend to provide an adequate education (the foundation) and by an aid percentage determined by the district's wealth. The result is the district's ECS grant." See Connecticut Office of Legislative Research, "Show Us the Money: School Finance in Connecticut" (1998), OLR Issue Brief, http://74.125.93.132/search?q=cache:XJFvYhUzn4oJ:www.cga.ct.gov/ps98/rpt/olr/98-r-1443.doc+school+funding+reform+connecticut+1977&cd=6&hl=en&ct=clnk&gl=us (accessed 12 January 2010).

12. See Connecticut General Statutes § 10-262f-h(13), (25) (1993). The funding formula for distribution of per-student state funds contained in Connecticut law specified that in addition to an annual allocation of 1.0 for each student in a school district, an additional 0.25 would be allocated for each student in that district from a poverty-level family and 0.25 more for each student whose performance on statewide tests fell below a prescribed level.

13. For an outline of a plan for improving Connecticut schools in the late 1980s, see Connecticut Board of Education, "Design for Excellence: Connecticut's Comprehensive Plan for Elementary, Secondary, Vocational, Career, and Adult Education, 1986–1990" (1986).

14. The state of Connecticut demonstrated during the *Sheff* trial that during the 1991–92 school year, Hartford received $4,915.36 per pupil in total state aid, compared to $1,758.47 received by the average suburban district.

15. In the early 1990s, combined state and federal funding for Hartford district students, at $8,126 per pupil, exceeded both surrounding suburban districts as well as the national average of $5,500. See Council of Great City Schools, ed., *National Urban Education Goals: Baseline Indicators, 1990–1991* (Washington, DC: CGCS, 1992), 85. See source cited in n. 17 and accompanying text.

16. See *Sheff v. O'Neill*, 1271. Connecticut's municipality-based school districting system had been in place since 1909.

17. Ibid., 1272–73.

18. *Sheff v. O'Neill*, Trial Transcript, 30 December 1992, at 66 (testimony of Dr. Gary Natriello); Plaintiff's Exhibit 163, at 38, table 2.

19. *Sheff*, 1292, n. 4.

20. *Sheff v. O'Neill*, Trial Transcript, Plaintiff's Exhibit 163, at 151, table 13.

21. Eaton, *Children in Room E-4*, 107.

22. Ibid., 89.

23. See *San Antonio Independent School District v. Rodriguez*, 411 U.S. 1 (1973), which ruled that education is not a federal "fundamental" right; *Milliken v. Bradley*, 418 U.S. 717 (1974), which held that suburban school districts can only be forced to desegregate where court finds evidence of intentional discrimination. "Taken together, [the two cases] . . . read the U.S. Constitution as providing no guarantee of 'equal' schools and no bar against racially separate ones either." Eaton, *Children in Room E-4*, 88. As John Brittain stated, "There was . . . a feeling that in terms of action, our watch was stuck—stuck in Milliken quicksand." Quoted in ibid., 83.

24. *Milliken*, 752–53.

25. See *Sheff*, 1274. In 1868 a town-enacted ordinance segregating African American students was overturned by state statute, providing for open enrollment in public schools. See Connecticut General Statutes § 10-15c (1868). This is the only example of "intentional" discrimination in the history of the Hartford school system.

26. See source cited in n. 17 and accompanying text.

27. See *Horton v. Meskill*, 1977 (Horton I); *Horton v. Meskill*, 1982 (Horton II); and *Horton v. Meskill*, 1985 (Horton III). In these cases the Connecticut courts "necessarily determined that the state's failure adequately to address school funding inequalities constituted the state action that is the constitutional prerequisite for affording judicial relief." See *Sheff*, 1277.

28. See nn. 12–13 and accompanying text.

29. See "Councilman Hernan LaFontaine," http://www.hartford.gov/government/Council/lafontainebio.htm (accessed 12 January 2010). Hernan LaFontaine was the first superintendent of Puerto Rican decent of any major mainland U.S. school district.

30. See nn. 8–9 and accompanying text.

31. See source cited in n. 17 and accompanying text. One program, Project Concern, for example, was established prior to the Horton litigation as a voluntary school choice program that bused urban minority students to more affluent schools in the Hartford suburbs. Although advocates called for the program to be expanded, the legislature cut funding. By the late 1980s only 747 students were enrolled in the program. Eaton, *Children in Room E-4*, 138.

32. J. Coleman et al., *Equality of Educational Opportunity Study* (Washington, DC: U.S. Department of Health, Education and Welfare, 1966), 22.

33. *Sheff*, 41–42.

34. *Green v. County School Board*, 391 U.S. 430 (1968).

35. *Swann v. Charlotte-Mecklenburg Board of Education*, 402 U.S. 1 (1971).

36. Despite initial legal challenges, Wake County, North Carolina, maintained a socioeconomic diversity policy from 2000 through mid-2010. See http://www.wcps.org. See G. Grant, *Hope and Despair in the American City: Why There Are No Bad Schools in Wake*

County (Cambridge: Harvard University Press, 2009). Grant provides an in-depth look at the success of Wake County's diversity policy, compared to those of other large, urban districts, in preventing socioeconomic and racial isolation.

37. *Missouri v. Jenkins*, 515 U.S. 70 (1995), 89.

38. See Kahlenberg essay.

39. See Scott essay.

40. See J. E. Ryan, "Sheff, Segregation and School Finance Litigation," *New York University Law Review* 74, no. 2 (1999): 559. Ryan's article discusses the possibility of utilizing school choice as an alternative to socioeconomic integration.

41. J. C. Boger, "Brown and the American South: Fateful Choices," in *School Resegregation: Must the South Turn Back?*, edited by J. C. Boger and G. Orfield (Chapel Hill: University of North Carolina Press, 2005), 305.

42. The Supreme Court's jurisprudence in the education area more generally has taken a libertarian stance, with decisions favoring choice. (See, e.g., *Zelman v. Simmons-Harris*, 536 U.S. 639 [2002], declaring that an Ohio voucher plan did not violate the establishment clause of the 1st Amendment.)

43. E. Frankenberg and C. Lee, *Race in American Public Schools: Rapidly Resegregating School Districts* (Cambridge: Civil Rights Project at Harvard University, 2002).

44. Indeed, the South is home to some of the most desegregated school systems in the country. However, according to recent reports, the South is losing this status. See E. Frankenberg, C. Lee, and G. Orfield, *A Multi-racial Society with Segregated Schools: Are We Losing the Dream?* (Cambridge: Civil Rights Project at Harvard University, 2002), 4. As the authors of the report suggest, "although the South remains the nation's most integrated region for both blacks and whites, it is the region that is most rapidly going backwards as the courts terminate many major and successful desegregation orders."

45. See M. Febbo-Hunt et al., *Reassignment, School Diversity and Student Outcomes* (Raleigh, NC: Wake County Public Schools Research Watch Report No. 04.16, 2004), 1–2, http://www.wcpss.net/evaluation-research/reports/2004/0416reassignment_diversity_outcomes.pdf (accessed 12 January 2010).

46. See Wake County Public Schools Attendance Policy, http://www.wcpss.net/policy-files/series/policies/6200-bp.html (accessed 12 January 2010).

47. See Kahlenberg essay.

48. See Kahlenberg, Reardon and Rhodes, and Siegel-Hawley essays. See also Williams and Frankenberg essay and Frankenberg essay.

49. Housing trends in many large cities resulting from suburban flight have created urban class and racial segregation. As a result, systems of "neighborhood schools" will inevitably reflect trends of racial and socioeconomic isolation. See Eaton, *Children in Room E-4*, 50–53.

50. See P. Gorman, *2009 Equity Report* (Charlotte, NC: Charlotte-Mecklenburg Board of Education, 2009), https://extranet.cms.k12.nc.us/news/stories/newsletters/pdf/1A30A200990827AM.pdf (accessed 12 January 2010); Ann Doss Helms, "College Prep

Lags at CMS Urban Schools," *Charlotte Observer*, 30 August 2009, http://www.charlotte observer.com/topstories/story/917366.html (accessed 12 January 2010).

51. *Leandro v. State*, 488 S.E. 2d. 249 (1997).

52. See White House Education Page, "Guiding Principles," http://www.whitehouse .gov/issues/education/ (accessed 12 January 2010).

53. *Brown v. Board of Education*.

54. See Brief of Swann Fellowship et al. as Amici Curiae Supporting Respondents at 6-20, *Parents Involved in Community Schools v. Seattle School District No. 1*, 2007. The brief discusses how the failure of the Charlotte-Mecklenburg public schools to actively pursue school integration while no longer under court order has negatively impacted its student population.

55. J. H. Braddock II et al., "A Long-Term View of School Desegregation: Some Recent Studies of Graduates as Adults," *Phi Delta Kappan* 66, no. 4 (1984): 259–64.

School Choice as a Civil Right

The Political Construction of a Claim and Its Implications for School Desegregation

Over the past two decades, media outlets, advocates, and advocacy-based researchers have often described school choice as the sole remaining civil rights issue. While there is ideological diversity undergirding the school choice movement, conservative choice adherents typically believe the state should assume a diminished role in the provision of public education, clearing the way for what they argue is a more competitive and accountable private sector to provide educational services. While belief in the superiority of markets is paramount to these choice advocates, they tend to argue that the primary reason to expand school choice is because of its benefits for poor parents of color. They often claim that justice and even morality are on their side, and they embrace linguistic signifiers of the civil rights movement, such as school choice's role in ensuring democracy, full citizenship, and equal educational opportunity. At the same time, they often privilege specific school choice policies,[1] such as vouchers and charter schools, and place less emphasis on other school choice plans, such as magnet schools and voluntary transfer plans, which were originally enacted to achieve desegregation.

The association between the market-based choice and civil rights has in some ways become so sacrosanct that opponents of market-based school choice have been lambasted by choice advocates as being opposed to equal educational opportunity. For example, in 2004, when Congress was considering voucher legislation for the Washington, D.C., public schools, the advocacy group D.C. Parents for Choice released an advertisement comparing Senator Edward Kennedy's opposition to vouchers to Bull Connor's use of dogs to attack civil rights demonstrators during one of the most violent moments in the modern civil rights movement. Other choice advocates have questioned the political legitimacy of traditional civil rights organizations, claiming that they fail to represent African Americans' desire for school choice.[2] The purpose of this essay is not simply to critique these claims[3] but rather to examine their origins and to consider their interaction with liberal or progressive advocacy and developments in law, social policy, and educational reform. This essay is a sociopolitical analysis of a central question: *Some four decades after it was used as a tool to preserve racial segregation in public education, how did school choice come to be constructed as a civil right?*[4] Drawing from historical, political, and sociological literatures as well as legal documents generated by advocacy organizations, I find three social and political factors have functioned together to construct market-based choice specifically as a civil right for poor parents of color. These include (1) conservative political framing coupled with progressive critiques of the state, (2) legal jurisprudence combined with the expansion of the suburbs and the subsequent race and social class isolation of many large urban school districts, and (3) the significant support of market-based choice by philanthropies, especially of charter school expansion and development.

There is significant historical and policy overlap between each of these factors. As I will discuss in the sections that follow, the first factor is the successful conservative framing of school choice as a civil right as one part of a broader neoliberal effort to diminish the state's role in providing public education; the ultimate goal of the agenda is a universal voucher and choice program that dismantles existing educational bureaucracies and teachers' unions. A part of this frame includes increasing the emphasis on "excellence" through the use of standards, testing, and accountability as measures of educational equity. The conservative reframing of equity focuses on expanding choice and high-stakes testing measures. This reframing of equity to look almost exclusively on outputs has led to a focus on replicating what has come to be termed "what's working" schools—often characterized by attempts to replicate high-achieving racially homogenous schools. Some liberals or progressives and communities of color support this policy direction, arguing that since urban school districts are already segregated and struggling, the expansion of high-quality schools of choice will give them access to better schools regardless of their racial homogeneity.

The second factor is that the courts have helped set boundaries for what kinds of choices are available to parents, and what tools school districts can use when establishing student assignment plans. While the courts have limited possibilities for school desegregation to be implemented by restricting the use of race in student assignments, geospatial alterations have resulted in racially identifiable suburbs and cities. With strict limits on the possibility of interdistrict choice and desegregation plans,[5] advocates are assured that any choice plan will keep urban students in their home districts, preserving what are often more highly resourced and white suburban school districts' demographic profiles.

A third factor helping to frame school choice as a civil right is related to the first: a recent group of philanthropists is supporting a rapid expansion of charter school reform in urban districts—specifically charter schools that are run by private management organizations—effectively driving public policy in key educational "markets" that serve high-poverty communities of color.

After discussing the essay's framework and each of these sociopolitical influences, I explore the policy and political implications of the construction of school choice as a civil right for racial integration in public schools across the United States. While the construction of school choice as a civil right has helped to diminish the stature of school desegregation as an educational reform tool and remedy for educational inequality, there remain opportunities for multiracial advocacy coalitions to renew and reconsider a desegregation reform agenda within the broader school choice movement.

Conceptual Framework

This essay joins linguistic analyses of political framing[6] with a consideration of political values and the sense-making in which citizens engage as they seek to realize public policy agendas in seemingly paradoxical ways. It assumes that social and political dynamics influence the framing of public policy, which is also informed by ideology, values, racial hierarchies, political power, and past social policy. As Deborah Stone argues, ideas and power work together to establish policy action, and the struggle over the multiple meanings of these ideas creates spaces for democratic action: "Political conflict is never simply over material conditions and choices, but over what is legitimate. The passion in politics comes from conflicting senses of fairness, justice, rightness, and goodness. . . . Political fights are conducted with money, with rules, with votes, and with favors, to be sure, but they are conducted above all with words and ideas."[7]

Under this frame, the association of school choice with civil rights emerges as a result of long-standing power struggles over American political and social values. Given this interaction, the school choice–civil rights claims must also be considered against their particular social and political contexts. This framing helps us to acknowledge the presence and importance of liberal or progressive support for school choice as well as the influence of conservative marketization of civil rights rhetoric in constructing choice as a civil rights claim. As a result of this interaction, much of the traditional discourse of equity and equality established in the civil rights era remains, but it is often removed from substantive critique of the distribution of social, political, and economic resources, and it tends to be silent on issues of racial segregation.[8]

Despite school choice reformers' silence on broader social inequality, African American and Latino support of contemporary school choice forms, whether it stems from progressive, conservative, or neoliberal philosophical commitments, makes sense. African Americans have a long history, after all, of utilizing alternatives to public education;, have a deep-seated dissatisfaction with their public schooling options, as well as a shared history in which they along with Latino students, bore most of the burden for the implementation of school desegregation; and often felt the brunt of within-school segregationist tactics.[9] For desegregation supporters who also value increasing options in public schooling, these experiences and perspectives present an opportunity to engage parental frustrations with public education and join them with broader, community-based grassroots efforts not only to reform schools, but also to create more equitable and responsive social policies in general.[10]

Political Ideology, Values, and Framing

School choice has had a complicated history with race in American society. African Americans have embraced alternative schooling forms for hundreds of years to realize goals of self-determination and culturally responsive schooling. But choice has also been a tool of segregationists. For example, early state sponsored school choice programs were mechanisms for southern segregated school systems to avoid implementing court-ordered desegregation.[11] In the North, desegregation-related school transfer plans largely relied on African American students' being bused from schools where they were the majority to schools where they were in the minority, placing the burden for school desegregation largely on the shoulders of those students who had been victims of state-sponsored segregation and educational inequality. Moreover, these students often found themselves tracked into low-level segregated classrooms once they entered their new schools, causing many African American parents and community members to decry school desegregation and instead embrace and advocate for community-based and controlled schools that better served the needs of students and communities of color.

Due to the massive resistance to school desegregation implementation in all regions of the country, school choice plans—such as magnet schools and controlled choice plans—were designed as less controversial compromises.[12] That is, reformers designed magnet schools to stabilize enrollments, particularly in urban schools, which were most vulnerable to white and middle-class flight. Thus magnet schools offered a particular curricular or career focus, and administrators monitored admission with an eye to achieving racial balance in student enrollment. Controlled choice plans allowed for choice of schools, but they also bounded that choice to maintain racial balance.[13] In terms of maintaining racial balance in schools, these forms of choice have been fairly successful, albeit certainly complicated by issues of resegregation in classrooms, selectivity in student admissions, and limited numbers of students served. In addition, they are politically vulnerable, especially after recent court decisions limiting the use of race in student assignment, most recently in Wake County, North Carolina, and also under the Supreme Court decisions striking down Louisville's and Seattle's student assignment plans.[14] Instead of equity-based choice, conservatives, and increasingly many liberals or progressives, are embracing market-based choice reforms.

Different forms of school choice have historically appealed to varying political ideologies, with progressives, conservatives, and others supporting an array of educational choice for different reasons, and with race usually implicated across ideological perspectives. Contemporary market-based choice forms, which involve competition and deregulation, generally owe their modern iteration to political conservatives.[15] This political construction largely, but by no means exclusively, emanates from conservatives who adopt civil rights rhetoric to support what is largely a reform movement led by white elites, what Michael Katz has called "the normalization of formerly radical rhetoric."[16] Traditional civil rights organizations like the National Association for the Advancement of Colored People (NAACP), which has long opposed vouchers,[17] are prime targets of conservative critique.

In order to challenge the authority of the NAACP and other civil rights groups, conservative donors have supported the creation of new civil rights groups.[18] These include the Black Alliance for Educational Options (BAEO), formed in 1999, and the Hispanic Council for Reform and Educational Options (HCREO), formed in 2001. The BAEO and the HCREO have similar missions of informing parents on their choice options, and they also serve as powerful examples of minority support for school choice. Yet unlike the NAACP and other civil rights groups, they are single-issue organizations; school choice is the only policy area on these organizations' respective agendas. Notably, desegregation choice plans are not mentioned on either organization's website; instead, charter schools, vouchers, and privately managed schools are touted. While these organizations advertise community-based and community-oriented agendas, their rhetoric in support of choice is much closer to that of their conservative supporters.

Political progressives have also advocated for forms of school choice during specific historical moments. They have tended to ground these efforts in concerns over community control and participation in school governance and curriculum, with a role for the state in regulating equal distribution of resources and allowing African American children to have access to schools historically restricted to white children.[19] An example is Herbert Gintis's progressive defense of vouchers if they are sufficiently large to have redistributive effects.[20] For liberals or progressives, having safeguards to ameliorate against what they see as limitations to school choice is critical to their tenuous support. Among liberal or progressive concerns about school choice are several critiques: it reaches a relatively small population, those best positioned to utilize it are relatively more privileged, and it can siphon off resources from public schools. As these examples indicate, school choice is a reservoir with multiple ideological tributaries. How conservatives moved from embracing it for segregation to championing it for minority empowerment bears scrutiny.

During the civil rights movement, choice became a controversial and popular tool for policy makers who wished to defy *Brown*'s mandate to desegregate public schools by providing "multiple escape routes" for white students.[21] This happened perhaps most infamously in Virginia, where in 1958 Governor J. Lindsay Almond closed schools in three cities for a full year and allowed white students tuition to attend all-white private schools. Choice was also a segregationist instrument in other states across the South, with instances in which the state paid teacher salaries in private schools, or exclusively allowed white students "freedom of choice" to avoid schooling with black students.[22]

In recent years, some researchers and advocates have argued that this depiction of school choice history fails to acknowledge the ways African Americans employed choice long before conservatives used it to maintain the social order, specifically by developing self-sustaining schools that reflected particular cultural, pedagogical, and political orientations.[23] Nor does it recognize liberal or progressive school choice proposals, which often include provisions for racial balance and adequate resources, or place limits on the involvement of private schools, such as the short-lived Alum Rock school voucher program in 1972.[24] For example, James Forman argues that African Americans have a long history of advocating for alternative schooling, at times pushing for choice within public education systems and often building self-supporting schools outside of it.[25] Their choice strategies were diverse and influenced by the political context in which they operated, with African Americans founding and operating schools after emancipation and community-control advocates demanding that they be given the reins of their local schools in the 1960s and 1970s. More recently, in the school voucher and charter school movements, African Americans are active participants in creating and utilizing private and public schools that they regard as more culturally and educationally responsive than what has been available to them in traditional public schools. What is common across these different forms of choice involvement is a sense that a quality education is key not only to social and economic mobility, but also to challenging the American racial hierarchy.[26] Yet even when African Americans have challenged public officials and the status quo in public education, they have generally called for greater inputs into public education; rather than the removal of the state from providing education, they demand that the state redistribute educational resources and opportunities, regulate equitable practices, and remedy past injustices.[27]

In contrast, one of the most influential strands of conservative support for school choice emanates from a desire to dismantle the public administration of education, leaving it instead to private entities to deliver. Milton Friedman first suggested that parents be given publicly funded vouchers that they could supplement with their own money to redeem schooling for their children from an array of providers: "The educational services could be rendered by private enterprises operated for profit, or by nonprofit institutions. The role of the government would be limited to insuring that the schools met certain minimum standards, such as the inclusion of a minimum content in their programs, much as it now inspects restaurants to insure that they maintain minimum sanitary standards."[28] While Friedman did not explicitly argue that choice was a civil right, he did frame educational choice as an issue of individual freedom from state control, setting the foundation for later choice arguments that would call for parental empowerment, and tie school choice to the long-standing desire of African Americans for liberation from inequality.

In the face of the social transformations brought by the civil rights movement in terms of redistributing downward resources and expanding access to public institutions, conservative opponents began to build a countermovement whose influence has shaped the school choice–civil rights framing. For instance, in 1971, Lewis Powell (who would go on to serve as a Supreme Court justice) wrote a confidential memo known as the Powell Manifesto. Addressed to the chair of the Education Committee of the U.S. Chamber of Commerce, the memo was titled "Attack of American Free Enterprise System." Powell argued that the social changes brought by the civil rights and related social movements were undermining individual liberties and American capitalism.[29] He called on corporations to provide financial support to develop conservative organizations that could challenge these changes. He called for the financing of a countermovement that would recruit students on university campuses, support conservative scholarship and researchers, and use the media to shape public opinion. This memo inspired wealthy conservative donors, such as the Scaife family, to become key supporters of think tanks, scholars, and advocacy organizations like the Heritage Foundation and Cato Institute, whose influence has directly shaped the conservative school choice–civil rights claim.[30]

The conceptualization of choice as an individual right, while not new, embraced, and arguably co-opted, civil rights language beginning in the 1980s. The Reagan administration's hostility to civil rights enforcement (following Richard Nixon's staunch opposition to busing to achieve desegregation) was coupled with a movement to focus more on educational "excellence" and less on educational equity.[31] With help from the publication of A Nation at Risk in 1983,[32] the popular discourse about public schooling became one of schools in steep decline. Improving them would require not more inputs, for those had been ineffective and even wasteful, but rather a different focus on standards, testing, competition, and choice.[33] This would be the new civil rights agenda: a focus on achievement in schools and individual responsibility. These arguments were the precursors to the current focus on the racial achievement gap in public education.

This reframing of educational equity was greatly assisted by the Heritage Foundation and the Landmark Legal Foundation. In 1989, these organizations convened a meeting in which participants articulated a conservative civil rights platform. As William Snider recounts: "The theme of this conservative platform, most participants agreed, should be 'individual dignity and empowerment' for minorities, with an emphasis on lifting regulatory barriers that conservatives say prevent minorities from pursuing economic advancement."[34] Besides choice, other components of this agenda were opposition to affirmative action, welfare, and regulation of businesses. Advocates began calling for school choice on the grounds that it would empower African Americans, freeing them from oppressive government regulations. In this rendering, civil rights became an individual commodity, as opposed to a community or civic good, and became a social imperative. A key architect of this rationale, Clint Bolick, has argued that "school choice is not a panacea, but it is a prerequisite to delivering on the promise of equal educational opportunities. Alone among school reforms, it promises to move children out of failing schools and into good schools, and to do so today—not ten years from now, not another wasted billion dollars from now, but *now*."[35] Much of the legal, scholarly, and political advocacy that has followed over the past several decades echoes this framing.[36]

For the framing of school choice as a civil right to gain popular currency, however, other social and political developments were necessary. My discussion turns now to an examination of how the courts have assisted in this framing by setting increasingly narrow legal possibilities for race-based student assignment given the spatial and racial isolation of cities and suburbs, while simultaneously expanding the boundaries of school choice policies.

School Choice, Geography, and Jurisprudence

U.S. Supreme Court decisions on race and education are best located on a spectrum of state action between *Plessy v. Ferguson* and *Brown v. Board of Education*. Where the former upheld the doctrine of separate but equal, the latter upended it by holding that state-sponsored, segregated schools were inherently unequal. With its decision in *Parents Involved in Community Schools v. Seattle School District No. 1* (*PICS*, 2007), the Court has come full circle by restricting the ability of school districts to take race into account when assigning students to schools to achieve diversity. Even before *PICS*, however, many U.S. public school systems that had once achieved desegregation had become, or were on their way to becoming resegregated, largely due to demographic trends, a series of court decisions that have declared school systems unitary, and state policies. This regression had happened in tandem with the expansion of market-based school choice policies and the Court's upholding of the constitutionality of publicly funded school voucher plans.[37]

Two voucher programs enacted by state legislators have been the subject of most controversy: Milwaukee's 1990 plan and Cleveland's 1995 plan, which became a statewide program in 2005. Both are targeted programs for poor families whose incomes are below a particular threshold. The Cleveland school voucher program allowed city students to attend school outside of Cleveland, but to date, no suburban district has opened its school doors to voucher families. The 1974 Supreme Court decision in *Milliken v. Bradley*[38] held that interdistrict school choice and transfer plans were no longer options as desegregation remedies, effectively reinforcing city-suburban racial divides that became more pronounced given labor, housing, and economic policy.[39]

As a result of these policy trends, predominantly white and middle-class suburban communities for the most part are protected from racial and class struggles over quality schools, since urban students are not likely to attend the relatively racially and socioeconomically homogenous schools in the suburbs.[40] This has led some critics of market-based school choice to argue that choice is nothing more than a "containment strategy" for ensuring that urban students stay out of suburban schools, while appeasing parents with an opportunity to choose among a closed set of schools that promise an alternative.[41]

In *Zelman v. Simmons-Harris* (2002), the Supreme Court not only upheld the constitutionality of Cleveland's school voucher program but also solidified the link between school choice and civil rights for African American students, most explicitly in Justice Clarence Thomas's opinion concurring with the majority. Thomas linked African American activist Frederick Douglass's notions of racial liberation and African Americans' quest for access to public schools during Reconstruction to the provision of school choice and vouchers in the inner city, and he criticized voucher opponents as indifferent elites. Recent U.S. Supreme Court decisions not only have helped frame the educational policy options available to federal and state policy makers by restricting even voluntary student assignment plans that consider the race of an individual student but also, by relying on advocacy-based school choice scholarship, have helped further concretize the association between school choice and civil rights.

The Court's restrictions on desegregation and support of school choice interact with the racial, geospatial development of cities and suburbs following World War II. Through the use of redlining, restrictive covenants, and federal highway subsidies, the suburbs developed and became enclaves that were largely racially homogenous. According to Harvey Kantor and Barbara Brenzel, "What changed most dramatically with the suburbanization of the American population was not just the relative proportion of the population living in cities and suburbs, but the racial and economic distribution of the population within the metropolitan areas."[42]

These shifts in urban-suburban demographics have had political consequences. Kevin Kruse argues that white flight after *Brown* solidified a conservative social agenda. Suburbs were home to one-fourth of the U.S. population in 1950; by 1990, half of the nation's inhabitants resided there.[43] According to Kruse, this population shift had ideological implications, "During the 1980s and 1990s, a powerful new political philosophy took hold in these post-secession suburbs. Finally free to pursue a politics that accepted as its normative values an individualistic interpretation of 'freedom of association,' a fervent faith in free enterprise, and a fierce hostility to the federal government, a new suburban conservatism took the now-familiar themes of isolation, individualism, and privatization to unprecedented levels."[44] In 1992, suburban voters outnumbered urban and rural voters combined.[45] In many states, then, suburban voters are largely responsible for electing the majority of state legislators who, in turn, are positioned to shape urban educational policies to meet their constituents' preferences.[46] According to Matthew Lassiter, white southern suburbs tend to possess a "meritocratic ethos" that privileges individual accomplishments, resulting in the belief "that children of privilege should receive every advantage of the consumer affluence accumulated by their parents instead of competing on an egalitarian playing field."[47]

These demographic trends, coupled with Supreme Court rulings and the marketization rhetoric of school choice as a civil right, have solidified the relationship between charter schools, vouchers, and race as particularly urban school reforms. Since legal remedies and constrained housing policies have all but ensured that city schools will be comprised of students of color and be poorly resourced, and suburban schools will be predominantly white and comparatively wealthy, many choice adherents argue that efforts to desegregate city schools are misplaced. Instead, dismantling unresponsive urban school district bureaucracies by developing alternative educational providers and expanding charter schools should be the preferred route to educational reform. Whites who are interested in preserving homogenous suburban schools can support school choice with the knowledge that their communities will be largely unaffected by it.

Charter Schools and Choice as a Civil Right

The marketization of publication has helped inform the development of charter school reform. Like other choice forms, charter schools have progressive and conservative roots, but they are increasingly associated with private, for-profit, and nonprofit management organizations, whose mission is to replicate their models across numerous urban school systems. Under this vision of charter school reform, parental choice comes to be defined as the ability to choose from an array of different school franchises.

Because many state constitutions explicitly forbid the use of state funds for private schools, vouchers have remained a relatively small item on the school choice menu, though the political rhetoric surrounding them has often been more expansive. In contrast, there are charter school laws in 41 states, and with more than 4,000 charter schools serving over 1.5 million children. Under the federal education legislation known as No Child Left Behind, charter schools are offered as a remedy to parents with students in schools failing to meet annual yearly progress. Recent federal initiatives under the Obama administration, such as Race to the Top (RttT) and the Investing in Innovation (13) programs, have also incentivized charter school expansion. Charter schools are also often the dominant educational reform in school districts under state takeover and under mayoral control, such as in New Orleans, Philadelphia, and New York. Reformers claim that the schools produce superior academic outcomes, and as I have argued, closing the achievement gap is a key educational goal of many choice supporters.[48]

Empirical evidence on charter school achievement is much more mixed than these claims reflect, however.[49] In response to the mixed achievement results across the charter school sector, a set of venture philanthropies such as the Broad Foundation, the Bill and Melinda Gates Foundation, and the NewSchools Venture Fund are pouring tens of millions of dollars into developing charter school management organizations that appear to produce high-achieving students.[50] For these philanthropic supporters, developing charter schools run by for-profit and nonprofit educational management organizations for poor children and children of color is a civil right because they believe such schools produce higher test scores. Equity is measured in a reduction of the racial achievement gap. In several cities, management organizations funded by these philanthropies now operate the majority of existing charter schools.[51]

Due to this political and philanthropic support, targeted cities are likely to see a dramatic increase in charter schools in the immediate future. A number of philanthropies, for example, have dedicated significant funds to the Knowledge Is Power Program (KIPP) charter school network to expand charter schools in Houston and Dallas, and many of these foundations are also active in the transformation of the New Orleans public schools by charter schools and management organizations.[52]

What is significant about these efforts is that instead of considering desegregation or fiscal equity in the development of school choice, they focus on specific pedagogical, disciplinary, and cultural approaches to schooling for low-income, predominantly African American and Latino children and, ultimately, on the re-creation of racially homogenous and racially isolated schooling.[53] Given the seeming success of some of these schools in posting high student achievement, and thereby, closing the racial achievement gap, advocates hold them up as reform models that both empower parents and provide high-quality schooling for students.[54]

Since charter school reform models are being developed specifically for

African American and Latino children in urban school districts, it is not surprising that data indicate that most charter schools are racially homogenous. While African American students are well represented in the aggregate charter school enrollment, they tend to go to schools that are majority African American.[55] Segregation measures become especially stark in individual charter schools; researchers have found extreme racial homogeneity across charter schools in particular school districts.[56]

The latest crop of charter school models not only reflects existing urban school segregation, but it also reinforces and, in essence, requires it. For if charter school founders have as their charge to prove that their models are effective and excellent places for students of color to perform at high levels on achievement measures, having racial diversity could undermine their ability to sell their models to donors and to policy makers. In this regard, the current direction of charter schools operated by management organizations seeks to provide parents with choices, but it also narrows the possibility for desegregated schooling when such schools are perhaps best positioned to achieve it, given their freedom to draw student populations from multiple attendance zones. The legislative flexibility charter schools have in being able to enroll students from across cities and districts is not enjoyed in any systematic way by school systems, and to target recruitment and enrollments to achieve racial homogeneity in effect squanders an opportunity to create racially diverse schools that the courts have otherwise limited for school districts.

The political construction of school choice as a civil right has created an environment that not only tolerates but also embraces segregation in U.S. public schooling at the exact moment when school choice is expanding across the country.[57] The interaction of charter schools with school districts that have had long-standing struggles over desegregation has been complex, and as charter school reform has expanded without an explicit policy mandate to create schools with diverse student enrollments, it has further complicated the racial and ethnic landscape, often resulting in racially homogenous charter schools and further segregating the students who remain in traditional public schools by race and socioeconomic status. While charter schools have been slow to take hold across the South, their numbers in that region are growing, and in key southern and southwestern states, such as Florida and Texas, charter schools are growing rapidly.

Despite the segregative trends in charter school reform, there exists an opportunity for lawyers, advocates, public school teachers, parents, unions, community members, and philanthropists to join in the policy design of school choice that might avoid the link between school choice and segregation, and remedy the segregation found across the broader national landscape. Despite the political construction that has made market-based school choice the last remaining civil right to be achieved, there is space for those committed to racially integrated schooling to redefine the kind of school choice and charter school reform that the South and the rest of the nation will pursue in the coming years, and to reframe the civil rights agenda as one that includes schools and other social institutions.

One promising development in national leadership around desegregation has come from the Obama administration. In 2009, on the 45th anniversary of the passage of Title VI of the Civil Rights Act of 1964, the U.S. Department of Justice's Civil Rights Division indicated it would take steps to strengthen its enforcement of the measure by enforcing antidiscrimination statutes and providing localities with technical assistance to bolster their civil rights compliance programs.[58] It is as yet unclear how these efforts will be linked with the U.S. Department of Education's support of charter school expansion, or if they will be connected at all. At minimum, however, it signals to local officials that federal funding could be linked to efforts to create diverse schools, and this signal could help local desegregation or integration advocates pressure school boards and charter school founders to make diverse schools a reality.

Such efforts might learn from the advocacy that resulted in the *Brown* decision. *Brown* was in many ways the result of a long-brewing social movement comprised of grassroots organizations, churches, and elite supporters. Their movement for educational and social opportunity included an argument for why desegregation, and ultimately, integration, was important for American society and the health of U.S. democracy, and why a remedy for past injustice and discrimination was in order. In other words, the movement articulated a civic benefit that would emanate from the realization of civil rights for disenfranchised communities.

Progressive or liberal support of market-based choice has often been strategic; advocates have embraced choice in the hopes that it would provide educational respite for communities whose public school systems have struggled or failed to serve them well. The alliances these advocates have formed with conservatives — especially those who favor more universal programs, are always tenuous. When Polly Williams, a prominent African American supporter of choice in Milwaukee, learned that efforts were afoot to expand vouchers to all Wisconsin students regardless of income, she decried the maneuver, noting that she was always aware that "white Republican and rich, right-wing foundations" had other agendas, but that she had hoped the voucher program would encourage public schools to serve children better. "I had hoped to nudge the public schools themselves to respond to the challenge and work harder to keep parents from wanting vouchers."[59]

Williams's experience in Milwaukee points to the political vulnerability of even modestly equity-minded choice plans, but it also demonstrates the potential power coalitions could have to reframe issues of equity to support and sustain school choice plans that make redistributive forms of equity a priority. The challenge for such coalitions is to successfully reclaim the civil rights terrain, place pressure on policy makers when they enact choice without equity provisions, provide support for school districts to operate more equitably, and reframe the discourse on school reform to focus on the role and benefits of equitable and quality schooling for an educated citizenry and a robust democracy. A potentially fruitful strategy would join housing, voting rights, and fair labor and employment advocates with educational supporters of integrated schooling to articulate a broad-based school reform agenda incorporating school choice.

This coalition would need to articulate a school choice agenda that embraces the importance of integrated schooling, while being flexible enough to allow for the paradoxical importance of racially homogenous charter schools that have provided parents and students with quality educational experiences. In doing so, this coalition would be able to counter market-based advocates whose agendas are not necessarily consistent with the long-term needs or complaints of communities of color. Such an agenda would include an expansion of magnet schools and controlled choice plans. With adequate resources and oversight, some of the issues that have vexed these choice programs, including selectivity and lack of capacity, could be mitigated. Researchers could also produce more and better evaluations of these programs, helping to establish their educational and social value so that policy makers feel more comfortable supporting them. Similarly, a coordinated advocacy effort that involves charter school leaders could tap into the Obama administration's emphasis on creating stimulating school reform by creating incentives for charter schools to develop racially, ethnically, linguistically, and socioeconomically diverse student bodies. There are currently no fiscal incentives for charter school developers to do so. Such incentives could help diminish the segregation and resegregation of students in charter schools, especially as charter school reform is posed to expand in the southern United States, where Latino students, especially, are vulnerable to such segregation.

While the Supreme Court has limited school districts' abilities to enact choice plans that consider race, the new charter school networks supported by philanthropists are not necessarily similarly restricted, and coalitions of advocates might begin a new movement for desegregated choice schools. Such a coalition would be well-positioned—given the indication of support from the federal government—to argue to local policy makers and philanthropists why they should support such an agenda, drawing from empirical studies demonstrating the effectiveness of well-designed school desegregation plans for students of all racial and ethnic backgrounds.

Finally, and perhaps most important, in order for choice to have a chance at helping create desegregated schools, suburban districts must also be participants in this coalition. Researchers have documented not only the racial divide between cities and suburbs, but also the growing segregation between many outer-ring suburbs themselves, which are often the communities in which African Americans and Latinos settle when they migrate from cities, often ending up in segregated suburban schools.[60] The creation of voluntary transfer and choice plans between these suburbs could help ease the hypersegregation that has evolved in these environments. So, too, could fiscal support for charter schools that are strategically located to maximize enrollments from adjoining cities, suburbs, and outer-ring suburbs.

The United States periodically revisits policy approaches aimed at reconciling past injustices. For example, in 2009, the Charlottesville, Virginia, City Council issued a public apology for its role in aiding the massive resistance to school desegregation following *Brown*. A renewed public education and reframed civil rights agenda that includes choice, desegregation, and equality of opportunity can be generated from these moments of recharged political spaces if civil rights and education advocates can mobilize and pressure policy makers to realize it.

NOTES

1. "Market-based choice" encompasses educational reforms whose hallmarks are competition, deregulation, private sector provision of education, and a focus on the rights of individual parents.

2. M. Holt, *Not Yet "Free at Last": The Unfinished Business of the Civil Rights Movement* (Oakland, CA: Institute for Contemporary Studies, 2000); T. Moe, *Schools, Vouchers, and the American Public* (Washington, DC: Brookings Institution Press, 2002).

3. For critiques, see B. Miner, "Distorting the Civil Rights Legacy," *Rethinking Schools Online* (2004), http://www.rethinkingschools.org/special_reports/voucher_report/v_kpsp183 .shtml (accessed 26 February 2009); People for the American Way, "Community Voice or Captive of the Right? A Closer Look at the Black Alliance for Educational Options" (Washington, DC: People for the American Way Foundation, 2001); and People for the American Way, "The Voucher Veneer: The Deeper Agenda to Privatize Public Education" (Washington, DC: People for the American Way Foundation, 2003).

4. For example, Georgia lawyer Glenn Delk has been pursuing the passage of school vouchers; one of his strategies has been to argue for the use of a state statute from 1961 that had previously provided whites access to private schools to avoid desegregation.

5. Under *Milliken v. Bradley* 418 U.S. 717 (1974), the Court held that urban school district student assignment plans could not require suburban districts to participate. For a good discussion, see F. Margonis and L. Parker, "Choice, Privatization, and Unspoken Strategies of Containment," *Educational Policy* 9, no. 4 (1995): 375–403.

6. K. Kumashiro, *The Seduction of Common Sense: How the Right Has Framed the Debate on America's Schools* (New York: Teachers College Press, 2008); G. Lakoff, *Don't Think of an Elephant! Know Your Values and Frame the Debate* (White River Junction, VT: Chelsea Green, 2002); G. Lakoff, *The Political Mind: Why You Can't Understand 21st-Century American Politics with an 18th-Century Brain* (New York: Viking, 2008).

7. D. Stone, *Policy Paradox: The Art of Political Decision Making* (New York: W. W. Norton, 2002), 34.

8. Kerner Commission, *Report of the National Advisory Commission on Civil Disorders* (Washington, DC: U.S. Government Printing Office, 1968); U.S. Commission on Civil Rights, *Racial Isolation in the Public Schools* (Washington, DC: U.S. Government Printing Office, 1967).

9. J. Oakes, *Keeping Track: How Schools Structure Inequality* (New Haven, CT: Yale University Press, 1985); A. S. Wells and R. Crain, *Steppin' Over the Color Line: African American Students in Suburban White Schools* (New Haven, CT: Yale University Press, 1997).

10. J. Anyon, *Radical Possibilities: Public Policy, Urban Education, and a New Social Movement* (New York: Routledge, 2005); T. Pedroni, *Market Movements: African American Involvement in School Voucher Reform* (New York: Routledge, 2007).

11. R. Kluger, *Simple Justice* (New York: Vintage, 1975).

12. O. Patterson, *The Ordeal of Integration: Progress and Resentment in America's "Racial" Crisis* (Washington, DC: Civitas, 1997).

13. C. V. Willie et al., *Student Diversity, Choice, and School Improvement* (Westport, CT: Bergin and Garvey, 2002).

14. *Parents Involved in Community Schools v. Seattle School District No. 1*, 05-908, 426 F. 3d 1162; *Meredith v. Jefferson County Board of Education*, 05-915, 416 F. 3d 513.

15. M. W. Apple, *Educating the "Right" Way: Markets, Standards, God, and Inequality* (New York: Routledge Falmer, 2001). An extensive discussion of political ideology is beyond the scope of this analysis. For the purposes of this essay, I define conservatives as people who favor limited state involvement and progressives as people who envision an active role for the state in providing for social and educational opportunity. Within conservative ranks are neoliberals, neoconservatives, authoritarian populists, and the managerial and professional class. Within progressive camps are those on the left, the center-left, and multiculturists. An African American nationalist and school choice supporter identifies African American ideological perspectives as Black Right, Middle, and Left, and argues that the Black Left is the only camp still in support of desegregation. See Holt, *Not Yet "Free at Last"*.

16. M. Katz, "Politics, Activism, and the History of America's Public Schools Conference," lecture delivered at University of Pennsylvania, 12 April 2008.

17. The national NAACP passed resolutions in 1970, 1971, 1992, and 2003 opposing vouchers on the grounds that voucher plans undermined school desegregation, siphoned money from public schools, and failed to provide sufficient tuition funds for poor black and Latino families to put them to use. Local affiliates have also opposed other school choice measures, such as the Seattle/King County NAACP's 2004 opposition to Washington's charter schools law, Referendum 55. See http://www.RejectR55.org.

18. J. Miller, *Strategic Investments in Ideas: How Two Foundations Changed America* (Washington, DC: Philanthropy Roundtable, 2003); E. DeBray-Pelot et al., "The Institutional Landscape of Interest-Group Politics and School Choice," *Peabody Journal of Education* 82, no. 2–3 (2007): 204–30.

19. Kluger, *Simple Justice*; D. Lewis and K. Nakagawa, *Race and Educational Reform in the American Metropolis: A Study of School Decentralization* (Albany: SUNY Press, 1997); A. S. Wells, *Time to Choose: America at the Crossroads of School Choice Policy* (New York: Hill and Wang, 1993).

20. H. Gintis, "The Political Economy of School Choice," *Teachers College Record* 93, no. 5 (1995): 492–511.

21. C. Clotfelter, *After Brown: The Rise and Retreat of School Desegregation* (Princeton, NJ: Princeton University Press, 2004).

22. A. Champagne, "The Segregation Academy and the Law," *Journal of Negro Education* 42, no. 1 (1973): 58–66; M. Lassiter and A. Davis, "Massive Resistance Revisited: Virginia's White Moderates and the Byrd Organization," in *The Moderate's Dilemma: Massive Resistance to School Desegregation in Virginia*, edited by M. Lassiter and A. Davis (Charlottesville: University Press of Virginia, 1998), 1–21.

23. Holt, *Not Yet "Free at Last"*; L. Stulberg, *Race, Schools, and Hope: African Americans and School Choice after Brown* (New York: Teachers College Press, 2008).

24. The federal Office of Economic Opportunity sponsored the Alum Rock, California, voucher program (1972–78). The program enabled parents to choose different public schools, but private schools were not a part of the choice menu. For a good discussion, see Jeffrey Henig, *Rethinking School Choice: Limits of the Market Metaphor* (Princeton, NJ: Princeton University Press, 1994).

25. J. Forman Jr., "The Secret History of School Choice: How Progressives Got There First," *Georgetown Law Journal* 93, no. 1287 (2005): 1287–319.

26. Mwalimu Shuuja, *Too Much Schooling, Too Little Education: The Paradox of Black Life in White Societies* (Trenton, NJ: Africa World, 1993); Amy Stuart Wells, Alejandra Lopez, Janelle Scott, and Jennifer Jellison, "Charter Schools as Postmodern Paradox: Rethinking Stratification in an Age of Deregulated School Choice," *Harvard Educational Review* 69, no. 2 (1999): 172–204.

27. A. S. Wells et al., "Charter School Reform and the Shifting Meaning of Educational Equity: Greater Voice and Greater Inequality?," in *Bringing Equity Back: Research for a*

New Era in American Educational Policy, edited by A. S. Wells and J. Petrovich (New York: Teachers College Press, 2005), 219–43.

28. M. Friedman, *Capitalism and Freedom* (Chicago: University of Chicago Press, 1962), 89.

29. L. Powell, "Confidential Memorandum: Attack of American Free Enterprise System" (1971), http://reclaimdemocracy.org/corporate_accountability/powell_memo_lewis .html (accessed 13 March 2008).

30. Kumashiro, *Seduction of Common Sense*; K. Demarrais, "'The Haves and the Have Mores': Fueling a Conservative Ideological War on Public Education (Or Tracking the Money)," *Educational Studies* 39, no. 3 (2006): 203–42.

31. J. Kahne, *Reframing Educational Policy: Democracy, Community and the Individual* (New York: Teachers College Press, 1996).

32. National Commission for Excellence in Education, *A Nation at Risk: The Imperative for Educational Reform* (Washington, DC: National Institute of Education, 1983).

33. D. Tyack and L. Cuban, *Tinkering toward Utopia: A Century of Public School Reform* (Cambridge: Harvard University Press, 1995).

34. W. Snider, "Conservatives' Civil-Rights Agenda Puts Spotlight on Choice," *Education Week*, 11 October 1989.

35. C. Bolick, *Transformation: The Promise and Politics of Empowerment* (Oakland, CA: Institute for Contemporary Studies, 1998), 52–53.

36. K. Blackwell, "School Choice and Civil Rights," *Townhall.com* (2007), http:// townhall.com/columnists/KenBlackwell/2007/04/06/school_choice_and_civil_rights (accessed 26 February 2009); L. G. Keegan, "'Our Gang . . .' A Reformer's Take on Injecting Sanity into the Education Wars," *School Choice Advocate*, 1, 3, 6 August; Sol Stern, "School Choice: The Last Civil Rights Battle" (electronic version), *City Journal* (Winter 1998), http://www.city-journal.org/html/8_1_school_choice.html (accessed 4 February 2009); Sol Stern, "School Choice Isn't Enough" (electronic version), *City Journal* (Winter 2008), http://www.city-journal.org/2008/18_1_instructional_reform.html (accessed 6 March 2009).

37. E. Frankenberg and C. Lee, *Charter Schools and Race: A Lost Opportunity for Integrated Education* (Cambridge: Civil Rights Project at Harvard University, 2003); J. Scott, ed., *School Choice and Diversity: What the Evidence Says* (New York: Teachers College Press, 2005).

38. *Milliken v. Bradley*, 418 U.S. (1974); *Milliken v. Bradley*, 433 U.S (1977).

39. D. Massey and N. Denton, *American Apartheid: Segregation and the Making of the Underclass* (Cambridge: Harvard University Press, 1993).

40. J. Ryan and M. Heise, "The Political Economy of School Choice," *Yale Law Journal* 111 (2002): 2043–2136.

41. Margonis and Parker, "Choice, Privatization."

42. H. Kantor and B. Brenzel, "Urban Education and the 'Truly Disadvantaged': The Historical Roots of the Contemporary Crisis, 1945–1990," in *The "Underclass" Debate: Views from History*, edited by M. Katz (Princeton: Princeton University Press, 1993), 370.

43. K. Kruse, *White Flight: Atlanta and the Making of Modern Conservatism* (Princeton: Princeton University Press, 2005), 259.

44. Ibid.

45. Ibid., 261.

46. M. Gittel, *State Power, Suburban Interests, and City School Reform* (New York: Howard Samuels State Management and Policy Center at the Graduate School and University Center of the City University of New York, 2001).

47. Lassiter and Davis, "Massive Resistance Revisited," 217.

48. J. Scott and C. DiMartino,"Hybridized, Franchised, Duplicated, and Replicated: Charter Schools and Management Organizations," in *The Charter School Experience: Expectations, Evidence, and Limitations*, edited by C. Lubienski and P. Weitzel (Cambridge: Harvard University Press, 2010), 171–96.

49. Center for Research on Education Options, *Multiple Choice: Charter School Performance in 16 States* (Palo Alto, CA: Stanford University Press, June 2009); C. Lubienski and S. Lubienski, "Charter, Private, Public Schools and Academic Achievement: New Evidence from NAEP Mathematics Data," http://www.ncspe.org (National Center for the Study of Privatization in Education, Teachers College, Columbia University, 2006) (accessed 1 February 2006).

50. J. Scott, "The Politics of Venture Philanthropy in School Choice Policy and Advocacy," *Educational Policy* 23, no. 1 (2009): 106–36.

51. Scott and DiMartino, "Hybridized, Franchised, Duplicated, and Replicated."

52. J. Bennett, "Brand-Name Charters," *Education Next* (2008), http://educationnext .org/brandname-charters/ (accessed 15 June 2008); J. Matthews, "Looking at KIPP, Coolly and Carefully," *Washington Post*, 24 April 2007, http://www.washingtonpost.com/wp-dyn/ content/article/2007/04/24/207 (accessed 29 February 2008); National Charter School Research Project, *Quantity Counts: The Growth of Charter School Management Organizations* (Seattle: Center on Reinventing Public Education, University of Washington); *Philanthropy Magazine*, "Mass-Producing Excellence," 1 July 2005, http://www.philanthropy roundtable.org/article.asp?article=747&paper=1&cat=149 (accessed 1 October 2007); P. Tough, "Can Teaching Poor Children to Act More Like Middle-Class Children Help Close the Achievement Gap?," *New York Times Magazine*, 26 November 2006.

53. J. Scott and A. Villavicencio, "School Context and Charter School Achievement: A Framework for Understanding the Performance 'Black Box,'" *Peabody Journal of Education* 84, no. 2 (2009): 227–42.

54. A. Thernstrom and S. Thernstrom, *No Excuses: Closing the Racial Achievement Gap in Learning* (New York: Simon and Schuster, 2003); U.S. Department of Education, *Successful Charter Schools* (Washington, DC: Office of Innovation and Improvement, 2005); D. Whitman, *Sweating the Small Stuff: Inner-City Schools and the New Paternalism* (Washington, DC: Thomas B. Fordham Institute Press, 2008).

55. Frankenberg and Lee, *Charter Schools and Race*, 53.

56. H. Fuller, "The Continuing Struggle of African Americans for the Power to Make Real Educational Choices," presentation at the "Second Annual Symposium on Educa-

tional Options for African Americans," Milwaukee, 2–5 March 2000; Institute for Race and Poverty, *Failed Promises: Assessing Charter Schools in the Twin Cities* (Minneapolis: University of Minnesota Law School, 2008), 1–59.

57. Thernstrom and Thernstrom, *No Excuses.*

58. See L. King, Acting Assistant Attorney General, "Memorandum: Strengthening of Enforcement of Title VI of the Civil Rights Act of 1964" (U.S. Department of Justice, Civil Rights Division, 10 July 2009).

59. Quoted in D. Jackson, "The Corruption of School Choice," *Boston Globe*, 28 October 1998.

60. G. Orfield, *Reviving the Goal of an Integrated Society: A 21st Century Challenge* (Los Angeles: Civil Rights Project/Proyecto Derechos Civiles at UCLA, 2009).

Integration after *Parents Involved*

What Does Research Suggest
about Available Options?

In the aftermath of separate, lengthy opinions by five members of the U.S. Supreme Court in the Louisville and Seattle voluntary school integration cases, educators in local districts have pondered whether their desegregation policies are legal and what their options are for maintaining racial diversity. In its 4-1-4 decision in *Parents Involved in Community Schools v. Seattle School District No. 1* (2007), the Court struck down the use of race as employed in the voluntary school desegregation plans in these districts. However, the Court also allowed for the use of race in some circumstances and affirmed maintaining diverse schools—as well as preventing racial isolation—as compelling state interests.

This essay reviews research and examples of options intended to achieve or maintain racial diversity in K–12 public schools. It is not an exhaustive review of different policies or evidence but instead provides a starting point for sorting through an array of options following this complex legal decision. The essay first reviews the demographics of today's student population. A discussion of the rationale for integration policies comes next because research has long noted the continuous need to educate the community about the rationale for such policies.[1] The bulk of the essay explores a variety of student assignment policies—both interdistrict and intradistrict—and considers what research says with respect to their effectiveness in creating racially integrated schools. The essay then examines whether housing integration efforts and other kinds of policies might enhance the effectiveness of traditional student assignment policies in creating racially diverse learning environments.

Although charter schools are a growing part of the educational landscape, this essay largely focuses on policies implemented by traditional school districts. Evidence suggests that in many places charter schools have high racial concentrations,[2] and they have arisen after the most intense policy focus on integration, making successful models of integration relatively rare.

Demographics

The demographics of the country today are rapidly changing. Nowhere is this clearer than in the public schools. In particular, the increasingly multiracial nature of school enrollment limits the usefulness of much of the early research on student assignment plans. This is because in the late 1960s, when the nation's first desegregation plans began, public school enrollment was still 80 percent white.[3] Desegregation efforts were most widespread in the South, where most districts included a mix of black and white students and were organized along county, rather than municipal, lines, thereby encompassing a diverse city and its often predominantly white suburbs.

Today, fewer than three out of every five public school students are white.[4] Latino students outnumber black students nationally, including in major urban and suburban districts. Most of the largest urban districts enroll very few white students, and rates of student poverty also are also high. Meanwhile, the patterns of racial segregation and concentrated poverty in these urban areas are being replicated in some parts of suburbia, while other suburban areas are experiencing substantial minority growth for the first time.[5] School segregation is not only multiracial but also multidimensional in that it affects various groups differently depending on location. Segregation exists within school districts and *between* school district boundary lines—between a city and its suburbs and now between certain "mixed" suburbs and other mostly white suburbs. Racial segregation is closely correlated with segregation by poverty and language.

Influenced by these demographic changes and changing judicial standards, segregation has been on the rise for black and Latino students since the late 1980s after a period of declining black-white segregation from the late 1960s through the 1980s. White students remain the most isolated of all groups, but their schools are slowly growing more diverse with increasing demographic change. Further, although the recent U.S. Supreme Court decision concerned within-district integration plans, some analyses suggest that segregation *between* districts is an even greater source of segregation across metropolitan areas than is segregation within a district.[6]

Rationale

Public education is critical for developing citizens and productive workers. Historically, public schools prepared future citizens for democratic participation; they are perhaps the last truly shared institutions of which everyone can be a part. In our increasingly diverse, interconnected nation and globalized economy, it is more important than ever that students not only gain important skills to compete in a changing economy but develop cross-cultural understanding; this is particularly urgent for white students, who, on average, grow up in the most isolated settings.[7]

Student Outcomes

Gordon Allport suggested that an essential condition for reducing prejudice was contact between various racial groups. It is particularly valuable, he stressed, that each group possess relatively equal status and work cooperatively toward a shared goal. Racially desegregated schools are not a panacea and the extent of benefits depends on whether racially diverse schools meet Allport's conditions. Research studies demonstrate that integrated schools tend to provide benefits not present in segregated schools.[8]

Learning in racially diverse classrooms, in which students have different backgrounds and experiences informing the perspectives they share in class, promotes complex thinking. Research in higher education settings, for example, finds that interactions with a racially diverse group of students can lead to deeper levels of thinking. Long-standing research finds a modest positive relationship between attending a racially diverse school and the academic achievement of African American students.[9] This positive relationship is stronger for younger students, and in voluntary programs. Additionally, depending on the nature of desegregation, Latinos students show modest gains. The achievement of white students is not harmed in desegregated schools, especially when schools remain majority white.[10]

Evidence suggests that previous attendance at a racially diverse school is related to important long-term life opportunities, particularly for students of color. These benefits include higher graduation rates than students in largely minority schools; higher college matriculation and graduation rates; and access to higher-status social and professional networks. Students who graduate from integrated schools may be more adept at working with people of other backgrounds, an important skill for workers in a global-knowledge economy.[11] Integrated schools benefit from higher levels of parental involvement and community support.

Research also indicates that communities with significant levels of school desegregation, particularly where desegregation is in place across the region, experience declines in residential segregation. Less residential segregation means students (and parents) are more likely to encounter people of different races and that neighborhood schools will be more diverse.

Public Opinion

One of the myths about school desegregation is that it lacks public support. In oral arguments, Supreme Court justices expressed skepticism about whether the public wanted integrated schools. However, most community members who experienced integration believe that such schools provide valuable learning opportunities. Because most school boards are elected, public support is critical to continuing voluntarily adopted desegregation plans.

A recent Gallup poll found that 90 percent of those surveyed believe educational opportunities for black children have improved since 1954. Half of respondents also believe that educational opportunities have improved for *white* students. A review of public opinion found Americans increasingly in favor of desegregation, and a more recent survey found that majorities of parents from all racial backgrounds believed integrated schools were better for their children.[12] This is particularly true among those with personal experience with desegregated schools.[13] Further, a majority also believed that the government should do more to integrate schools.[14] Teachers believe it is important for students of different races to interact for student learning and societal participation,[15] though fewer teachers and students believed their schools were integrated.[16]

This is not to say that educational policy or the constitutional rights of students should hinge on parental preferences. It does indicate, however, that the public supports racially diverse schools and the policies that create them.

Permissible Strategies for Creating Racially and Ethnically Diverse Schools

Within-District Strategies

Regardless of what strategies a district chooses, social science research points to specific conditions that help ensure a desegregation plan does not end up unintentionally stratifying students by race or ethnicity. For example, the provision of free transportation to school should be a component of any plan to ensure that choices of working or poor families are not severely constrained. Another important component is a provision that information about the plan and the choices available under the plan be presented in accessible languages. The strategies explored in the following section involve, in turn, race-conscious student assignment plans and race-neutral alternatives for achieving diversity. The third section turns to interdistrict strategies, which are options for largely homogeneous districts near districts of a different racial composition. Some strategies discussed have been elements of court-ordered desegregation plans. Others were included in voluntarily adopted integration plans. Still more did not necessarily have integration as an aim but should be permissible under *Parents Involved* and, if combined with other strategies, might achieve racially diverse schools.

Race-Conscious Approaches[17]

The National Association of Education panel concluded that race-conscious policies are the most effective way to achieve racially diverse schools.[18] One permissible strategy is to use a student's individual race in a manner similar to that permitted by *Grutter*. This approach would include a student's race-ethnicity as one element of a multifactor index, to be considered in magnet school admissions or when making assignments within a managed choice system. These strategies should be constitutional so long as a student's race is not the determining factor in assignments. It is not clear that any district has implemented such an approach or what specific mechanisms would make it appropriate for younger students (e.g., what would replace college applicant essays).

Berkeley Unified School District uses a plan that manages parents' choices for elementary schools using several factors to assign a "diversity code" to planning areas (four to eight neighborhood blocks). The diversity code is calculated from the percentage of students of color; household income level; and adults' educational attainment in each planning area. This plan has been successful in maintaining racial diversity[19] and has been upheld as constitutional under California's Proposition 209, which forbids preference based on an individual's race or ethnicity.[20]

Despite evidence to the contrary,[21] plans based on geographical considerations might achieve racial diversity. Because such plans consider the racial composition of a neighborhood, and not of an individual student, they comply with *Parents Involved*. Such considerations of geography may not even be formal policy given the need to craft plans unique to each district.

One of the race-conscious suggestions in Justice Anthony Kennedy's opinion was to draw boundary lines to maximize diversity in schools. Some student assignment plans divide large districts into zones. Educators give students who live within such zones preferential treatment in choosing schools in that area. (One component of Louisville's plan *not* deemed unconstitutional was similar "resides zones.") Such zones are usually designed to equally distribute students of each racial group and educational opportunities across each zone.

Siting schools in areas that would naturally draw a diverse student body was another race-conscious suggestion in Kennedy's opinion. Acknowledging the reciprocal link between housing and schooling segregation patterns is crucial to designing stable plans: school segregation is both a cause and an effect of residential segregation. In the past, some districts provided an exemption from busing as an incentive for families to live in desegregated neighborhoods. An earlier study suggested that zoning might cause parents to relocate to another zone where they deemed the racial composition more desirable.[22] Under certain circumstances, such as the pairing of adjoining, opposite-race neighborhoods, drawing school boundary lines might destabilize pockets of integration within districts. One of the difficulties is that many of the organically diverse areas are on the border between a predominantly minority central city and an overwhelmingly white suburban area. Students in such areas might be viewed as potential participants to integrate more isolated city or suburban areas and not remain in what could be diverse neighborhood schools. Plans should be based not only on demographics at the time of the plan's implementation but also account for demographic projections in every part of the district over several years, including differential birth rates by race or ethnicity and regional immigration trends.[23] Zones should be monitored to ensure they do not imbalance the district.

Race-Neutral Alternatives

Race-neutral policies to create racially diverse schools have received enormous attention after *Parents Involved*. This section considers evidence about their efficacy. In general, the link between inequality and race (and poverty status) accounts for why race-neutral alternatives may not be as effective in creating—or maintaining—integrated schools in many communities as were race-conscious policies.[24] It has been less than a decade since educators who desired voluntary integration began to consider alternatives to race-conscious student assignment plans, which might explain why there is so little research available on several strategies explored here.

After the passage of Proposition 209, and while still subject to a desegregation consent decree, San Francisco adopted a multifactor, race-neutral diversity index to manage students' choices. The index accounted for (1) socioeconomic status, (2) academic achievement, (3) English Language Learner status, (4) mother's educational background, (5) prior academic performance, (6) home language, and (7) geographic location. A judge ultimately discontinued its use, concluding from the court monitor's report that the index may have exacerbated district segregation.[25] While this approach failed in San Francisco, it still might be successful in a district where racial status is highly correlated with one or more factors, in a system of approximately equal schools, or both, thereby making most, if not all, schools "desirable."

Similarly, the Kirwan Institute at Ohio State University constructed a model that involves the identification of "low educational opportunity" neighborhoods.[26] Kirwan constructed models of districts with publicly available census and educational data. The factors included in the institute's analysis include median income, median home value, poverty, educational attainment for adults, child poverty, and school poverty. Using these factors, Kirwan identified neighborhoods where the characteristics of neighborhood residents are of "low educational opportunity." Several districts are using this information to draw school boundaries or grant student choices to ensure that students from neighborhoods characterized by low educational opportunity are spread across schools in the district.

Most uses of socioeconomically based approaches for desegregating schools have been relatively recent. Advocates of this approach tout the use of socioeconomic status (SES) as a politically and judicially viable alternative to employing race to assign students to schools, and they claim that scores of districts across the country use such policies.[27] Some of these districts (Berkeley, San Francisco) use additional factors besides SES in assignment. They also employ SES in different ways—sometimes to prioritize transfer requests or other instances when making initial assignment decisions.[28] Many of the districts that first used SES to assign students were relatively small (Wake County is the exception), largely enrolled white students, or both.[29]

Analysis of five districts that use SES-based plans endorsed by the U.S. Department of Education as successful race-neutral alternatives, in fact, shows that in two districts, schools resegregated after implementation of the plan. In three districts, racial isolation actually increased.[30] A separate analysis suggests that, because of the racial distribution of poor and nonpoor students, SES-based assignment plans would be unlikely to produce racial diversity in most of the nation's largest school districts. This is true particularly if socioeconomic status were measured only by students' free-lunch eligibility.[31] More precise measures, such as annual household income or wealth, are likely to be considered too invasive for parents to provide.

The largest district that was using a student assignment plan based on students' SES, Wake County, North Carolina, attained racial integration as a by-product of its plan, but this is due to the unusual demographics in the Raleigh area, not to the plan per se. In Wake County, 88 percent of poor families are black while 12 percent are white. Since the district's plan aims to spread poor students evenly through the district, nine of ten times when they assigned a poor student, that student was also a black student. While racial segregation rose in the aftermath of the implementation of the socioeconomic status plan, the district remained relatively desegregated.[32] The district voted in 2010 to end its diversity policy.

Other districts, such as Charlotte-Mecklenburg, give preference to low-income students if they are transferring from a school with a higher concentration of poor students to a school that is lower than the system average of poor students. In general, an approach that only uses socioeconomic status (or another factor) to give preference in transfer requests will be limited in its effectiveness at creating a larger system of more balanced schools because it would, in this case, require (1) space in low-poverty schools, (2) knowledge about the policy among those eligible to transfer, (3) information about alternative schools, (4) that low-income students feel welcome in schools in potentially distant neighborhoods serving predominantly higher-status families, and (5) transportation to lower-poverty schools. While this may create small gains in diversity, it will come entirely at the initiative of low-income families concentrated in low-income schools, neighborhoods, or both.

CHOICE-BASED APPROACH

Most plans incorporate some form of family choice into student assignments. Sociological theory and evidence from the implementation of choice-based student assignment plans suggest that choice plans often lead to further racial stratification *not* integration.[33] One reason is that due to racially segregated social networks not everyone is knowledgeable about available choice options.[34] Further, if transportation is not provided, socioeconomic factors may make it impossible for working families in the city, for example, to transport their children to suburban schools. A second reason is the segregative nature of choice requests: a study of San Diego's choice programs found the applicants were choosing schools with higher percentages of white students.[35] Understanding choice preferences and ensuring that schools are similarly attractive to applicants of all races will help achieve diversity.

While still under court order, Charlotte-Mecklenburg (CMS) used a systematic race-conscious student assignment plan that thoroughly desegregated schools, although in the early 1990s, CMS moved to a system where about half of its schools were converted to magnets and segregation rose.[36] Once the district was declared unitary in 2002, Charlotte's race-neutral approach to student assignment was coupled with more resources targeted to predominantly minority schools. This strategy, too, was unsuccessful in closing the achievement gaps for black and Latino students, nor did it address the underlying problem of racial segregation.[37] Further, when the district adopted the choice-based plan, demand was high for schools in white neighborhoods. Given the policy's preference for allowing students to attend schools in their "neighborhood," these schools became largely inaccessible to children of color, which again emphasizes the significant role that housing segregation plays in school segregation.[38] CMS also failed to provide transportation for students who wanted to attend schools not among their zone's designated schools.

The No Child Left Behind Act (NCLB) allows students in schools judged to be chronically low-performing to transfer out of these schools, but only 1.6 percent of eligible students had used this option as of 2006.[39] As the provision stands now, students generally must choose a school within their district, except for the rare instances when schools outside the district have agreed to accept transfers. An analysis of nine urban districts found students using the NCLB choice provision generally transferred to more racially balanced schools—though that is at least partially because schools designated as "low performing" tend to have high concentrations of minority students.[40]

Originally, educators used magnet schools as part of a court-ordered remedy. Magnet programs typically had a curricular theme, guidelines that ensured a diverse enrollment, and provided transportation. These schools were often popular among parents.[41] Under the second Bush administration, however, the Education Department began requiring that recipients of funding from the Magnet School Assistance Program (MSAP) use race-neutral admissions criteria. The department's own review of MSAP concluded that in almost half of the nearly 300 magnet schools receiving funding, the percentage of students in predominantly minority schools increased or did not change. The report concluded that "limitations placed on the use of race as a factor in selection of students" as a "potentially important factor" in admissions may "help explain why more than 40 percent of desegregation-targeted schools were not successful in making progress on their desegregation objective."[42] Further, more than half of the MSAP recipient districts, 35 out of 57, had more students in 90–100 percent minority schools than they did prior to the grant.[43] This suggests that race-neutral magnet schools may not be effective in creating racially diverse schools and can exacerbate districtwide racial isolation.

GEOGRAPHICALLY BASED APPROACHES

The plans of most districts, whether race-conscious or race-neutral, have some geographic component. Under a choice plan, students' proximity to a school may give them preference over students who reside in more distant locations. Plans like that of Cambridge, Massachusetts, while most prominently weighting a student's socioeconomic status, give preference to students who choose one of their two "proximity" schools. In this section I discuss plans in which school assignments are primarily based on where students reside.

The high levels of residential segregation in numerous communities are exactly why voluntary integration policies have been deemed necessary. Segregation by race is much more widespread than segregation by income *within* a racial group. Studies have long found that while current demographic patterns stem from a combination of factors, segregation is a result, in part, of past governmental policies and discrimination in the housing market, which is difficult to remedy due to the fragmented nature of that market. Race-neutral policies, such as where public housing is built and zoning regulations—in conjunction with the market forces of the real estate market—can still have a substantial effect in reinforcing and perpetuating such patterns. Thus, in residentially segregated areas, "neighborhood" schools also will be segregated schools.

Examples of districts declared unitary illustrate the difficulties of maintaining integrated schools with neighborhood-based policies. After the Denver school district was released from its court order in 1995, educators returned to a "neighborhood" school system. Within six years there was a rise in racially isolated schools in the district.[44] Even though there was an overall decline in the percentage of white students enrolled in the school district, the number of racially isolated white schools actually increased. The Norfolk, Virginia, school district was declared unitary in the mid-1980s and decided to dismantle desegregation based on court testimony from social scientists who concluded that the city's neighborhoods were integrated enough to create diverse schools and that ending mandatory desegregation would trigger a return of white students. In the first year post-desegregation, there were ten nearly all-black schools and three nearly all-white schools. While the district retained a majority-to-minority transfer option, it was rarely used and not advertised.[45] White flight out of the school system continued: by 2003, only 26 percent of Norfolk's students were white.[46]

Political Considerations

There are political considerations for school districts wanting to pursue diverse schools. Districts that have voluntarily adopted race-conscious integration plans are generally committed to overcoming the historical racial segregation in their communities. There may not be the same commitment, or perhaps moral imperative, to diversifying by other factors. Officials from some largely white suburban Boston school districts questioned whether they would continue participating in a city-suburban interdistrict desegregation program if they switched to eligibility by SES since they value the program's ability to racially diversify their schools. The program coordinator in one suburban district commented, "We don't need more white children. . . . Not that they're not deserving of a quality education, but it's not desegregation."[47]

While Justice Kennedy's opinion provides for race-conscious approaches to integrate schools, the possibilities he outlines are limited in scope.[48] Less systemic approaches to desegregating schools, such as using diversity factors only to decide whether to grant transfer requests, can lead to instability and white flight. Under a choice-based system, parents may send their children to schools where they imagine they will feel most comfortable. As in studies of housing preferences, this could be influenced by interracial anxiety, since the racial diversity parents will "tolerate" varies.[49] A system with small differences in school racial composition may find these differences exacerbated over time as families perceive some schools as places where their children will not be comfortable. If racial diversity is an educational goal, it stands to reason that a district would want every student in the district to attend a school with a diverse learning environment—and not create a situation where diversity is merely an option.

What Can Be Done above the District Level?
The 1974 *Milliken* decision made it difficult to create desegregation plans across district boundary lines. In many districts, integration plans will have limited effect in creating racial integration within district boundaries alone since metropolitan areas across the country are now divided into black and Latino central cities and white suburbs.[50] A comparison of the racial inte-

gration in districts with various types of desegregation plans or none at all found that districts with the most comprehensive, metrowide plan had the most stable integration.[51]

This section reviews strategies that encompass more than one district. As these strategies are used less frequently, there is also less research on them. Interdistrict policies may sometimes be considered politically undesirable, particularly where town boundaries or notions of "local control" are entrenched. But they may offer integration opportunities not otherwise available and provide promising approaches for some communities. Most of the examples discussed below were part of a court-ordered desegregation remedy. While some of these policies may have to be altered in order to comply with *Parents Involved* (i.e., to expand eligibility criteria), many of the programs have enjoyed political support in crossing lines of race and class in metropolitan areas.

Similar to some of the strategies discussed above that, for example, give preference to low-income students in schools of concentrated poverty, NCLB's transfer provision could be invoked to allow students in schools judged to be low-performing to transfer across district boundaries to high-performing schools. According to one analysis, only 8 percent of eligible students transferred across district boundaries.[52] To ensure that this choice can be used effectively, districts with capacity in high-performing schools should be required to take students from another district, provide free transportation, and have states pay suburban districts for any extra costs incurred.

Interdistrict magnet schools are one of the remedies that Connecticut adopted in response to a state court ruling to desegregate schools in the Hartford region. Students are chosen by lottery from both Hartford and surrounding suburban districts. In 2006–7, 7,000 students were attending these magnets schools, including nearly 1,000 students of color from Hartford, but not all schools complied with the racial guidelines set by the settlement agreement. Approximately 40 percent of all minority students were from the suburbs, *not* the urban areas. White suburban students are less likely to participate, and many of the magnets are heavily minority. While some interdistrict magnet schools provide integrated schooling experiences for their students, they are less effective at integrating a metropolitan region overall.

Maggie Walker Governor's School, in Richmond, Virginia, is an example of an interdistrict magnet school voluntarily begun in the 1990s that accepts applications from students in eleven surrounding districts. The admissions criteria are academically selective, but a certain number of spaces are allotted for each participating district. Although the school is disproportionately white, it allows selected students to experience a more diverse school than either the largely white suburban districts or the racially isolated Richmond city district.

Kansas City's desegregation remedy was remarkable for the amount of money spent to create a system of magnet schools. The theory was that the schools would be so attractive that they would lure surrounding suburban families into the city to desegregate schools. While the racial distribution of students in Kansas City was more even after the implementation of the magnet schools, the percentage of white students being educated in the district declined slightly from 1986 to 1992.[53] The state phased out funding for the magnet school program following the 1995 *Missouri v. Jenkins* decision. As funding dried up—demonstrating the precarious nature of integration programs whose funding is regularly allocated—and the district was released from court supervision, black students' exposure to white students fell sharply.[54]

St. Louis and Hartford operate two-way interdistrict programs: a city-suburban transfer program and interdistrict magnets. St. Louis has operated the nation's largest interdistrict desegregation program, implemented in the early 1980s under court order and continued under voluntary terms since 1999. Unlike Kansas City and Hartford, St. Louis suburban districts were required to participate and to accept enough St. Louis urban students to meet targets for minority percentage.[55] The state initially funded the program (e.g., transportation and staff), but since 1999 a voter-approved tax increase pays for the programs. The Metropolitan Council for Educational Opportunity (METCO) is a similar program, begun voluntarily in Boston in the 1960s, serving 3,300 students and 38 participating suburban districts, funded by a state law to reduce racial imbalance. The popular program has a long waiting list, and students have had remarkable academic success. Although parents value the program's interracial experiences for their children, the most important reason cited for participation is the academic quality of suburban schools.[56]

Minneapolis may offer a promising race-neutral interdistrict model. The program, called The Choice Is Yours, began in 2001–2 in response to a city-suburban segregation lawsuit. Unlike the other interdistrict programs profiled here, Minneapolis's effort bases student eligibility on family socioeconomic status.[57] By 2006–7, nearly 2,000 students placed in nine suburban districts were participating, and the program was voluntarily continued. Suburban districts, in general, have become more diverse because most participating students are students of color.[58]

During the 20th century, the overall number of school districts declined as states came to see that consolidating districts would be more efficient.[59] Southern states have generally had larger countywide districts. North Carolina policy, for example, encourages district consolidation and has just more than 100 school districts for 1.4 million students; Florida has only 67 countywide districts enrolling 2.7 million students. Michigan and New Jersey, in contrast, each have more than 500 districts educating fewer than 1.5 million students.[60]

Several decades ago, the cities of Raleigh, Charlotte, and Nashville consolidated with other districts in their county prior to desegregation. In other places like metropolitan Louisville, consolidation occurred under pressure from federal judges in 1975. More recently, local districts consolidate for purposes other than desegregation, such as for financial efficiency (e.g., Chattanooga and Knoxville, Tennessee). Several of these districts have had decades of stable integration, which would have been unlikely if the city and suburban districts had been separate.

Delaware offers an interesting example of consolidation. Courts found the state liable for reinforcing segregation across metropolitan Wilmington and ordered the consolidation of all thirteen districts in New Castle County. The county was subsequently divided into four pie-shaped districts, each containing urban and suburban areas. The districts were under court order until 1996, and during this time Delaware had among the highest levels of desegregation for black students.[61]

Housing Integration Strategies

Some communities' school desegregation efforts also have recognized the importance of partnering with housing efforts in order to sustain school efforts. Ultimately, if housing integration is successful, there will be less need for school-based policies. A common suggestion regarding the partnership of housing and school integration efforts is that existing governmental housing programs be altered so that racial integration becomes a byproduct. Some of the programs below have been implemented on a small scale—or are currently mere suggestions. One identified policy is improving the counseling of prospective renters or buyers about housing choices that would help reduce residential segregation. An oft-cited example is counseling conducted by the Kentucky Human Rights Commission where a staff member drove Section 8 recipients who are black to areas with a higher percentage of white residents in order to more evenly spread black recipients.[62] A few states have provided low-cost mortgage financing for residents who make moves contributing to integration. Seattle, for example, provided $2,000 tax credits to low- or moderate-income home buyers—which, the school superintendent noted, could pay for itself by eliminating the costs to the district of busing those children elsewhere.[63]

A second suggestion is to require that new housing, including affordable housing, aid racial integration. For example, the Low-Income Housing Tax Credit is the federal government's largest program providing housing opportunities for low-income families. Research shows that, as administered, the program concentrates affordable housing in poor, urban neighborhoods.[64] One positive change would require that a share of low-income units be built in low-poverty neighborhoods. This would ensure that the government does not subsidize housing that exacerbates racial segregation or poverty. A number of states require scattered-site affordable housing to avoid concentration of below–market cost housing. Thousands of units in suburban areas have been produced which, if combined with counseling for minority residents about such opportunities, could lead to more racially integrated communities.

Research documents the positive effects of the Gautreaux Assisted Housing Program in Chicago. Under this program, counseling and housing subsidies provide low-income families access to well-functioning, desegregated schools in low-poverty, predominantly white suburban neighborhoods as a way to deconcentrate poverty and reduce racial segregation in Chicago, problems exacerbated by densely populated public housing.[65] Thousands of low-income black families participated in the relocation to predominantly white suburban Chicago communities. After nearly two decades, 70 percent of these families remained in suburbia.[66] Despite initial hesitation about moving to such a different environment, families and students succeeded in their new schools.[67]

Other efforts focus on partnerships between individual school districts, housing developers, and planners. In some suburban communities planning new developments, school boards promised to build a new school if a portion of new development units went to residents of color.[68] Charlotte-Mecklenburg, for instance, worked with housing officials to ensure that new schools or new affordable or public housing would not impede desegregation efforts. Minneapolis's interdistrict school program connects participating families with low-cost housing in the suburban communities where their children attend schools. These parents already have a significant connection to the community through their children's school, and their relocation would reduce transportation time and costs for students commuting from Minneapolis each day.

Other Variables to Consider in Making Diversity Work

A National Institute of Education (NIE) panel of desegregation experts in the early 1980s suggested several components of successful desegregation. In addition to implementing a student assignment strategy such as those described above, the NIE experts stressed that educators must constantly gather and analyze data, partner with housing efforts, involve parents and the community, provide teacher and principal professional development, create healthy environments and organizational changes within desegregated schools such as inclusive curriculum and instruction, structure extracurricular activities to encourage diversity, create a shared vision embracing diversity, and implement policies to eliminate any perceived racial inequality or discrimination in school rules.[69] Disseminating information and providing transportation are critical to the success of choice-based strategies.

In light of the judicial skepticism toward any use of race, it is more important than ever to gather and analyze data to remain aware of changing demographics. First, district demographics are important to consider in determining which plan will most effectively create diverse schools. Wake County's demographics, for example, are one reason why the socioeconomically based plan maintained racial integration but might not work in other districts.[70] Second, demographic changes may not be apparent when one looks at the overall school enrollment at one point in time. Thus, examining the lowest grade in a school may project trends and help administrators adjust policies accordingly before schools become segregated.[71] Third, data help educate community members as to why desegregation plans are needed in the first place. If families make transfer requests that exacerbate segregation, and a district manages these choices according to a prescribed set of factors, the district, with appropriate data, can explain the need to maintain such an assignment policy. Relative stability in assignments also helps parents know what to expect and may lead to greater support for the district's policy. Finally, demonstrating successes and areas needing improvement contributes to parental and community support.

Given the overwhelming percentage of white female teachers, and the fact that many of these teachers grew up in white, middle-class environments, teachers need professional development to ensure that they effectively reach all students in their classrooms.[72] School districts and teacher preparation institutions have important roles in educating teachers for the nation's increasingly multiracial student population. School and district leaders must assess data to ensure that racial and ethnic segregation or inequality does not occur within schools.[73]

Studies demonstrate that even in some schools that were diverse at the school level, students are often not exposed to students of other races and ethnicities due to within-school segregation. Simply designing effective student assignment plans is therefore not enough. For example, tracking is a method of assigning students to classes based on perceived academic ability or achievement, which often sorts students—unintentionally—by race.[74] Detracking is an approach to eliminate these segregating mechanisms by creating heterogeneously grouped classes in terms of race or ethnicity and ability. A case study of a district in New York that detracked its curriculum by offering college-preparatory classes to all students demonstrated that many of the above points about data collection, analysis, and community buy-in also are relevant to policy changes within schools.[75] Research in this area is important both in terms of demonstrating a comprehensive, systemic approach to diversity and because of voluminous research findings on the benefits that come when schools are appropriately structured.

The available research demonstrates that race-neutral alternatives have been less effective than race-conscious ones. This is not to imply that districts should not consider alternatives; partially, this is a reflection of the lack of research (and research funding) on available alternatives. Often too, adopting policies that seek to create integrated schools—even if not completely successful in fully desegregating all district schools by race—may be more effective than trying to do nothing at all, at least until we learn more about what works in different contexts. In fact, a number of examples of policies portray "works in progress" as districts continue to try to understand what motivates families' choices or how to make more schools attractive to more families. This information can help ensure that policies intended to create diverse schools do not unintentionally result in racially isolated schools.

It remains essential to think about integration efforts outside of K–12 school districts. If all the strategies school districts have been left with are partially successful plans, educators must collaborate with housing officials, regional planners, and others to mitigate the well-established detrimental effects of racial and class stratification in American society.

NOTES

This essay is drawn from a working paper drafted for the Charles Hamilton Houston Institute for Race and Justice.

1. See, e.g., W. D. Hawley et al., *Strategies for Effective School Desegregation* (Lexington, MA: Lexington, 1983), chap. 5.

2. E. Frankenberg, G. Siegel-Hawley, and J. Wang, "Choice without Equity: Charter School Segregation," *Education Policy Analysis Archives* 19 (2011), http://epaa.asu.edu/ojs/article/view/779.

3. In the past three decades, the federal government has considerably underfunded re-

search about the importance of school racial context as the nation grows increasingly diverse.

4. G. Orfield, *Reviving the Goal of an Integrated Society* (Los Angeles: Civil Rights Project/Proyecto Derechos Civiles at UCLA, 2009).

5. W. Frey, *Melting Pot Suburbs: A Census 2000 Study of Suburban Diversity* (Washington, DC: Brookings Institution, 2001).

6. C. Clotfelter, *Public School Segregation in Metropolitan Areas* (Cambridge, MA: National Bureau of Economic Research, 1998).

7. This section is drawn from research summarized in the 553 Social Scientists Brief; more detail and citations can be found at http://civilrightsproject.ucla.edu/legal-developments/court-decisions/statement-of-american-social-scientists-of-research-on-school-desegregation-submitted-to-us-supreme-court/amicus_parents_v_seatle.pdf (accessed 20 March 2011).

8. T. Pettigrew and L. Tropp, "A Meta-analytic Test of Intergroup Contact Theory," *Journal of Personality and Social Psychology* 90 (2006): 751–83.

9. More recent, methodologically rigorous research finds even stronger benefits. See R. L. Linn and K. G. Welner, eds., *Race-Conscious Policies for Assigning Students to Schools: Social Science Research and the Supreme Court Cases* (Washington, DC: National Academy of Education, 2007).

10. J. W. Schofield, "Review of Research on School Desegregation's Impact on Elementary and Secondary School Students," in *Handbook of Research on Multicultural Education*, edited by J. A. Banks and C. A. McGee Banks (New York: Simon and Schuster Macmillan, 1995), 597–617.

11. W. D. Hawley, "Designing Schools That Use Student Diversity to Enhance Learning of All Students," in *Lessons in Integration: Realizing the Promise of Racial Diversity in America's Schools*, edited by E. Frankenberg and G. Orfield (Charlottesville: University of Virginia Press, 2007), 31–56.

12. Metropolitan Center for Urban Education, *"With All Deliberate Speed": Achievement, Citizenship and Diversity in American Education* (New York: Steinhardt School of Education, New York University, 2005).

13. G. Orfield, "Public Opinion and School Desegregation," *Teachers College Record* 96, no. 4 (1995): 654–70.

14. 1994 Gallup poll cited in Orfield, "Public Opinion and School Desegregation."

15. E. Goldring and C. Smrekar, "Magnet Schools and the Pursuit of Racial Balance," *Education and Urban Society* 33 (2000): 17–35.

16. K. Bagnishi and M. R. Sheer, "Brown v. Board of Education: Fifty Years Later," *Trends and Tudes Newsletter of Harris Interactive Youth* 3, no. 6 (June 2004).

17. Districts' student assignment plans often have race-conscious *and* race-neutral elements.

18. Linn and Welner, *Race-Conscious Policies for Assigning Students.*

19. L. Chavez and E. Frankenberg, *Integration Defended: Berkeley Unified's Strategy to*

Maintain School Diversity (Los Angeles: Civil Rights Project/Proyecto Derechos Civiles at UCLA, 2009). See also Williams and Frankenberg essay.

20. *American Civil Rights Foundation v. Berkeley Unified School District* (no. A121137) (Cal. App. Mar. 17, 2009).

21. Most geographically based plans we discuss in this essay are race-neutral—color-blind. They do not simply forgo integration as a goal; more likely than not, they do not attain racial integration.

22. Cited in Hawley et al., *Strategies for Effective School Desegregation*.

23. Ibid.

24. See essays by Kahlenberg, Reardon and Rhodes, and Siegel-Hawley on socioeconomic status (SES) assignment plans.

25. S. Biegel, "Court-Mandated Education Reform: The San Francisco Experience and the Shaping of Educational Policy after *Seattle-Louisville* and *Brian Ho v. SFUSD*," *Stanford Journal of Civil Rights and Civil Liberties* 4 (2008): 159–213.

26. M. Baek et al., "K–12 Diversity: Strategies for Diverse and Successful Schools" (Columbus, OH: Kirwan Institute, 2007).

27. R. Kahlenberg, *Rescuing Brown v. Board of Education: Profiles of Twelve School Districts Pursuing Socioeconomic School Integration* (New York: Century Foundation, 2007).

28. See Kahlenberg essay.

29. Department of Education, Office for Civil Rights of the United States, "Achieving Diversity: Race-Neutral Alternatives in American Education" (Washington, DC: U.S. Department of Education, 2004). A recent report by Richard Kahlenberg notes several districts with few white students using such approaches, which suggests that where racial integration difficult, SES policies might limit concentrations of poverty in segregated minority schools.

30. Brief Amicus Curiae of the American Civil Liberties Union, the ACLU of Kentucky, and the ACLU of Washington in Support of Respondents, *Parents Involved in Community Schools v. Seattle School District No. 1, et al.* and *Crystal D. Meredith v. Jefferson County Board of Education et al.* (nos. 05-908 and 05-915) (Sp. Ct. 2006).

31. S. F. Reardon, J. T. Yun, and M. Kurlaender, "Implications of Income-Based School Assignment Policies for Racial School Segregation," *Educational Evaluation and Policy Analysis* 28, no. 1 (2006): 49–75.

32. S. L. Flinspach and K. E. Banks, "Moving beyond Race: Socioeconomic Diversity as a Race-Neutral Approach to Desegregation in the Wake County Schools," in *School Resegregation: Must the South Turn Back?*, edited by J. C. Boger and G. Orfield (Chapel Hill: University of North Carolina Press, 2005), 261–80.

33. S. Saporito and D. Sohoni, "Coloring Outside the Lines: Racial Segregation in Public Schools and Their Attendance Boundaries," *Sociology of Education* 79 (April 2006): 81–105.

34. B. Fuller, R. F. Elmore, and G. Orfield, eds., *Who Chooses, Who Loses? Culture, Institutions, and the Unequal Effects of School Choice* (New York: Teachers College Press, 1996).

35. J. R. Betts et al., *Does School Choice Work? Effects on Student Integration and Achievement* (San Francisco: Public Policy Institute of California, August 2006).

36. R. A. Mickelson, "Subverting *Swann*: First and Second Generation Segregation in Charlotte-Mecklenburg Schools," *American Educational Research Journal* 38 (2001): 215–52.

37. R. A. Mickelson, "The Academic Consequences of Desegregation and Segregation: Evidence from the Charlotte-Mecklenburg Schools," *North Carolina Law Review* 81 (2003): 1513–62.

38. R. K. Godwin et al., "Sinking *Swann*: Public School Choice and the Resegregation of Charlotte's Public Schools," *Review of Policy Research* 23 (2006): 983–97.

39. Center for Education Policy, *From the Capital to the Classroom: Year Four of the No Child Left Behind Act* (Washington, DC: Center for Education Policy, 2006); G. L. Sunderman, J. S. Kim, and G. Orfield, *NCLB Meets School Realities: Lessons from the Field* (Thousands Oaks, CA: Corwin, 2005).

40. See R. Zimmer et al., *State and Local Implementation of the No Child Left Behind Act*, vol. 1 (Washington, DC: U.S. Department of Education, 2007).

41. L. Steel and R. Levine, *Educational Innovation in Multiracial Contexts: The Growth of Magnet Schools in American Education* (Palo Alto, CA: American Institutes for Research, 1991). See also Smrekar and Goldring essay.

42. U.S. Department of Education, *Evaluation of the Magnet Schools Assistance Program, 1998 Grantees* (Washington, DC: U.S. Department of Education, 2003), IV-11.

43. Brief of ACLU.

44. C. Lee, *Denver Public Schools: Resegregation, Latino Style* (Cambridge: Civil Rights Project at Harvard University, 2006).

45. G. Orfield and S. E. Eaton, eds., *Dismantling Desegregation* (New York: New Press, 1996), chap. 4.

46. G. Orfield and C. Lee, *Racial Transformation and the Changing Nature of Segregation* (Cambridge: Civil Rights Project at Harvard University, 2006).

47. T. Jan, "Metco Fears for Its Future," *Boston Globe*, 26 July 2007.

48. *Parents Involved in Community Schools v. Seattle School District No. 1*, 127 S. Ct. 2738, 2792 (2007).

49. C. Z. Charles, "Can We Live Together? Racial Preferences and Neighborhood Outcomes," in *The Geography of Opportunity: Race and Housing Choice in Metropolitan America*, edited by X. D. S. Briggs (Washington, DC: Brookings Institution Press, 2005), 45–80.

50. Reardon, Yun, and Kurlaender, "Implications of Income-Based School Assignment Policies."

51. E. Frankenberg and C. Lee, *Race in American Public Schools: Rapidly Resegregating School Districts* (Cambridge: Civil Rights Project at Harvard University, 2002).

52. Center for Education Policy, *From the Capital to the Classroom*.

53. A. Morantz, "Money and Choice in Kansas City: Major Investments with Modest

Returns," in *Dismantling Desegregation: The Quiet Reversal of Brown v. Board of Education*, edited by G. Orfield and S. E. Eaton (New York: New Press, 1996), 241–63.

54. G. Orfield and C. Lee, *Brown at 50: King's Dream or Plessy's Nightmare?* (Cambridge: Civil Rights Project at Harvard University, 2004).

55. G. W. Heaney and S. Uchitelle, *Unending Struggle: The Long Road to an Equal Education in St. Louis* (Lincoln: University of Nebraska Press, 2004).

56. G. Orfield et al., *City-Suburban Desegregation: Parent and Student Perspectives in Metropolitan Boston* (Cambridge: Civil Rights Project at Harvard University, 1997).

57. Omaha is beginning to implement an interdistrict learning community that also uses socioeconomic status to diversify. See Holme et al. essay.

58. IRP, *The Choice Is Ours: Expanding Educational Opportunity for All Twin Cities Children* (Minneapolis: University of Minnesota Law School, May 2006).

59. G. Orfield, "Metropolitan School Desegregation," in *In Pursuit of a Dream Deferred: Linking Housing and Education Policy*, edited by j. a. powell, G. Kearney, and V. Kay (New York: Peter Lang, 2001), 121–57.

60. Student enrollment data taken from NCES Common Core of Data, 2005–6. See J. Tilove, "Pressed by a New Invasion of Yankees, Schools of the New South Resegregate," *Newhouse News Service*, 30 June 2005.

61. Orfield and Lee, *Brown at 50*.

62. Described in Orfield and Eaton, *Dismantling Desegregation*.

63. Ibid.

64. L. Freeman, *Siting Affordable Housing: Location and Neighborhood Trends of Low Income Housing Tax Credit Developments in the 1990s* (Washington, DC: Brookings Institution, 2004).

65. See, generally, A. Polikoff, *Waiting for Gautreaux: A Story of Segregation, Housing, and the Black Ghetto* (Evanston, IL: Northwestern University Press, 2006).

66. J. Rosenbaum, S. DeLuca, and T. Tuck, "New Capabilities in New Places: Low-Income Black Families in Suburbia," in *The Geography of Opportunity*, edited by X. Briggs (Washington, DC: Brookings Institution, 2005), 150–75.

67. J. Rosenbaum, "School Experiences of Low-Income Black Children in White Suburbs," paper presented at National Conference on School Desegregation, University of Chicago, June 1986.

68. Orfield and Eaton, *Dismantling Desegregation*.

69. Hawley et al., *Strategies for Effective School Desegregation*; Hawley, "Designing Schools That Use Student Diversity."

70. They also had a prior voluntary racial integration plan in place for several decades prior to the current SES plan.

71. E. Frankenberg, "School Segregation, Desegregation, and Integration: What Do These Terms Mean in a Post-PICS, Racially Transitioning Society?," *Seattle Journal for Social Justice* 6 (2008): 553–90.

72. See Hawley and Irvine essay.

73. See, generally, E. Frankenberg and G. Orfield, eds., *Lessons in Integration: Realizing the Promise of Racial Diversity in American Schools* (Charlottesville: University of Virginia Press, 2007).

74. J. Oakes, *Keeping Track: How Schools Structure Inequality*, 2nd ed. (New Haven, CT: Yale University Press, 2005).

75. C. C. Burris and K. G. Welner, "Classroom Integration and Accelerated Learning through Detracking," in *Lessons in Integration: Realizing the Promise of Racial Diversity in American Schools*, edited by E. Frankenberg and G. Orfield (Charlottesville: University of Virginia Press, 2007), 207–27.

Advancing the Integration Agenda under the Obama Administration and Beyond

When it comes to racial and ethnic integration in our nation's public schools, it matters significantly whether the federal government is friend or foe. According to the U.S. Supreme Court, the Constitution does not guarantee a fundamental right to education, let alone an equal or racially integrated education.[1] School districts once subject to court-ordered desegregation decrees may emerge from their long history of de jure acts after just a few years of reasonable compliance with formal orders, regardless of whether the compliance resulted in any sustainable desegregation. Even voluntary efforts to provide some modicum of racial integration, once encouraged by the courts, are constitutionally suspect.[2] These days, it seems the courts only loosely enforce (and hardly expand) education rights, so executive and congressional leadership is sorely needed if we are ever to realize the vision articulated in *Brown v. Board of Education* more than a half century ago.

This essay, roughly divided into two sections, offers concrete political, legal, and policy recommendations to break the stalemate. The first section sets forth a proposal to address the hundreds of traditional school desegregation cases on the federal government's docket that remain under judicial supervision, as well as the unknown number of "voluntary" school desegregation agreements that technically remain under agency supervision. Recognizing the limited reach of these traditional desegregation cases, the second section offers a series of recommendations on how the federal government can develop an affirmative school integration agenda that not only includes efforts to assist school districts adopt student assignment methods that promote racial and ethnic diversity in their schools but also infuses an integrationist approach into all of its public policy initiatives.

The School Desegregation Docket

Arguably, it has been more than forty years since the U.S. Department of Justice (DOJ) last took a truly transparent, comprehensive, and strategic approach to its school desegregation docket, which includes approximately 200 cases at present.[3] Meanwhile, hundreds of school systems have been declared unitary in the past two decades alone, and in many of these districts, troubling patterns of resegregation have emerged almost overnight.[4] The combination of the Supreme Court's vagueness in *Freeman* and *Dowell* and a dearth of recent district and appellate court guidance on the appropriate standards to apply in unitary-status proceedings has led to an ad hoc approach to school desegregation litigation. Maximizing the integration possibilities of these cases, therefore, requires collaboration between DOJ's Civil Rights Division and the U.S. Department of Education's Office of Civil Rights (OCR) to develop a clear philosophy on and approach to their respective desegregation dockets.

As an initial matter, OCR and DOJ should issue much-needed formal guidance on preconditions for unitary status that would maximize the ability of school districts under court order to realize their integration potential.[5] Similar guidelines could be developed through OCR to address the districts theoretically still subject to "Form 441-B" voluntary desegregation plans, negotiated in the 1960s and 1970s by the Department of Health, Education, and Welfare (HEW). Not only could the government use these guidelines, in assessing the active cases on OCR's and DOJ's school-desegregation docket, but so could private plaintiffs, in litigating cases that do not involve DOJ; school districts, in initiating self-evaluations of their own desegregation progress; and even the courts, in assessing litigation claims and motions for unitary status.[6]

Substantively, the guidelines could address a number of issues. For instance, they could set forth in greater detail the specific facets of school operations, beyond the six contemplated in *Green*, for which the vestiges of desegregation must be eliminated "to the extent practicable" under *Dowell*. Lawyers in school desegregation cases often have examined a wide range of school operations in which racial disparities may exist, for example, in student achievement, discipline, the enrollment in advanced, gifted, or remedial courses, the assignment of students to alternative schools, or the identification of students for (and in the provision of) special education. These areas, and perhaps others, should be formally codified in the government's guidelines, which would allow more uniform assessment of progress under court order.

The guidelines also should clarify that once plaintiffs identify disparities, the defendant school district bears the burden of demonstrating that they are not proximately caused by the prior de jure discrimination and segregation. Racial disparities are quite common, but the key question in a school desegregation case is whether they can be traced to the district's prior unlawful acts (in which case it has a legal duty to remedy them) or caused by factors outside of the district's control (in which case it is permitted, but not obligated, to address them). Making this rebuttable presumption explicit is helpful because federal courts have not always stated clearly which party bears that burden; making it more challenging for integration advocates, some courts have placed the burden on plaintiffs. Given the difficulty of proving proximate cause, shifting the burden to the school district may be a fair but remedy-maximizing interpretation of the law.

Beyond identifying these discrete areas that should be examined, the guidelines should address the issue of demographic changes. Almost all school districts still under court order have experienced vast demographic changes since the desegregation cases against them were filed.[7] Insofar as some dormant, decades-old orders no longer reflect the communities they are intended to serve, OCR and DOJ should define how the demographic changes should be treated. If there is a legal basis to do so, perhaps the burden should be explicitly placed, again, on school districts (rather than plaintiffs) to explain why they are not responsible for disparities that were not addressed in the original order, or to account for disparities pertaining to racial groups on whom the original order was silent.

Last, but not least, the guidelines should address one of the most pressing issue that advocates have identified—the resegregation that often immediately follows a finding of unitary status. The guidelines might require a court or parties, first, to determine which desegregative student assignment strategies the school district in question employs, and second, to assess how unitary status likely will affect the continued use of these strategies and the resulting impact. If resegregation appears likely, the school district should called on to explain—under the "continuing good faith compliance" prong of the *Dowell* test—how it intends to continue to assign students in a way that effectively demonstrates its commitment to avoid racial isolation and to promote racial integration, while complying with the Constitution and the requirements of *Parents Involved*. The guidelines should also establish a presumption that districts may continue to use assignment strategies established under court order (such as satellite zones and school siting and pairings arrangements) beyond the order's dissolution, on the theory that eliminating them may not only disrupt feeding patterns but also knowingly re-create segregated conditions. Such assurance might give school districts the comfort of knowing that they can exist after unitary status without completely altering or overhauling something that works well as is.

With the guidelines established, DOJ and OCR should revisit their respective school desegregation dockets in a systematic way to seek sustainable, constitutional, integration-maximizing solutions in the districts that remain under supervision. The sad reality is that law is stacked against school-desegregation plaintiffs. Given the state of the law, and the general resistance of the federal judiciary to continued supervision, it is hard to imagine what kind of conditions a court would need to find to reject outright a school district's request for unitary status and to order more aggressive relief. For minority students and parents, knowing that a dormant court order exists in their school district is of limited benefit.

By reviving desegregation cases and using them to focus school districts on existing racial disparities, these cases may still serve some good. DOJ and OCR, therefore, should seriously consider a more proactive approach to desegregation cases on their respective dockets. Proceeding proactively in this way need not mean, as it might have under some prior administrations less interested in desegregation, immediately negotiating unitary status for every school district in question. But it would mean that the government might negotiate the terms of an eventual dissolution of the order, if DOJ or OCR finds that the school district has indeed met all of its constitutional obligations.

While there is that risk, the benefits could significantly outweigh it. First, revisiting the order allows the government an opportunity to conduct site visits, meet with the community and with district officials, complete an on-the-ground assessment of the continuing racial disparities and school segregation, and strategize with key stakeholders about how best to address these problems given the school district's continuing constitutional obligations.

Second, the government's case review would be comprehensive and uniform, and conducted at the government's initiation and on the government's terms, rather than at a school district's, or court's, or private intervenor's behest. Such a posture allows the government to establish its goals proactively, use its own metrics to evaluate the efforts of the school districts in meeting their obligations, and negotiate the best possible result for all of the parties involved.

Third, negotiating a modified order or, if appropriate, terms for the eventual dissolution of a court order, may provide opportunities for concessions from a defendant school district that may not have been possible through litigation. Given the stringent standards under *Freeman* and *Jenkins*, it seems unlikely that a court would find disparities in achievement, assignment, or discipline in existence today traceable to constitutional violations that occurred decades prior. A school district, however, might agree to take actions in these areas, and a court might be willing to approve a stipulation that includes such relief because the parties assessed their likelihood of success at trial and decided that the settlement fairly recognizes the litigation risks.

Fourth, should any such negotiated unitary status agreement containing race-conscious elements be challenged by a dissatisfied parent in the future, the hope is that a court evaluating its validity may find some of the following justifications for it: (1) the vestiges of any remaining duties to eliminate de jure segregation; (2) demonstration of a continuing commitment to sustain gains obtained while under court order; and (3) pursuit of the compelling interest of racially integrated education as established in *Parents Involved*. And because all parties will have agreed to any negotiated settlement, they will be in the position of working together to defend the agreement together, should a court or private intervenor challenge school district actions.

Affirmative Strategies for Voluntary School Integration

A large number of desegregation cases remain on the books, but they do not apply to the vast majority of school districts in the nation, and the Supreme Court has already declared that their reach and duration are limited, as is the relief that can be achieved through them. An administration committed to educational equity and integrated schooling therefore should put the bulk of its resources behind political, legislative, and policy efforts, and to coordinating federal agency functions that promote racial integration and equity.

Reframing the School Integration Debate and
Advancing Research to Support It

For the past several decades, advocates of school integration have been playing defense in the courts of law as well as in the court of public opinion. To advance an agenda that prioritizes racially integrated public education, the president and Congress must make clear that *Brown*'s vision of equal, integrated public schools continues to be relevant and critical to the health and prosperity of our democracy. Indeed, as our nation has become more racially and ethnically diverse, and our society more global than ever, *Brown*'s goal is only more compelling.

Public education and messaging are crucial, and the U.S. Department of

Education (ED) specifically can play a key role in better informing the public about the benefits of integration and the harms of racial isolation. A substantial body of research already exists from which the government can draw,[8] but its reach does not extend to those who work and write outside the halls of universities, where the research is conducted and discussed, or courtrooms, where these matters are sometimes litigated. To be sure, many Americans have unwavering views on the subject, but a significant number can still be informed and persuaded of the value of school integration. ED officials, therefore, should use the "bully pulpit" to provide leadership to help the public better understand how and why racial and ethnic integration improves the educational experience and life opportunity of all students.

Beyond democratizing knowledge that already exists, the Obama administration also should support researchers to develop more of it. As much as is known about race and schooling today, there remains much more to learn. As I have noted, the nation's demographics have shifted radically since the 1950s and 1960s, when the foundational research was conducted on the harms of racial isolation. Today, not only are there far more nonwhite students in public school, but also students are diverse in many other areas of life, including language, class, ethnicity, religion, and culture.[9] Issues of integration and isolation are increasingly layered, with some students facing segregation, for example, by race and poverty, as well as language. Public schools constantly struggle with which training, teaching, and learning methods are most effective (and for whom). Some of this thinking is certainly already being done by innovative teachers and researchers, and funded by private foundations, but there is a limit to how much privately funded work can accomplish and no reason why the government should not participate in, if not lead, the dialogue.

Undoing Obstacles to Integration Innovation

The Obama administration must move quickly to reverse policies and programs put in place by the Bush administration that undermine civil rights enforcement[10] or, as related to issues of integrated schooling, stifle the development of innovative, constitutionally sound practices of local communities and school districts. Two examples come immediately to mind. First, OCR should withdraw or amend "Dear Colleague" letters and other guidance it issued in the waning days under Bush purporting to provide legal advice on the use of race in K–12 student assignment and in higher education admissions.[11] Any revisions should energetically encourage, rather than discourage, school districts' and institutions' exploring legally permissible strategies to expand educational opportunities and expose students to diverse educational settings.

Second, OCR should use its technical assistance to assist, not inhibit, entities that want to promote voluntary integration in ways consistent with the law. To be sure, strategies that take race into account must satisfy strict scrutiny. But, race-conscious policies and programs are by no means invalid per se, and OCR should not treat them as if they are. Insofar as the docket of magnet school technical assistance reviews and affirmative compliance reviews that OCR inherits include actions initiated under the prior administration that were ideologically motivated, those reviews or investigations should be approached with a balanced eye and, if appropriate, brought to a responsible and ethical close.

Reforming Choice in "Traditional" Public Schools: NCLB and Magnets

School choice has undoubtedly captured the modern American imagination as an integral part of the cure for our educational ills.[12] At the federal level, two examples of public education choice programs immediately come to mind: The federal magnet schools program, now nearly four decades old, continues to (purport to) offer unique curricula and exposure to greater student diversity, even as that latter promise has been diluted over the years.[13] And more recently, the No Child Left Behind Act gives students in failing schools the right, theoretically, to transfer elsewhere.

With regard to these choice options, however, the federal government has taken a weak, sometimes counterproductive, stance toward integration. NCLB, for example, does not have any structures in place to encourage integrative transfers or discourage segregative ones, and as a result some commentators have observed that its choice provisions contribute to greater racial isolation.[14] And though certainly the more effective public school choice tool available, magnets in recent years also are increasingly less successful at achieving meaningful levels of integration, despite their origins as an explicit desegregation tool.[15] A full discussion of the shortcomings of and possible reforms to NCLB and magnets is beyond the scope of this essay, but to advance the integration agenda, any reforms must, at a minimum, eliminate the perverse incentives that the choice mechanisms create, and replace them with positive ones.

For instance, the federal government should create incentives for districts to offer or encourage integrative NCLB transfers and to promote greater cooperation among neighboring school districts, especially at the borders along which substantial residential segregation exists. Providing parents with access to complete information about the full range of NCLB transfer options and assistance in the decision-making process may also empower individuals with the knowledge and ability to make integrative choices.

Further, as it revamps the landscape of school choice, this administration and those that follow it can do more to elevate the status of magnet schools as an important contributor to the patchwork of options available to parents and students. Properly conceived and designed, magnet schools provide specialized curricula and programs, include free transportation, draw a diverse core of teachers and administrators, and offer the opportunity to learn in an integrated educational setting.[16] To the extent that some of them are not actually doing these things, or are not doing them well, the federal government should pour its resources into strengthening magnets, rather than draining funds from them in order to fund other, less-tested programs that may not hold the same promise.

Finally, across all of its school choice programs, the federal government should facilitate regional solutions. Because substantially more school segregation exists *between* school districts than *within* them,[17] encouraging more interdistrict magnet schools, incentivizing cooperation between and among (especially urban and suburban) school systems, and creating opportunities for interdistrict NCLB transfers.

Incentivizing Integrated Charter Schools

Although magnet schools currently enroll twice as many students as charter schools do and have enjoyed a modicum of success in drawing together a diverse student body,[18] the Obama administration has already made clear that the expansion of charter schools is central to its education reform vision. The evidence on student diversity in charters is mixed, but to date and on the whole, it appears that they do not tend to be centers of racial or socioeconomic integration.[19] Indeed, a recent report that examined federal data collected for charter schools in 40 states and the District of Columbia found that 70 percent of all black charter school students attend schools that are 90–100 percent minority, and in many Western states with the largest concentrations of Latino students, Latino charter school students are similarly isolated in intensely segregated schools.[20] The fact that charters tend to be located in urban areas provides a partial explanation for the higher enrollment of black (and in some areas, Latino) students, but it fails to account for the disparities entirely. Moreover, the absence of federally maintained data in key areas of charter school enrollment and success severely limits the ability of researchers to assess fully which students they are serving and how well they are serving them.[21]

The Obama administration's focus on charters may provide a unique opportunity to create incentives for integration and equity among schools that are serving more and more students each year. As significant federal funds become available for charter schools, grant applicants should be expected to consider, if not required to take, affirmative steps to attract a diverse body of teachers and students, as magnets are expected to do, and to document targeted outreach and recruitment efforts. The federal grant process should also require that applicant states commit to enacting or enforcing state laws mandating that charter schools take affirmative steps to promote integration, which may include an expectation that, where appropriate, charter schools seek to enroll students from multiple school districts within a region. Federal funds should also be available to such schools for transportation, so that families of limited means have access to schools beyond the neighborhoods in which they live. Finally, separate and apart from its grant process for new and existing charter schools, ED should immediately begin collecting uniform charter school data regarding enrollment and graduation rates, achievement, discipline, and so on, broken down by race, English Language Learner characteristics, and low-income students.

Promoting Smart School District Consolidation

Facilitating student mobility between districts is one way to address the problem of the growing segregation between and not within school districts. Another strategy is simply attempting to erase altogether the lines that divide racially and socioeconomically distinct communities. Different state governments have tried, at times, to require consolidation, usually for fiscal and administrative reasons, but it is unclear whether there has ever been a real federal effort to facilitate that objective on a broad scale. School district consolidation, however, can also be an attractive possibility as a means of increasing school integration in parts of the country where residential segregation tracks district lines. ED therefore should give some consideration to involving the federal government, strategically, in consolidation conversations that serve important national educational objectives as well. While consolidation has long been desired by integration advocates in the abstract, not enough thought has been given to using the government's resources to encourage what is otherwise primarily a state and local decision. This administration may provide an opportunity to do just that.

Prioritizing Fair Housing and Housing Integration Initiatives

As described elsewhere in this book, researchers have long recognized the complicated relationship between residential segregation and school segregation.[22] Because the vast majority of school districts assign students to public schools based on where they live, public policy and private acts and "choices" that result in residentially segregated housing patterns are reflected in segregated schools. To the extent that enforcement of fair housing laws can have a dramatic impact on where people live, therefore, it can also affect where children go to school.

Under the Fair Housing Act of 1968 (FHA), the U.S. Department of Housing and Urban Development (HUD) has the responsibility to conduct impartial investigations of fair housing complaints through its administrative processes, and DOJ's Civil Rights Division has broad authority to initiate or intervene in litigation raising issues of general public importance involving charges of systematic housing discrimination. HUD and DOJ should work to revitalize these federal entities and vigorously enforce federal fair housing laws at both the administrative and "pattern and practice" levels.[23] Moreover, HUD should develop guidance for grantees of federal housing funds and other governmental agencies, clearly defining what must be shown to meet FHA's requirement that the federal government and the moneys it disburses "affirmatively further fair housing."[24]

Beyond this, DOJ, with strong support and advocacy from the administration, should join those civil rights lawyers who have tried for decades to pursue legal theories and remedies that explore the relationship between housing discrimination and school segregation. The late-1970s witnessed some attempts by DOJ to coordinate such litigation, but the effort was short-lived. In addition to straight-up enforcement of fair housing and civil rights laws, therefore, DOJ's Civil Rights Division should take this opportunity to reexplore more intersection work in order to attack the complex barriers to equal opportunity for all Americans. Doing so would entail forging relationships across the division's related practice areas and with other federal agencies to develop innovative, cross-disciplinary litigation strategies.

Coordinating Legal and Policy Work on Integration Issues

On the campaign trail, Barack Obama seemed committed to using White House leadership to develop and advance a social justice policy agenda. Now after more than two years in office, he must focus and follow through on that vision by dispatching key White House staff to coordinate nonlitigation, interagency strategies that connect schools and housing and complement the work done by DOJ's Civil Rights Division. Dozens of independently operated federal education and housing programs currently exist to promote integration, explicitly or implicitly—but they seem to function independently. Federal executive leadership is needed to promote cooperation among existing federal programs, to develop and implement cross-disciplinary initiatives, and to build better bridges across the relevant federal agencies. The White House, perhaps through its Domestic Policy Council, also can work with HUD, ED, the Department of Transportation, the newly created Office of Urban Affairs, and other federal (and state and local) agencies to develop new, proactive policies or legislation that goes even further in addressing school and housing issues comprehensively, and then, if necessary, champion such proposals through Congress.

President Obama assumed office in something of a time of crisis, but it was also a time of opportunity. Despite all of the challenges that confronted the country, his administration elected to prioritize a few major items on its affirmative domestic agenda—health care, financial regulation, job creation, and budget and deficit reduction, to name a few. While charter schools might also belong on this list, it's not clear to date that educational equity or diversity does.

Civil rights and school integration advocates must not miss the opportunity to demand that the federal government prioritize their issues too. They should continue to think big, and rethink big, about how to enlist the government's assistance in reversing this two-decades-long trend toward resegregated public schools. The political landscape has shifted substantially for the president, halfway through his (first) term, and undoubtedly, so has his agenda. Yet for the trajectory of our system of public education to change, this administration and those that will follow it must remain mindful of the promise of *Brown*, firmly endorse its goals and vision, and commit the federal government to actively working to make that promise a reality for all children.

NOTES

A longer version of this essay was published as "Racially Integrated Education and the Role of the Federal Government," *North Carolina Law Review* 88 (2010): 725–86.

1. *San Antonio School District v. Rodriguez*, 411 U.S. 1, 35 (1973).

2. *Parents Involved in Community Schools v. Seattle School District No. 1*, 551 U.S. 701 (2007).

3. U.S. Commission on Civil Rights, *Becoming Less Separate? School Desegregation, Justice Department Enforcement, and the Pursuit of Unitary Status*, September 2007, 23–28.

4. See, e.g., G. Orfield and C. Lee, *Historic Reversals, Accelerating Resegregation, and the Need for New Integration Strategies* (Los Angeles: Civil Rights Project/Proyecto Derechos Civiles at UCLA, August 2007), 42–44; S. F. Reardon and J. T. Yun, "Integrating Neighborhoods, Segregating Schools: The Retreat from School Desegregation in the South, 1990–2000," in *School Resegregation: Must the South Turn Back?*, edited by J. C. Boger and G. Orfield (Chapel Hill: University of North Carolina Press, 2005), 51, 64–66.

5. See, e.g., G. Orfield, *Reviving the Goal of an Integrated Society: A 21st-Century Chal-*

lenge (Los Angeles: Civil Rights Project/Proyecto Derechos Civiles at UCLA, January 2009), 31; M. L. Moore, "Unclear Standards Create an Unclear Future: Developing a Better Definition of Unitary Status," *Yale Law Journal* 112 (2002): 311, 315–17, 319–23.

6. Federal courts deferred to similar guidelines created by HEW in the 1960s. See J. H. Wilkinson, *From Brown to Bakke: The Supreme Court and School Integration, 1954 to 1978* (New York: Oxford University Press, 1979), 102–8. Indeed, in some instances, HEW's guidelines were incorporated into federal court orders, giving them additional credence and weight. Ibid., 107, 111–14. See also J. R. Dunn, "Title VI, the Guidelines, and School Desegregation in the South," *Virginia Law Review* 53 (1967): 42, 53–87.

7. Nationally, whereas in 1968 whites made up 80 percent of public school students, and blacks were the dominant minority at 14 percent, today, whites comprise only 56.5 percent of the public school population, and the largest minority group is Latino students, at 20.5 percent. G. Orfield and C. Lee, *Racial Transformation and the Changing Nature of Segregation* (Cambridge: Civil Rights Project at Harvard University, January 2006), 13; Orfield, *Reviving the Goal of an Integrated Society.*

8. See, e.g., Brief of 553 Social Scientists as Amici Curiae in Support of Respondents, *Parents Involved in Community Schools v. Seattle School District No. 1*, 551 U.S. 701 (2007) (nos. 05-908, 05-915).

9. See, generally, Orfield and Lee, *Racial Transformation.*

10. C. Q. Le, "Racially Integrated Education and the Role of the Federal Government," *North Carolina Law Review* 88 (2010): 725.

11. S. J. Monroe, "'Dear Colleague' Letter Re: The Use of Race in Assigning Students to Elementary and Secondary Schools" (28 August 2008); S. J. Monroe, "'Dear Colleague' Letter Re: The Use of Race in Postsecondary Student Admissions" (28 August 2008), http://www2.ed.gov/about/offices/list/ocr/letters/raceassignmentese.html.

12. E. Frankenberg and C. Q. Le, "The Post-*Parents Involved* Challenge: Confronting Extralegal Obstacles to Integration," *Ohio State Law Journal* 69 (2008): 1041–45.

13. Ibid., 1056–59.

14. See, e.g., J. J. Holme and A. S. Wells, "School Choice beyond District Borders: Lessons for Reauthorization of NCLB from Interdistrict Desegregation and Open Enrollment Plans," in *Improving on No Child Left Behind: Getting Education Reform Back on Track*, edited by R. Kahlenberg (New York: Century Foundation Press, 2008), 139. Not only does the text of NCLB itself lack such positive incentives, but a "Dear Colleague" letter issued by OCR during the Bush administration explicitly rejects any interpretation of NCLB that would allow school districts to harmonize their voluntary integration efforts with the statute if doing so would limit the transfer option in any way. See S. J. Monroe, "'Dear Colleague' Letter Re: Anti-Discrimination Obligations of School Districts under No Child Left Behind" (8 January 2009).

15. Frankenberg and Le, "Post-*Parents Involved* Challenge," 145–55.

16. See, generally, E. Frankenberg and G. Siegel-Hawley, *The Forgotten Choice? Rethinking Magnet Schools in a Changing Landscape* (Los Angeles: Civil Rights Project/Proyecto Derechos Civiles at UCLA, 2008).

17. C. Clotfelter, *After Brown: The Rise and Retreat of School Desegregation* (Princeton, NJ: Princeton University Press, 2004), 59–73; Reardon and Yun, "Integrating Neighborhoods," 51–69.

18. See, generally, Frankenberg and Siegel-Hawley, *Forgotten Choice?*

19. See, e.g., Institute on Race and Poverty, *Failed Promises: Assessing Charter Schools in Twin Cities*, November 2008, 3–15; E. Frankenberg and C. Lee, *Charter Schools and Race: A Lost Opportunity for Integrated Education* (Cambridge: Civil Rights Project at Harvard University, July 2003); A. S. Wells et al., "Charter Schools and Racial and Social Class Segregation: Yet Another Sorting Machine?," in *A Notion at Risk: Preserving Public Education as an Engine for Social Mobility*, edited by R. Kahlenberg (New York: Century Foundation Press, 2000), 169.

20. E. Frankenberg, G. Siegel-Hawley, and J. Wang, *Choice without Equity: Charter School Segregation and the Need for Civil Rights Standards* (Los Angeles: Civil Rights Project/Proyecto Derechos Civiles at UCLA, January 2010).

21. Ibid.

22. See, e.g., Brief of Housing Scholars and Research and Advocacy Organizations as Amici Curiae in Support of Respondents, *Parents Involved in Community Schools v. Seattle School District No. 1*, 551 U.S. 701 (2007) (nos. 05-908, 05-915); N. A. Denton, "The Persistence of Segregation: Links between Residential Segregation and School Segregation," in *In Pursuit of a Dream Deferred: Linking Housing and Education Policy*, edited by j. a. powell, G. Kearney, and V. Kay (New York: Peter Lang, 2001), 89, 89–120.

23. National Commission on Fair Housing and Equal Opportunity, *The Future of Fair Housing*, December 2008, 13–14, 22–24.

24. 42 U.S.C. § 3608(e) (2009); Exec. Order 12,892, 59 Fed. Reg. 2939 (20 January 1994). See also U.S. *ex rel. Antidiscrimination Center of Metro New York, Inc. v. Westchester County, New York*, 2009 WL 455269 (S.D.N.Y., 24 February 2009).

PART II

The Case for Integration

DOUGLAS D. READY & MEGAN R. SILANDER

School Racial and Ethnic Composition and Young Children's Cognitive Development
Isolating Family, Neighborhood, and School Influences

Racial and ethnic disparities in cognitive ability are evident even among very young children. Nonwhite and non-Asian students enter kindergarten academically behind their more advantaged peers,[1] and these initial cognitive differences increase as children progress through school.[2] Myriad explanations have been offered for these differential learning rates, including inequalities in family and neighborhood resources, the persistent associations between race and socioeconomic status, and sociocultural disconnects between home and school environments.[3] Another prominent hypothesis—and the focus of this essay—highlights the concentration of minority children in racially and ethnically isolated schools. In this essay we explore the extent to which school racial composition influences young children's academic development after accounting for the characteristics of students themselves.

The essay also addresses a fundamental issue salient to a wide array of research on education policy. Any nonexperimental study that seeks to attribute academic development to school policies and practices faces serious questions of selection and unmeasured variable bias. Within the context of our present essay, estimates of the effects of school racial composition on student learning may be spurious, reflecting instead other influences related to the characteristics of students, families, and the neighborhoods in which they live. Fortunately, the analytic approach and data structure we employ here are able to distinguish cognitive development that occurs during the school year (when school, family, and neighborhood effects are in operation) from learning during the summer months (when school effects are absent). Our results suggest that even after adjusting for a host of student and school characteristics, students attending schools with high minority enrollment typically gain fewer mathematics skills in both kindergarten and first grade, and they develop fewer literacy skills during first grade.

Background

An early empirical assertion regarding the influences of school contexts was offered by James Coleman and his colleagues in their landmark study *Equality of Educational Opportunity*: "The social composition of the student body is more highly related to achievement, independent of the student's own social background, than is any school factor."[4] More recent studies also suggest strong associations between school sociodemographic characteristics and student cognitive development. Our focus here is on a growing body of research that finds negative effects of concentrated minority enrollments on academic development. Even after controlling for child- and school-level demographic characteristics, high minority racial enrollments are linked to lower student achievement.[5]

But why would school racial composition influence cognitive development after accounting for student-level characteristics? Explanations for the link generally fall under two broad categories: (1) disparities in institutional resources related to minority enrollments and (2) differences in peer norms, behaviors, and expectations across low and high minority enrollment schools. Authors have also advanced a third explanation for the phenomenon that is unrelated to the characteristics of schools themselves, and even calls into question findings that school racial composition directly influences child outcomes.

Institutional Resources

Schools that enroll substantial proportions of minority and low-income students tend to provide students fewer human and material resources.[6] In particular, such schools have greater difficulty attracting quality teachers, suffer higher teacher turnover rates, and employ teachers with fewer years of classroom experience.[7] Teachers in high-poverty schools are also less likely to be credentialed, tend to score lower on teacher exams, have fewer years of experience, and are less likely to have graduate degrees.[8] Similar inequalities are evident in the allocation of other types of school resources. Students in high minority, low-income schools are typically enrolled in larger classes,[9] experience less productive social and academic climates,[10] are more often subject to rote teaching that focuses on basic skills, and are less likely to encounter more complex and higher-order thinking.[11] This can be attributed in part to the lower expectations teachers tend to have for students in high-poverty schools,[12] and to the fact that teachers in disadvantaged schools are less likely to take responsibility for their students' learning.[13] Authors using data from the Early Childhood Longitudinal Study, Kindergarten Cohort (ECLS-K)—the same data we employ in this essay—have also suggested that differences in the types of schools attended by black and white children may contribute to disparities in early cognitive development. These authors report that the achievement gap between black and white children attending the same elementary school widens only one-third as much as does the overall gap between black and white students.[14]

Social and Academic Peer Effects

In addition to the enhanced social and material resources associated with advantaged schools, peer quality represents another important contextual resource that varies by school demographic composition. Sociologists have long described the influence of normative student climates on student behaviors and outcomes.[15] Shortly after publication of *Equality of Educational Opportunity*, Coleman stated that "the educational resources provided by a child's fellow students are more important for his achievement than are the resources provided by the school board."[16] Indeed, Coleman and his colleagues had earlier concluded that the relationships they found between racial and ethnic school composition and student achievement were not due to race per se but to the fact that, on average, white students possessed comparably higher academic abilities and aspirations.[17]

Subsequent studies have confirmed positive relationships between aggregate school-level achievement and student-level learning.[18] Moreover, the impact of peer achievement on student performance is stronger for low-ability than high-ability students.[19] This is important within any study that examines the racial isolation of schools, as students in high minority schools more often encounter low-achieving peers.[20] Elevated peer abilities may also reflect increased motivation and academic peer pressure, and shared beliefs, values, and habits that promote academic success indirectly via classroom disciplinary environments, as well as teacher expectations and pedagogy.[21] In an effort to explain why achievement gaps grow fastest between high-achieving black and white children, authors have noted that the average black student attends a school with considerably lower average achievement.[22] As such, high-achieving black students will be farther from their school's mean than the average high-achieving white student. If classroom practices and teacher expectations are aimed at the modal child, high-achieving black children will be more likely to receive inappropriate instruction and limited opportunities for academic growth.

Methodological Challenges:
Unmeasured Family and Neighborhood Effects

Schools that serve large proportions of minority and low-income children are more often located in neighborhoods with increased levels of social disorganization, crime, gang activity, unemployment, and family instability.[23] Social problems related to health, substance abuse, and teen pregnancy also tend to cluster geographically.[24] Children raised in such communities often have reduced access to out-of-school resources and social networks, and they are more likely to drop out of school and be unemployed.[25] Conversely, proximity to middle-class neighbors is associated with improved student outcomes, even after accounting for the student's own family background.[26] In addition to negative environmental impacts, racially isolated neighborhoods with high concentrations of poverty tend to lack other resources—such as playgrounds, health and child care facilities, and after-school programs—that positively influence child development. In sum, neighborhood characteristics have serious implications for children's out-of-school experiences and their opportunities for social and cognitive development.[27]

From a methodological standpoint, family and neighborhood effects present a considerable challenge to researchers seeking to estimate the effects of schooling on child outcomes.[28] Indeed, an important consideration is the systematic and nonrandom sorting of individuals and families into schools and neighborhoods based on many unmeasured and unobservable characteristics.[29] One methodological solution to isolating neighborhood effects is to randomly assign children and families living in high minority communities to racially heterogeneous schools and neighborhoods. The Gautreaux experiment[30] in Chicago and other studies associated with the Moving to Opportunity (MTO) demonstration projects have sought to approximate such a design.[31] However, within nonexperimental studies, the finding that students in racially or economically isolated schools learn less may be explained by the environments they experience after school and during the summer months, not the characteristics of schools. As such, unmeasured characteristics likely produce artificially inflated estimates of school effects. The methods we describe below begin to address this important limitation in the extant literature on the links between school racial and ethnic composition and student academic performance.

Research Focus

Using longitudinal data and growth-curve modeling within a three-level hierarchical framework, this essay examines how school racial and ethnic composition influences children's literacy and mathematics development during kindergarten, first grade, and the intervening summer. It is important to stress that we do not directly address the effectiveness of school desegregation or economic integration as a policy lever. Rather, we examine school sociodemographic composition, without considering the social, economic, or political forces that produced given levels of racial isolation. However, our findings clearly have implications for policies surrounding integration efforts. Specifically, this essay addresses the following questions:

1. How do schools' racial and ethnic compositions influence cognitive development controlling for the characteristics of students they serve?
2. Do these influences vary by student racial and socioeconomic background?
3. To what extent are these compositional effects spurious, reflecting instead unmeasured characteristics of families and neighborhoods?

Data and Methods

Our essay employs data from the ECLS-K, sponsored by the National Center for Education Statistics (NCES). These data are ideal for studying the relationship between school racial composition and student learning, particularly with the statistical methods discussed below. We draw from the first four data waves of ECLS-K, which include information on the same children in the fall and spring of kindergarten (waves 1 and 2) and the fall and spring of first grade, with a random subsample in the fall (waves 3 and 4). Our analytic sample includes 29,900 literacy and mathematics test scores nested within 9,049 children, who are nested within 698 public and nonpublic schools.[32]

Analytic Approach

We employ hierarchical linear modeling (HLM) within a three-level growth-curve framework.[33] Specifically, we nest learning trajectories within children, who are nested within schools. Our level 1 HLM models estimate children's individual learning trajectories. At level 2, we model these learning trajectories as a function of children's social and academic background. Our level 3 models, the focus of this essay, estimate the relationship between school racial composition and student learning, adjusted for the characteristics of students and schools that are associated with high minority school concentrations.

The dates on which the ECLS-K cognitive assessments were administered varied considerably across children, both within and between schools. In addition to variability in testing dates, the starting and ending dates of academic years also varied across schools. The result of this variability in school exposure at each assessment is that children's opportunities to learn differed both within and between schools. Further complicating the analyses, on average, children were in school for approximately half of the "summer vacation" between the spring kindergarten and fall first-grade assessments. This variability in school exposure, however, allows us to isolate learning that occurs during the school year from learning during the summer months.[34] A finding that school racial and ethnic composition was a significant predictor of *summer* learning would suggest unmeasured variable bias—namely, characteristics of families and neighborhoods that are simply associated with school racial and ethnic composition, and not racial and ethnic composition itself.

Measures

LITERACY AND MATHEMATICS ASSESSMENTS

As outcomes, these analyses employ the ECLS-K cognitive assessments, which were administered individually by an adult assessor who spent between 50 and 70 minutes with each child at each data collection wave. The literacy assessment measured both basic literacy skills and advanced reading comprehension ability. The mathematics assessment items attended to conceptual and procedural knowledge as well as to problem-solving skills.[35]

SCHOOL CHARACTERISTICS

In this essay we focus on our level 3 results, particularly the relationships between school racial composition and student learning. Due to the nonnormal distribution of school racial composition—most schools either enroll many or few minority children—we created a dummy variable indicating high minority enrollment (nonwhite, non-Asian enrollments > 70% = 1, otherwise = 0). Our school-level models also employ a continuous measure of school-average socioeconomic status (SES). This measure is central, considering the strong links between school racial, ethnic, and socioeconomic characteristics.[36]

The school-level models include additional controls that adjust for school characteristics related to both racial and ethnic composition and student learning. We employ dummy-coded indicators of school location (urban and rural or small-town schools each compared to suburban schools), school sector (Catholic and non-Catholic private schools compared to public schools), and average kindergarten and first-grade class sizes (small classes [< 17 students] and large classes [> 25] compared to medium-size classes [17–25 students]). To account for peer academic climate, we include separate continuous indicators of kindergarteners' and first graders' approaches to learning (e.g., their attentiveness, task persistence) as reported by their teachers. We also consider differences in teacher background across schools and incorporate a measure of school-average kindergarten and first-grade teacher experience, as well as a standardized composite measure of kindergarten and first-grade teacher preparation (the highest degree attained and the number of college courses completed in mathematics and literacy pedagogy, child development, early childhood education, and elementary education).

CHILD CHARACTERISTICS

Our level 2 (child-level) models include dummy-coded measures that identify whether the child was black, Asian, Hispanic, Native American, or multiracial, with whites serving as the uncoded comparison group. Children's socioeconomic status is captured with a composite measure of parents' income, education, and occupational prestige. We also employ a child-level SES quadratic term to account for nonlinearity. The models further account for children's age, gender, single-parent status, whether a language other than English was the primary one spoken at home, and whether the child was repeating kindergarten or attended full-day kindergarten. Within the HLM models, the race and ethnicity measures are group-mean centered, while the remaining covariates are grand-mean centered.[37]

Results

Descriptive Results

Table 5.1 displays school and student descriptive statistics organized by school minority enrollment. We define schools with greater than 70 percent nonwhite and non-Asian enrollments as high minority; schools with 10 to 70 percent nonwhite and non-Asian enrollments as average minority; and those with fewer than 10 percent minority children as low minority enrollment schools. Note first that high minority schools tend to enroll kindergarteners who possess considerably fewer academic skills even at the beginning of kindergarten. Well over one full standard deviation separates the measured literacy and mathematics abilities of children in high and low minority enrollment schools.[38] Severe socioeconomic disadvantage also characterizes high

TABLE 5.1. *Descriptive Statistics for Schools and Students, by School Minority Enrollment (n = 9,049 children within 698 schools)*

	Low Minority Enrollment[a]	Average Minority Enrollment	High Minority Enrollment
Schools (n = 698)	n = 274	n = 307	n = 118
Initial literacy skills,[c] M	0.254***[b]	0.113***	−0.883
SD	(0.725)	(0.952)	(1.183)
Initial math skills,[c] M	0.293***	0.067***	−0.857
SD	(0.827)	(1.039)	(0.768)
School-average SES,[c] M	0.213***	0.113***	−0.778
SD	(0.886)	(0.967)	(0.888)
School sector (%)			
Public	69.7	80.1**	76.1
Catholic	16.4	12.7**	12.0
Private, non-Catholic	13.9	7.2	12.0
School location (%)			
Large city	3.3***	16.9***	39.0
Medium city	17.2	30.3***	18.6
Suburban	33.9***	40.7***	22.9
Small town/rural	45.6***	12.1***	19.5
Kindergarten class size, M	19.0*	20.0	20.6
SD	(6.3)	(4.6)	(5.5)
First-grade class size, M	19.9	20.3	19.9
SD	(4.3)	(4.0)	(4.9)
Average kindergarten approaches to learning,[c] M	0.335***	0.007***	−0.552
SD	(1.035)	(1.031)	(0.951)
Average first-grade approaches to learning,[c] M	0.271***	−0.052	−0.309
SD	(0.969)	(0.980)	(1.103)
Students (n = 9,049)	n = 3,524	n = 4,164	n = 1,360
Race/ethnicity (%)			
White	92.2***	65.4***	8.0
Black	0.8***	13.5***	42.0
Hispanic	4.1***	13.9***	34.3
Asian	1.1***	3.3***	7.5
Native American	0.3***	0.8**	7.0
Multiracial	1.5	3.0***	1.2
Socioeconomic status,[c] M	0.118***	0.006***	−0.638
SD	(0.887)	(0.967)	(0.964)
Age (months), M	66.5***	66.0	65.7
SD	(4.3)	(4.3)	(4.2)
% Female	50.8	47.2**	50.6
% Single-parent family	12.4***	21.5***	40.1

TABLE 5.1. *(continued)*

	Low Minority Enrollment[a]	Average Minority Enrollment	High Minority Enrollment
% Repeating kindergarten	3.3	3.6	3.2
% Full-day kindergarten	48.4***	54.7***	74.4
% Non-English household	1.5***	7.6***	25.1

*p < .05; **p < .01; ***p < .001.
[a] Low minority enrollment = < 10% nonwhite/non-Asian; middle = 10–70%; high = > 70%.
[b] Significance tests compared to high minority enrollment schools.
[c] Measure is z-scored ($M = 0$, $SD = 1$).

minority schools: school-average SES is more than three-quarters of a standard deviation higher for both average and low minority enrollment schools compared to high minority enrollment schools.[39]

Although one might assume that high minority schools would be overwhelmingly public, school sector and minority enrollments are only weakly related; a slightly lower proportion of high minority enrollment schools are public schools compared to average minority enrollment schools. However, these descriptive findings do highlight the geographic nature of racial and ethnic segregation. High minority schools are far more likely to be located in urban centers, while average minority enrollment schools are typically found in midsize cities and suburban communities, and low minority enrollment schools are normally situated in rural areas and small towns. Important differences also distinguish low minority enrollment schools in terms of their peer academic climates. Kindergarten teachers in both low and average minority enrollment schools view their students' approaches to learning more favorably than do teachers in high minority enrollment schools. Similarly, roughly one-half standard deviation separates first graders' approaches to learning in low and high minority enrollment schools.

Necessarily reflecting the school-level aggregate measure, students attending high minority schools are much more likely to be black or Hispanic and socioeconomically disadvantaged: a three-quarter standard deviation SES gap separates students in low and high minority enrollment schools. Put differently, the average family income of children attending high minority schools is roughly $33,000 compared to more than $57,000 for children in low minority enrollment schools. Further evincing this disadvantage, students in high minority enrollment schools are two to three times more likely to come from

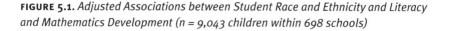

FIGURE 5.1. *Adjusted Associations between Student Race and Ethnicity and Literacy and Mathematics Development (n = 9,043 children within 698 schools)*

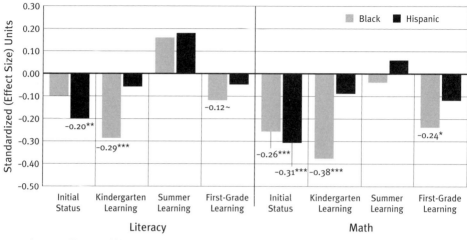

$*p < .05; **p < .01; ***p < .001.$

Note: Within-school estimates adjusted for SES, gender, age, single-parent status, home language, kindergarten repetition, and full-day kindergarten attendance. Comparison is to white children, represented by the zero line.

single-parent families, and between three and sixteen times more likely to live in a home where English is not the primary language. Indicating kindergarten's frequent use as a compensatory program, three-quarters of children in high minority enrollment schools attend full-day kindergarten, compared to roughly half of those in average and low minority enrollment schools.

Analytic Results: Within-School Models

Figure 5.1 summarizes our within-school HLM estimates of black and Hispanic children's academic skills at kindergarten entry and their cognitive development during kindergarten, first grade, and the intervening summer (for the full within-school results, see tables 5.2 and 5.3). These results, which compare children attending the same schools, are adjusted for SES, gender, age, single-parent and home-language status, kindergarten repetition, and full-day kindergarten attendance.[40] Once we adjust for these sociodemographic differences, we find no differences between black and white children in literacy ability at kindergarten entry.[41] However, black students gain literacy skills at a slower pace than their white peers during both kindergarten and first grade.[42] Black children tend to enter formal schooling with weaker mathematics skills than white children, and this initial gap widens further during both kinder-

TABLE 5.2. *Within-School HLM Estimates of Kindergarten, Summer, and First-Grade Literacy Learning (n = 9,049 children within 698 schools)*

	Initial Status	Kindergarten Learning	Summer Learning	First-Grade Learning
Black[a]	−0.69[b]	−0.24***	0.30	−0.15~
Hispanic	−1.34**	−0.05	0.34	−0.06
Asian	1.90**	0.09	0.32	0.15
Native American	−0.77	−0.15	0.82*	−0.45*
Multiracial	0.26	−0.02	−0.09	0.06
Socioeconomic status[c]	2.12***	0.10***	0.09	0.16***
Socioeconomic status squared[c]	0.24***	0.00		
Age (months)	0.33***	0.00	0.05**	−0.01
Female	1.43***	0.13***	0.22~	0.05
Single-parent family	−1.42***	−0.08**	−0.33*	−0.11~
Repeating kindergarten	1.60*	−0.38***	−0.61*	−0.45***
Non-English household	−2.61***	0.05	−0.22	−0.05
Full-day kindergarten		0.24***	−0.01	−0.31***
Intercept	23.71***[d]	1.84***	−0.09	3.42***

~*p* < .10; **p* < .05; ***p* < .01; ****p* < .001.
[a]All racial/ethnic groups compared to whites.
[b]Estimates reflect points-per-month of learning.
[c]Measure is standardized (z-scored; *M* = 0, *SD* = 1).
[d]*SD* initial status = 6.85; *SD* kindergarten slope = 0.82; *SD* summer slope = 1.85; *SD* first-grade slope = 1.24.

garten and first grade, even after controlling for other social and academic inequalities. Conversely, Hispanic children begin kindergarten with fewer literacy and mathematics skills, but they gain these skills at rates comparable to their white peers in both kindergarten and first grade (although they continue to achieve at lower levels). In other words, the initial disadvantages evident at kindergarten entry do not grow larger for Hispanic children. During the summer between kindergarten and first grade, adjusting for background differences, we find that race and ethnicity are unrelated to either literacy or mathematics development.[43] We turn now to the primary focus of this essay—the relationship between school minority enrollment and cognitive development.

Analytic Results: Between-School Models

Figure 5.2 summarizes our between-school findings regarding the relationship between high minority school enrollment and children's initial achievement and subsequent academic development (for the full between-school results,

TABLE 5.3. *Within-School HLM Estimates of Kindergarten, Summer, and First-Grade Mathematics Learning (n = 9,049 children within 698 schools)*

	Initial Status	Kindergarten Learning	Summer Learning	First-Grade Learning
Black[a]	−1.59***[b]	−0.24***	−0.06	−0.23*
Hispanic	−1.89***	−0.06	0.09	−0.11
Asian	0.54	0.10	0.36	−0.35**
Native American	−0.77	−0.12	0.49	−0.39~
Multiracial	−0.84	−0.10	−0.48	0.06
Socioeconomic status[c]	1.93***	0.09***	0.09	0.08**
Socioeconomic status squared[c]	0.14**	0.02*		
Age (months)	0.46***	0.01***	0.01	−0.01
Female	0.05	−0.03	−0.07	−0.10**
Single-parent family	−1.37***	−0.07*	−0.15	−0.00
Repeating kindergarten	−0.83	−0.27***	−0.02	−0.26**
Non-English household	−1.86***	−0.06	−0.11	0.04
Full-day kindergarten		0.11**	0.04	−0.17**
Intercept	18.79***[d]	1.66***	0.41***	2.45***

~$p < .10$; *$p < .05$; **$p < .01$; ***$p < .001$.
[a]All racial/ethnic groups compared to whites.
[b]Estimates reflect points-per-month of learning.
[c]Measure is standardized (z-scored; $M = 0$, $SD = 1$).
[d]Within-school SD initial status = 6.09; SD kindergarten slope = 0.64; SD summer slope = 1.42; SD first-grade slope = 0.94.

see table 5.4).[44] It is important to stress that these estimates are fully adjusted for the sociodemographic backgrounds of children who tend to enroll in high minority schools, and for a host of school characteristics associated with school racial and ethnic composition. The estimates of initial status are descriptive in nature and simply reflect the relationships between school racial composition and children's school readiness. As our descriptive results also indicated, children who begin formal schooling in high minority enrollment schools do so at a considerable mathematics disadvantage.[45]

In terms of student learning in literacy and mathematics, even after adjusting for a host of student and school characteristics, we find that students attending high minority enrollment schools gain fewer literacy skills during first grade (ES = −0.60 SD) and fewer mathematics skills during both kindergarten (ES = −0.42 SD) and first grade (ES = −0.70 SD). These estimates, which are substantial even after controlling for myriad child and school characteristics, suggest that the racial and ethnic isolation of black and Hispanic chil-

FIGURE 5.2. *Adjusted Associations between High Minority Enrollment and Literacy and Mathematics Development (n = 9,043 children within 698 schools)*

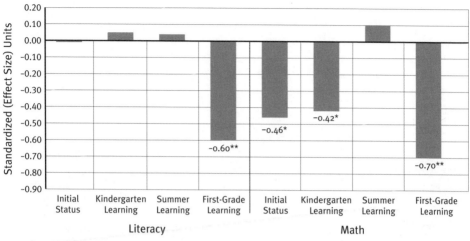

*p < .05; **p < .01.

Note: Between-school estimates adjusted for all child-level covariates in figure 5.1, plus school-level characteristics including school-average SES, average K and average first-grade class size, school sector, urbanicity, and school-average peer approaches to learning. Comparison is to schools without high minority enrollments, represented by the zero line.

dren plays an important role in exacerbating educational inequality. Bear in mind that these results do not suggest that children in high minority schools are losing academic skills during kindergarten and first grade. Rather, these children are generally learning a great deal each year, but at a slower rate than children attending non–high minority schools.

A central focus of this essay is the possibility that these associations between school racial composition and student learning are spurious, reflecting the influence of families and neighborhoods rather than schools. A finding that the links between high minority enrollment and student learning were equally strong during the summer—when these children were not enrolled in school—would cast doubt on the school-year estimates. One would likely conclude that the kindergarten and first-grade estimates were tapping the unmeasured attributes of families and neighborhoods rather than the effects of school racial and ethnic compositions. However, figure 5.2 provides no evidence of school racial compositional effects on learning during the summer months between kindergarten and first grade (note the nonsignificant effects on summer learning; see also table 5.4). This affords relatively robust evidence that the school composition effects are not spurious and instead reflect the

TABLE 5.4. *Between-School HLM Estimates of Kindergarten, Summer, and First-Grade Literacy and Mathematics Learning (n = 9,049 children within 698 schools)*

	Literacy		Math	
	Model 1	Model 2	Model 1	Model 2
Initial Status				
High minority enrollment school[a]	**−1.08****[b]	**−0.02**	**−1.86*****	**−0.69***
School-average SES		1.20***		1.46***
K class size ≤ 17[c]		0.07		0.37
K class size ≥ 25[c]		0.22		0.19
Kindergarteners' approaches to learning		0.52**		0.37*
Catholic[d]		0.49		0.89*
Non-Catholic private[d]		1.30~		0.94~
Large city[e]		0.27		0.36
Mid-size city[e]		−0.54		−0.36
Rural/small town[e]		−1.31***		−0.74**
Intercept	24.00***	23.87***	19.24***	18.86***
Kindergarten Learning				
High minority enrollment school	**−0.02**	**0.02**	**−0.11***	**−0.11***
School-average SES		0.04		−0.03
K class size ≤ 17		−0.01		0.00
K class size ≥ 25		−0.18**		−0.09*
Kindergarteners' approaches to learning		−0.01		0.02
Catholic		−0.00		0.08
Non-Catholic private		0.02		0.09
Large city		0.11		0.07
Midsize city		0.08		0.01
Rural/small town		0.02		0.02
Intercept	1.85***	1.83***	1.68***	1.68***

	Literacy		Math	
	Model 1	Model 2	Model 3	Model 4
Summer Learning				
High minority enrollment school	**0.02**	**0.02**	**−0.03**	**0.09**
School-average SES		−0.01		0.26**
K class size ≤ 17		−0.10		−0.06
K class size ≥ 25		0.27*		0.08
Kindergarteners' approaches to learning		0.14*		−0.01
Catholic		−0.08		−0.18
Non-Catholic private		0.80*		−0.16
Large city		−0.06		−0.35
Midsize city		−0.30~		−0.41*

TABLE 5.4. *(continued)*

	Literacy		Math	
	Model 1	Model 2	Model 3	Model 4
Rural/small town		−0.10		−0.14
Intercept	−0.08	−0.15	0.43***	0.61***
First-Grade Learning				
High minority enrollment school	**−0.37***	**−0.27****	**−0.24****	**−0.21****
School-average SES		0.10*		−0.04
1st-grade class size ≤ 17		0.11~		0.02
1st-grade class size ≥ 25		−0.15~		−0.17***
First-graders' approaches to learning		0.10***		0.04*
Catholic		0.05		−0.03
Non-Catholic private		−0.07		−0.07
Large city		0.13		0.05
Midsize city		0.10		0.19**
Rural/small town		0.02		0.02
Intercept	3.49***	3.43***f	2.45***	2.46***

~$p < .10$; *$p < .05$; **$p < .01$; ***$p < .001$.

[a] School enrollment ≥ 70% nonwhite, non-Asian.

[b] Estimates reflect points-per-month of learning; all estimates are adjusted for the child-level characteristics in Tables 5.2 and 5.3.

[c] Compared to schools with class sizes between 17 and 25.

[d] Compared to public schools.

[e] Compared to suburban schools.

[f] Between-school SD (model 2) initial-status literacy = 1.82; SD kindergarten slope = 0.37; SD summer slope = 0.57; SD first-grade slope = 0.45. SD initial-status math = 1.54; SD kindergarten slope = 0.26; SD summer slope = 0.86; SD first-grade slope = 0.30.

genuine disadvantage associated with racial and ethnic isolation. Indeed, the presence of unmeasured variable bias in this regard should have produced racial composition effects that were *stronger* during the summer months when school was not in session. We also modeled summer learning using first-grade school effects and found virtually identical relationships.[46]

Discussion

Speaking to the policy implications of *Equality of Educational Opportunity*, Coleman noted that "the facts themselves point to no obvious solution."[47] Indeed, the fifty years since *Brown v. Board of Education* have witnessed hundreds of local, state, and federal policy efforts aimed at reducing racial isolation in public schooling. These efforts, however, have faced considerable logistical and legal challenges. Logistically, due to housing segregation within major metropolitan areas, the majority of segregation lies between (rather than within) school districts.[48] As a result, racially integrating every school *district* in the United States would have limited influence on overall levels of school segregation. The authors of several essays in this book point to promising approaches—such as school assignments based on parental workplace, and interdistrict choice programs—that operate beyond the traditional confines of school district boundaries.

The ability of school districts and states to influence school social compositions, particularly their racial and ethnic enrollments, has also faced increased legal scrutiny.[49] The Supreme Court's narrow rejection of the use of "racial classifications" as one factor in voluntary school assignment programs has reinvigorated policy interest in educational segregation and sparked efforts to identify alternate routes to school integration.[50] One common proposal is that school districts develop *economic* integration programs, as approximately 40 districts already have.[51] Given the strong associations between race and socioeconomic status, integration along socioeconomic lines seems reasonable. Substantive demographic trends have also highlighted these concerns, as economic segregation has steadily increased since the 1970s.[52] However, despite holding both student- and school-level SES constant, we find that students still gain fewer academic skills in high minority elementary schools.

Our findings may also have important implications for early childhood policies and programs, which have again been placed in the national spotlight. Proponents of universal access have argued that quality preschool has the potential to reduce social, economic, and educational inequalities.[53] Indeed, over the past several decades dozens of studies have found short-term positive cognitive effects of Head Start, the nation's primary preschool program for low-income children.[54] However, these and other studies conclude that the initial advantages Head Start affords quickly fade.[55] Among the most common explanations for these dissipating effects is the lower average quality of schools Head Start children subsequently attend. For example, Head Start children typically start kindergarten in schools with higher poverty rates and lower levels of academic achievement.[56] Important to our current findings, the benefits of Head Start fade more quickly for black compared to white children.[57] We noted above that school quality may be implicated by the fact that the achievement gap between black and white children grows only one-third as fast among black and white children attending the same school.[58] Given our findings here, it seems plausible that school racial and ethnic segregation during the early elementary school years plays an important role in the erosion of the otherwise positive effects of compensatory preschool programs.

This essay focused on yearly effects of attending high minority schools. However, many students attend high minority schools for their entire public school careers. Even if we only consider kindergarten through sixth grade—the normal span of elementary schools—these effects would be multiplied by seven. In the case of mathematics skills development, holding other student and school-level characteristics constant, a student attending a high minority school from kindergarten through sixth grade would be over five months behind a similar child who attended a non–high minority school. Black students who attend high minority enrollment schools—as the majority in this nationally representative sample do—are doubly disadvantaged. Again controlling for student and school characteristics, a black student in a high minority school would gain over 12 months fewer mathematics skills that her white peer in a non–high minority school—the equivalent of 1.25 academic years less cognitive development. Clearly, the assumption that these kindergarten and first-grade relationships are constant through sixth grade is not entirely warranted. However, even if we reduce these effects by half, the ramifications for educational equity are considerable.

Finally, it is important to bear in mind that *explaining* racial inequalities in young children's learning is a far simpler task than *reducing* or *eliminating* racial differences in student learning. Although we use statistical adjustments to help us understand the links between school racial composition and children's cognitive development, the fact is that such differences remain and are observable every day in schools. Put simply, schools do not educate statistically "adjusted" children. The multiple disadvantages of minority status and attendance at high minority enrollment schools reflect the cumulative realities that teachers and schools must confront. The actual, continuing, and widening disadvantage is a further reality that is associated with the unequal resources available to children, families, neighborhoods, and schools.

NOTES

1. J. Brooks-Gunn and G. J. Duncan, "The Effects of Poverty on Children," *Future of Children* 7, no. 2 (1997): 55–71; D. R. Entwisle, K. L. Alexander, and L. S. Olson, *Children, Schools, and Inequality* (Boulder, CO: Westview, 1997); V. E. Lee and D. T. Burkam, *Inequality at the Starting Gate: Social Background Differences in Achievement as Children Begin School* (Washington, DC: Economic Policy Institute, 2002).

2. D. B. Downey, P. T. Hippel, and B. A. Broh, "Are Schools the Great Equalizer? Cognitive Inequality during the Summer Months and the School Year," *American Sociological Review* 69, no. 5 (2004): 613–35; M. Phillips, J. Crouse, and J. Ralph, "Does the Black-White Test Score Gap Widen after Children Enter School?," in *The Black-White Test Score Gap*, edited by C. Jencks and M. Phillips (Washington, DC: Brookings Institution Press, 1998), 229–72; S. Reardon, *Sources of Educational Inequality: The Growth of Racial/Ethnic and Socioeconomic Test Score Gaps in Kindergarten and First Grade* (University Park: Population Research Institute, Pennsylvania State University, 2003).

3. See G. J. Duncan and K. A. Magnuson, "Can Family Socioeconomic Resources Account for Racial and Ethnic Test Score Gaps?," *Future of Children* 15, no. 1 (2005): 35–54; C. Jencks and S. E. Mayer, "The Social Consequences of Growing Up in a Poor Neighborhood," in *Inner-City Poverty in the United States*, edited by L. E. Lynn and M. G. H. McGeary (Washington, DC: National Academy Press, 1990), 111–86; A. Lareau, *Unequal Childhoods: Class, Race, and Family Life* (Berkeley: University of California Press, 2003).

4. J. Coleman et al., *Equality of Educational Opportunity* (Washington, DC: U.S. Government Printing Office, 1966), 119.

5. C. Bankston and S. J. Caldas, "Majority Black Schools and the Perpetuation of Social Injustice: The Influence of de Facto Segregation on Academic Achievement," *Social Forces* 75, no. 2 (1996): 535–55; K. Borman et al., "Accountability in a Postdesegregation Era: The Continuing Significance of Racial Segregation in Florida's Schools," *American Educational Research Journal* 41, no. 3 (2004): 605–31; E. Hanushek, J. Kain, and S. Rivkin, *New Evidence about Brown v. Board of Education: The Complex Effects of School Racial Composition on Achievement*, Working Paper 8741 (Cambridge, MA: National Bureau of Economic Research, 2002); C. Lleras, "Race, Racial Concentration and the Dynamics of Educational Inequality across Urban and Suburban Schools," *American Educational Research Journal* 45, no. 4 (2008): 886–912; R. Rumberger and G. Palardy, "Does Segregation Still Matter? The Impact of Student Composition on Academic Achievement in High School," *Teachers College Record* 107, no. 9 (2005): 1999–2045.

6. B. Jacob, "The Challenges of Staffing Urban Schools with Effective Teachers," *Future of Children* 17, no. 1 (2007): 129–53; Lee and Burkam, *Inequality at the Starting Gate*.

7. Jacob, "Challenges of Staffing Urban Schools"; S. L. Loeb, L. Darling-Hammond, and J. Luczak, "How Teaching Conditions Predict Teacher Turnover in California Schools," *Peabody Journal of Education* 80, no. 3 (2005): 44–70.

8. H. Lankford, S. Loeb, and J. Wyckoff, "Teacher Sorting and the Plight of Urban Schools: A Descriptive Analysis," *Education Evaluation and Policy Analysis* 24 (2002): 37–62; National Center for Education Statistics, *America's Teachers: Profile of a Profession, 1993–94* (Washington, DC: U.S. Department of Education, Institute for Education Sciences, 1997).

9. Loeb, Darling-Hammond, and Luczak, "How Teaching Conditions"; D. D. Ready and V. E. Lee, "Optimal Context Size in Elementary Schools: Disentangling the Effects of Class Size and School Size," in *Brookings Papers on Education Policy, 2006/2007*, edited by T. Loveless and F. M. Hess (Washington, DC: Brookings Institution, 2007), 99–135.

10. Rumberger and Palardy, "Does Segregation Still Matter?"; A. S. Wells and R. L. Crain, *Stepping Over the Color Line: African-American Students in White Suburban Schools* (New Haven, CT: Yale University Press, 1997); A. S. Wells and R. L. Crain, "Perpetuation Theory and the Long-Term Effects of School Desegregation," *Review of Educational Research* 64, no. 4 (1994): 531–55; J. D. Willms, "Social Class Segregation and Its Relationship to Pupils' Examination Results in Scotland," *American Sociological Review* 51, no. 2 (1986): 224–41.

11. H. Levin, "On the Relationship between Poverty and Curriculum," *North Carolina Law Review Association* 85, no. 5 (2007): 1381–418.

12. T. L. Good and J. E. Brophy, *Looking in Classrooms* (New York: Longman Higher Education, 1987).

13. Lee and Burkam, *Inequality at the Starting Gate*; V. Lee and S. Loeb, "School Size in Chicago Elementary Schools: Effects on Teachers' Attitudes and Students' Achievement," *American Educational Research Journal* 37, no. 1 (2000): 3–31.

14. R. Fryer and S. Levitt, "Understanding the Black-White Test Score Gap in the First Two Years of School," *Review of Economics and Statistics* 86, no. 2 (2004): 447–64.

15. See A. B. Hollingshead, *Elmtown's Youth: The Impact of Social Classes on Adolescents* (New York: Wiley, 1949); A. Wilson, "Residential Segregation of Social Classes and Aspirations of High School Boys," *American Sociological Review* 24, no. 6 (1959): 836–45; J. Coleman, *The Adolescent Society: The Social Life of the Teenager and Its Impact on Education* (New York: Free Press of Glencoe, 1961).

16. J. Coleman, "Toward Open Schools," *Public Interest* 9 (1967): 21.

17. Coleman et al., *Equality of Educational Opportunity*.

18. E. A. Hanushek et al., "Does Peer Ability Affect Student Achievement?," *Journal of Applied Econometrics* 18 (2003): 527–44; V. Henderson, P. Miezkowski, and Y. Sauvageau, "Peer Group Effects and Educational Production Functions," *Journal of Public Economics* 10 (1978): 97–106; R. W. Zimmer and E. F. Toma, "Peer Effects in Private and Public Schools across Countries," *Journal of Policy Analysis and Management* 19, no. 1 (2000): 75–92.

19. B. Barber, "Social-Class Differences in Educational Life-Chances," *Teachers College Record* 63 (1961): 102–13; A. Summers and B. Wolfe, "Do Schools Make a Difference?," *American Economic Review* 67 (1977): 639–52; Zimmer and Toma, "Peer Effects in Private and Public Schools."

20. Rumberger and Palardy, "Does Segregation Still Matter?"

21. S. J. Caldas and C. L. Bankston, "Baton Rouge, Desegregation, and White Flight," *Research in the Schools* 8, no. 2 (2001): 21–32; R. Dreeben and R. Barr, "Classroom Composition and the Design of Instruction," *Sociology of Education* 61, no. 3 (1988): 129–42; E. P. Lazear, "Educational Production," *Quarterly Journal of Economics* 116, no. 3 (2001): 777–803.

22. S. Reardon, *Differential Growth in the Black-White Achievement Gap during Elementary School among Low Scoring Students*, Working Paper 2008-07 (Palo Alto, CA: Stanford University Institute for Research on Education Policy and Practice, 2008).

23. T. Leventhal and J. Brooks-Gunn, "A Randomized Study of Neighborhood Effects

on Low-Income Children's Educational Outcomes," *Developmental Psychology* 40, no. 4 (2004): 488–507; Jencks and Mayer, "Social Consequences"; M. Orfield, *American Metropolitics: The New Suburban Reality* (Washington, DC: Brookings Institution, 2002); J. E. Rosenbaum, "Changing the Geography of Opportunity by Expanding Residential Choice: Lessons from the Gautreaux Program," *Housing Policy Debate* 6, no. 1 (1995): 231–69; R. J. Sampson, J. D. Morenoff, and T. Gannon-Rowley, "Assessing 'Neighborhood Effects': Social Processes and New Directions in Research," *Annual Review of Sociology* 28 (2002): 443–78; W. J. Wilson, *When Work Disappears* (New York: Vintage, 1996).

24. J. Brooks-Gunn, G. Duncan, and J. L. Aber, eds., *Neighborhood Poverty*, vol. 1, *Context and Consequences for Children*, edited by J. Brooks-Gunn, G. J. Duncan, and J. L. Aber, (New York: Russell Sage Foundation, 1997); Sampson, Morenoff, and Gannon-Rowley, "Assessing 'Neighborhood Effects'"; Wilson, *When Work Disappears*.

25. G. Orfield and S. E. Easton, *Dismantling Desegregation: The Quiet Reversal of Brown v. Board of Education* (New York: New Press, 1997); Wilson, *When Work Disappears*.

26. Brooks-Gunn, Duncan, and Aber, *Neighborhood Poverty*; G. J. Duncan and S. W. Raudenbush, "Assessing the Effects of Context in Studies of Youth and Child Development," *Educational Psychologist* 34, no. 1 (1999): 29–41; L. F. Katz, J. R. Kling, and J. B. Liebman, "Moving to Opportunity in Boston: Early Results of a Randomized Mobility Experiment," *Quarterly Journal of Economics* 116, no. 2 (2001): 607–54; A. R. Pebley and N. Sastry, *Concentrated Poverty vs. Concentrated Affluence: Effects on Neighborhood Social Environments and Children's Outcomes*, Working Paper 03-24 (Santa Monica, CA: RAND, 2003).

27. D. S. Massey and N. Denton, *American Apartheid: Segregation and the Making of the Underclass* (Cambridge: Harvard University Press, 1993).

28. Jencks and Mayer, "Social Consequences"; G. J. Duncan, J. P. Connell, and P. K. Klebanov, "Conceptual and Methodological Issues in Estimating Causal Effects of Neighborhoods and Family Conditions on Individual Development," in *Neighborhood Poverty*, vol. 1, *Context and Consequences for Children*, 219–50; M. E. Sobel, "Spatial Concentration and Social Stratification: Does the Clustering of Disadvantage 'Beget' Bad Outcomes?," in *Poverty Traps*, edited by S. Bowles, S. N. Durlauf, and K. Hoff (New York: Russell Sage Foundation, 2006), 204–29.

29. C. E. Bidwell and J. D. Kasarda, "Conceptualizing and Measuring the Effects of School and Schooling," *American Journal of Education* 88, no. 4 (1980): 401–30; Jencks and Mayer, "Social Consequences"; Katz, Kling, and Liebman, "Moving to Opportunity"; Sobel, "Spatial Concentration."

30. See Rosenbaum, "Changing the Geography of Opportunity."

31. See Katz, Kling and Liebman, "Moving to Opportunity."

32. This analytic subsample is somewhat more socioeconomically advantaged than the full ECLS-K sample, with fewer language-minority children. The loss of lower-SES and language-minority children mostly occurred when restricting the sample by available test scores. Because our sample of children attending high minority schools is somewhat more advantaged than the typical child attending such schools, our findings here may be some-

what conservative (i.e., the negative effects of high minority concentration may actually be slightly larger).

33. S. W. Raudenbush and A. S. Bryk, *Hierarchical Linear Models: Applications and Data Analysis Methods* (Thousand Oaks, CA: Sage, 2002); J. D. Singer and J. B. Willett, *Applied Longitudinal Data Analysis: Modeling Change and Event Occurrence* (New York: Oxford University Press, 2003).

34. For a full description of the modeling technique, see D. D. Ready, "Socioeconomic Disadvantage, School Attendance, and Early Cognitive Development: The Differential Effects of School Exposure," *Sociology of Education* 83, no. 4 (2010): 271–86.

35. The scores on both the reading and mathematics assessments were separately equated using Item Response Theory (IRT) in order to make them appropriate measures of change over time. The reliabilities for all eight assessments are quite high, ranging from 0.92 to 0.97. Our models employ the raw IRT scale scores as outcomes. However, we report results in effect sizes calculated using the standard deviations of the parameter-specific within- or between-school slopes. For more information, see National Center for Education Statistics, *User's Manual for the ECLS-K First Grade Public-Use Data Files and Electronic Codebook* (Washington, DC: U.S. Department of Education, 2002).

36. We also incorporated a school-level high minority by school-average SES interaction term. It was nonsignificant in all models.

37. As with other longitudinal NCES data sets, analyses using the ECLS-K data require the use of weights to compensate for unequal probabilities of selection within and between schools (e.g., the intentional oversampling of private schools and Asian/Pacific Islander children), and for nonresponse effects. Our descriptive and analytic analyses employ child-level (C124CW0) and school-level weights (S2SAQW0). Both weights are normalized to a mean of 1 to reflect the actual (smaller) sample sizes.

38. All differences are statistically significant. For specific p-values, refer to table 5.1.

39. A substantive interpretation of standard deviation (effect size) differences is that they are *large* if 0.5 SD or greater, *moderate* if 0.3–0.5 SD, *small* if 0.1–0.3 SD, and *trivial* if less than 0.1 SD; see R. Rosenthal and R. L. Rosnow, *Essentials of Behavioral Research: Methods and Data Analysis* (New York: McGraw-Hill, 1984).

40. Because children attending the same school are generally more alike than children randomly selected from the population, the racial or ethnic and social-class gaps reported here tend to be smaller than those produced using traditional ordinary least squares (OLS) regression techniques. For example, if we do not nest children within schools, the unadjusted gap between black and white in entering literacy skills within our sample is 0.42 SDs—larger than the 0.27 SD within-school HLM estimate reported above.

41. The unadjusted within-school differences (not presented here) are considerable (ES = −0.27 SD; $p < .001$).

42. Reflecting our second research question, our aim was to model the race and ethnicity slopes as a function of high minority enrollments. However, the learning slopes did not vary across schools (i.e., learning rates among blacks and among Hispanics—relative to whites—were constant across schools).

43. This is largely a function of the fact that children in general gain very few literacy skills during the summer months. Note the *negative* intercept for summer literacy learning in table 5.2; the average child actually *loses* literacy skills during the summer when he or she is not in school. This finding, which scholars have reported for decades, has been found more recently using the ECLS-K data; see D. T. Burkam et al., "Social-Class Differences in Summer Learning between Kindergarten and First Grade: Model Specification and Estimation," *Sociology of Education* 77, no. 1 (2004): 1–31.

44. Because teacher characteristics were unrelated to student learning in either literacy or mathematics, we removed these measures from the models. Given that our methods and analytic approach did not permit us to nest children in teachers, the teacher estimates surely included a considerable amount of noise due to the aggregate nature of the measures.

45. ES = −0.45 SD. Effect sizes here are calculated by dividing the coefficient by the SD of the related intercept or slope (e.g., −0.69/1.54 = −0.45).

46. However, children who attend higher-SES schools—even holding their own SES constant—tend to spend the summer months in contexts that are positively associated with mathematics learning (see table 5.4; ES = 0.30 SD; $p < .001$). Moreover, the results further indicate school-year peer effects on summer learning; children whose peers have more positive approaches to learning in the classroom gain more literacy skills during the summer months (ES = 0.16 SD; $p < .05$). This is reasonable, as children's school-year peer networks often function during the summer as well.

47. Coleman, "Toward Open Schools."

48. See S. G. Rivkin, "Residential Segregation and School Integration," *Sociology of Education* 67, no. 4 (1994): 279–92.

49. R. A. Mickelson, "The Academic Consequences of Desegregation and Segregation: Evidence from the Charlotte-Mecklenburg Schools," *North Carolina Law Review* 61 (2003): 1513.

50. See R. L. Linn and K. G. Welner, eds., *Race-Conscious Policies for Assigning Students to Schools: Social Science Research and the Supreme Court Cases* (Washington, DC: National Academy of Education, 2007).

51. R. Kahlenberg, *All Together Now: Creating Middle-Class Schools through Public School Choice* (Washington, DC: Brookings Institution, 2001).

52. P. A. Jargowsky, "Take the Money and Run," *American Sociological Review* 61, no. 6 (1996): 984–98; Orfield, *American Metropolitics.*

53. See B. T. Bowman, M. S. Donovan, and M. S. Burns, eds., *Eager to Learn: Educating Our Preschoolers* (Washington, DC: National Academies Press, 2000); and D. L. Kirp, *The Sandbox Investment* (Cambridge: Harvard University Press, 2007).

54. J. Currie and D. Thomas, "Does Head Start Make a Difference?," *American Economic Review* 85, no. 3 (1995): 341–64; J. Currie and D. Thomas, "School Quality and the Longer-Term Effects of Head Start," *Journal of Human Resources* 35, no. 4 (2000): 755–74; V. Lee et al., "Are Head Start Effects Sustained?," *Child Development* 61, no. 2 (1990): 495–507.

55. Currie and Thomas, "Does Head Start Make a Difference?"; Lee et al., "Are Head Start Effects Sustained?"

56. Lee and Burkam, *Inequality at the Starting Gate*. Other studies indicate that Head Start children also attend lower-quality middle schools (see V. Lee and S. Loeb, "Where Do Head Start Attendees End Up? One Reason Why Preschool Effects Fade Out," *Educational Evaluation and Policy Analysis* 17, no. 1 [1995]: 62–82).

57. Currie and Thomas, "Does Head Start Make a Difference?"; Currie and Thomas, "School Quality."

58. Fryer and Levitt, "Understanding the Black-White Test Score Gap."

AMY STUART WELLS, JACQUELYN DURAN, & TERRENDA WHITE

Southern Graduates of School Desegregation

A Double Consciousness of Resegregation yet Hope

Recent research on the graduates of school desegregation explores the complicated relationship between how individuals were fundamentally changed by their educational experiences in racially diverse schools and, paradoxically, how little our racially divided society has changed since they were in school, making their adult lives far more segregated.[1] In other words, the story of school desegregation's graduates illustrates how the dismantling of racial segregation within the public schools was intended to be only one part of a broader social reform. Yet many other parts of that reform, including the War on Poverty, serious fair-housing enforcement, and policies to revive urban communities, were never implemented or quickly abandoned. This meant the burden of transforming a racially polarized society was placed almost entirely on public schools and their desegregation policies.[2] Schools alone could not do this, although they did have a strong impact on those who attended them during that era.

Echoing findings from the quantitative survey data on school desegregation and racial attitudes, this in-depth, qualitative research finds that most graduates of desegregation say their experiences in racially diverse schools made them more comfortable in their interactions with people of other racial and ethnic backgrounds. They compare themselves to spouses, friends, and siblings who attended more racially isolated schools and who are far less at ease around people of other racial and ethnic backgrounds. At the same time, however, school desegregation in and of itself did not change the still segregated and unequal larger society into which these graduates matriculated to buy homes, get jobs, and rear their own children.

When they were in high school, the graduates believed their desegregated public schools were preparing them for a "real world" that would be more racially integrated and equal. When they graduated, however, they learned that in fact this was not the case. Most of their adult lives were lived under presidential administrations and federal courts that were dismantling major parts of the civil rights revolution, including school desegregation. While the

public schools they attended were part of a bold effort in the field of education—both court-imposed and voluntary—to bring people together across
color lines, little had occurred in the other sectors of society to prepare for
a generation of graduates who, because of their schooling experience, were
more open to living in racially diverse neighborhoods, churches, and workplaces than prior generations. As one graduate of school desegregation aptly
described this phenomenon, it was as if the public schools were at the forefront of the first phase of desegregation, but that beyond this, there was no
"second gear" for the civil rights movement, which required other institutions
to follow suit. And while more progress has been made in the employment
sector to diversify workplaces than in the housing sector to integrate neighborhoods, even at work, the graduates of desegregation say their offices are
stratified by race, with whites generally in charge of lower-paid employees of
color.[3]

Nowhere was this lost momentum of the civil rights movement and racial
desegregation felt more strongly than in the South, where high school graduates of the 1980s recognized that through their participation in school desegregation, they helped rewrite the history of what had always been a rigidly
segregated society with de jure segregation and massive white resistance to
civil rights. Furthermore, only in the South were large-scale increases in the
levels of school integration achieved and sustained for several decades. In re-
calling the racial tension and violence that symbolized the breakdown of a
formal system of racial apartheid, the southern graduates clearly distinguished
themselves from their parents' and grandparents' generations and thus saw
themselves as central to the development of a "new" forward-looking South.
Believing they had been somewhat successful in this endeavor by the time they
left high school, which most of them did, they were filled with a great sense
of accomplishment and fulfillment. Similarly, their later understanding that
they, as former high school students, had moved further toward embracing an
integrated society than most people or institutions in the South contributed
to their even deeper sense of the lost momentum related to these issues after
graduation.

A sense of "double consciousness"—or a "twoness" as W. E. B. Du Bois[4]
would have referred to it—emerges from these graduates' frustration from
being both prepared for a more racially integrated society and yet living in a
society that has not become much more integrated at all. How this sense of
twoness plays out differs for the graduates according to which side of the color
line they reside on. White graduates of desegregated schools, for instance,
may yearn for a more progressive, racially integrated society but at the same

time benefit in material ways from the separation and inequality of society as it is—a society in which segregated white property values, school rankings, and employment access are much greater. The most privileged, upper-middle-class, and affluent white parents make school choices from a particular standpoint, at a particular moment in history when their anxiety about the education of their children is quite high and the choices available are too often racially segregated and unequal. And yet these white parents know intuitively that diversity is important in preparing their children and the larger society for the future, even as they choose schools that are not at all diverse.[5]

Graduates of color, for their part, not only bemoan the lack of progress around issues of race and segregation in society, but also fight back against segregation more because of the material and structural consequence they face as a result. They therefore are more likely than their white counterparts to seek racially diverse neighborhoods and schools for their children, knowing as they do the high costs and harms of segregation. At the same time, they realize what is gained and what is lost when they enroll their children in predominantly white schools with high test scores and challenging curriculum but also administrators and teachers who may or may not understand their culture or ways of knowing the world.[6]

In order to capture the uniqueness of the southern context and its impact on graduates of desegregation, we focus on studies we have conducted of 1980 high school graduates from Charlotte, North Carolina, and 1986 high school graduates from Louisville, Kentucky, as well as 2009 follow-up interviews with several 1980 Charlotte graduates to understand whether the election of the first African American president and the 2008–11 economic crisis had affected their attitudes. We learned that the recent history in the United States has given all the graduates interviewed a sense of hope that perhaps issues of racial segregation and inequality will once again be addressed—or even discussed—by policy makers and the public. But it is also clear that absent a bold social movement and a related policy agenda aimed at supporting and sustaining more diverse communities and schools, these graduates, like most Americans, will remain mired in the separate and unequal structures we created and sustained through prior policies.

Louisville and Charlotte School Desegregation Plans

Both the Charlotte-Mecklenburg Public Schools and the Jefferson County Public Schools in Louisville were desegregated via federal court orders in the

1970s. In both instances, these large, countywide, suburban-and-urban districts—both formed from a merger of city and suburban districts prior to the beginning of school desegregation—were required to implement desegregation plans that reassigned students from racially segregated to desegregated schools.

Charlotte's court order: In Charlotte, the school desegregation case went all the way to the U.S. Supreme Court, resulting in the landmark decision *Swann v. Charlotte-Mecklenburg* (1971). This ruling sanctioned the use of transportation of students to racially diverse schools and initiated desegregation of cities across the South. Over the next 30 years, thousands of students enrolled in the Charlotte-Mecklenburg Schools (CMS) were reassigned outside of their neighborhoods to desegregate the schools. Thus, between 1969 and the mid-1970s, the racial makeup of West Charlotte High School—the only historically black high school that remained open after the desegregation plan was implemented—shifted demographically from nearly 100 percent black to about 50 percent white. The graduates interviewed for this chapter attended West Charlotte when it was still racially balanced. Then, in the early 1990s, the CMS administration began slowly dismantling the school desegregation plan, and West Charlotte lost virtually all of its white student population. Furthermore, since the court order was dissolved in 2002, all of Charlotte's public schools have become increasingly racially segregated, with some schools 90 percent African American and others more than 80 percent white. Nearly half of CMS's African American students now attend racially segregated, predominantly black schools.

Louisville's court order: The original Louisville school desegregation case resulted in a comprehensive student reassignment plan mandated by a federal district court judge in 1975. Although there had been racial violence and resistance to school desegregation in Charlotte, particularly before the Supreme Court ruling in 1971, it was nothing like what was unfurled in Louisville when white students were reassigned to schools in black communities. Armed police officers rode on school buses as they transported children across racial dividing lines. It was not uncommon during those early days of desegregation in Louisville to see angry white parents jeering the buses and waving antibusing signs.[7] By the time the class of 1980 reached high school in Charlotte and the class of 1986 entered high school in Louisville, things had been deeply transformed, but there were still powerful memories of the battles. Louisville retained a comprehensive desegregation plan until it was overturned by the 2007 Supreme Court ruling in *Parents Involved in Community Schools v. Seattle School District No. 1*. Following that decision, the school board in Louisville devised a creative way to maintain a substantial income-based and neighborhood-based desegregation plan.

In the following sections of this essay, we describe the central themes and findings to emerge from our in-depth interviews with graduates of school desegregation from these two southern sites. Given the social and political contexts into which these former students were born and raised, the impact of school desegregation on how they make sense of race and difference is all the more striking, as is the cost of the failure of other segments of the society to follow suit.

Why Desegregation Was Worth It
A Universal Theme of Adult Graduates

The most powerful theme to emerge from these studies of school desegregation's graduates runs counter to much of the popular "wisdom" about the failure of school desegregation policy. When we listen to those who lived through school desegregation and experienced it firsthand, they tell us that it was one of the most valuable experiences of their lives because it taught them to be more open, accepting, and comfortable around people of different racial and ethnic backgrounds.[8] Southern graduates of desegregated schools in the 1980s thought they were at the forefront (or at least a part) of a sea change toward a more open, accepting, and racially integrated southern society and left with a sense of accomplishment and fulfillment.

The De Jure Segregation Context of the South

The children of school desegregation who were born and raised in Louisville, Kentucky, in the 1960s and 1970s can still remember—often quite vividly—Ku Klux Klan members, in their long white robes and hoods, standing next to their parents' cars and handing out their anti-desegregation literature at stoplights in the white neighborhoods. This left lasting impressions. As one white Louisville graduate we interviewed recalled, "Now looking back, I can't believe the KKK was hanging out two miles from where I grew up, recruiting[,] . . . and that's when they covered their faces. . . . And I remember an older kid went up and got their literature, and we were reading it, and I didn't really understand it. Yeah, you just think it wasn't that long ago they were doing that. . . . I vividly remember that, just thinking, 'What are these guys doing with sheets on walking around?'" (laughs).

Yet while several white Louisville graduates recall seeing KKK members, the black graduates, who were more physically removed from the hooded Klansmen, said they knew that the Klan was out there, in the neighborhoods of the white students they were interacting with in desegregated schools.

One African American graduate of Louisville's Central High School noted that her mother temporarily put her in a private school when she was young because of the violence and sense of threat in the public schools. Because of that constant tension during elementary school, she ended up having a nervous condition that she attributes to being bused at a young age into a white neighborhood known for racial hatred: "It was like they'd be throwing bricks and always taunting us. It was like rough, when you're trying to go to school, wondering if you're going to make it to school the next day, 'cause we were so far out there. . . . And back in that day, it was like the Ku Klux Klan area, and they didn't want us out there as it was, so it was just rough."

Even when the KKK was not involved, there was enough racial tension, violence, and raw, blatant prejudice in the streets and airways of these two metro areas that the graduates were not immune to it. As a white graduate of West Charlotte High School explained, by the time she and her classmates enrolled in that historically black high school, there was a great deal of pride in the school. But a mere ten years prior to her cohort's arrival at West Charlotte High School, when desegregation was first implemented in Charlotte, she recalled white people in her neighborhood angry about desegregation and referring to blacks and West Charlotte High School with derogatory names.

Similarly, the students who attended desegregated public schools in these two cities were well aware that many of the white students assigned to those schools did not come. They knew that private schools—aka segregation academies—were cropping up in both contexts. As one African American graduate from Charlotte noted, "The private schools in Charlotte got their start because of busing. . . . They exploded when busing started."

Given this larger context of racial tension and avoidance, graduates who grew up on the black side of the color line in these two cities were even more aware of the burden being placed on their generation to rewrite the history of the South. In the process of doing this, these African American graduates were conscious that giving up their "safe spaces" in segregated black schools meant they were being more directly exposed to the kind of discrimination and racism that their parents had known only at a distance.

Black graduates and educators in Charlotte, for instance, recalled the process of resegregation in desegregated schools—even when the desegregated school was a historically black school where black students had once filled the highest level classes. As one black community activist in Charlotte noted, when members of the black community began voicing criticism about within-school segregation across tracks, classes, and opportunities, funds and resources to support their schools were withdrawn by the district officials.

As an African American graduate of West Charlotte High School noted: "I think from an African American perspective, there were things that were gained, but there were things that were lost as well. We lost the sense of community and the school being a rallying point for persons in the community and a source of pride. We had teachers that we knew really—well." Like virtually all of his classmates in Charlotte and Louisville, however, this graduate argues that more was ultimately gained than lost by having attended a racially diverse public school.

At the Forefront of Change

Whatever costs or fears were associated with school desegregation on each side of the color line in Charlotte and Louisville, the strongest and clearest finding from our data is that it was still "worth it" to endure them. In fact, in great part *because* of this larger context of Jim Crow and the legacy of racial tension that it spawned, the southern experience was even more valuable because it allowed these cohorts of graduates to feel that they were indeed at the forefront of major change in their communities. For many of the graduates of West Charlotte High School, in particular, being part of this sea change was "cool," "hip," and very much a part of their adult identity today.

According to one African American graduate who reminisced about her years at West Charlotte in the late 1970s, "In my day, we just thought it was the coolest thing that we all got along so well. I mean, we really did. We just thought we was something! [laughs] And that's a good feeling for a young person."

A white West Charlotte graduate, echoing the sense of change and historical significance of where the class of 1980 fit into the larger history of the South, recalled "being proud [of the racial diversity at West Charlotte,] . . . especially 'cause we had been aware that not everyone had gotten along in recent years, you know, throughout the South or throughout the country and that . . . we were proud that we were racially diverse . . . and that we got along and worked together on things like the newspaper and clubs."

When pressed to respond with more detail about the substantive aspects of attending desegregated schools, graduates of desegregation tended to come up with the same set of themes we see in other studies. They almost all reported a greater sense of comfort around people of other racial and ethnic backgrounds. For whites, this often signifies that they have overcome significant fears and dispelled major stereotypes of people of color that whites often harbor even if they do not articulate them. For African Americans and Latinos, this sense of comfort often relates to overcoming feelings of inferiority in their interactions with whites. On both sides of the color line, the graduates explained how they have grown as individuals due to their exposure to and interactions with people different from them.

According to a white male graduate from Louisville's Male High School, a magnet school that drew a mix of black and white students from all over the district: "I think it benefited me not to be stuck with the same guys . . . I grew up with in the same neighborhood, because I got to see different people, I got to see different people act in different ways, and their thinking was different."

A white West Charlotte graduate noted that because he went to a 50 percent black high school, he "saw a bunch of [black] kids that weren't out to, you know, rob, steal, undermine white people as a group. . . . I saw people that were human beings and that had good days, bad days, problems, concerns, just like I did and other white kids did, who were trying to figure out, what do I do to get an A on this test or to pass the class or whatever." Another white West Charlotte graduate explained: "Honestly it taught me not to judge people until I get to know [them]. That has been one of the best lessons I think I ever learned."

At the same time, an African American graduate of Fern Creek High School in Louisville, class of 1986, said that early exposure to people of different racial backgrounds and cultures taught him to be more comfortable with whites, especially in an adult work environment. He argued that if he had lacked that interracial exposure in desegregated schools as a child and then suddenly found himself working around white people, "it would be different. . . . I'd feel probably like a lot of eyes were on me at work and everybody's watching what I'm doing or something like that, versus you know, trying to be a little more at ease and then get along."

As if demonstrating Gordon Allport's "contact hypothesis" theory,[9] graduates of desegregated schools almost always report that attending racially diverse schools made them far more at ease with people who are culturally and racially or ethnically different from them. This sense of comfort, understanding, and dispelled fears and stereotypes is discussed again and again by these graduates.

The Double Consciousness of Graduates Prepared for a "Real World" That Does Not Exist

The graduates we interviewed found that when they left high school, the "real world" was much more segregated than their schools. While they all discuss this theme in slightly different ways—and some of them, particularly the graduates of color, have worked harder to find racially diverse neighborhoods and schools for their own children—there is much evidence that the society writ large did not keep up with their expectations, given the emphasis on racial desegregation that shaped their schooling experiences in the 1970s and 1980s. Some of the graduates of desegregation talk about this in terms of the missing "second gear" for the civil rights movement—a much-needed post-1960s renewed commitment to racial integration and equality that never occurred. Such a second gear would have assured that the burden of solving all the problems of racial inequality was spread more evenly across different institutions in the society and not placed only on the public schools.[10]

Without school desegregation, most of these now 40-something adults would have led their entire lives within racially isolated institutions. In a society in which housing patterns, places of worship, and social circles are often segregated by race, diverse public schools have been, for many students, the only institutions in which cross-racial interaction and understanding can occur. They have also often been historically the only institutions in our society in which students of color can gain access to predominantly white and prestigious institutions.

We know from social science research on segregation that U.S. housing patterns are, and have been for several decades, highly divided along racial lines, with African American residents the most segregated population.[11] These segregated patterns peaked nationally in the 1970s, as the class of 1986 entered kindergarten. Since then, segregation in housing has decreased significantly except in the largest cities but far less than would be predicted given the growth of the black middle class over the last 40 years. There is evidence that housing integration increased more in areas with comprehensive metropolitan desegregation plans.[12] Furthermore, churches and other places of worship and social circles have also remained highly segregated.[13]

It is not surprising, therefore, that we learned from our research that the public schools were often the only institutions in which these former students had any meaningful interactions with people of other races. A white graduate of Louisville's historically black high school, Central High, explained that if the Jefferson County Public Schools had not desegregated, she would have grown up in a virtually all-white environment, and she would have always thought of downtown Louisville as a crime-ridden place where white people did not go. Had she not attended her urban high school, she said, she "would have been much more apprehensive about people[,] . . . not just African Americans, but of any other race. I certainly would have been much more sheltered because, you know, living in this area, everything that you need is right here, so there would never be any reason for me to have a lot of interaction with anyone who wasn't middle-class and white."

On the other side of town, this white Central High graduate's classmate, an African American woman, described the neighborhood where she grew up as almost exclusively black: "I think there was only one white . . . there was one, an older white lady there." Of her interactions with people of other races, she said, "mostly it was at school."

But the fact that these patterns of out-of-school segregation changed very little as these graduates left high school and went on to higher education and/or the workforce, purchased homes, joined churches, made adult friends, and had children who then needed to be sent to school meant that their adult lives became more racially isolated than their adolescent lives had been.

Throughout all the interviews with desegregation's graduates it is clear that they were much more optimistic about the future of racial integration in the United States when they were enrolled in their desegregated schools than they were 20-plus years later when we interviewed them as adults. Even those graduates who were exposed occasionally to other races in their adult lives—which was most likely to occur in their workplace—were quick to point out the many other aspects of their lives that remained highly segregated, including their neighborhoods, children's schools, places of worship, and their social networks. This was not the 21st-century society they had envisioned back when the system of state-enforced apartheid schooling was being dismantled in the South.

The pattern of resegregation for adult West Charlotte graduates held for housing but not as much for their children's public schools because the school desegregation plan—especially magnet schools—was still partially operating at the time we interviewed these parents. Thus, in terms of housing, 88 percent of the white West Charlotte graduates we interviewed described their neighborhoods as mostly white. Meanwhile, of those with school-aged children, 52 percent had them enrolled in what they described as racially diverse schools. For African American graduates in Charlotte, only 38 percent lived in self-described diverse neighborhoods, while 50 percent of them were sending their children to "diverse" schools.

The graduates of Louisville were more likely to live in diverse neighborhoods—with one-third of whites and virtually all blacks living in communities they described as having some racial or ethnic diversity. Furthermore, because the Louisville school desegregation plan was still in place when we interviewed these graduates, the majority—60 percent—of white Louisville graduates and 100 percent of the black graduates of 1986 who had children enrolled them in racially diverse schools at that time (2006).

These southern graduates were also more likely to work in diverse settings than they were to live in them, but for the most part, their children's public schools remained, like the schools of their own childhoods, the most racially diverse institutions they interacted with on a regular basis. In thinking about what these trends say about the larger, political context of their lives, the graduates, especially those from Charlotte, bemoan the loss of their integrationist dream. According to one white Charlotte graduate, not only was there no "second gear" for the civil rights movement, we actually went into reverse. "There was no second gear. Just first gear, then back up."

Another white graduate who works for an organization serving disadvantaged youth in Charlotte bemoans the fact that West Charlotte High School, and so many other schools in that district, are now extremely segregated and unequal: "There's still such a disparity I think, and the neighborhoods have not become integrated, so . . . if you're going to have neighborhood schools, you're going to have schools that have families that have money, and you're going to have schools that have families that don't have money. . . . I mean, you know, it's basically segregated again here."

This lost momentum is felt more deeply, we argue, among southern graduates. For instance, an African American graduate of West Charlotte's class of 1980 explained that her daughter is in one of the city's remaining magnet school programs, but that because it is in a predominantly black neighborhood, on the "black" side of town, many of the white students have left. "It's starting to look a lot different than when she started in kindergarten. . . . But you see less and less diversity in the program, because I guess certain parents don't choose to send their child to a school in certain areas. And see, now they choose."

Another African American graduate of West Charlotte High School noted that "if you want to take a snapshot of the Charlotte schools, they are pretty much segregated, which I think is unfortunate because I think what happens is when you're not interacting on a daily basis with folks of different races, genders, socioeconomic backgrounds, your thoughts about those people are pretty much determined by what you see in the media, which is not always accurate."

The graduates of Louisville have been less affected by this retrenchment because their public schools have remained more integrated. Thus, while they acknowledge the ongoing segregation in their neighborhoods, due to the commitment of the local school officials to maintain school-level diversity, their children's public schools have remained far more diverse even after a 2007 Supreme Court decision forced revisions of the local plan.

"That Was a Different Time"
The Rationale for Segregation and White Privilege

As much as white graduates of school desegregation bemoan the lack of integration in their adult lives, and often in the lives of their children, it is true that many of the white graduates—particularly those who grew up middle- or upper-middle-class—have benefited in material and thus structural ways from the changing economic and political context that has fostered greater income inequality.

This duality of outcomes and benefits has led to a sense of double consciousness among white graduates in particular about where they find themselves today—yearning for greater diversity but demanding separate and unequal educational opportunities for their children.[14] These economically successful white graduates of desegregation know both the benefits of learning to get along with others who are different from them and the benefits of separating themselves from too much racial diversity in order to maintain the distinction needed to drive up their property values and their children's chances of getting into better colleges.

In other words, because they know that the rewards are greater for those who win in the seemingly zero-sum game of economic mobility in this country, they note that this is "a different time" from when they were in school, and they reconcile the differences between their children's school experiences and their own in this way.

In the data on southern graduates of school desegregation, this theme is much more pronounced among the white West Charlotte graduates, almost half of whom have their children in elite private schools, an option they say their parents never would have considered. This sense of pressure to help their children get "ahead" in a rat race to the top of a highly stratified society is powerful and prevalent among the most affluent white West Charlotte graduates in particular. One West Charlotte graduate whose children attended one of the most elite private schools in the city said that he and a former classmate of his whose children are in this same school often talk about the contrast between societal priorities when they were in high school in the 1970s and today: "The measure of success today or up until today, I think, has been primarily financial things, whereas in the sixties, that was not the case. It was to make a difference in the world, to stand for something, to be a leader, to be creative, solve a major social or medical problem or issue—that was a measure of success. Not being the CEO of a company or making millions of dollars as a hedge-fund manager or being a philanthropist. It was getting in the trenches and doing the work to make the world a better place."

White, upper-middle-class graduates of school desegregation (as well as some of the graduates of color)—in the South and the other regions of the country—will talk for hours at a time about how competitive the educational system is today for parents and children who want to have an edge, who want to get ahead. They talked about parents who dedicate their lives to orchestrating their children's academic, social, and professional success. One white West Charlotte graduate who has two children in high school reflected on the changes in parenting and the stress of getting children into the "right" college, sorority, job, and on and on: "And I'm not sure how that has evolved. I think there might be more people applying to college right now than there were when we were in high school. But I mean, the whole competition thing, and it starts on the soccer field when they're five. It started a long, long, long time ago, and I think it's the parents."

Parents who do not participate—who do not try to get their children in the most exclusive, high-status schools—are made to feel they are bad parents. In this way, what being a "good upper-middle-class parent" is in these contexts is socially constructed. In fact, West Charlotte white graduates from the affluent side of town talked about how many of their friends from high school now have their children in prestigious private schools. Only one of the graduates we reinterviewed in 2009 still had her children in a public school—a neighborhood high school that has become predominantly white since the desegregation plan ended in 2002 and which, according to this parent, is highly segregated by race across classrooms. As this white graduate noted, "All of my best friends that I went through West Charlotte with have their kids in private schools."

When asked why she thought so many parents in her generation, who went to public school—and often very diverse public schools—have put their own children into competitive private schools, one of the West Charlotte white graduates answered: "Some of it is kind of an affluent thing. . . . It's just that highly competitive nature. . . . I mean, some people are so competitive, and I do think a lot of it is based on fear."

In Louisville, where the public schools were still racially balanced when we conducted our interviews, only three of the 19 graduates had their children in private schools. One of these three graduates said she chose a private school because she wanted her children to go to the school affiliated with her mostly white church. Yet in thinking about her decision more as it related to diversity, she noted that her son "needs more diversity."

Clearly, the increased parental anxiety at the top and upper-middle section of the income distribution in Charlotte if not in Louisville that is pushing more families toward private or elite, racially isolated public schools is related to the growing inequality in incomes since the late 1970s. Contrasted to the prior era (1950s–1970s) when there was a compression of incomes and the creation of a strong and more prosperous middle class, the last quarter century has seen deeper and wider divisions in income and wealth.[15]

This theme of greater parental anxiety at the top of the highly stratified society is tightly interwoven with a moment in our nation's history when efforts to make our society more equal have been all but abandoned. Today, the white, affluent graduates of West Charlotte High School, in particular, can simultaneously talk about how meaningful and worthwhile their high school experience was and how they could never, ever send their own children to a 50-percent-black public school today. This is a different time, they note, so West Charlotte, for instance, is not really an option for their children.

One mother who graduated from a racially and ethnically and socioeconomically diverse high school less than 30 years ago sends her two children to a mostly white, elite private Christian school in which there are virtually no poor students. One of the few students of color, she told me, has her picture on the front of every brochure and page of the school's website. She explained that her way of keeping the part of her that is West Charlotte alive is by encouraging her children to participate in philanthropic efforts.

At the same time, this graduate possesses an awareness and a critique of the larger inequality in Charlotte, particularly in the housing market. She said that the real problem of inequality and segregation in Charlotte is "very much a housing issue because in the late seventies, early eighties, up until the past I would say five years or so, there were a lot of more diverse housing opportunities and . . . neighborhoods."

But the idea of trying to change local zoning laws or housing policy does not yet appear to be on the radar screen of these graduates of school desegregation, even as they are increasingly sensing the need to give something back to their community—in part because of their own experiences in desegregated schools. As one of the more affluent white West Charlotte graduates explained, she has two of her children working with a local foundation through a youth program where teenagers are able to volunteer to award grants to local non-profits. She thinks this process of learning how to give (tax-deductible) money from rich people to needy organizations is a good learning experience. But she also admitted that this particular learning experience will help them get into the college of their choice, which is, after all, but a means to yet another "end."

The Post–Obama Election Conclusion

We have learned from the graduates of school desegregation that much of what has evolved politically, socially, and economically in this country in the past 30 years has worked against many of the gains made in the 1960s and 1970s toward greater racial integration and equality. Yet in the first and most powerful finding from this qualitative research on school desegregation— namely, that attending racially diverse schools did change individuals, making them fundamentally different from their peers and parents—we do find hope. This hope is that perhaps there is a latent majority out there that still believes the civil rights movement needs a "second gear."

The November 2008 election of President Barack Obama and the economic crisis of 2008 and 2009 may well be two catalytic factors that influence how the graduates of school desegregation make sense of their fairly segregated adult lives. In our follow-up interviews with graduates of West Charlotte High School in February 2009, we heard a great deal of soul-searching—searching for a different time, when there was less of a rat race to the top of a highly unequal society, less of a focus on giving kids material things and opportunities to build their college résumés as opposed to meaningful experiences that could transform the world as we know it. These reflections from class of 1980 graduates as they move into their late 40s and watch their children apply to college and begin to make choices about their adult lives are not earth-shattering. But they do strongly suggest some reframing of how they make sense of what is important to them and which experiences have been most meaningful to them.

One of the African American West Charlotte graduates from 1980 noted that after President Obama was elected, she began hoping for a brighter future—that things will change and issues of diversity and equity will become more important again. She said that the naysayers on the issue of diverse schools tell her that "times are different," and that it wouldn't make a difference. But she knows from her experience and that of her former classmates that it did make a huge difference. "They say we're past that, but we're really not. [laughs] You know what I'm saying, we're really not. . . . But I'm just saying with Obama being elected, I'm hoping that maybe we're going back . . . to the days of 1980 West Charlotte. . . . Where anybody can be anything. That's what we all found. We found we could be anything we wanted to be . . . because that seed was planted." She added that when she looks at the president, she sees the spirit of West Charlotte during its heyday as the symbol successful desegregation in Charlotte.

Perhaps what is most interesting and hopeful about the West Charlotte graduates' reflections on how things are currently changing and possibly re-aligning is that they are drawn back to their old high school and the people who were there with them, as well as to the spirit from that time that so many say they carry inside. For instance, one of the African American West Charlotte graduates noted that at a recent high school reunion, he and his white and black former classmates were discussing how they felt about having been part of the social experiment that was southern school desegregation. "And thirty years later, if you ask the folks in my class if we thought the experiment worked or it didn't, the majority would say that it worked. . . . And I think in large part because a lot of times, when you are at the forefront of any change, you don't know the results of that change immediately."

While he admits there have been setbacks since his class graduated, he believes it is not too late to try to move that agenda forward in a new political and economic era. He believes enough people like him, who are products of a different era, want to continue to move forward, particularly in the area of race relations. "It just remains to be seen," he said. "There's definitely potential, and I think the election has given people hope who in the past didn't have it."

Reflecting on his generation, Obama's generation, and this moment in history, one white graduate of a historically black high school in a formerly de jure segregated state in the southern United States noted: "We [could] sit in the back seat when we were kids[,] . . . [but] now we're on deck; it's time to start taking some swings. . . . It's our time. . . . And it's daunting." After a pause, he added: "It's really daunting. But I hope that we can remember and think back to our experiences at West Charlotte and other schools like that and bring that to bear."

NOTES

1. A. S. Wells et al., *Both Sides Now: The Story of Desegregation's Graduates* (Berkeley: University of California Press, 2009).

2. A. S. Wells, "Our Children's Burden: A History of Federal Education Policies That Ask (Now Require) Our Public Schools to Solve Societal Inequality," in *NCLB at the Crossroads: Re-examining America's Commitment to Closing Our Nation's Achievement Gaps*, edited by M. A. Rebell and J. Wolff (New York: Teachers College Press, 2009), 1–42.

3. Ibid.; Wells et al., *Both Sides Now*.

4. W. E. B. Du Bois, *The Souls of Black Folk*, 100th anniversary ed. (Boulder, CO: Paradigm, 2003).

5. A. S. Wells and A. Roda, "White Parents, Diversity and School Choice Policies: Where Good Intentions, Anxiety and Privilege Collide," paper presented at the Vanderbilt School Choice Conference, Nashville, 25 October 2009; A. S. Wells et al., *Why Boundaries Matter: A Study of Five Separate and Unequal Long Island School Districts* (New York: Teachers College, Columbia University, 2009).

6. See Wells et al., *Both Sides Now*; see also A. S. Wells, J. Duran, and T. White, "Refusing to Leave Desegregation Behind: From Graduates of Racially Diverse Schools to the Supreme Court," *Teachers College Record* 110, no. 12 (2008): 2532–70.

7. S. Garland, *Divided We Fail: The Fight for Equal Schools in a Post-Desegregation Era* (New York: Beacon, forthcoming).

8. Wells et al., *Both Sides Now*; Wells, Duran, and White, "Refusing to Leave Desegregation Behind."

9. G. Allport, *The Nature of Prejudice* (Reading, MA: Addison-Wesley, 1954).

10. Wells, Duran, and White, "Refusing to Leave Desegregation Behind."

11. D. M. Cutler, E. L. Glaeser, and J. L. Vigdor, "The Rise and Decline of the American Ghetto," *Journal of Political Economy* 107, no. 3 (1999): 455–507; J. E. Farley and G. D. Squires, "Fences and Neighbors: Segregation in 21st-Century America," *Contexts* 4, no. 1 (2005): 33–39.

12. R. Sethi and R. Somanathan, "Inequality and Segregation," *Journal of Political Economy* 112, no. 6 (2004): 1296–322.

13. Correspondents of the New York Times, *How Race Is Lived in America: Pulling Together, Pulling Apart* (New York: Times Books, 2001).

14. Ibid.

15. Paul Krugman, "Losing Our Country," *New York Times*, 10 June 2005.

CASEY D. COBB, ROBERT BIFULCO, & COURTNEY BELL

Legally Viable Desegregation Strategies
The Case of Connecticut

In this essay, we consider the impact of two school choice programs explicitly focused on reducing the racial and economic isolation of black and Latino students living in Connecticut's cities. The programs, interdistrict magnet schools and Open Choice, are particularly relevant in the legal environment since *Parents Involved in Community Schools v. Seattle School District No. 1* (PICS, 2007) because they appear to adhere to the legal precedents laid out in the PICS decision. Specifically, the programs are designed to integrate students across district lines, which in many regions is crucial for achieving racial integration. The programs are entirely voluntary; neither districts nor families are required to participate. Finally, the race of individual students is not used in determining admissions to the programs or to individual schools. These two Connecticut programs thus offer models of choice-based, interdistrict desegregation plans that appear to satisfy current legal constraints and hold the promise of racial integration.

This essay summarizes recent analyses examining the effects of these two programs on racial, ethnic, and economic isolation, individual student experiences and attitudes, and academic achievement. Few other studies provide similar analyses of interdistrict choice programs designed to promote integration. Our findings indicate that both programs provide participating students more integrated environments than they would otherwise experience, that interdistrict magnet high schools offer environments more conducive to academic learning and cross-cultural understanding than nonmagnet schools in the central city, and that the programs have positive effects on academic achievement. Despite these successes the programs may not be reaching enough students. Of most importance, the number of central city students participating in these programs remains relatively small, and as a result the majority of central city students remain isolated in overwhelmingly minority and economically disadvantaged schools.

The essay is organized as follows. First, we briefly describe desegregation policy in Connecticut. Second, we summarize our analyses of the effects of interdistrict magnet schools on a range of student outcomes. We then turn our attention to the Open Choice program, examining its effects on integration and student achievement. Finally, we draw conclusions about the work and make suggestions for next steps.

Desegregation Policy in Connecticut

In 1989, Elizabeth Horton Sheff of Hartford and other concerned parents filed a lawsuit against the governor of Connecticut claiming that the state had failed to provide students in Hartford with an education equal to that of their suburban counterparts. In 1996, the Connecticut Supreme Court ruled that due to racial, ethnic, and economic isolation, students in Hartford had been denied equal educational opportunity in violation of the state's constitution. The Court left remedies to the state legislature, without providing specific goals or timetables.

The state responded by renewing a long-standing interdistrict student transfer program called Project Concern, substantially increasing the number of interdistrict magnet schools and adopting a number of other programs to encourage contact among students from different backgrounds. Dissatisfied with progress toward reducing the isolation of Hartford students, the plaintiffs filed suit again, resulting in a 2003 settlement agreement with the state. The agreement called for at least 30 percent of Hartford's minority public school students to be enrolled in a reduced-isolation setting at the end of four years. It mandated additional funding to support existing programs, expanding the number of seats in Open Choice and adding at least two new magnet schools per year. Following the expiration of the 2003 agreement, new deliberations led to a second *Sheff* settlement agreement in 2008 resulting in a Comprehensive Management Plan (CMP) to be honored through at least September 2012. The new CMP aims at increasing participation in magnet schools and the Open Choice program via more suburban participation, a Regional School Choice Office that oversees a more streamlined and well-advertised application process for families, more aggressive interim performance benchmarks, and a new goal of meeting at least 80 percent of the demand for seats in reduced-isolation settings.[1]

Interdistrict Magnet Schools

An interdistrict magnet school is a publicly funded school operated by a local school district, regional educational service center, or institution of higher education. The purposes of Connecticut's interdistrict magnet schools are "to reduce, eliminate or prevent racial, ethnic or economic isolation while offering a high-quality curriculum that supports educational improvement."[2] The operators of each magnet school establish with individual school districts agreements that determine whether the district will participate in the magnet school and in some cases how many seats in the school will be reserved for district students. All students in the participating school districts are eligible to attend, and the magnet school operators must hold a lottery if there are more applicants than spaces.[3] The state allocates special funding to sending districts and the magnet schools, and it provides transportation funding for students who attend an interdistrict magnet school located outside the district in which they live.

Following the decision in *Sheff v. O'Neill*, the number of interdistrict magnet schools in the state increased significantly. As of October 2007, 53 interdistrict magnet schools served 18,928 students. In the 2008–9 school year, there were a total of 60 operating magnet schools. Six of the interdistrict magnet high schools are half-time programs, where students attend part of the school day at the magnet and part in their home school. Approximately two-thirds of the magnets are located in the Hartford and New Haven areas, and the magnets in these areas serve roughly 75 percent of all magnet school students in the state.

Our magnet school research focused mainly on middle schools and high schools. We were interested in the extent to which interdistrict magnet schools provide students in Connecticut's central cities access to less isolated environments and improve student achievement. Analyses of the schools' impact on racial isolation and academic achievement were conducted using Connecticut State Department of Education administrative datasets spanning several academic years. The analysis of magnet school environments and students' academic and intergroup attitudes were based on a survey conducted in spring 2008.

Effects on Reducing Racial, Ethnic, and Economic Isolation

Interdistrict magnet schools in Connecticut clearly provide some students of color the opportunity to join less isolated learning environments. Figure 7.1

compares the racial and economic composition of both traditional city and interdistrict magnet high schools (similar results were found at the elementary- and middle-school levels). Racial and ethnic isolation in Connecticut's central city districts is very high. The students of color from these districts who attend magnet schools are, on average, in substantially more integrated peer environments than their counterparts in central city district schools. The percent free-lunch eligible in these magnet schools is also much lower than in the central city district schools.

Although informative, the comparisons in Figure 7.1 do not tell us how magnet schools change the peer environments of individual magnet school students, who may have been attending schools less isolated than the typical school in their home district. For an alternative view of the impact of interdistrict magnet schools on the racial and economic isolation of individual students, we used information from state test score files to identify all eighth and tenth graders attending an interdistrict magnet school in the Hartford, New Haven, or Waterbury areas during the 2005–6 or 2006–7 school year. For 69.4 percent of the eighth graders and 70.0 percent of the tenth graders, we were able to identify the school they attended prior to enrolling in their current magnet.

Comparison of the peer environments in magnet schools to the peer environments in the schools magnet school students attended prior to enrolling in their current magnet confirms that interdistrict magnet schools reduce the racial and economic isolation for the city students who attend them. As shown in table 7.1, the current magnet schools attended by city students have a significantly higher percentage white, lower percentage free-lunch eligible, and higher average test scores than their previous school. These differences are, however, considerably more marked for middle school magnet students than for high school magnet students. For typical suburban magnet school students, their current magnet school has a higher percentage of minority and free-lunch eligible students, and also slightly higher average test scores than their previous school. This last comparison suggests that most suburban students who choose magnet schools would otherwise attend relatively low-performing suburban schools.

Although interdistrict magnet schools are more diverse than traditional city schools, they provide access to less isolated learning environments for only a small percentage of students of color in the state's central cities, limiting the overall effect of the program on racial, ethnic, and economic isolation. Only 12 percent of black students and 6 percent of Latino students in Hartford attend magnet schools with more than 20 percent white students. Similarly,

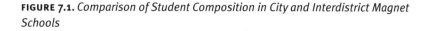

FIGURE 7.1. *Comparison of Student Composition in City and Interdistrict Magnet Schools*

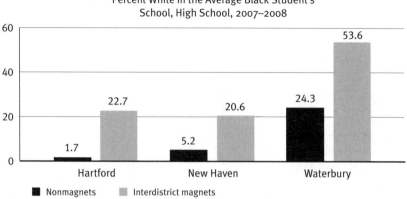

Percent White in the Average Black Student's
School, High School, 2007–2008

Hartford: Nonmagnets 1.7, Interdistrict magnets 22.7
New Haven: Nonmagnets 5.2, Interdistrict magnets 20.6
Waterbury: Nonmagnets 24.3, Interdistrict magnets 53.6

- Nonmagnets
- Interdistrict magnets

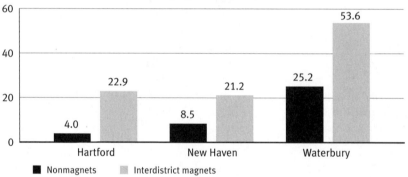

Percent White in the Average Hispanic Student's
School, High School, 2007–2008

Hartford: Nonmagnets 4.0, Interdistrict magnets 22.9
New Haven: Nonmagnets 8.5, Interdistrict magnets 21.2
Waterbury: Nonmagnets 25.2, Interdistrict magnets 53.6

- Nonmagnets
- Interdistrict magnets

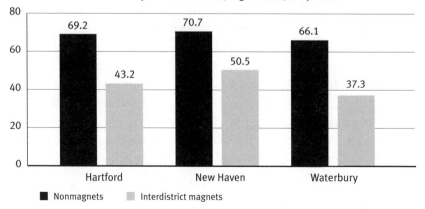

Percent Free-Lunch Eligible in the Average
Minority Student's School, High School, 2007–2008

Hartford: Nonmagnets 69.2, Interdistrict magnets 43.2
New Haven: Nonmagnets 70.7, Interdistrict magnets 50.5
Waterbury: Nonmagnets 66.1, Interdistrict magnets 37.3

- Nonmagnets
- Interdistrict magnets

TABLE 7.1. *Change in Peer Environments for Magnet-School Students*

Tenth Graders

	Urban Students (n = 970)		Suburban Students (n = 626)	
	Previous School	*Magnet School*	*Previous School*	*Magnet School*
% Black	47.2	50.6*	39.8	50.8*
% Latino	33.2	25.8*	18.1	21.4*
% White	16.4	21.7*	39.0	24.9*
% Free-lunch eligible	69.6	56.8*	45.5	51.2*
Mean grade 8 math score	225.2	231.6*	235.2	234.9
Mean grade 8 reading score	225.7	237.9*	239.6	241.9*

Eighth Graders

	Urban Students (n = 675)		Suburban Students (n = 581)	
	Previous School	*Magnet School*	*Previous School*	*Magnet School*
% Black	44.4	42.8	29.3	36.8*
% Latino	40.1	26.3*	17.2	21.4*
% White	15.1	29.7*	50.2	39.4*
% Free-lunch eligible	72.1	53.8*	33.8	38.8*
Mean grade 4 math score	218.3	240.1*	241.0	247.8*
Mean grade 4 reading score	211.5	236.5*	240.6	245.3*

Note: Samples consist of students in a magnet schools serving students in Hartford, Waterbury, or New Haven during 2005–6 or 2006–7, and that we can place in a school prior to enrollment in their current magnet school.
* Significantly different than the previous school at 0.01 level.

only 6 percent of minority students from Hartford attend magnet schools in which less than 40 percent of the students are eligible for free lunches.

Effects on Student Achievement

In order to better understand how magnets influenced academic achievement, we developed estimates of average achievement effects for a set of 12 interdistrict magnet high schools and another set of seven interdistrict middle schools.[4] These schools include all of the full-day interdistrict magnet high schools and all but two of the interdistrict magnet middle schools that serve students from Hartford, New Haven, or Waterbury.[5] We estimate the effects of the interdistrict magnet high schools on tenth-grade reading and math scores on the Connecticut Academic Performance Test (CAPT), and the effects of the interdistrict magnet middle schools on eighth-grade math and reading achievement on the Connecticut Mastery Test.

To construct our student sample for the analysis of the 12 interdistrict magnet high schools, we matched 2005–6 and 2006–7 tenth-grade CAPT records for all of the students attending either one of these interdistrict magnets or a high school in a district that sends at least ten students to one of these interdistrict magnets to student records from earlier eighth- and sixth-grade test score files. Our sample for the middle school analysis was constructed in an analogous manner. A sample of 1,731 magnet high school students and 11,091 students from feeder districts were extracted from the tenth-grade test score files; of these, 74.6 percent were matched to eighth-grade test score records and 60.4 percent to both eighth- and sixth-grade test score records. Of the sample of 1,188 magnet school students and 11,231 students from feeder districts from the eighth-grade test score files, 80.1 percent matched to sixth-grade test score records and 63.6 percent to both fourth- and sixth-grade test score records.[6]

To estimate the effects of attending a magnet school on academic achievement we use regression analysis, which allows us to estimate differences in achievement between magnet school students and students in regular public schools, controlling for student background characteristics and earlier measures of achievement.[7] These estimates tell us whether the test scores of magnet school students are higher or lower than those of other students who have similar background characteristics and similar test scores at two earlier points in time. If we assume that, in the absence of magnet schools, magnet school students would have had the same achievement growth as non–magnet school students who have a similar background and similar prior achievement, then these estimates can be interpreted as the effect of magnet schools on student achievement.[8]

The results of our analysis indicate that both interdistrict magnet high schools and middle schools have statistically significant positive effects on the reading and math achievement of students who reside in Connecticut's cities and attend magnet schools for two or three years. For city high school students, the estimated effects of two years of magnet school exposure are a 0.153 standard deviation gain in reading, and a 0.135 standard deviation gain in math. For three years exposure to a magnet school during the middle school grades, we see a gain of 0.152 standard deviations in reading and 0.126

standard deviations in math.[9] The estimated effects suggest the effect of both middle school and high school magnets is roughly 13 percent of the overall achievement gap between whites and minorities in math and roughly 17 percent of the gap in reading.[10]

Interdistrict magnet high schools also have positive effects on the achievement of students who reside in the suburbs; however, these positive effect estimates are smaller than the estimates for city students and are not statistically distinguishable from zero. These estimates suggest that suburban students who attend interdistrict magnet high schools improve their achievement at least as much as they would in their home district school. Interdistrict magnet middle schools show positive but statistically insignificant effects on the math achievement of their suburban students and large, statistically significant, positive effects on the reading achievement of these students, suggesting that middle school suburban students benefit from attending magnet schools.

Differences in School Climate, Attitudes, and Behaviors
Because they attract a diverse set of students, magnet schools are intended to enhance multicultural understanding, broaden worldviews, and help students develop the skills and orientations to successfully engage in a global society. In addition, magnets are designed to improve student engagement and academic aspirations by organizing around a common curricular theme. We administered a student questionnaire to examine these expectations and better understand the experiences of students in magnet high schools.

We targeted magnet high schools and comparison high schools in the Hartford and New Haven regions. Students in 13 interdistrict magnet high schools in these areas completed the survey.[11] In addition, three nonmagnet high schools served as comparison schools; two were predominantly minority high schools located in a central city and the third was a predominantly nonminority high school in an affluent suburb. For each high school, we surveyed ninth and twelfth graders.[12] In the magnet schools, which are considerably smaller than nearby nonmagnet high schools, we attempted to survey all students in the targeted grades. In the nonmagnet schools, which are larger, we worked with principals to obtain a reasonably representative sample of classrooms. In total, we administered the survey to 1,282 magnet school students and 504 non–magnet school students. The 100-item survey measured several constructs, including those related to academic achievement, college expectations, teacher-student relationships, classroom climate, sense of safety and belonging, attendance, intergroup relations, racial tension, and multicultural interests.[13]

Our sample allowed us to compare the experiences and perceptions of ninth- and twelfth-grade magnet school students with their counterparts in a comparison group of nonmagnet high schools. The fact that both magnet and non–magnet school students selected different types of schools suggests they may be systematically different than one another. It is possible that magnet school students could have developed different attitudes toward achievement and other groups than non–magnet school students even in the absence of any magnet school effect. Thus, differences in attitudes between magnet and non–magnet school students cannot be interpreted as resulting from attending a magnet school. Nonetheless, these comparisons provide a good indication of how the environment that students encounter in magnet schools differs from the environment in comparison schools.

Our initial analyses involved comparisons of school climate among magnet high schools, city high schools, and suburban high schools in our sample. Table 7.2 presents comparisons among twelfth graders only and indicates statistically significant differences between magnet schools and both city schools and suburban schools. Magnet schools appear to provide an academic climate similar to that found in a wealthy, suburban school, and they appear to be more supportive of achievement than city schools. Specifically, compared to their counterparts in city schools, central city students who attend a magnet school reported more positive influences of adults in their school on their college expectations, stronger peer norms supporting achievement, fewer social sanctions of academic achievement and efforts, and fewer classroom disruptions. These differences between magnet students and city students tend to be larger among twelfth graders than ninth graders, suggesting that the differences might emerge over the course of students' high school careers. Magnet school students also report better intergroup relations and less racial tension in their schools than either students in the traditional city or suburban schools in our sample.

Compared to students in the traditional suburban high school, twelfth graders in magnets reported a considerably lower sense of safety and belonging. Ninth-grade magnet students also reported less positive student-teacher relationships than ninth graders in either traditional city or traditional suburban high schools, but those differences were not found among twelfth graders. These differences suggest that the typical magnet school environment may not be more positive along every dimension compared to the environments in other schools.

We also examined a range of student attitudes and behaviors believed to be important for future success. Magnet students who reside in a central city

TABLE 7.2. *Differences between Magnet Schools and City or Suburban Schools, Grade 12*

Measure	*Difference in sᴅ Units between Magnet and City Samples*	*Difference in sᴅ Units between Magnet and Suburban Samples*
School Climate		
Academic press	.08	.11
Influence on college expectations	.40**	−.19
Peer academic norms	.71**	−.06
Social sanctions for achievement	−.60*	−.07
Classroom disruptions	−.58**	.10
Teacher-student relationships	−.19	.04
Safety and belonging	.23	−.74**
Intergroup relations	.44**	.31*
Racial tension	−.90**	−.36**
Attitudes and Behaviors		
Academic aspirations	.29	.29**
College expectations	1.00**	−.27**
Average number of absences (2 weeks)	−.67**	−.32**
Average number of classes skipped (2 weeks)	−1.18**	−.34**
Social closeness to minorities (among whites)*	Could not be calculated	.95**
Social closeness to whites (among minorities)	.34**	−.36**
Future multicultural interests	.23	.43**
	% Difference	*% Difference*
% White students with multiple minority friends	Could not be calculated	45.50**
% Minority students with multiple white friends	25.30**	−23.60**
% Reporting that school has helped understanding of other groups	1.10	32.40**

Note: Differences in sᴅ units were calculated by the formulas (magnet − city)/sᴅ$_{magnet}$ and (magnet − suburban)/sᴅ$_{magnet}$. Positive figures indicate the magnet scored higher than the comparison group. "Could not be calculated" indicates statistical comparisons were not possible because so few white student attended city schools in our sample.

* Significantly different than value among magnet-school students at 0.10 level.

** Significantly different than value among magnet-school students at 0.05 level.

appear to have higher academic aspirations and college expectations than students in traditional city schools.[14] Further, magnet school students generally have higher academic aspirations but lower college expectations than students in suburban schools. Magnet school students are also much less likely to miss school and skip classes than students in both the traditional city schools and traditional suburban schools in our sample. In terms of racial attitudes, white magnet school students reported higher levels of "social closeness" to students of color than did suburban students. Likewise, magnet students of color reported greater closeness to white students than city students reported; suburban students of color, however, indicated greater closeness to whites than magnet students reported. Finally, magnet students indicated greater "future multicultural interests" than suburban ninth and twelfth graders and twelfth-grade city students.

Twelfth-grade magnet school students were significantly more likely than students in the suburban school to report that their school experience helped them understand people from other groups. Magnet students also reported having larger percentages of friends from other races or ethnicities than suburban students. In particular, among twelfth graders, the percentage of white magnet school students who reported having multiple minority friends was significantly higher compared to suburban white students.

To examine whether the difference in attitudes between magnet school and non–magnet school students from the city might be due to differences in their high school experiences, we estimated regression models that control for observed differences in family background characteristics between magnet school students and non–magnet school students.[15] These background characteristics include the student's race, primary home language, access to resources in the home including a space to do schoolwork, a regular newspaper subscription, a home computer, and the frequency with which students discuss school activities and college with their parents. The results of these regressions estimate the differences in attitudes and behaviors between magnet and nonmagnet students among students with similar background characteristics and reveal similar patterns to those detailed in table 7.2.[16] While we cannot conclude that magnets are improving attitudes, the differences suggest that the magnet school environment is substantially different than what students might otherwise encounter.

Open Choice Program

Four decades ago, the Connecticut state legislature established an urban-to-suburban district student transfer program in Hartford called Project Concern. Under Project Concern, suburban and mostly white school districts voluntarily accepted small numbers of students of color from Hartford. Between 1966 and 1996, the program served 24,714 students.[17] Following *Sheff*, the Open Choice program replaced Project Concern.

The structure of Open Choice is similar to the former Project Concern.[18] Participation by school districts—providing "seats"—is encouraged but completely voluntary. As in previous years, virtually all the transfers go in the direction of urban-to-suburban schools. The program expanded beyond Hartford to other cities and now includes New Haven and Bridgeport. The state subsidizes transportation of Open Choice students at $3,200 per pupil and gives the receiving district $2,500 per Open Choice student.

The Open Choice program allows urban residents to indicate their preference for attending kindergarten through twelfth grade in participating suburban districts. Suburban districts open a certain number of Open Choice seats, which are then filled using a lottery. Total participation in Hartford, New Haven, and Bridgeport has steadily grown from 1,498 urban-to-suburban transfers in 2002 to 1,724 transfers in 2007. The 2008 *Sheff* settlement agreement calls for increased participation by suburban districts, as growth has fallen short of desired targets.

In recent years, Project Choice Early Beginnings (PCEB) has been developed to support kindergarteners from the city of Hartford that participate in the Open Choice program. In the first three years of its existence, PCEB served 224 Open Choice students in 16 suburban districts, 29 schools, and 80 kindergarten classrooms. The kindergarten experience takes place in different formats and locations. Whatever their kindergarten experience, PCEB students are able to remain in the suburban district for their entire school career, provided they maintain residency in the city of Hartford. PCEB supports both students and teachers. Students participate in orientation activities at the beginning of the year as well as ongoing literacy support and monitoring. Teachers receive specialized training to help them develop the talents of all the students in their classrooms. Literacy facilitators are assigned to schools that enroll four or more PCEB students to help teachers build and improve receptive vocabulary skills—as studies suggest vocabulary is a predictor of future school success. These facilitators also monitor the progress of students in the program and work with PCEB parents or guardians to encourage language and literacy development as well as to resolve any issues or concerns that arise with their children.

Effects on Reducing Racial, Ethnic, and Economic Isolation

Using program application data for the Hartford area Open Choice program and data from student test score files, we examined the effects of the Open Choice program on racial, ethnic, and economic isolation and on student achievement. The application data include 3,669 applications to Open Choice from 2002 through 2006. Based on the grade level of the applicant at the time of application, we would expect 1,864 of these students to be in a tested grade during the spring of 2006 or the spring of 2007. Of these, 1,344 were successfully matched to at least one test score record—a matching rate of 72 percent. Students who could not be matched either enrolled in private schools, left the Hartford area, or had a name or date of birth (or both) in the application files that differed from that used in the test score files. These data indicate that nearly all participants in Open Choice are black or Latino; black students, however, are both more likely to apply to Open Choice and to accept an offer to participate than are Latino students. In addition, males and females are equally likely to apply to Open Choice, but females are more likely to accept an offer to participate.

Reduced isolation of Hartford students of color is the primary aim of all *Sheff* remedies, including the Open Choice program. A secondary goal is to increase the exposure of white students to students of diverse races, cultures, and economic backgrounds. We found that Open Choice contributes to both of these goals. Our data allowed us to determine the school an Open Choice student is placed in for 570 of the 984 applicants who were placed. The data also provided home addresses for 563 of these 570 students, which allowed us to identify the Hartford public school that a student would have attended if he or she had not opted for Open Choice or any other school choice option.

The Hartford schools that Open Choice students would be assigned to are, on average, almost entirely black or Latino (96.7 percent combined) and are considerably poor (76.1 percent of students are eligible for free lunches). In stark contrast, in the typical school of an Open Choice student, roughly 9 of 10 students are white or Asian (88.4 percent combined), and only 12.5 percent of the students are eligible for free lunches.

Open Choice also serves to increase diversity in participating suburban schools. Black, Latino, and free-lunch- eligible students are substantially over-represented in the home schools of Open Choice students and substantially underrepresented in the schools where Open Choice students are placed. Nearly all Open Choice students are black or Latino, and the majority are eligible for free lunches. Thus, not only does Open Choice reduce the isolation of the low-income and minority students who participate, it also increases the exposure of white and nonpoor students in relatively isolated suburban schools to students from different racial, ethnic, and economic backgrounds.

Our ability to estimate the impact of Open Choice on the student composition of Hartford public schools is limited, but it suggests that, on average, Open Choice has very little effect on the racial, ethnic, and gender composition of Hartford public elementary schools. Some schools, however, do show somewhat larger estimated effects. The fact that Open Choice draws sizeable proportions of students from the attendance zones of particular schools suggests that the program could have significant effects on the student composition of at least some Hartford schools.

Effects on Student Achievement

When the number of applications to Open Choice exceeds the number of grade-level seats available, lotteries are held. Admission lotteries serve to randomly assign students to a treatment group that has a chance to participate in Open Choice and a control group of applicants who are denied admission to Open Choice, which helps to ensure that treatment and control group members have no systematic differences that might bias estimates of program impacts. After removing lotteries in which there were either too few students denied admission or too few placements made, we were able to assess the effects of Open Choice on the academic achievement of students who apply to begin Open Choice between grades three and seven.[19]

Our estimates indicate that despite having slightly lower test scores at the beginning of sixth grade, students who are admitted to Open Choice in sixth or seventh grade have higher test scores in eighth grade than those students who applied to Open Choice but were denied admission because of the lottery number they received (table 7.3).[20] Entering Open Choice in sixth or seventh grade has a large, statistically significant positive effect on eighth-grade reading achievement (0.33 standard deviations) and a positive but statistically insignificant effect on eighth-grade math achievement. Entering Open Choice in grades three, four, or five has no discernible impact on sixth-grade academic achievement. Although we think these findings are informative, one must be mindful that the effect estimates are fairly imprecise, and we cannot completely rule out potential biases due to our inability to observe the achievement of all lottery participants.

TABLE 7.3. *Comparison of Admission Lottery Winners and Losers*

Applicants for Grades 6 & 7

	Pretreatment Difference in Grade 6 Scores	*Posttreatment Difference in Grade 8 Scores*	*Estimated Impact Controlling for Pretreatment Differences*
Reading	−0.085	0.252	0.329*
	(0.194)	(0.252)	(0.138)
Math	−0.047	0.06	0.094
	(0.188)	(0.206)	(0.107)

Applicants for Grades 3, 4, & 5

	Pretreatment Difference in Grade 4 Scores	*Posttreatment Difference in Grade 6 Scores*	*Estimated Impact Controlling for Pretreatment Differences*
Reading	0.115	0.052	−0.098
	(0.219)	(0.187)	(0.098)
Math	0.070	−0.031	−0.043
	(0.163)	(0.142)	(0.065)

Note: Figures are regression coefficients with standard error robust to clustering within school in parentheses. All regressions include lottery fixed effects.
* Statistically different from 0 at 0.10 level.

Effects of the PCEB Program

Using data from 2004–7, we examined the achievement of PCEB students on two common measures of early school learning: the Peabody Picture Vocabulary Test (PPVT) and the Dynamic Indicators of Basic Early Literacy Skills. Because the PCEB program was not oversubscribed in the years we examine, admission lotteries were not held. Thus, our analyses relied on statistical comparisons and correlational techniques.[21] We compared PCEB students' performance with similar Hartford students and with suburban peers in PCEB students' classrooms. We found that PCEB and Hartford students begin and end the kindergarten year in different places. PCEB students have significantly higher scores than their Hartford counterparts when they enter kindergarten. Once students' initial achievement levels are controlled for, we find little difference in achievement, on average, between kindergarteners in the PCEB

TABLE 7.4. *Estimated Differences between PCEB and Hartford Public School Students, Controlling for Gender and Fall Test Score*

	PPVT	Initial Sound	Letter Naming
All students			
N	284	290	282
Estimated difference	0.746	1.722	−0.582
Standard error	(1.223)	(3.847)	(2.958)
Female students			
N	127	129	126
Estimated difference	3.245*	2.708	−0.899
Standard error	(1.548)	(4.379)	(2.085)
Male students			
N	157	161	156
Estimated difference	−1.066	0.816	−0.260
Standard error	(1.681)	(3.503)	(3.831)

Note: Estimates are from regressions of spring (or winter) test score on an indicator of PCEB participation controlling for fall test score and gender. Standard errors are adjusted for clustering within schools.
* Significant at 0.05 level.

program and in a sample of Hartford Public Schools. This is true regardless of whether PCEB students participate in full-day kindergarten or part-day kindergarten. PCEB girls, however, develop their vocabularies more than girls in the Hartford Public School sample who started kindergarten with similar PPVT scores (table 7.4). Similar gains, however, are not realized among the PCEB boys.

When comparing PCEB students' achievement to that of their suburban classmates, we find that PCEB students start and end the kindergarten year with lower average achievement scores. After controlling for initial scores, however, we find little difference between the achievement of PCEB students and their suburban classmates. Finally, there is little evidence that differences in achievement gains between PCEB students and their suburban classmates vary significantly by the length of the program (full-day versus half-day kindergarten), the program location (center or school-based), or the year a student participated in the program.

The findings suggest that PCEB students and their suburban classmates who start with the same test scores make similar achievement gains over the kindergarten year. Further, the program might be helping to reduce achievement gaps, in at least one domain, for girls. Strong conclusions should not be drawn from results that occur strictly during kindergarten and focus on literacy measures. Evaluation results over a longer time period and a wider array of student outcomes are needed.

This essay describes two voluntary, controlled school choice programs Connecticut has used to reduce the racial and economic isolation of central city students. These programs came into being as a result of concerned activists and received significant financial and legislative support as a result of the *Sheff v. O'Neill* decision. Although these court-instigated programs are not subject to the PICS decision, their student assignment provisions appear to be consistent with the majority ruling in PICS; neither program uses explicit race-based criteria in the assignment of students. Instead, these programs encourage voluntary participation across urban and suburban districts that are highly stratified by race, ethnicity, and income.

Our research indicates that interdistrict magnet schools provide reduced-isolation settings, offering environments conducive to learning and cross-cultural understanding, and improving student achievement. Open Choice also provides central city students access to less racially and economically isolated schools. Further, for suburban students, who are relatively racially and economically isolated, the program increases exposure to students of color. Although the evidence that participation in Open Choice and PCEB helps to improve student achievement is less definitive than it is in our analyses of interdistrict magnet schools, there is evidence of positive impacts for some groups of students.

These results are encouraging and suggest that carefully designed interdistrict choice programs can help to further the goals of integration. However, a few caveats on these positive findings are warranted. Although interdistrict magnets and Open Choice do create benefits for students who participate in these programs, it is not clear how they benefit, or if they benefit at all, the majority of central city students in Connecticut who remain in very racially and economically isolated settings. Also, the costs of these programs need to be considered as well as their benefits. These costs include pecuniary costs such as those related to transportation, as well as the potential impact these programs have on the peer environments of other public schools in the central city. Despite these important caveats, our investigations of interdistrict magnet schools and Open Choice suggest that they provide promising models for promoting integration and improving student achievement.

NOTES

We wish to acknowledge the Connecticut State Department of Education for providing the funding to support much of the research reported on here. We also wish to thank the Capitol Region Education Council for providing data and assistance. Finally, we thank the Magnet Schools of America for helping with the dissemination of this research.

1. A reduced-isolation setting is defined by the Desegregation Standard as stipulated in the 2008 agreement. The Desegregation Standard is established by the aggregate percent minority in the *Sheff* region plus 30 percentage points or 75 percent minority, whichever is less.

2. Connecticut State Department of Education, *Public School Choice in Connecticut: A Guide for Students and Their Families* (Hartford: Connecticut State Department of Education, 2006).

3. In cases where the agreements between magnet school operators and participating districts establish the number of seats allocated for students from the district, district-specific lotteries are held.

4. High schools here are schools that serve grades nine through twelve, and middle schools are schools that begin in grade six or seven. Four of the six "middle schools" end in grade eight, but three serve high school grades as well.

5. Two interdistrict magnet middle schools that serve students from New Haven start in grade five and are not included in this analysis.

6. For both the middle school and high school samples, students whom we were able to successfully match to prior year test scores are less likely to be black, Latino, free-lunch eligible, and male and are on average three to four months younger and have higher average test scores than students for whom we did not find matches. Our estimation sample, on average, is thus somewhat more educationally advantaged than the larger sample. Magnet and non–magnet school students, however, were equally likely to find a match to prior year test scores, and magnet school status was not significantly related to whether or not a student found a match in regressions that control for observable student characteristics. Because selection into our estimation sample does not depend on magnet school status, the nonrandom nature of our sample is unlikely to bias estimates of magnet school effects.

7. We also used propensity score procedures as an alternative method of controlling for student background and earlier measures of achievement. In some circumstances, regression analysis and propensity score methods can provide quite different estimates of program effects (E. A. Stuart, "Estimating Causal Effects Using School-Level Data Sets," *Educational Researcher* 36, no. 4 [2007]: 187–98), but in this case, the propensity score methods provide effect estimates very similar to those derived from regression analysis.

8. To test whether or not our estimates suffered from substantial biases, we obtained information on admission lotteries for two schools. Data on lottery admissions allow us to measure program effects by comparing the average outcomes of lottery winners who enroll in a given school to the average outcomes of students who apply but are denied admission because they lost the lottery. Because lottery winners and losers are determined through a random process, we expect that the two groups will not differ significantly from

each other on either observed or unobserved characteristics. Comparisons of average outcomes across the two groups will, then, be free of systematic bias. We find that for these two schools the regression based estimates that control for pre–magnet school test scores provide effect estimates very close to those obtained using the lottery data. This important robustness check provides confidence that our estimates of magnet school impacts do not have substantial bias. For details on the lottery analysis and the comparison of results from the lottery and the regression-based analysis, see R. Bifulco, C. D. Cobb, and C. A. Bell, "Can Interdistrict Choice Boost Student Achievement?," *Educational Evaluation and Policy Analysis* 31, no. 4 (2009): 323–45.

9. We are not able to directly observe how long an individual student has attended the magnet high school in which we observe him or her. However, all of the magnets in the high school sample begin with ninth grade, the CAPT exams are administered in the spring of tenth grade, and turnover rates in magnet high schools are low. Thus, the great majority of magnet school students in our high school sample have attended a magnet school for nearly two years at the time achievement is observed. For middle schoolers we are able to observe whether or not they were enrolled in their current schools in the fall of sixth grade; our estimates are based on a sample limited to students who have been in their current schools for nearly three years at the time that eighth-grade achievement is observed.

10. Gaps between the test scores of minority and white students in Connecticut are 0.91 standard deviations in reading in grades eight and ten, 0.95 standard deviations in grade-eight math, and 1.04 standard deviations in grade ten math.

11. The sample includes students who attend two half-day magnet schools and students in two schools that serve grades six through twelve as well as nine of the twelve magnet high schools included in the achievement analysis above.

12. In cases where a school did not serve students in ninth or twelfth grade, students in the next nearest grade were surveyed.

13. For more details on the survey and survey results, including sampling procedures, administration, response rates, and measures, see C. D. Cobb, R. Bifulco, and C. A. Bell, "Magnet School Effects on Student Achievement and Racial Isolation: The Case of Connecticut," paper presented at the annual meeting of the American Educational Research Association, New York, 24–28 March 2008.

14. *Academic aspirations* are students' views about the importance of grades and learning. *College expectations* reflect students' intentions to apply to and enroll in college.

15. Specifically, we regressed each student attitude and behavior measure on an indicator of whether or not a student attends a magnet school, an interaction of that variable and an indicator of what grade the student is in, and an extensive set of student background characteristics that we collected as part of the survey.

16. Specifically, regarding academic attitudes, twelfth-grade magnet students have significantly higher expectations for college, fewer absences, and fewer skipped classes than twelfth-grade nonmagnet students with similar family background characteristics. Ninth-grade magnet school students also show higher college expectations and lower propensity to skip class than ninth-grade nonmagnet students, but the estimated differences be-

tween ninth graders are smaller than those among twelfth graders. With regard to racial and intergroup attitudes, twelfth-grade magnet school students report greater closeness to minorities and to whites and are more likely to report having multiple white friends than non-magnet school students with similar family background characteristics. No such differences are found across ninth graders.

17. E. Frankenberg, *Project Choice Campaign: Improving and Expanding Hartford's Project Choice Program* (Washington, DC: Poverty and Race Research Action Council, 2007).

18. Open Choice is sometimes referred to as Project Choice. Project Choice is the Hartford region's implementation of Open Choice.

19. Specifically, we were able to use students who applied for admission to Open Choice in sixth or seventh grade to estimate the impacts of entering Open Choice near the transition to middle school on eighth-grade test scores, and students who applied for admission in third, fourth, or fifth grade to estimate the impacts of entering Open Choice in the later elementary school grades on sixth-grade achievement. Among the 337 students who participated in the sixth- and seventh-grade lotteries, 153 students had lottery numbers low enough to be offered admission and 184 were not offered the chance to participate in Open Choice. We were able to obtain eighth-grade test scores for 110 of the students offered admission and 88 of the students who were not offered admission. The third-, fourth-, and fifth-grade admission lotteries that we were able to use included 301 students, of whom 120 had lottery numbers low enough to be offered admission and 181 were not offered the chance to participate in Open Choice. We were able to observe sixth-grade test scores for 89 of the lottery winners and only 103 of the lottery losers. The fact that we are unable to observe achievement for a high percentage of the lottery participants and the fact that whether or not we can observe a student's test scores is statistically related to whether or not the student was offered admission to Open Choice are potential sources of bias in our estimates of program effects. Nonetheless, we believe comparisons of the lottery participants that we can observe are suggestive.

20. The figures in table 7.3 are based on students who participated in Open Choice lotteries and for whom we could observe a test score both prior to and following their participation in the lottery.

21. For a complete description of the PCEB study design and results, see Bifulco, Cobb, and Bell, "Can Interdistrict Choice Boost Student Achievement?"

JENNIFER JELLISON HOLME, SARAH L. DIEM, &
KATHERINE CUMINGS MANSFIELD

Regional Coalitions and Educational Policy
Lessons from the Nebraska Learning
Community Agreement

In May 2007, Nebraska's governor signed a law requiring 11 public school districts in the Omaha metropolitan area to form a cooperative "Learning Community." The agreement is distinctive in that it secured the commitment of all 11 school districts across two counties in the Omaha metro area to an interdistrict choice-based socioeconomic desegregation plan without a court order. The plan is also unusual in that it is funded not through a legislative allotment (which can be politically vulnerable) but through a tax-base sharing plan. The Learning Community is governed by a regional governing council charged with implementing the agreement and overseeing the construction of new interdistrict schools of choice and early childhood centers in high-poverty communities. The governance council was established in January 2009, and the choice plan and early childhood centers will be established beginning in the 2010–11 school year.

While cross-jurisdictional agreements to reduce inequality are not novel, to date few agreements have been designed explicitly to address educational inequality. Indeed, while regional equity scholars have examined the ways cross-jurisdictional collaboration on transportation, housing, and employment helps to reduce isolation for low-income families and families of color, few have paid serious attention to the potential of regional *educational* policy to promote opportunity for children. Regional equity experts acknowledge that schools and school districts are a key driver of regional stratification; educational collaboratives offer an important and yet underexamined policy tool to counter these processes.

This essay begins by discussing why regional agreements like the one enacted in Omaha are increasingly important as a mechanism to address stratification and segregation between districts in metropolitan areas. It then describes the features of the agreement and examines the process by which the agreement in Omaha unfolded. The essay concludes with an analysis of the current state of the agreement, an illustration of the fragility of such arrangements, and a discussion of policy recommendations.

Toward Regional Educational Policy
Characteristics of the Omaha Plan Problem Statement

Although U.S. schools are more racially diverse than ever before, they are also growing increasingly segregated with African American and Latino students attending more segregated schools than at any time in the past 20 years. Poverty concentration has also worsened, as increasing numbers of students of color attend schools that have a majority of low-income students.[1]

While current levels of school segregation are reminiscent of the era before *Brown v. Board of Education*, the nature of segregation today is fundamentally different and poses a unique set of challenges for district administrators and state policy makers. Decades ago students from different racial, ethnic, and economic backgrounds resided within the boundaries of the same school districts but were segregated into separate buildings; today, with the growth of metropolitan areas and the expansion of suburban development, students from different racial, ethnic, and economic backgrounds are likely to reside in separate school districts entirely, resulting in high levels of "between-district" segregation.[2]

This between-district segregation is more severe in metropolitan areas with large numbers of school districts, where district boundaries exacerbate racial isolation and resource inequality by aggravating fiscal competition and stratification along racial and ethnic lines.[3] In these metropolitan areas, urban and inner-ring suburban school districts most affected by racial segregation, poverty concentration, and dwindling resources have little power to address these issues alone. In such contexts, cooperative agreements between school districts are one of the few remaining policy tools available to reduce racial and economic isolation. As john powell observes, "The critical problems associated with the hollowing out of the urban core cannot be addressed without a regional approach."[4]

Regional policies in education and in other public sectors remain few in number because they are so difficult to create. Many regional policies in the past were forged at the behest of urban politicians, who used their political power in state legislatures to force suburban cooperation.[5] As a result, they have tended historically to run up against intense resistance from suburbs, which resent the loss of resources and fear the loss of political power and identity.[6] Urban-core neighborhoods have also had reason to resist these policies, due to a fear of losing or diluting what little political power they possess.[7]

The Omaha agreement represents a newer type of regional collaboration, what powell refers to as "federated regionalism," which balances "the need for an integrated regional approach with the need to preserve local control on some issues."[8] Thus school districts retain control over their core functions (curriculum, hiring, budgeting, student enrollment) while at the same time committing on some level to the pursuit of regional goals. The legislation is also the result of what Margaret Weir, Harold Wolman, and Todd Swanstrom refer to as an interest-based coalition politics, in which many (though not all) of the school districts involved receive some sort of benefit from the arrangement.[9]

The Learning Community (LC) contains four central elements. First, the LC is mandated to create an 11-district socioeconomically based desegregation plan with the goal of fostering diversity across all buildings in the 11-district area. The law states that "the goal of the diversity plan shall be to annually increase the socioeconomic diversity of enrollment at each grade level in each school building within the Learning Community until such enrollment reflects the average socioeconomic diversity of the entire enrollment of the Learning Community."[10] The law also provides for interdistrict cooperative magnet schools (called "focus schools") and magnet school matriculation "pathways" that foster diverse learning opportunities across the 11 districts.

Second, the LC legislation establishes a tax-base sharing plan by authorizing a common levy. The levy is assessed across the property wealth of all 11 districts combined, then redistributed back to individual districts based on need per the state funding formula. Local school districts are allowed to levy slightly above the common levy to maintain some of their tax base advantages. This common levy will be fully implemented by 2012–13.

Third, the LC is governed by the Learning Community Coordinating Council (LCCC), a 21-member elected governing board. Twelve members are elected via a general election, with six electoral subdistricts electing two members each. Six additional members are voted in via a caucus of school board members, to represent local school boards. An additional three nonvoting members are appointed by the school boards of districts that fail to win a seat through either election or the caucus process. The 11 school superintendents serve in an advisory role to the Coordinating Council.

Fourth, the LC is required to establish elementary learning centers, intended to provide social and academic support services to children and parents outside of school hours (i.e., literacy and English classes for families, and health services). The LC is required to establish "at least one" elementary learning center for every 25 high-poverty elementary schools—defined as elementary schools "in which at least 35 percent of the students attending the school who reside in the attendance area of such school qualify for free or reduced price lunch."[11]

The Learning Community, therefore, can be distinguished from other interdistrict transfer and interdistrict desegregation plans in two central ways: first is its inclusion of tax-base sharing, which is used to redistribute revenue more equitably, to fund student transfers, and to fund elementary learning centers. Second is its governance structure and authority: the regional governing council, which is elected, is granted significant taxation, construction, and programmatic powers.

Forging Regional Solutions
Moving from Conflict to Collaboration

The process that led to the creation of the Learning Community included many key features that prior research has shown to be critical to the creation of regional policies.[12] This case study, which explores the process by which the LC was created, identifies a number of these parallels, as well as additional factors that may be relevant in the creation of regional educational policies in other contexts.

This case study draws from interviews with 14 key informants who were involved in the creation of the LC, including current and former legislators, school district superintendents and school board members, community activists, and representatives from the community's major philanthropic organizations. The case study is augmented by news reports from the city's major newspaper, the *Omaha World-Herald*, which provided extensive news coverage of the process. The analysis also utilizes other documents, including legislative documents, demographic reports, and research reports.

As this discussion will illustrate, the process by which the LC agreement was forged began with older urban coalition-building strategies that involved a mixture of legal threats and legislative appeals in an attempt to force suburban acquiescence. Over time, however, the policy debate in the Omaha metro area and in the Nebraska state legislature evolved from a battle between city and suburbs into a broader conversation about metropolitan regional equity. As we will illustrate below, the ultimate agreement resulted from a combination of behind-the-scenes brokering as well as involvement of key community actors. While some of the factors we identified as critical to the creation of the Learning Community are consistent with prior literature on the development of regional policies, several factors are unique to regional *educational* policy making. We discuss each in detail below.

Redefining the Issue as a Metropolitan Problem

As Margaret Weir found in her case studies of regional governance, a key factor in the creation of metropolitan regional solutions is the framing of the "problem" as a metropolitan issue. In the case of the Learning Community, this "problem framing" began with a legal maneuver by the Omaha Public Schools (OPS) aimed at addressing its growing poverty and declining resources. Increasingly frustrated with the legislature's lack of response to its appeals for financial assistance, the Omaha School Board in June 2006 passed a resolution to follow a long-forgotten 19th-century law that gave the district the right to expand the Omaha school district boundaries to "capture" territory within the city limits of Omaha. At the time, the Omaha city boundaries were significantly larger than the OPS boundaries, encompassing 21 school buildings in the territory of suburban school districts. This resolution by the Omaha School Board meant that the district would annex both territory with higher tax valuation and schools with larger proportions of middle-class students. The maneuver set off a political uproar in the Omaha metropolitan area.

Yet, while it generated tremendous political fallout, as a school board member in Omaha reflected, the decision by the OPS school board reframed the conversation from one of an "urban problem" into one that centered on racial and economic isolation, and the role of geopolitical boundaries and divisions between school districts: "We defined the problem. We said, 'There's racial isolation, socioeconomic isolation, we don't have the resources to do what we need to do.' . . . We came up with the policy, where it is we wanted to go, and then we executed it, and we did it without worrying about . . . what our future would be, whether we would be school board members, whether we would . . . continue on as the superintendent. We said, 'We're doing it because this is what is best, best for kids, but best for the community, and ultimately it's gonna be best for the community.'"

A key ally in framing the problem in Omaha was the press, specifically the publisher of the city's major newspaper, the *Omaha World-Herald*. Eager to facilitate a solution to the stalemate between city and suburbs, the publisher made a decision to steer clear from publishing stories on this conflict and instead ran a series of articles about the issues of racial and socioeconomic isolation at the heart of the debate. The superintendent of the Omaha school district noted of the coverage, "Out of all of that, came understanding, came awareness, I think came embarrassment. This is a can-do state, we're in a good-life state, it is for some, not for all, and I believe out of that came exactly what educators believed, that through education, through awareness, through understanding, you can effect change. I think the newspaper, specifically the *Omaha World-Herald*, did a tremendous job, in an unbiased, objective manner, looking at the issues of race, looking at the issues of poverty, looking and forecasting."

Prior case studies of efforts to diversify schools in other cities have found that the news media worked against efforts to diversify schools through unfavorable reporting or simply failing to report on the positive outcomes of school desegregation.[13] These efforts by the major publisher in Omaha to encourage a solution that focused on issues of racial isolation and poverty were, therefore, relatively unusual.

Initiative from Groups outside the Formal Political System

Research on metropolitan agreements has shown that the support of community groups outside the formal political system is crucial to devising any long-term metropolitan regional solution. In Omaha, a number of community organizations, civil rights organizations, key religious leaders, and business leaders came together to voice support for a solution that was equitable to all districts across the regions. The OPS superintendent noted the importance of this common cause:

> There isn't any doubt in my mind that had it not been for the philanthropy component, had it not been for editors in the newspaper, had it not been for advocacy leaders of this community, had it not been for long-standing institutions that advocated for kids, specifically the NAACP, Chicano Awareness Center, all coming together and saying, as a result of awareness, through understanding, lessons that had been communicated for years, I don't believe for one moment we would be at this point. We asked that the right thing be done for a decade, and what we found is the hole was being dug deeper and deeper and deeper. So, do I celebrate the fact that a pending miracle exists, yeah, I do, I think that this holds tremendous promise.

This support became critical when the legislation was passed and required the signature of the governor. The OPS superintendent recalled, "We literally got on a bus one night, these are guys that I would never have a . . . it was a CEO—a very wealthy individual—Warren Buffet, and [a major philanthropist], all, bless their hearts, got on a bus on a winter night, we drove down to the governor's mansion to a dinner, with [a suburban superintendent] and myself, simply saying, we have a solution, we're working this thing out, if you can endorse it."

In part as a result of these appeals, the governor, who was elected in part due to antiurban sentiment that arose after the ops tried to recapture land, ultimately signed the legislation.

Educational Leadership and Collaboration

What is unique to this particular type of agreement between school districts was the leadership of the metro area school superintendents. While a number of the superintendents in the Omaha metro area had, prior to the Learning Community negotiations, met as part of a metropolitan collaborative called the Metropolitan Omaha Educational Consortium, none of these discussions or arrangements dealt substantively with issues of finance equity or racial isolation.

It was only in the aftermath of the Omaha resolution to recapture territory that substantive talks began among the majority of superintendents across the two counties in the metropolitan area. Initially, the conversations involved a coalition of suburban superintendents formed to oppose ops. Ironically, it was out of this group that proposals for interdistrict desegregation initially arose in an effort to offer an incentive for ops to drop its recapture resolution and allow suburbs to preserve their boundaries.

It was only after a long stalemate that the ops superintendent and the suburban superintendents came together to begin to talk about solutions. According to the ops superintendent, "We sat down and simply said, 'We know what the right thing to do is, we all are paid employees of particular school districts, but let's set that aside and look at education policy, let's look at principles.' . . . And what I can tell you is that the principles [we discussed in that conversation] are ultimately contained in every piece of legislation was crafted, drafted, hammered out."

In creating regional metropolitan educational policy in this instance, superintendents' leadership was critical in crafting policy and in marshalling political support across the metro area.

Interest Convergence: The Common Tax Levy

One of the aspects of metropolitan regional cooperation that is most difficult to achieve is tax-base sharing, which allows resources to be redistributed more equitably across a metropolitan area.[14] While revenue sharing redistributes revenue toward property-poor school districts (in a "Robin Hood" fashion) it can also create an "interest convergence" between cities and inner-ring suburbs by providing needed assistance to suburban districts with growing levels of poverty.

The reason the common levy was initially included in the LC, according to late state Senator Ron Raikes, the key architect of the legislation, was not only to provide more equity in terms of revenue, but also to create a shared sense of financial responsibility across all 11 districts, thereby quieting complaints about the cost of interdistrict desegregation and focus schools. According to Raikes, "A lot of this stuff was aimed at . . . the complaints that are gonna come. . . . 'OK, this is sharing, great, . . . and joint education is great, but I'm getting hosed on this deal. I'm having to pay for educating kids that I shouldn't have to pay for.' So . . . at least part of is based on that, I think."

When the common levy was included in the legislation, it was not immediately apparent what impact the levy would have on different districts in the metro area. The *Omaha World-Herald* analyzed the new levy system and assessed which districts would gain and lose under the new levy system. "The ones that got more money served 75 percent of the students and 90 percent of the at-risk kids," Raikes recalled.

As a result of the distribution of revenue to districts with growing poverty, the levy was reluctantly supported by a number of suburban superintendents. The superintendent of the suburban Millard School District, Keith Lutz, reflected, "We don't like to look at winners and losers, but it's about money and you'll live and die without the money, and we come out better than most. So if you're a large school district, and you're growing; and your poverty and minority numbers are growing, you're gonna come out a winner, and we are, and we did, and we will."

The common levy also created savings for the state, according to an analysis conducted by the *Omaha World-Herald*, because the state would no longer have to use equalization payments to equalize resources among districts. Because the levy shares property taxes among districts, the need for additional state aid is reduced.[15]

Yet the common levy was not supported by all the suburbs. Especially wary were those suburban districts projected to lose funding by several different analyses—one by the *Omaha World-Herald*, another by school districts themselves. It remains unclear, however, whether these losses will be significant given the increase in state aid that will be funneled to growing districts.[16]

Federated Regionalism: Advancing Regional Equity While Preserving Local Control

One of the greatest appeals of this legislation across multiple constituencies is the balance it strikes between regional equity and local autonomy. While the Learning Community fosters tax sharing and integration, it also allows local school districts to maintain their boundaries as well as local authority over budgeting and curriculum. In addition, the voluntary interdistrict desegregation program provides choice-based options that appeal to parents with different goals. For the chair of the nonprofit African American Achievement Council, appealing to a diverse community of families was the goal: "I think over a period of time you will see that from this Learning Community because it does not include busing, unless you want to be bused, and it continues to maintain, if you want strong neighborhood schools, and it provides an opportunity for students who want to specialize to engage in the process of specialization by going to those schools that fit what they want to do."

The finance structure also provides "something for everyone" by providing support to low-wealth and high-poverty districts while at the same time allowing the high-wealth districts to maintain some of their taxing advantage. As Senator Raikes observed, "We maintain that in the Learning Community, so . . . the high valuation districts don't give up every advantage of their high valuation. In that discretionary levy, they get to levy on the valuation base they have in their school district, and if that happens to be high per student, they get the advantage, if it's low per student, then they don't."

In the end, Raikes said, the idea was to allow school boards to maintain their autonomy while fostering cooperation across the metropolitan area.

> You still have individual school boards, each district is governed individually, but they all become a part of the Learning Community, which has a governance. . . . The idea is that school districts still have a competitive relationship, you want to, in fact, foster that; you want school districts to compete with each other in providing the best opportunities for students and thereby attract . . . the students, and so on, but you also want them to cooperate with each other in the sense of these students that live in east Omaha, or wherever they happen to live, are, in fact, students that we're all responsible for, so we all need to have programs to serve those students.

The Fragility of Metropolitan Solutions

While the legislation as it was enacted contained many promising components, as Weir notes, "metropolitan regionalism is best conceived as a political process that develops over time, rather than something that is achieved in a single blow."[17] While the actors involved did strike the "single blow" in passing the LC legislation, over time the legislation's provisions have been contested and diluted. There are a number of reasons for these shifts.

The primary reason is the relatively weak nature of the legislative provisions. In order to get compromise and ensure passage, the provisions around equity were either watered down or intentionally vague. While Weir observes that "much can grow from even modest legislation,"[18] she notes that to prevent dilution or dissolution, regional solutions require ongoing political mobilization. This entails the existence of a strong and "readily mobilized" base of support in the face of challenges; this does not thus far appear to be occurring in Omaha. In fact the coalition that formed behind this agreement has fallen apart to some degree: the key architect of the legislation has passed away, and key community leaders appear to have moved on to other, more pressing issues. The momentum that led to the creation of the legislation appears to have dissipated, leaving few to argue against efforts to weaken the law's provisions.

Suburban districts have already pushed back against some of the legislation's core features. Below we discuss two of the most contentious aspects of the plan and the potential fragility in their implementation.

The Common Levy and Funding Cuts

While the common levy was supported by most of the districts initially resistant to the legislation, it has also been one of the more contentious aspects of the law. In the 2009 legislative session, the levy authority that the Learning Community was given to raise money to build and renovate interdistrict magnet schools and elementary learning centers was slightly reduced.[19] In that same session, the legislature also reduced the state appropriations to the LC slightly.[20] However, at the same time the legislature did give the LC additional taxation authority to raise funds for programs aimed at helping disadvantaged students, effectively diverting some funding aimed at actually diversifying schools toward other programs.

In January 2010, the levy was challenged in court by a coalition of rural property interests. While the court initially ruled that the suit could proceed, it later threw out the case because the plaintiffs missed the filing deadline by 11 days. In his ruling, the judge also stated that any challenge to the statute must be filed in the same tax year that the tax was levied.[21]

Despite these setbacks, the Learning Community Coordinating Council did pass its levy in August 2010. In a 17-0 vote, the LCCC approved a new levy on property in Douglas and Sarpy County school districts that would raise $5.5 million for Learning Community programs.[22] Of these funds, $585,000 will be used for leasing, renovating, and building facilities for learning centers as well as paying half the cost of building the interdistrict magnet schools (or "focus schools").[23]

Diversity Provisions

One of the more significant weaknesses in the Learning Community law is the lack of clear targets and timelines for the diversity provision, which were left out intentionally in order to ensure passage. As a result, there are no provisions in the legislation that hold either the Learning Community or member school districts accountable for making progress on the diversity targets or subgroup achievement (beyond the accountability provisions that will likely be developed in a revamped state law).

Another potential weakness in the law is the nature of the diversity provisions: currently, the provisions require only that districts seek to achieve socioeconomic, not racial, diversity. As research has shown, the extent to which socioeconomic status–based student assignment plans are successful in diversifying schools along either racial or socioeconomic lines depends on the socioeconomic factors that are used. While research has found that the more successful plans include multiple measures beyond free and reduced-price lunches, the Learning Community currently used only free and reduced-price lunches as the measure of diversity.[24]

The design of the choice plan is already proving to be one of its more contentious aspects, as suburban districts have sought more influence and control over admissions and enrollment. One major sticking point has been the issue of choice transfer priority, as the law did not specify whether interdistrict choice students would get priority over intradistrict choice students. Because many suburban districts allow within-district transfers, suburban parents grew concerned that their children would be denied their choice of schools within their home districts as a result of priority given to interdistrict "diversity transfers." Suburban districts have already successfully appealed to the LCCC for the right to give priority to their own resident students seeking within-district transfers before any interdistrict admissions can occur.[25]

The issue of capacity is also likely to become an issue in the implementation of the plan. While the LCCC is charged with establishing a process to determine school and district capacity so that districts are not able to use lack of space as an excuse to deny transfers, the suburban districts have also successfully lobbied the LCCC to allow them more input in establishing capacity.

Suburban pushback was also apparent in a legislative proposal that challenged the structure of the Learning Community governing board. In 2011, legislation was introduced that would have changed the LC governance structure from the 21-member elected board to a 9-member elected board.[26] This proposal, which was backed by a number of the suburban districts, was voted down by the legislature in March 2011.[27]

Looking to the Future

The compromises that were negotiated in the creation of the Learning Community legislation sought to balance demands for local autonomy with regional equity. Yet suburban districts have been capitalizing on the ambiguity in the law to assert their interests and slowly chip away at the law's provisions. This pushback has been facilitated by a lack of clear political base in support of the LC.

While metropolitan regional solutions will be an increasingly important policy tool to address growing between-district isolation in metropolitan areas across the United States, there are a number of important lessons to be drawn from the Omaha case, in terms of both creating and implementing a sustainable agreement that is not weakened over time. The first is the need to keep momentum beyond the "single blow"—the need to organize an ongoing base of support and to continually rearticulate the rationale for the law's provisions, and to continue to involve key community players. Equally important is the need to work to anticipate and preempt suburban efforts to dilute the power of the legislation.

Despite these challenges in Omaha, regional structures are a critically important tool to address problems that stem from fragmentation and segregation between districts. These types of agreements must be given serious consideration by policy makers. As powell notes, "As long as we continue to allow and support a racialized and fragmented jurisdictional structure, we will continue to limit the reach of civil rights, social justice, and environmental protection. Federated regionalism can begin to meet these challenges."[28]

NOTES

The research for this essay was generously supported by a grant from the Charles Hamilton Houston Institute for Race and Justice at Harvard Law School.

1. G. Orfield, *Reviving the Goal of an Integrated Society: A 21st Century Challenge* (Los Angeles: Civil Rights Project/Proyecto Derechos Civiles at UCLA, 2009).

2. C. T. Clotfelter, *After Brown: The Rise and Retreat of School Desegregation* (Princeton, NJ: Princeton University Press, 2004).

3. K. Bischoff, "School District Fragmentation and Racial Residential Segregation: How Do Boundaries Matter?," *Urban Affairs Review* 44 no. 2 (1998): 182–217; M. Orfield, *American Metropolitics* (Washington, DC: Urban Institute Press, 2002).

4. j. powell, "Addressing Regional Dilemmas for Minority Communities," in *Reflections on Regionalism*, edited by B. Katz (Washington, DC: Brookings Institution Press, 2000), 220.

5. M. Weir, "Coalition Building for Regionalism," in *Reflections on Regionalism*, edited by B. Katz (Washington, DC: Brookings Institution Press, 2000), 127–53.

6. powell, "Addressing Regional Dilemmas."

7. Ibid.

8. Ibid., 222.

9. M. Weir, H. Wolman, and T. Swanstrom, "The Calculus of Coalitions: Cities, Suburbs and the Metropolitan Agenda," *Urban Affairs Review* 40 (2005): 730.

10. Nebraska Unicameral Legislature, *Change Provisions Relating to Learning Communities, Schools, Educational Service Units, and Job Training Grants*, LB 1154, sec. 26 (1) (2008), http://nebraskalegislature.gov/FloorDocs/100/PDF/Final/LB1154.pdf (accessed 23 May 2010); Nebraska Unicameral Legislature, *Change Provisions Relating to Schools, Learning Communities, School Governance, and School Finance*, LB 641 (2007), http://nebraskalegislature.gov/FloorDocs/100/PDF/Final/LB641.pdf.

11. LB 1154, sec. 23 (1).

12. Weir, "Coalition Building"; Weir, Wolman, and Swanstrom, "Calculus of Coalitions."

13. C. V. Willie, "What We Learned about Urban Education Planning and Governance from the Boston School Desegregation Experience," *Equity and Excellence in Education* 30, no. 3 (1997): 13–20; A. S. Wells et al., *Both Sides Now: The Story of Desegregation's Graduates* (Berkeley: University of California Press, 2009).

14. R. D. Yaro, "Growing and Governing Smart: A Case Study of the New York Region," in *Reflections on Regionalism*, edited by B. Katz (Washington, DC: Brookings Institution Press, 2000), 43–75.

15. P. Goodsell and J. Robb, "Financial Loss Is a Sore Point in Seven Districts," *Omaha World-Herald*, 8 July 2007.

16. J. Robb, "Stakes Get Clearer for Schools: Smaller Districts Likely See Blow to Wallet," *Omaha World-Herald*, 11 December 2008.

17. Weir, "Coalition Building," 149.

18. Ibid.

19. J. Dejka, "Council Unveils Tax Levy," *Omaha World-Herald*, 13 August 2010.

20. Ibid.

21. J. Dejka, "Learning Community Tax Fight Rejected," *Omaha World-Herald*, 24 August 2010.

22. M. Saunders, "Learning Comm. Tax Levy Approved," *Omaha World-Herald*, 27 August 2010.

23. Dejka, "Council Unveils Tax Levy."

24. S. F. Reardon and L. Rhodes, "The Effects of Socioeconomic School Integration Plans on Racial School Desegregation," paper presented at the conference "Looking to the Future: Legal and Policy Options for Racially Integrated Education in the South and the Nation," Chapel Hill, NC, 2 April 2009.

25. J. Dejka, "Vote Eases Suburban Concerns," *Omaha World-Herald*, 2 October 2009.

26. J. Dejka, "Downsizing Proposal Draws Reaction," *Omaha World-Herald*, 2 September 2010.

27. J. Dejka, "Learning Community Bill Fails," *Omaha World Herald*, 3 March 2011.

28. powell, "Addressing Regional Dilemmas," 243.

PART III

Student Assignment Policy

Choices and Evidence

Socioeconomic School Integration
Preliminary Lessons from More Than 80 Districts

The U.S. Supreme Court's decision in *Parents Involved in Community Schools v. Seattle School District No. 1* (PICS, 2007) restricting the ability of school districts to use race in student assignment has increased interest in using socioeconomic status, either as an alternative to race or as a supplement in designing integration plans.[1] Proponents argue that economic school-integration plans can indirectly produce racial diversity and increase academic achievement, in a manner that is legally bulletproof.[2] While the idea of socioeconomic school integration has been discussed since the 1970s, it was not until the early 21st century that school districts began implementing socioeconomic integration plans in earnest. Consequently, relatively little is known about these programs, certainly far less than is known about race-based integration plans.

This essay seeks to expand our understanding of socioeconomic integration plans and proceeds in four parts. The first section provides a brief historical overview examining why a number of school districts began placing an emphasis on socioeconomic integration, particularly over the past decade. The second part provides a survey of more than 80 districts that are now using socioeconomic status as a factor in student assignment, describing the major ways in which the plans differ. The third section draws some preliminary lessons about how well the existing programs are working to raise academic achievement and to produce racial diversity as a by-product and makes recommendations about what could be done to improve outcomes further. The final section briefly discusses ways forward.

History of Socioeconomic Integration

La Crosse, Wisconsin, a town of 50,000, with a student population of about 7,000, was the first school district in the country to pursue socioeconomic school integration. In the late 1970s, the school board voted to change the boundary lines between La Crosse's two high schools so that some affluent students began attending the "blue collar" high school in town.[3] The high school plan proved successful in equalizing educational opportunity in the two schools, and in the early 1990s, when the district needed to open two new elementary schools, teachers approached their principals, who in turn approached the superintendent, arguing that the education of children in La Crosse could be improved by breaking up concentrations of poverty. The school board agreed and set 10 guidelines for redistricting, one of which stated the following goal: "Redistricting shall attain a balance in each school which as nearly as possible reflects the socio-economic student profile in the total district." Across the district, 30 percent of students were eligible for free lunch, and the board set its goal accordingly: socioeconomic integration is reached when 15–45 percent of the student body in every school consists of free-lunch recipients.[4]

The economic integration plan initially proved contentious, and several school board members were voted out of office, but then prointegration forces came back in power, and the boundary lines drawn to achieve integration remained in place.[5] The plan has been quite successful, as low-income students in La Crosse generally perform better than low-income students statewide. The differences tend to grow over time and are larger in math than in reading.[6]

La Crosse's plan remained an outlier, however, until the turn of the millennium, when a number of school districts—most notably that of Wake County, North Carolina, which includes Raleigh and its surrounding suburbs—began adopting programs of socioeconomic integration. Two main factors drove these plans: (1) legal concerns about using race in student assignment and (2) educational concerns about the difficulty of raising academic achievement in high-poverty schools, a concern accelerated by the standards-based reform movement that sought increases in student test scores.

Promoting Racial Diversity through Socioeconomic Integration

In the early 1990s, the U.S. Supreme Court grew increasingly hostile to continued court-ordered desegregation. In a trio of cases—*Board of Education of Oklahoma v. Dowell* (1991), *Freeman v. Pitts* (1992), and *Missouri v. Jenkins* (1995)—the Court relaxed the standards under which districts could be released from desegregation orders and declared unitary.[7] But in the late 1990s, the Fourth Circuit Court of Appeals went further and struck down the use of race in *voluntary* integration programs in the cases of *Tuttle v. Arlington County School Board* (1999) and *Eisenberg v. Montgomery County Public Schools* (1999).[8]

In Wake County (which today has 138,000 students, making it the 18th-largest district nationally), officials worried that its long-standing, voluntary racial integration plan, which provided that all schools should have racial minority student populations of between 15 percent and 45 percent, was legally vulnerable. Wake officials believed that racial integration was good for children and did not wish to go back a system of neighborhood schools that would reflect economically and racially segregated residential patterns.

Wake officials began to explore the idea of using socioeconomic status rather than race as a factor in student assignment. Unlike voluntary racial integration plans, socioeconomic integration programs are on very sound legal footing. Under the U.S. Supreme Court's reading of the 14th Amendment's equal protection clause, any use of race—even for the benign purpose of promoting integration—is subject to "strict scrutiny," a very exacting standard of review that requires government to offer a "compelling" interest and ensure that the means employed are "narrowly tailored." By contrast, the government's use of economic status need meet only the more relaxed "rational basis" test. In later years, even opponents of using race in student assignment—such as the George W. Bush administration, the conservative Pacific Legal Foundation, the American Civil Rights Institute, and the Center for Equal Opportunity—would concede that using socioeconomic status in student assignment is perfectly legal.[9]

In Wake County, there was a strong relationship between socioeconomic status and race.[10] The same is true nationally. African American and other minority students are almost three times as likely to be low-income as white students, and they are 12 times as likely as whites to attend schools with high concentrations of poverty.[11]

Promoting Positive Educational Outcomes through Socioeconomic Integration

While Wake County was interested in preserving racial diversity, its interest in socioeconomic integration also had a powerful educational rationale: to raise student achievement. Indeed, years later, a legal challenge to Wake County's socioeconomic integration program—alleging that economic status was just a proxy for race—was denied because Wake County had "legitimate nondiscriminatory reasons" for using socioeconomic status.[12]

In 1998, Wake had set an ambitious goal of raising student achievement, and officials believed a policy of socioeconomic school integration would help them reach that objective. Indeed, four decades of research has found that the single most important predictor of academic achievement is the socioeconomic status of the family a child comes from, and the second most important predictor is the socioeconomic makeup of the school she or he attends.[13] Students generally perform significantly better in schools with strong middle-class populations than they do in high-poverty schools. Virtually everything that educators talk about as desirable in a school—high standards and expectations, good teachers, active parents, a safe and orderly environment, a stable student and teacher population—are more likely to be found in economically mixed schools than in high-poverty schools.

As other essays in this book show, a growing number of studies have linked a school's socioeconomic status with student achievement, after controlling for the individual socioeconomic status of a student's family.[14] Indeed, research generally finds that socioeconomic school integration is an even more powerful lever for raising academic achievement than racial integration per se.[15]

In January 2000, the Wake County School Board voted to replace its long-standing 15–45 percent minority integration plan with a goal that no school in the district should have more than 40 percent of students eligible for free and reduced-price lunch, and no school should have more than 25 percent of students reading below grade level (averaged over two years). Some residents in Wake County were concerned that middle-class children might suffer academically under the socioeconomic integration plan, but research has long found no such negative effects to attending economically mixed (as opposed to high-poverty) schools.[16] The policy was adopted without dissent by the school board, but the unanimity belied undercurrents of discontent with the policy that a decade later would break out into the open.

Survey of Districts Pursuing Socioeconomic School Integration Today

In recent years, dozens of school districts across the country have joined La Crosse and Wake County in considering socioeconomic status in student assignment.

In the late 1990s, there were only a few districts with about 20,000 students where economic status was a factor in assigning students. By the time of the PICS decision in 2007, there were an estimated 40 such school districts, educating some 2.5 million students.[17] Today, there are more than 80 districts educating roughly 4 million students in which socioeconomic status is a factor in assigning children to magnet schools and other schools of choice, in student transfers, or in school boundary decisions.[18]

Within the universe of school districts employing socioeconomic status as a factor in student assignment, a variety of methods have emerged.

1. *Different breadths of school integration efforts.* Some districts have systemwide goals applying to all schools; others limit socioeconomic considerations to oversubscribed schools or magnet schools or some other subset of district schools.

2. *Different methods of achieving integration.* Some districts use socioeconomic status as a factor in redrawing school district lines. Others use it as a factor in public school choice and magnet school admissions. Some combine these two approaches.

3. *Different methods of identifying disadvantaged and non-disadvantaged students.* Some districts consider the individual socioeconomic status of student families, while others categorize students by the socioeconomic status of neighborhoods in which students reside. Some districts rely on eligibility for free or reduced-price meals as an indicator of low-income status. Other districts look at parental education levels as well as income. Others include limited proficiency in English. Some combine an effort to avoid concentrations of poverty with efforts to avoid concentrations of low-achieving students.

4. *Different ways of handling race.* Some districts employ socioeconomic status alone and are completely race-neutral in their approach to integration. Others use socioeconomic status as a primary factor, reserving the use of race as a last resort. Still others use socioeconomic status and race simultaneously.

Four school districts illustrate the range of alternative approaches to socioeconomic school integration: Wake County (Raleigh), North Carolina; Charlotte-Mecklenburg, North Carolina; Cambridge, Massachusetts; and (discussed later) Jefferson County (Louisville), Kentucky.

Wake County, North Carolina

As I noted above, the Wake County board adopted a policy guideline in 2000 that no school should have more than 40 percent of students eligible for free or reduced-price lunch or more than 25 percent of students reading below grade level. The policy has been implemented through redrawing school boundaries and by using income rather than race in magnet school admissions. Assignment is based not on whether an individual child receives free and reduced-price lunch but on whether the children in her or his local neighborhood do. According to school officials, the more than 700 neighborhood zones in Wake

TABLE 9.1. *Wake County High-Poverty Schools (60% + low-income), Percentage of Students at or above Grade Level in Reading and Math, 2007–2008*

School (Percentage Low-Income), 2008–2009	All	Black	Hispanic	White	Low-Income	Middle-Class
Brentwood Elementary (69.8%)	35.3	26.0	27.6	73.9	34.3	38.0
Creech Road Elementary (64.3%)	34.7	25.7	34.1	56.1	25.8	51.2
Fox Road Elementary (60.5%)	42.6	35.5	31.6	64.9	30.3	58.2
Smith Elementary (68.1%)	35.3	30.9	25.5	51.2	28.7	52.1
Wakelon Elementary (66.7%)	30.3	28.7	24.6	42.7	22.3	44.5
District average	**61.0**	**33.4**	**35.1**	**78.7**	**31.3**	**74.5**

Source: Wake County Public School System, "School General Information, 2008–09," Reports of Supplemental Disaggregated State, School System (LEA) and School Performance Data, 2007–8, End of Grade (Reading and Mathematics), Grades 3 through 8.
Note: "Low-income" = students eligible for free- and reduced-price lunch.

County, known as "nodes," align very closely with the socioeconomic status of individuals in the node.[19]

Redistricting each year has drawn political opposition; and although almost 80 percent of the need for redistricting is spurred primarily by explosive growth (rather than socioeconomic balancing), the economic policy has become a convenient political target.[20] In the 2009 elections, opponents of integration won a 5-4 majority on the school board, and even before that, the board had allowed schools to fall out of compliance with the guidelines rather than take on additional battles. By 2007, 51 of 149 schools had fallen out of compliance with the 40 percent or below free- and reduced-price-lunch cap, up from seven noncomplying schools in 2000.[21] This has had a deleterious impact on achievement, particularly at the highest ranges. Five elementary schools now exceed 60 percent free and reduced-price lunch, and disaggregated data show that virtually all categories of students in those five schools—blacks, Hispanics, whites, low-income, and middle-class—do worse than the district average for these groups (see table 9.1).

Still, overall, Wake County's schools remain far more socioeconomically integrated than most districts throughout the country, and they include far fewer high-poverty schools than other large North Carolina districts. As such, Wake County's program has rightly received national attention.[22]

Following the 2009 elections, Wake County has been the scene of great turmoil. As the new board majority sought to dismantle the diversity policy, civil rights groups pushed back, staging protests and threatening legal action.[23] The board chairman, Ron Margiotta, said that despite his opposition to the diversity policy, he did not want to create new high-poverty schools; and the Chamber of Commerce released a compromise plan in 2011 written by Michael Alves, an author of controlled choice integration plans across the country, to marry the goals of choice, integration, and stability in student assignment.[24] As of this writing, the issue remains very much in flux.

Charlotte-Mecklenburg, North Carolina

Like Wake, Charlotte-Mecklenburg is a large urban-suburban district in North Carolina. Encompassing the city of Charlotte and surrounding suburban areas, it has 133,664 students, 48.7 percent of whom qualify for free or reduced-price lunch. The student body is 41.2 percent African American, 33.5 percent white, 15.9 percent Hispanic, 4.9 percent Asian, and 4.1 percent American Indian or multiracial. The system has 103 elementary schools, 33 middle schools, 31 high schools, and 40 magnet schools.[25]

As a remedy to long-standing racial segregation of the schools, Charlotte, beginning in 1969, was ordered to desegregate its schools through busing to achieve racial balance between the district, which was then 40 percent black and 60 percent white (and other) population. The program was successful in raising academic achievement and was widely lauded as a national model.[26] In 2001, the district was declared unitary, and the Charlotte Board of Education voted to drop its long-standing racial desegregation plan and implement a public school choice plan, with a socioeconomic component.

The choice plan allowed parents to rank preferences among schools and gave special consideration to students who are eligible for free and reduced-price lunch and currently attend schools whose free and reduced-lunch numbers are thirty percentage points above the district average. Priority was also given to low-income students whose choice to transfer "would enhance the free and reduced lunch status but not create a concentration of free-reduced lunch status above 50 percent in the receiving school." Beginning in 2004–5, a priority was also given when the student reads below grade level and the home school performs 10 percentage points below the district average for reading. The goal was to ensure that "schools don't have a concentration of low-income students or students who perform below grade level."[27] Significantly, however, the plan provided a guarantee of admissions to a neighborhood school, and low-income students were provided choice to higher performing schools only if seats were available.[28]

Cambridge, Massachusetts

Cambridge, Massachusetts, a city of more than 100,000 located near Boston, is the site of one of the nation's best-known public school choice programs. Although many people associate Cambridge with Harvard and the Massachusetts Institute of Technology, it is also home to substantial numbers of disadvantaged families. Among students in the district, 44.9 percent were eligible for free and reduced-price lunch during the 2007–8 school year. The schools have a very diverse student population, which is 36.6 percent white, 35.0 percent African American, 14.1 percent Hispanic, and 11.2 percent Asian. The district has approximately 6,000 students attending 12 K–8 schools and one high school. The school system is nationally known as one of the first districts to adopt a "controlled choice" system of student assignment—in which parents rank their preferences among schools and the district honors choices in a way to ensure that all schools are integrated.[29] Between 1981 and 2001, Cambridge used a controlled choice plan in which all families chose from a variety of K–8 schools, each with a distinctive offering, subject to strict guidelines for racial integration.

In November 2001, Cambridge officials, citing "the growing body of research that shows that high concentrations of students of poverty in a school may have a negative impact on achievement of students of poverty within that school," urged that socioeconomic status be the primary factor in integrating schools.[30] In December 2001, the Cambridge school committee voted to amend its public school choice program to require that all public schools fall within a range of plus or minus 15 percentage points of the districtwide percentage of students eligible for free and reduced-price lunch. The board also put in a mechanism to continue weighting race as a backup, should socioeconomic diversity not produce sufficient racial diversity.[31] Current students would continue attending the school they had been assigned to under the old race-based system, but beginning in the 2002–3 school year, kindergartners each year would be assigned under the new socioeconomic plan. The transition from a race-conscious to a socioeconomic controlled choice plan has been carried out without controversy or any organized resistance from parents and community leaders.

Preliminary Lessons

What can be learned from the early experiences of districts? We begin by reviewing the results in a few jurisdictions and then attempt to draw some broader lessons.

Particular Outcomes in Districts Employing Socioeconomic School Integration on Racial Diversity and Academic Outcomes

COMPARING WAKE COUNTY AND CHARLOTTE-MECKLENBURG OUTCOMES

Wake County's full-fledged economic integration plan has produced robust racial diversity. When the school district switched from a policy of racial integration to one that emphasizes socioeconomic integration in 2000, much of the previous racial integration was preserved. Susan Leigh Flinspach of the University of California and Karen Banks of Wake County found that under the old racial integration policy, 64.6 percent of Wake County schools were racially desegregated in 1999–2000 and, two years later, under the new socioeconomic integration policy, 63.3 percent of schools were racially desegregated.[32] A 2008 news report found that the proportion of Wake students in racially segregated schools had climbed modestly to 32 percent, up from 25 percent over the previous decade.[33] But the increase may have been less a function of the switch from race to class than of the reduced compliance with the socioeconomic integration plan, noted earlier, where one-third of schools exceed the cap of 40 percent free and reduced-price lunch. The new economic mechanism also differs from Wake's old racial approach in another important respect: the economic policy sets a ceiling on low-income students (40 percent), whereas the old racial policy set both a ceiling (45 percent minority) and a floor (15 percent minority). In any event, even after Wake County's slippage, its schools remain far more racially and economically integrated than most other districts in North Carolina or in the nation as a whole. By contrast, Charlotte-Mecklenburg's highly circumscribed socioeconomic integration plan has proven deeply flawed and permitted substantial racial resegregation. Between 2001–2 (prior to unitary status) and 2003–4 (two years after unitary status was declared), the percentage of racially balanced schools declined by 22.6 percent at the elementary level, 7.4 percent at the middle school level, and 20.6 percent at the high school level.[34]

In terms of academic outcomes, over the past several years, Wake County's low-income and minority students have performed better than low-income and minority students in other large North Carolina districts that fail to break up concentrations of poverty.[35] This comparison is more relevant than Wake County vis-à-vis statewide averages because North Carolina includes many rural districts that are more naturally integrated than urban areas typically are. Wake County schools are considerably less likely to have concentrations of poverty than other large North Carolina districts such as Forsyth, Guilford, Durham, and Charlotte-Mecklenburg.[36]

In the past few years, Wake County has continued to outperform Durham, Forsyth, and Guilford Counties, but Wake County and Charlotte-Mecklenburg have performed at comparable levels. One explanation may be that Charlotte-Mecklenburg, despite its less integrated system, is seeing the fruits of its nationally recognized pre-K program, Bright Beginnings, first instituted in the fall of 1997.[37] The "gold standard" program recruits the lowest-performing pre-schoolers and gives them access to a literacy-rich curriculum, with highly trained teachers and low teacher-pupil ratios for six and a half hours a day—a much different environment than that found in typical Head Start programs. Bright Beginnings has a steady funding stream, using more than 80 percent of the district's federal Title I allocation, and has yielded substantial academic benefits for students on math and reading tests, compared with nonparticipating students.[38] These positive benefits are consistent with the findings from other high-quality pre-K programs throughout the nation, particularly in Oklahoma and New Jersey.[39] Wake County, by contrast, does not have a nationally recognized Title I–funded pre-K program. It seems probable, in other words, that while Wake is right on school integration, Charlotte is right on pre-K programs. A policy that combined Charlotte's pre-K program with Wake's commitment to integrated schooling would likely deliver the strongest total results. This approach would address both prongs of the Coleman Report's findings—that public policy should address both the inequality rooted in family socioeconomic status (pre-K programs) and inequality rooted in a school's socioeconomic makeup (socioeconomic integration).

CAMBRIDGE OUTCOMES

The controlled choice economic integration plan in Cambridge has produced substantial racial diversity without using race as a determining factor in assigning students to a school. As I noted earlier, under the plan, which went into effect in the 2002–3 school year, race remains a potential factor in student assignment for schools in which race-neutral assignments would result in school segregation. In the years since it was enacted, however, the plan's socioeconomic diversity requirement in assigning low- and non-low-income students has by itself led to racially diverse schools at a level similar to the race-conscious plan. According to school district enrollment figures, Cambridge had only two schools not within the guideline of plus or minus 15 percentage points for white and nonwhite racial integration in 2001–2, and seven years later, in 2008–9, Cambridge still had only two schools that did not meet this desegregation standard. Michael Alves of Enroll Edu, which administers the Cambridge controlled choice economic integration kindergarten assignment lottery, attributes the plan's racial integration to the strong association between race and socioeconomic status among the school district's student population. In the 2009–10 school year, the assignment lottery for kindergarten students showed 67 percent of African American students to be eligible for free or reduced-price lunch compared to only 14 percent of white students, 29 percent of Asian students, and 47 percent of Hispanic students. "Although Cambridge retains race as a potential factor in its computerized assignment algorithm," Alves notes, "it appears that to date the 'additional weight' provided to the randomly assigned applicants from an underrepresented racial group has not been a determinative factor in the assignment of any kindergarten students. In future years, race may prove to be determinative, but so far socioeconomic guidelines have produced racial diversity by themselves and no student has been denied a spot because of race."[40]

The early data on academic outcomes—test scores and graduation rates—also suggest that Cambridge's integration plan is working well. The socioeconomic plan was first implemented for incoming kindergartners in the 2002–3 school year. These kindergartners reached sixth grade in 2008–9, the latest year for which test score data are available. Massachusetts Department of Education data show that low-income and minority sixth graders in Cambridge's economically desegregated schools performed better than low-income third graders statewide on the Massachusetts Comprehensive Assessment System (MCAS) for language arts in the 2008–9 school year. Cambridge's middle-class sixth graders performed about the same. On the Composite Performance Index (CPI), low-income Cambridge sixth graders had a 75.5, compared with a 73.9 for low-income sixth graders statewide.[41] Cambridge black students had a 77.0 score, compared with 75.3 for black students statewide; and Cambridge Hispanic students had an 81.1 score compared with a 70.9 for Hispanic students statewide. Meanwhile, there is no evidence that the middle-class students in Cambridge were in any way harmed academically by the system's socioeconomic integration program. Their CPI was 91.0, roughly comparable to the state score for middle-class students of 91.2.[42]

Even more notable, Cambridge, with its long-standing commitment to integration by race and class, produced a 2008 high school class in which 88.3 percent of students graduated in four years, compared with 81.2 percent of students statewide and 59.9 percent in Boston. Broken down into subgroups, 88.8 percent of Cambridge's low-income students graduated in four years, compared with 64.8 percent of low-income students statewide and 59.1 percent of low-income students in Boston. Cambridge's black and Hispanic students also far surpassed blacks and Hispanics in Boston and statewide in graduation rates, while whites graduated at the same level as whites statewide, and far ahead of Boston's whites.

BROADER LESSONS

From these experiences, and those of other districts, it is possible to draw four broad lessons that can help guide others on how best to shape socioeconomic school integration plans:

Lesson 1: Systemwide socioeconomic school integration programs with clearly stated goals are generally more effective in raising achievement and promoting racial diversity than narrower, more modest ad hoc programs. While Wake County has had general success with its districtwide 40 percent cap on low-income students, districts such as Charlotte-Mecklenburg with more passive and narrow socioeconomic integration programs have been far less successful in preserving racial diversity. Likewise, academic achievement is more modest when programs are less robust. When Wake County, for example, began to let more schools drop out of compliance with the 40 percent cap on low-income students, all students suffered, particularly in those schools with more than 60 percent of students eligible for free and reduced-price lunch (see table 9.1).

Lesson 2: Using public school choice and magnet schools tends to be more politically acceptable than redrawing school boundaries to achieve socioeconomic integration. School districts have learned a great deal about how to integrate students voluntarily since the crisis over implementing court-ordered racial busing in the 1970s. Today, most successful districts rely primarily on student assignment systems that utilize magnet schools and public school choice, rather than mandatory assignment and compulsory busing, to achieve socioeconomic integration. The model developed in Cambridge is the purest example of this new approach, in which all schools have been designated magnet schools of choice.

The biggest public backlash against integration tends to come from compulsory redistricting, which offers parents no say in where their children attend school and little incentive for middle-class families to support integration. In places such as Manatee, Florida, for example, there was huge political fallout when some students were redistricted from high-performing schools, designated as "A" schools in Florida's parlance, to "F" schools in order to achieve greater economic balance. Manatee's subsequent plan to use economic status as a factor in its public school choice program, by contrast, generated little opposition.[43] Likewise, the compulsory element of Wake County's socioeconomic integration plan—reassignment and rezoning of schools—has produced far greater political concern than its use of magnet schools. In large districts, the Cambridge "controlled choice" model can be implemented successfully by carving the district into racially and economically heterogeneous zones within which choice options are exercised.[44]

Lesson 3: In defining students as poor or middle class, there are advantages and disadvantages to considering the individual socioeconomic status of student *families*, compared with categorizing students by the socioeconomic status of *neighborhoods* in which students reside. In some cases, it may be appropriate to consider both sets of data.

A number of the newer plans, like one found in Berkeley, California, examine the socioeconomic status of neighborhoods rather than individuals. This approach has three main advantages.

First, districts that categorize students by neighborhood (often Census tract) typically have access to more sophisticated residential-based data about parental education and income than could be easily attainable from individual families.[45] Census tract data is more finely grained than individualized binary considerations such as eligibility for free and reduced-price lunch, and it can be broken into three tiers, quartiles, quintiles, or more, in relationship to the neighborhood where a child resides. This is important as an educational matter because many elements of school quality appear to be complex and tiered. Recall, for example, that it is an advantage to have classmates with large vocabularies. Research suggests this factor is tiered by socioeconomic status. At 36 months, children from professional families have 1,116 words in their vocabularies, and children from welfare families have 525. But children from working-class families fall neatly in between, with 749 words.[46]

Second, if a district is hoping that socioeconomic integration will produce racial integration as a by-product, considering Census data as well as individual family data may produce a larger racial dividend. As noted earlier, while there is a strong association between income and race, there is often an even stronger connection between neighborhood concentrations of poverty and race. Indeed, middle-class African Americans are more likely to live in neighborhoods of concentrated poverty than low-income whites.[47]

Third, if a district is planning to use racial characteristics alongside socioeconomic ones (see discussion below), considering the socioeconomic status and race of neighborhoods is less likely to draw legal attack than considering the socioeconomic status and race of individual students—a practice Justice Anthony Kennedy, the swing vote in the PICS case, found particularly objectionable.

At the same time, there are two advantages to using individualized family

FIGURE 9.1. *Voluntary School Integration Continuum of School Districts*

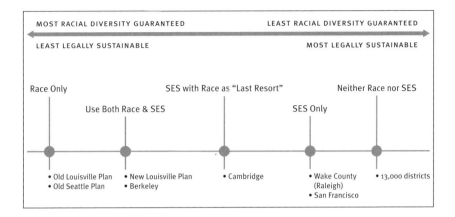

data in socioeconomic integration programs. First, the practice is more finely tuned to ensure socioeconomic integration in a school than the geographic approach. A magnet school program that provides a preference to students residing in a low-income neighborhood, for example, could end up favoring a wealthy student living in the corner of a low-income Census tract. Individualized family data avoid this problem of neighborhood outliers. Second, Census data grows old over time and may not reflect current neighborhood realities. Some neighborhoods gentrify and others decline economically, so Census data, collected every 10 years, may not accurately capture the latest demographic trends in a neighborhood. It is possible for districts to pay to update Census data, but that can prove expensive.

It may be that districts will ultimately want to rely on some combination of individualized family and neighborhood data to create the strongest possible program.

Lesson 4: There is a tension between socioeconomic plans that produce the most racial diversity and those that are most legally sustainable—and the best solution for districts may be to lead with socioeconomic factors and use race only as a last resort.

Figure 9.1 outlines a continuum of district approaches to voluntary school integration. Those on the far left (like the old Louisville and Seattle integration plans) use the race of individual students and have been struck down as illegal. Those on the far right (probably the vast majority of American school districts) do nothing to integrate by either race or class and usually produce segregated outcomes. In the middle three categories are those districts that are purely race neutral and use socioeconomic status by itself (Wake County,

Charlotte, etc.), those that use race and socioeconomic status simultaneously (Berkeley), and those that lead with socioeconomic status and reserve the use of race as a "last resort" (the Cambridge plan).

The completely race-neutral plans run the danger of not producing sufficient racial diversity. Although race and class are closely associated, by definition there is no better way to ensure a certain racial result than by employing race per se. Meanwhile, the plans that use race plus socioeconomic status simultaneously run the risk of violating the requirement that schools use race only as a last resort. Even plans using race at the geographic level have invited litigation.

Looking Forward

For those of us committed to racial integration, the U.S. Supreme Court's 2007 decision in PICS was a disappointment. But the experience in Louisville itself paints a more heartening picture. Instead of giving up on integration entirely, Louisville officials began to consider alternatives and came up with something even better than their old plan focused exclusively on racial diversity. The new plan points to one future for school integration: a focus on socioeconomic status alongside of race.

The new system considers socioeconomic status (parental income and education) and race, rather than race alone, based on the geographic areas in which students reside, rather than their individual economic status or race. Under the new program, the school district is divided into six clusters, each of which was drawn to be racially and economically diverse. Families will choose schools within the cluster, and their choices will be honored so long as there is room and the placement furthers the diversity requirements. To be diverse, each school is required to have between 15 percent and 50 percent of students from elementary school enrollment areas that are designated as "Geographic Area A"—those where the majority of students reside in census blocks that are below the district's average median household income, below the district average educational attainment, and above the district average for public school minority students. (Currently, 48 percent of the district's 98,000 students are from minority groups.) All students in a geographic area are designated by their neighborhood demographics, regardless of their individual race or economic status. All other areas—poor white areas, middle-class minority areas, and middle-class white areas—are designated as "Geographic Area B." The plan went into effect in the 2009–10 school year.[48]

The addition of socioeconomic status is something many within the community had long argued should be part of the district's integration plan. In 1993, Superintendent Stephen Daeschner said the uneven distribution of poor children "bothers me more than anything. . . . That question is as powerful as the (racial) integration one in my mind." The principal at Roosevelt Perry Elementary, which was racially integrated but 99 percent low income, urged a plan to "equalize schools by socioeconomic status as well as race."[49] A few years later, a poll of Louisville teachers found that educationally they were more concerned about income integration than racial integration.[50] An April 2002 analysis by the Jefferson County school district found that low-income students in middle-class schools performed better than low-income students in high-poverty schools.[51] Louisville's system, like Wake County's, faces political challenges, particularly from upper-middle-class families that are new to the system and expect neighborhood schools, even if those schools are segregated.[52] Combining integration with extensive parental choice—as employed in places like Cambridge—may offer the most politically viable alternative for proponents of integrated education.

Whether districts embrace a Louisville-type plan (race along with socioeconomic status), a Wake County-type plan (socioeconomic status alone), or a Cambridge-type plan (socioeconomic status, with race available as a last resort), it seems clear that the socioeconomic component, an unusual feature only a decade ago, is likely to be a mainstay of integration plans in the coming decades.

NOTES

1. *Parents Involved in Community Schools v. Seattle School District No. 1*, 127 U.S. 2738 (2007).

2. See R. D. Kahlenberg, *All Together Now: Creating Middle-Class Schools through Public School Choice* (Washington, DC: Brookings Institution Press, 2001).

3. R. Mial, "La Crosse: One School District's Drive to Create Socioeconomic Balance," in *Divided We Fail: Coming Together through Public School Choice—The Report of the Century Foundation Task Force on the Common School* (New York: Century Foundation Press, 2002), 115–40.

4. R. D. Kahlenberg, *Rescuing Brown v. Board of Education: Profiles of Twelve School Districts Pursuing Socioeconomic School Integration* (New York: Century Foundation, 28 June 2007), 16–19.

5. See Mial, "La Crosse"; Kahlenberg, *All Together Now*, 228–51.

6. See Kahlenberg, *All Together Now*, 228–51; Kahlenberg, *Rescuing Brown*, 26.

7. See *Board of Education of Oklahoma v. Dowell*, 498 U.S. 237 (1991); *Freeman v. Pitts*, 503 U.S. 467 (1992); and *Missouri v. Jenkins*, 515 U.S. 1139 (1995).

8. See *Tuttle v. Arlington County School Board*, 195 F.3d 698 (4th Cir. 1999), cert. dismissed, 529 U.S. 1050 (2000); *Eisenberg v. Montgomery County Public Schools*, 197 F.3d 123 (4th Cir. 1999), cert. denied, 529 U.S. 1019 (1999).

9. See Brief for the United States as Amicus Curiae Supporting Petitioner, 2006, *Parents Involved in Community Schools v. Seattle School District No. 1*, 25–27; and Brief Amicus Curiae of the Pacific Legal Foundation, American Civil Rights Institute, and Center for Equal Opportunity in Support of the Petitioner, 2006, *Meredith v. Jefferson County Board of Education*, 25.

10. Todd Silberman, "Wake County Schools: A Question of Balance," in *Divided We Fail*, 151.

11. U.S. Department of Education, Condition of Education 2006, table 6.1; G. Orfield, *Reviving the Goal of an Integrated Society: A 21st Century Challenge* (Los Angeles: Civil Rights Project/Proyecto Derechos Civiles at UCLA, January 2009), 15.

12. U.S. Department of Education, Office of Civil Rights, Southern Division, letter to William R. McNeal, Superintendent, Wake County Public School System, 29 August 2003 (re: OCR Complaint Nos. 11-02-1044, 11-02-1104, and 11-02-1111).

13. See J. S. Coleman et al., *Equality of Educational Opportunity* (Washington, DC: U.S. Government Printing Office, 1966). The basic findings of the report have been affirmed again and again in the research literature. See Kahlenberg, *All Together Now*, 25–35 (reviewing numerous studies).

14. Kahlenberg, *All Together Now*, 25–42; D. Rusk, "Classmates Count: A Study of the Interrelationship between Socioeconomic Background and Standardized Test Scores of Fourth Grade Pupils in the Madison–Dane County Public Schools," 5 July 2002, http://www.schoolinfosystem.org/archives/Unifiedfinalreport.pdf; R. W. Rumberger and G. J. Palardy, "Does Segregation Still Matter? The Impact of Student Composition on Academic Achievement in High School," *Teachers College Record* 107, no. 9 (2005): 1999–2045; D. N. Harris, *Lost Learning, Forgotten Promises: A National Analysis of School Racial Segregation, Student Achievement, and "Controlled Choice" Plans* (Washington, DC: Center for American Progress, 24 November 2006), 14, 18, 22.

15. Coleman et al., *Equality of Educational Opportunity*, 307; G. Orfield, *Must We Bus? Segregated Schools and National Policy* (Washington, DC: Brookings Institution Press, 1978), 69; Kahlenberg, *All Together Now*, 36 (n. 61); R. W. Rumberger and G. J. Palardy, "Does Resegregation Matter?," in *School Resegregation: Must the South Turn Back?*, edited by J. C. Boger and G. Orfield (Chapel Hill: University of North Carolina Press, 2005), 137; G. Orfield and C. Lee, *Why Segregation Matters: Poverty and Educational Inequality* (Cambridge: Civil Rights Project at Harvard University, January 2005), 8–9; R. D. Kahlenberg, *A New Way on School Integration* (New York: Century Foundation, November 2006), 4–6, http://www.tcf.org/publications/education/schoolintegration.pdf.

16. Kahlenberg, *All Together Now*, 37–42; Rusk, "Classmates Count."

17. Kahlenberg, *Rescuing Brown*.

18. See R. D. Kahlenberg, *Turnaround Schools That Work: Moving beyond Separate but Equal* (New York: Century Foundation, November 2009), 20–21, listing 69 districts. Sub-

sequently, a number of new districts or charter schools have adopted socioeconomic integration plans, including Alachua County Public Schools, FL (29,533); Allen Independent School District, TX (18,715); Bloomington Public Schools, MN (10,070); Brunswick School Department, ME (2,962); Burnsville-Eagan-Savage Independent School District 191, MN (9,897); Chicago Public Schools, IL (435,000); Denver School of Sciences and Technology, CO (728) (charter school); East Baton Rouge Parish School System, LA (49,197); Eden Prairie Schools, MN (9,700); Farmington Public Schools, MI (12,000); High Tech High, San Diego, CA (3,500) (charter schools); Kalamazoo Public Schools, MI (11,588); Little Rock School District, AR (25,899); Seattle Public Schools, WA (45,581); and Tucson Unified School District, AZ (54,907).

19. Silberman, "Wake County Schools," 148.

20. T. K. Hui and K. W. Epps, "Schools: Trust Us, Diversity Works," *Raleigh News and Observer*, 4 February 2008.

21. T. K. Hui, "Schools Relax Goals on Diversity," *Raleigh News and Observer*, 25 September 2007.

22. See, e.g., A. Finder, "As Test Scores Jump, Raleigh Credits Integration by Income," *New York Times*, 25 September 2005.

23. See, e.g., T. Goldsmith, "Wake Schools Fight Stays Hot," *Raleigh News and Observer*, 21 June 2010.

24. See Editorial, "Eyeing the Models," *Raleigh News and Observer*, 29 July 2010; and Richard Kahlenberg, "Chamber of Commerce vs. Tea Party over Wake County Schools," The Answer Sheet, *Washington Post*, 17 February 2011.

25. Charlotte Mecklenburg School District, "Fast Facts," http://www.cms.k12.nc.us/mediaroom/aboutus/Pages/FastFacts.aspx.

26. R. A. Mickelson, "The Incomplete Desegregation of the Charlotte-Mecklenburg Schools and Its Consequences, 1971–2004," in *School Resegregation: Must the South Turn Back?*, edited by J. C. Boger and Gary Orfield (Chapel Hill: University of North Carolina Press, 2005), 87–88.

27. See Charlotte-Mecklenburg Schools, "Adopted Student Assignment Plan, 2002–03," http://www.cms.k12.nc.us/k12/assign/choice_priorities_0203.htm; Charlotte-Mecklenburg Schools, "Applying for Choice," http://www.cms.k12.nc.us/k12/choice/brochure/priorities.asp; K. S. Reid, "Charlotte District, Still in Limbo, Presses Ahead with Choice Plan," *Education Week*, 5 September 2001, 10; K. S. Reid, "Charlotte Schools Desegregated, Court Rules," *Education Week*, 3 October 2001, 3. See also Mickelson, "Incomplete Desegregation," 87.

28. Mickelson, "Incomplete Desegregation," 99.

29. Fiske, E. B., "Controlled Choice in Cambridge, Massachusetts," in *Divided We Fail*, 167.

30. Ibid., 192.

31. See Cambridge Public Schools Controlled Choice Plan, 18 December 2001, http://www.cpsd.us/Web/PubInfo/ControlledChoice.pdf; Brief of 553 Social Scientists as Amicus Curiae in Support of Respondents, Appendix, 46 (n. 149) (noting that Cambridge's stu-

dent assignment plan "does include socioeconomic status as one factor [but] it retains race as a factor in assignments where significant resegregation appears"); S. Rimer, "Schools Try Integration by Income, Not Race," *New York Times*, 3 May 2003 (noting that Cambridge relies on socioeconomic factors and uses race "as a last resort if schools fall out of racial balance"); and Fiske, "Controlled Choice in Cambridge, Massachusetts," 196–97.

32. S. L. Flinspach and K. E. Banks, "Moving beyond Race: Socioeconomic Diversity as a Race-Neutral Approach to Desegregation in the Wake County Public Schools," in *School Resegregation*, edited by J. C. Boger and G. Orfield (2005), 275.

33. E. Bazelon, "The Next Kind of Integration," *New York Times Magazine*, 20 July 2008.

34. Mickelson, "Incomplete Desegregation," 100. See also Brief Amicus Curiae of the American Civil Liberties Union, the ACLU of Kentucky, and the ACLU of Washington in Support of Respondents, *Parents Involved in Community Schools v. Seattle School District No. 1* and *Meredith v. Jefferson County Board of Education*, pp. 13–14; Brief of 553 Social Scientists, App. 52.

35. See Kahlenberg, *Rescuing Brown*, 13.

36. R. D. Kahlenberg, "Using Socioeconomic Diversity to Improve School Outcomes," paper presented at Rochester State of Fair Housing Conference, 11 October 2007, http://www.tcf.org/list.asp?type=PB&pubid=628.

37. See P. Tough, *Whatever It Takes: Geoffrey Canada's Quest to Change Harlem and America* (Boston: Houghton Mifflin, 2008), 210–11.

38. See S. B. Neuman, *Changing the Odds for Children at Risk: Seven Essential Principles of Educational Programs That Break the Cycle of Poverty* (Westport, CT: Praeger, 2009), 106–12.

39. For a recent summary of the research, see G. Anrig, *Building on Success: Educational Strategies That Work* (New York: Century Foundation, 2009), 3–5, http://www.tcf.org/Publications/Education/Greg_Education.pdf.

40. Michael Alves, interview with author, 13 November 2006.

41. The CPI is a 100-point index that measures student progress toward proficiency in English, language arts, and mathematics on the standard MCAS tests and the MCAS–Alternate Assessment. See http://www.doe.mass.edu/sda/ayp/cycleIV/glossary.html.

42. See 2009–10 NCLB Report Card—Cambridge, http://profiles.doe.mass.edu/reportcard/rc.aspx?linkid=38&orgcode=00490000&fycode=2009&orgtypecode=5&.

43. See Kahlenberg, *Rescuing Brown*, 36–37.

44. See C. V. Willie, R. Edwards, and M. J. Alves, *Student Diversity, Choice, and School Improvement* (Westport, CT: Bergin and Garvey, 2002).

45. Although the 2010 Census eliminated the "long form," which included detailed data from roughly one-sixth of households, the Census Bureau's American Community Survey will continue to gather extensive data of the type that were collected in the Census's long form. See U.S. Census Bureau, "American Community Survey—Key Facts," http://www.census.gov/newsroom/releases/pdf/09ACS_keyfacts.pdf.

46. P. Barton and R. Coley, *Windows on Achievement and Inequality* (Princeton, NJ: Educational Testing Service, 2008), 9, figure 2.

47. See J. R. Logan, *Separate and Unequal: The Neighborhood Gap for Blacks and Hispanics in Metropolitan America* (Albany, NY: Lewis Mumford Center for Comparative Urban and Regional Research, October 2002); D. Fears, "Disparity Marks Black Ethnic Groups, Report Says," *Washington Post*, 9 March 2003, http://www.nytimes.com/2008/03/18/us/politics/18text-obama.html?_r=1.

48. See "Choices: A Guide to Jefferson County Public Schools" (2008), http://www.jefferson.k12.ky.us/Pubs/Choices.pdf; R. D. Kahlenberg, "The New Look of School Integration," *American Prospect*, 2 June 2008, http://www.prospect.org/cs/articles?article=the_new_look_of_school_integration.

49. H. Holland, "Schools Worried by Clusters of Poverty," *Louisville Courier-Journal*, 11 December 1993.

50. A. Trotter, "Teachers Propose Integrating Schools by Socioeconomic Status," *Education Week*, 25 November 1998, 5.

51. C. Kenning, "Income May Impact Student Assignments," *Louisville Courier-Journal*, 1 September 2002.

52. C. Kenning, "N.C. District Turnabout Chills JCPS Busing Supporters," *Louisville Courier-Journal*, 14 March 2010.

The Effects of Socioeconomic School Integration Policies on Racial School Desegregation

Given the Supreme Court's decision in *Parents Involved in Community Schools v. Seattle School District No. 1* (*PICS*, 2007), the use of individual student race in voluntarily adopted school assignment plans (as opposed to court-ordered plans) is no longer legally permissible in most cases.[1] However, because socioeconomic status does not create a protected class under the 14th Amendment, the use of individual socioeconomic status in school assignment plans is legally permissible. Richard Kahlenberg, among others, has argued that socioeconomic integration will produce racial desegregation as a by-product, given the strong correlation between race and socioeconomic status in the United States.[2] Sean Reardon, John Yun, and Michal Kurlaender demonstrate, however, that socioeconomic integration need not necessarily lead to increased racial desegregation.[3] Their analysis suggests that socioeconomic integration is most likely to lead to reduced racial segregation in districts where racial residential segregation is relatively low and where socioeconomic integration is based on a measure such as family income or parental education, rather than only on student free or reduced-price lunch eligibility.

As yet, however, there is no systematic empirical study of the claims made by Kahlenberg or of the analysis of Reardon, Yun, and Kurlaender regarding the effects of socioeconomic status (SES)–based student assignment plans on racial desegregation.[4] In fact, there is not even any systematic empirical evidence regarding the effects of SES-based student assignment plans on *socioeconomic* desegregation. Our goal in this essay is to provide evidence on these two issues.

A Brief History of Socioeconomic Status–Based Student Assignment Plans

As the name implies, socioeconomic status–based student assignment (SBSA) plans use socioeconomic characteristics of students' families or neighborhoods as factors in determining which schools students attend. Typically, this means that districts classify students by one or more socioeconomic characteristics (free or reduced-price lunch eligibility, parental education, neighborhood poverty rate) and seek to assign students to schools in ways that roughly balance these characteristics among schools so that poor students are not concentrated in a subset of the district's schools. The defining characteristic of an SBSA plan, then, is the aim of constructing school enrollments so that each school is relatively socioeconomically representative of the district enrollment as a whole, at least with regard to the set of socioeconomic factors used in the plan.

Socioeconomic status–based school assignment plans are relatively new. A few districts began using SES-based student assignment plans more than a decade ago (Montgomery County, Maryland, in 1986; Topeka, Kansas, in 1991; La Crosse, Wisconsin, in 1992). Most of the districts using some form of SBSA plan, however, began doing so in the last decade. Thirty-two districts implemented some form of SBSA plan between fall 1998 and fall 2008; three more have plans to begin SBSA in the next two years (we give details on our data collection procedures below). In the fall of 1997, roughly 200,000 students were enrolled in districts with SBSA plans; in the fall of 2008, there were 1.6 million students in such districts, an eightfold increase in a decade.

In part, the impetus for such plans likely comes from the courts' relatively recent retreat from racial desegregation policies, which in some cases has resulted in a rapid—and troubling—resegregation of schools. As Reardon and Yun describe, three Supreme Court decisions in the early 1990s, *Board of Education of Oklahoma City Public Schools v. Dowell, Freeman v. Pitts*, and *Missouri v. Jenkins*,[5] made it easier for districts to be released from court-ordered desegregation:

> In *Dowell*, the court emphasized that desegregation orders were intended to be temporary and that a return to local control was preferable, once a district had "complied in good faith with the desegregation decree since it was entered, and . . . the vestiges of past discrimination had been eliminated to the extent practicable" (*Dowell*, 498 U.S. at 249–50). In *Freeman*, the Court ruled that districts could be released from desegregation orders piecemeal—district courts might end their judicial oversight in areas where sufficient progress had been shown, for example, in student or faculty assignments, while retaining oversight in other areas where progress was still needed. See *Freeman*, 503 U.S. at 489–90. Moreover, the Court emphasized the need for a district's "good faith commit-

ment" to end segregation, see *Freeman* at 491, rather than the stronger requirement that desegregation efforts "work, and . . . work *now*," an approach the Court had previously emphasized. *Green v. County Sch. Bd.*, 391 U.S. 430, 439 (1968). Most recently, in *Missouri v. Jenkins*, 515 U.S. 70 (1995), the Court appeared to shift the burden of proof from school districts (who, since *Green*, had been required to explain racial disparities) to plaintiffs, who, it said, must identify "the incremental effect" that prior de jure segregation had upon any continuing racial disparities if they are to be considered by federal courts. *See id.* at 101.[6]

As a result of these decisions, a large number of school districts have been released from court order in the past decade. In some cases, school districts have responded by implementing SES-based student assignment plans, in the hope that such plans will ameliorate some of the potential resegregation of schools.

The courts' retreat from race-based desegregation strategies is not the only factor leading to the adoption of SBSA plans, however. The impetus for SBSA plans likely also stems from a growing societal deemphasis on race and race-based remedies for racial and social inequality, as evident in the PICS decision. Although most of the plans in effect today predate the Supreme Court's decision in PICS, they may stem from the same societal move away from race-based remedies. Moreover, research suggests that the concentration of low-income students in schools leads to negative educational outcomes,[7] a finding that many districts adopting SBSA plans cite as part of their rationale for such assignment plans.

Prevalence of Socioeconomic Status–Based Student Assignment Plans

There is no comprehensive national data source identifying all public school districts that use some form of SBSA plan. As a result, we conducted a comprehensive search to identify districts using SBSA plans.[8] We identified 40 school districts using, or planning to use, socioeconomic status factors in determining student assignments (details below).[9] These districts are widely distributed across the United States; few states have more than one or two such districts. Although the 40 districts using SBSA plans comprise only roughly one-quarter of one percent of all districts in the United States, most of them are relatively large districts (averaging roughly 42,000 students enrolled in 2006–7); collec-

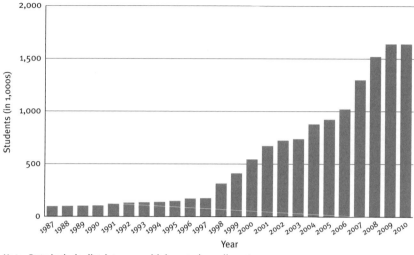

FIGURE 10.1. *Number of Students in All Districts with SES Integration Plan by Year*

Note: Data include district years with imputed enrollments.

tively they enroll more than 1.6 million students (roughly 3.5 percent of U.S. public school enrollment) (see figure 10.1).

Not only are the districts that have implemented SBSA plans larger than the typical U.S. school district, they are also much more racially and ethnically diverse than the population of U.S. students as a whole: in 2005–6, 42 percent of students in these districts were non-Hispanic white; 28 percent were non-Hispanic black; 24 percent were Hispanic; and 6 percent were Asian.[10] It appears, therefore, that large, racially and ethnically diverse districts are much more likely to have adopted SBSA plans in the past decade than smaller and more racially homogenous districts. Almost half a million black and a quarter of a million Hispanic students currently attend school in districts with SBSA plans (close to 6 percent of all black and 3 percent of all Hispanic students in the United States).

The Effects of Socioeconomic Status–Based Student Assignment Plans

Before turning to our analysis of the effects of SBSA plans on segregation patterns, it is useful to consider how different features of SBSA plans may affect patterns of socioeconomic segregation, racial segregation, or both. There are three broad mechanisms used by SBSA plans to reduce socioeconomic seg-regation: (1) explicit socioeconomic balancing of school composition (SES-balancing plans), (2) the use of attendance zones to produce socioeconomic diversity (attendance-zone plans), and (3) SES-based preferences in school choice or transfer practices (transfer priority plans). SBSA plans that rely on the first of these mechanisms (SES-balancing plans) are potentially the strong-est type of plan, because they explicitly attend to how evenly students are dis-tributed among schools. Even among SBSA plans that rely on SES balancing, however, the extent to which such balancing affects socioeconomic segrega-tion levels will likely depend on what socioeconomic factors are used, and the level of socioeconomic balance required by a plan. For example, SBSA plans that rely on information about parental education levels and family in-come (measured with some reasonable detail) are likely to distinguish poor and middle-class students more effectively (and so will likely produce greater socioeconomic integration, all else being equal) than plans that rely solely on students' eligibility for free or reduced-price lunch. Such eligibility is a weak measure of poverty, both because it dichotomizes continuous family income and because it is error-prone. Likewise, SBSA plans that require relatively strict balance among schools in student socioeconomic characteristics (such as re-quiring that no school have socioeconomic characteristics that differ by more than 5–10 percent from the district average) are likely to produce greater inte-gration than those requiring only a much cruder level of balance.[11]

SBSA plans that rely on attendance zones also have the potential to have strong effects on socioeconomic segregation levels, but this will depend, again, largely on the particulars and context of the plan. In districts where large num-bers of poor students live near large numbers of nonpoor students, it will be relatively easy to draw school attendance-zone boundaries in such a way that each school draws its student body from both high- and low-poverty neigh-borhoods, resulting in a situation where most students attend schools that are both near their homes and socioeconomically diverse. If poor and nonpoor students live, on average, very far from one another, it will be much harder, or impossible, to delineate compact attendance zones that are socioeconomically diverse. Moreover, drawing attendance zones to include both high- and low-poverty neighborhoods does not guarantee that each school will have equal proportions of poor and nonpoor students. Salvatore Saporito and Deeneesh Sohoni, for example, show that school compositions often do not mirror the racial and socioeconomic compositions of the school-age population living in their attendance zones, because of differential patterns of private-school en-rollment and use of school-transfer options.[12]

In contrast to SES-balancing plans and attendance-zone plans, SBSA plans that rely on SES-based preferences in transfer or school choice decisions are likely to have little substantial impact on segregation patterns. Transfer priority plans typically give low-income students priority in transferring into low-poverty schools (and give higher-income students priority in transferring into high-poverty schools), but such transfers are generally rare. Relatively few students seek to transfer schools in most school districts (often because transportation to a school out of one's neighborhood poses a substantial barrier). Moreover, lower-poverty schools are less likely to be underenrolled than are high-poverty schools, so there are generally few available seats for poor students to apply for in low-poverty schools. Conversely, few nonpoor students apply to transfer to high-poverty schools. As a result, transfer priority SBSA plans are likely to have little effect on overall segregation levels, because the number of students affected by a SES-based transfer priority system is likely to be very small.

One additional feature of student assignment plans may affect their ability to influence socioeconomic segregation levels. Student assignment plans that focus solely on socioeconomic integration may be more effective than those that attend to many factors and use other nonsocioeconomic factors in determining school assignments (such as prior achievement, language, proximity to schools, etc.) because the latter have to balance many competing demands. Attempting to balance schools on a number of factors, for example, makes it less likely that optimal balance will be attained on any one factor.

The effects of SBSA plans on racial segregation also may depend on a variety of factors. Reardon, Yun, and Kurlaender argue that SBSA plans are most likely to produce racial integration as a by-product if the correlation between race and socioeconomic status is strong within a district's population (so that socioeconomic status serves as a good proxy for race) and if residential patterns are characterized by high levels of socioeconomic segregation within racial groups.[13] If there is high racial segregation but little socioeconomic segregation within racial groups (i.e., if poor and nonpoor blacks live near one another but far from poor and nonpoor whites), many students could attend neighborhoods schools and the system could have relatively high levels of socioeconomic integration without achieving much racial desegregation. Reardon, Yun, and Kurlaender show that such residential patterns are typical of most large urban school districts.[14]

The effects of SBSA plans on racial segregation may also depend on whether the SBSA plan replaces a preexisting race-based student assignment (RBSA) plan, operates in conjunction with it, or is introduced in a district with no prior plan. In the case where SBSA plans are implemented when race-based student assignment plans end (as has happened in some cases when desegregation orders have ended or when districts have moved away from voluntary race-based plans to socioeconomic plans), for example, it is quite possible that the implementation of the SBSA plan may—seemingly paradoxically—lead to an increase in racial segregation among schools. We might expect that SBSA plans produce less racial integration than do RBSAs but more racial integration than no plan at all. As a result, in our analyses, we investigate whether the effects of SBSA plans differ depending on whether there was a prior RBSA plan and whether the SBSA plan supplanted or supplemented the RBSA.

Data and Methods

As noted above, we attempted to identify every school district currently using some form of SES-based student assignment plan. Table 10.1 lists the 40 districts we identified that have some form of SBSA plan. We contacted district officials and interviewed them regarding the characteristics of the SBSA plans. Based on these interviews and other information (district websites, school board meeting minutes, other published articles and reports), we coded SBSA plans along several key dimensions. Most important, we coded districts as using SES balancing, attendance zones, transfer priority strategies, or some combination of these. These are not mutually exclusive: districts can, and often do, employ more than one feature in their SBSA plans. Specifically, we defined these categories as follows.

SES-*balancing plan*: Districts were coded as using an SES-balancing plan if their SBSA policy explicitly seeks to ensure that each school has socioeconomic student characteristics that fall within some specified range (e.g., districts where each school must have proportions of students eligible for free or reduced-price lunch within some specified range of the district proportion; or districts where all schools must have fewer than 40 percent of students from high-poverty neighborhoods).

Attendance-zone plan: Districts were coded as using an attendance-zone plan if their student assignment plan relies primarily on neighborhood schools but draws school attendance-zone boundaries in order that each school enrolls students from a socioeconomically diverse set of neighborhoods.

Transfer priority plan: Districts were coded as using a transfer priority plan

TABLE 10.1. *Student Assignment–Plan Characteristics in School DIstricts with Socioeconomic-Based Student Assignment Plans*

| District | State | Plan Mechanisms | | | |
		SES Balancing	Attendance Zones	Transfer Priority	Strong Plan
Beaumont	TX	0	0	1	0
Berkeley	CA	1	0	0	1
Boulder Valley RE 2	CO	0	0	1	0
Brandywine	DE	1	1	0	1
Burlington	IA	0	1	0	0
Burlington	VT	0	0	1	0
Cambridge	MA	1	0	0	1
Chapel Hill–Carrboro City	NC	0	1	0	1
Christina	DE	0	0	1	0
Davenport	IA	0	0	1	0
Des Moines	IA	0	0	1	0
Duval County	FL	0	0	1	0
Eugene 4J	OR	0	0	1	0
Greenville County	SC	0	1	0	0
Guilford County	NC	0	0	1	0
Hamilton County	TN	0	0	1	0
Jefferson County	KY	1	0	0	1
La Crosse	WI	0	1	1	0
Lafayette Parish	LA	0	0	1	0
Manatee County	FL	0	1	1	1
McKinney	TX	0	1	0	1
Minneapolis	MN	0	0	1	0
Montgomery County	MD	0	1	1	0
Moorpark	CA	0	0	1	0
Napa Valley	CA	0	0	1	0
Omaha	NE	0	0	1	0
Palm Beach County	FL	0	1	1	0
Portland 1J	OR	0	0	1	0
Rock Hill Three	SC	1	0	0	1
Rosemount–Apple Valley–Eagan	MN	0	0	1	0
San Diego	CA	0	0	1	0
San Francisco	CA	1	0	0	1
San Jose	CA	0	0	1	0
Seminole County	FL	0	0	1	0
St. Lucie County	FL	1	0	0	1
Stamford	CT	0	1	0	1
Topeka	KS	0	0	1	0
Troup County	GA	0	1	1	1
Wake County	NC	1	0	0	1
Waterloo	IA	0	0	1	0
All (Proportions)		**0.20**	**0.28**	**0.68**	**0.33**

			Student Factors Used			
Free Lunch Eligibility	Neighborhood Poverty	Other SES Measures	Non-SES Measures	Never Used Race	Prior RSBA Plan	Currently Uses Race
1	0	0	1	0	1	0
0	1	1	1	0	0	1
1	1	0	0	1	0	0
1	0	0	0	1	0	0
1	0	0	0	0	0	1
1	0	0	1	1	0	0
1	0	0	1	0	0	1
1	1	0	1	0	1	0
1	0	0	0	0	1	0
1	0	1	1	0	1	0
1	0	0	1	0	1	0
1	0	0	0	0	1	0
1	0	0	0	1	0	0
1	0	0	1	0	1	0
1	0	0	0	1	0	0
1	0	0	0	1	0	0
0	0	1	0	0	0	1
1	0	0	0	1	0	0
1	0	0	1	0	1	0
1	0	0	1	0	1	0
1	0	0	1	1	0	0
1	1	0	0	1	0	0
1	0	0	1	0	0	1
1	0	0	1	0	0	1
1	0	0	0	1	0	0
1	0	0	1	0	1	0
1	0	0	1	1	0	0
0	0	0	0	1	0	0
1	0	0	1	1	0	0
1	0	0	0	1	0	0
1	0	0	1	1	0	0
1	0	1	1	0	1	0
1	0	0	1	0	1	0
1	0	0	1	0	1	0
1	0	0	1	0	1	0
1	1	0	1	0	1	0
1	0	0	1	0	0	1
1	0	0	1	0	1	0
1	1	0	1	0	1	0
1	0	0	0	0	1	0
0.93	0.15	0.10	0.63	0.38	0.45	0.18

if they use SES factors in determining whether a given student can voluntarily transfer from his or her neighborhood or assigned school to another school in the district (e.g., districts that give low-income students preference in transferring to schools with low proportions of low-income students). Some districts with transfer priority SBSA plans use SES factors in all voluntary transfers; others use SES factors only in voluntary transfers to some specific subset of schools in the district, such as magnet schools.

For descriptive purposes, we characterize SBSA plans that rely solely on SES-based transfer priority as *weak* SBSA plans. Those that use SES balancing we characterize as *strong* plans. Those that use SES-based attendance zones but not SES balancing we characterize as either *weak* or *strong* SBSA plans depending on how we read the plans' particulars. The distinction between weak and strong plans is intended to capture our hypotheses regarding the potential of the SBSA plan to reduce segregation levels.

In addition to coding the SBSA plans of the 40 districts according to the features of the plans, we also collected information from each district on when the SBSA plan was first implemented (coded as the fall of the school year in which the plan was first in effect). We also gathered information on what SES factors the SBSA plan uses (eligibility for free or reduced-price lunch, neighborhood poverty rate, parental education) and whether student assignments are also based on other, non-SES factors (such as race, sibling priority, prior achievement, language spoken at home, and gender). Finally, we also collected information on whether each district formerly had or currently has a race-based student assignment plan. Table 10.1 lists the characteristics of the SBSA plans in the 40 districts in our sample.

In order to investigate the effect of SES-based assignment plans on segregation levels, we compute segregation levels for each district in each year for which data are available. We use data from the Common Core of Data (CCD), which covers the school years 1987–88 to 2006–7, to compute racial composition, enrollment, and segregation levels. For our longitudinal analyses, we include only districts for which we observe at least one year's data prior to the implementation of the SBSA policy and at least one year following it. This excludes data from 17 districts: one whose plan began in 1986, prior to the start of the CCD availability (Montgomery County, Maryland); one whose plan began in 1991 but for whom the CCD contains no data prior to 1992 (Topeka, Kansas); and 15 whose plans began, or are scheduled to begin, after the 2006–7 school year, the latest available year of CCD data available at the time of writing). Because some schools are missing enrollment counts by race, eligibility for free or reduced-price lunch, or both in some years of the CCD (particularly in the early years of our data), we include in our analysis only district-by-year observations in which the CCD includes enrollment counts by race and free or reduced-price lunch for at least 90 percent of the students in the district.[15] This excludes 70 district-by-year observations (57 of which are from the school years 1987–88 to 1996–97), leaving us with a final analytic sample of 390 valid observations in 23 school districts.

We measure segregation using the information theory index (H), developed by Henri Theil.[16] The information theory index measures the extent to which students of two groups are evenly distributed among schools. The index ranges from a minimum of 0, indicating no segregation (each school has identical proportions of each group) to a maximum of 1, indicating complete segregation (no student of one group attends school with any member of another group). Using this index, we compute segregation between white and black students, white and Hispanic students, white and nonwhite students, and between students who are eligible for free or reduced-price lunch and those who are not.

Models

Following some brief description of the characteristics of existing SBSA plans, we conduct several analyses to estimate the effects of such plans on segregation levels. We begin by estimating the effect of the SBSA policy in each district separately.[17] We then fit a series of models to test whether the size of the SBSA effect within each district is related to characteristics of the districts and their plans.[18] Because we have only 23 districts in them, these models are necessarily parsimonious. In particular, we fit models including the following SBSA characteristics: (1) the mechanisms the SBSA plan uses to create socioeconomic desegregation (SES balancing, attendance zones, or both, with transfer priority–only plans as the omitted category) and (2) the district's use of an RBSA plan (we include an indicator for districts that never used an RBSA plan and an indicator for districts that used an RBSA plan both prior to and after the implementation of the SBSA plan, with districts that substituted SBSA plans for RBSA plans as the omitted category). We fit several versions of this model for each of the four outcomes of interest (segregation levels between poor and nonpoor, white and black, white and Hispanic, and white and nonwhite students).

Results

Before turning to the estimated effects of SBSA plans, it is useful to examine some of the characteristics of these plans (table 10.2). Districts with "strong" SBSA plans are, on average, somewhat larger than those with "weak" plans, but otherwise the racial and socioeconomic characteristics of districts with each type of plan are relatively similar. The characteristics of strong and weak SBSA plans differ substantially, however, as we expect. Strong plans are much more likely to use SES balancing or attendance-zone boundaries than are weak plans (largely because these are the features that determine whether a plan is coded as strong or weak). Moreover, strong plans typically rely on a broader range of socioeconomic factors than weak plans—only 3 of 27 weak plans use neighborhood poverty or any family socioeconomic factor other than eligibility for free or reduced-price lunch, compared to 6 of 13 strong plans.

In 18 of the 40 districts using SBSA plans, the SBSA plan replaced a prior race-based school assignment plan. Fifteen of the districts had no RBSA plan in the years immediately prior to implementing their SBSA plan. SBSA plans in such districts are generally weak plans that rely only on transfer priority provisions to reduce segregation. Finally, in 7 of the 40 districts, SBSA plans were implemented to supplement existing (and continuing) RBSA plans. Most of these districts have had voluntary RBSA plans to which socioeconomic factors were added (e.g., Berkeley, California; Cambridge, Massachusetts; Burlington, Iowa; Montgomery County, Maryland; and Jefferson County, Kentucky). In general, table 10.2 suggests that strong SBSA plans are somewhat more likely than weak plans to have been implemented in districts that previously used an RBSA; weak SBSA plans are more common in districts that have not used an RBSA in recent years.

In order to investigate the effects of SBSA plans on segregation levels, we begin by plotting trends in segregation levels for each of the school districts in our analytic sample, in order to get a sense of whether segregation levels appear to change sharply following the implementation of SBSA plans. Figure 10.2 shows the trends in socioeconomic and racial segregation for each of the nine districts with SBSA plans coded as "strong" and for which we have segregation data before and after the start of the plan. For the most part, the trend lines suggest little effect of SBSA plans on segregation levels, with a few exceptions. For example, in San Francisco, racial segregation sharply reversed its upward trend at the same time as the SBSA plan was implemented. In Cambridge, Massachusetts, socioeconomic segregation levels declined sharply fol-

TABLE 10.2. *Descriptive Characteristics of* SBSA *Plan Districts, by Plan Strength*

	Strong	Weak	Total
Number of districts	13	27	40
District Characteristics			
Average enrollment	34,164	45,551	41,851
Average percentage white	50	48	48
Average percentage black	28	26	27
Average percentage Hispanic	12	18	17
Average percentage poor	31	35	34
Student Assignment–Plan Features			
SES balancing	8 (62%)	0 (0%)	8 (20%)
Attendance zones	6 (46%)	5 (19%)	11 (28%)
Transfer priority	2 (15%)	25 (93%)	27 (68%)
Uses free/reduced-price lunch eligibility	11 (85%)	26 (96%)	37 (93%)
Uses neighborhood poverty	4 (31%)	2 (7%)	6 (15%)
Uses other SES measures	3 (23%)	1 (4%)	4 (10%)
Uses non-SES measures	11 (85%)	14 (52%)	25 (63%)
Never used RSBA plan[a]	3 (23%)	12 (44%)	15 (38%)
Currently uses RSBA plan	3 (23%)	4 (15%)	7 (18%)
RSBA plan before SBSA plan	7 (54%)	11 (41%)	18 (45%)

[a] "Never used RSBA plan" applies to districts that did not use an RBSA plan in the two years prior to the implementation of the SBSA plan.

lowing the implementation of the SBSA plan, though segregation levels were declining before the plan started as well. Although we do not show segregation trends for "weak plans," they are similar to those shown in that there is no evident average effect of the SBSA plans on segregation levels.

After estimating the effects in each district separately (as described in note 18), we investigate whether the magnitude and direction of the effects are associated with several characteristics of the SBSA plan itself. Recall that we hypothesize the effects will be larger (a greater reduction in segregation levels) in districts that had no race-based plan prior to the start of the SBSA or that had a race-based plan that remained in place when the SBSA plan was implemented. In districts where an SBSA plan replaced an RBSA plan, we expect that segregation will not change or may even increase. In addition, we expect SBSA plans to have larger effects in districts that use stronger mechanisms for producing socioeconomic integration, such as SES balancing and attendance zones, than in districts that use only transfer priority mechanisms.

FIGURE 10.2. *Trends in Racial, Ethnic, and Socioeconomic Segregation: Nine Districts with "Strong" Socioeconomic Status–Based Student Assignment Plans, 1990–2006*

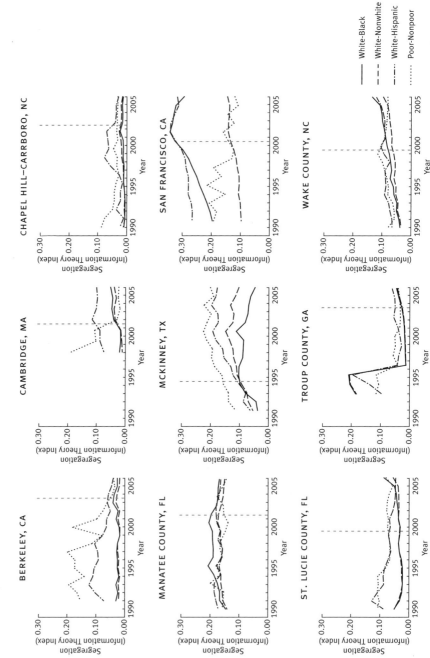

The results of the models testing these hypotheses are shown in table 10.3. For each of the three segregation outcomes (between poor and nonpoor, white and black, white and Hispanic, and white and nonwhite), we fit three models: one including only the SBSA plan mechanism variables, a second including only the district RBSA status variables, and a third containing both sets of variables.

In the models predicting the magnitude of segregation between poor and nonpoor students, the plan features are not predictive of the effect, but the RBSA status variables are. In districts that substituted an SBSA plan for an RBSA plan, segregation by poverty status *increased* slightly (by 0.011 in model 2), on average, while in districts that kept an RBSA plan in place, segregation by poverty status *decreased* by 0.036 (0.011 + −0.047; see model 2), on average. This suggests that SBSA plans may be effective at reducing socioeconomic segregation when they augment race-based plans but not when they supplant them.

A somewhat similar pattern is evident in the models predicting the effect of SBSA plans on levels of segregation of black and white children. First, note that the intercept in model 3 is positive, indicating that, on average, districts that replace race-based student assignment plans with SES-based plans that rely solely on transfer priority provisions (the weakest type of SBSA plans) tend to experience significant increases in segregation of whites and blacks (+0.40 on average, a moderate increase).[19] The effects of SBSA plans on segregation of whites and blacks, however, are stronger (meaning they increase segregation less, or even reduce it) when SBSA plans use SES balancing or attendance-zone mechanisms or when SBSA plans are implemented in districts with no prior RBSA plan (rather than supplanting prior RBSA plans). For example, model 3 predicts that an SBSA plan using only transfer priority mechanisms that is implemented in a district with no prior RBSA plan will have no impact on segregation of whites and blacks (0.040 − 0.042 = −0.002). Likewise, model 3 predicts that an SBSA plan that uses either SES balancing or attendance zones and that replaces a prior RBSA plan will result in no significant change in levels of segregation of whites and blacks. This suggests that strong SBSA plans may be as effective as the race-based plans they replace (though whether that is because the RBSA plans they replace are relatively weak or because the SBSA plans are particularly effective is unclear). We caution, however, against over-interpreting these results, as they are based on a very small sample of districts and there are few districts in the sample with any particular set of characteristics.

TABLE 10.3. *Estimated Effects of Socioeconomic-Based Student Assignment–Plan Characteristics on Segregation Levels (H)*

	Free Lunch–Non-Free Lunch			White-Black		
	Model 1	Model 2	Model 3	Model 1	Model 2	Model 3
Plan Features						
Attendance zones	0.006		−0.006	−0.005		−0.036+
	(0.017)		(0.017)	(0.017)		(0.019)
SES balancing	0.004		−0.006	−0.011		−0.042*
	(0.010)		(0.010)	(0.013)		(0.016)
RBSA Status						
Never used RBSA plan		−0.016*	−0.019+		−0.011	−0.042*
		(0.007)	(0.009)		(0.012)	(0.015)
Uses RBSA plan		−0.047*	−0.047+		−0.004	−0.008
		(0.022)	(0.023)		(0.027)	(0.025)
Constant	0.000	0.011*	0.015+	0.007	0.007	0.040*
	(0.005)	(0.005)	(0.008)	(0.008)	(0.008)	(0.014)
N	23	23	23	23	23	23

+ p < .10; * p < .05.
Note: All models are weighted by the inverse of the sampling variance of the district-specific SBSA effects. For plan features, omitted category is districts that use only transfer priority provisions. For race status variables, omitted category is districts that used an RBSA plan prior to the SBSA plan but have not used an RBSA plan since implementing the SBSA plan (those that substituted an SBSA plan for an RBSA plan).

Relatively little pattern of effects is evident in the models predicting the magnitude of the effect of SBSA plans on segregation of whites and Hispanics, likely because the correlation between income and Hispanicity is less strong than the correlation between race and income, and because most RBSA plans do not target Hispanic students. Finally, the last set of models, predicting the effect of SBSA plans on white/nonwhite segregation show patterns similar to the white/black models, albeit weaker, as we would expect given the lack of pattern in the white/Hispanic models.

Socioeconomic status–based student assignment plans hold the promise of producing two beneficial outcomes: they may be effective in reducing racial school segregation in the absence of race-based assignment plans; and they may produce socioeconomic integration, a valuable end in its own right. Our analyses here, however, suggest that the SES-based plans that have been implemented to date are few and weak. We are able to identify only 40 school districts using some form of explicit SBSA plan; two-thirds of these use plans

	White-Hispanic			White-Nonwhite	
Model 1	Model 2	Model 3	Model 1	Model 2	Model 3
0.020		0.013	−0.005		−0.023
(0.010)		(0.013)	(0.012)		(0.015)
−0.012		−0.016	−0.014		−0.030*
(0.011)		(0.012)	(0.008)		(0.011)
	0.010	0.010		−0.001	−0.022+
	(0.010)	(0.010)		(0.008)	(0.011)
	0.023*	0.019		0.003	0.000
	(0.011)	(0.012)		(0.020)	(0.019)
0.011+	0.006	0.006	0.007	0.003	0.025*
(0.005)	(0.006)	(0.007)	(0.005)	(0.006)	(0.010)
23	23	23	23	23	23

that employ weak mechanisms and so are likely to have little or no impact on racial or socioeconomic segregation patterns. Of the 13 districts we identified that use mechanisms that appear, on their face, strong enough to have some effect on segregation levels, only 9 have been in place long enough to evaluate. Our graphical and district-specific analyses of segregation trends in these districts suggest little impact on either racial or socioeconomic segregation levels.

Our analyses suggest that one reason that SES-based student assignment plans have relatively little apparent effect on segregation levels is that they supplant prior race-based plans. Indeed, six of the nine districts we evaluate that have relatively strong SBSA plans implemented their SBSA plan to replace a prior race-based plan. On average, in these districts the change from RBSA to SBSA plans has yielded little change in either racial or socioeconomic segregation. The other reason that SES-based student assignment plans appear to have little effect on segregation levels is that most such plans use only very weak mechanisms, typically relying on SES-based priority (in conjunction with non-SES factors) in school assignments for a small number of students requesting school transfers. Such plans have no effect on segregation levels when implemented in districts that had no prior RBSA plan. We do find evidence indicating that such plans are poor proxies for race-based plans, however. Both racial and socioeconomic segregation appear to increase, on average, when race-based student assignment plans are replaced by weak SES-based plans. In sum, then, when SBSA plans do not supplant RBSA plans, or when SBSA plans use SES-balancing or attendance-zone strategies to reduce socioeconomic segregation, they appear to lead to modest reductions in socioeconomic segregation and to no change in racial segregation.

Our findings here should be considered tentative, given that they are based on only a small number of school districts. Nonetheless, they do suggest that districts interested in using SES-based school assignment plans to create more integrated schools should use SES-balancing and/or attendance-zone boundary mechanisms. Our data suggest that such plans may be able to substitute for race-based assignment plans, but it is unclear whether that is because the RBSA plans replaced by strong SBSA plans are weak or because the SBSA plans are sufficiently strong. With only six districts where RBSA plans are replaced by strong SBSA plans, we have little empirical evidence from which to generalize.

Finally, our evidence suggests that weaker mechanisms, such as SES-based transfer priority mechanisms, are poor substitutes for race-based assignment plans, leading to higher levels of both racial and socioeconomic segregation than the RBSA plans they replace. And when implemented in districts with no prior RBSA plan, these weak SBSA plans have no effect on segregation levels. SES-based transfer mechanisms appear to be ineffective methods of producing either racial or socioeconomic balance among school enrollments.

NOTES

We thank Doug Lauen for his comments on an earlier draft. We are indebted to the staff members at dozens of schools districts who took time to answer our questions and explain their student assignment plans to us. In addition, we thank Richard Kahlenberg for sharing data on school district student assignment plans. Demetra Kalogrides provided excellent research assistance. Any errors in the essay remain our responsibility.

1. *Parents Involved in Community Schools v. Seattle School District No. 1,* 551 U.S. 701 (2007).

2. R. D. Kahlenberg, *All Together Now: Creating Middle-Class Schools through Public School Choice* (Washington, DC: Brookings Institution Press, 2001); R. D. Kahlenberg, *A New Way on School Integration* (New York: Century Foundation Press, 2006).

3. S. F. Reardon, J. T. Yun, and M. Kurlaender, "Implications of Income-Based School

Assignment Policies for Racial School Segregation," *Educational Evaluation and Policy Analysis* 28 (2006): 49–75.

4. See R. D. Kahlenberg, *Rescuing Brown v. Board of Education: Profiles of Twelve School Districts Pursuing Socioeconomic School Integration* (New York: Century Foundation Press, 2007). Although Kahlenberg presents case studies of 12 districts that use socioeconomic integration, his analysis is more descriptive than causal and so does not provide clear estimates of the average effect of the socioeconomic integration plans on racial desegregation.

5. *Board of Education of Oklahoma City Public Schools v. Dowell*, 498 U.S. 237 (1991); *Freeman v. Pitts*, 503 U.S. 467 (1992); *Missouri v. Jenkins*, 515 U.S. 70 (1995).

6. S. F. Reardon and J. T. Yun, "Integrating Neighborhoods, Segregating Schools: The Retreat from School Desegregation in the South, 1990–2000," *North Carolina Law Review* 81 (2003): 1566 (n. 7).

7. J. Anyon, *Ghetto Schooling: A Political Economy of Urban Educational Reform* (New York: Teachers College Press, 1997); J. S. Coleman et al., *Equality of Educational Opportunity* (Washington, DC: U.S. Department of Health, Education, and Welfare, Office of Education, 1966); D. R. Entwisle, K. L. Alexander, and L. S. Olson, *Children, Schools, and Inequality* (Boulder, CO: Westview, 1997); S. E. Mayer, "How Economic Segregation Affects Children's Educational Attainment," *Social Forces* 81 (2002): 153–76; G. Natriello, E. L. McDill, and A. L. Pallas, *Disadvantaged Children: Racing against Catastrophe* (New York: Teachers College Press, 1990).

8. In order to identify districts with SBSA plans, we used several search methods. First, we began with several lists of school districts identified by Kahlenberg as using some form of SBSA plan; Kahlenberg, *Rescuing Brown v. Board of Education*. Kahlenberg lists 40 districts using some form of SBSA. In the fall of 2008, Kahlenberg (personal communication) provided us with a list of an additional 20 districts that he had subsequently identified as using some form of SBSA. A more recent essay by Kahlenberg lists 65 districts identified as using an SBSA plan, including four districts neither he nor we had previously identified; R. D. Kahlenberg, "Socioeconomic School Integration: Preliminary Lessons from More than 60 Districts," paper presented at the conference "Looking to the Future: Legal and Policy Options for Racially Integrated Education in the South and the Nation," Chapel Hill, NC, 2 April 2009. Second, we searched the scholarly literature for articles about SBSA plans. Third, we conducted Internet searches of school-district websites and media sites for references to SBSA plans. These methods yielded an initial list of 116 districts (64 initially identified by Kahlenberg; 52 we identified through other sources) using some form of SBSA plan. We contacted each of these districts by phone or e-mail (we also examined their websites for information on their student assignment plan when possible) in order to verify that the district had some form of SBSA plan and to determine the particulars of the plan. This exercise revealed that many of the districts initially identified do not, in fact, use any form of socioeconomic status measure in their student assignment plan. Many districts that were initially identified as potentially using SBSA plans turned out not to use an SBSA plan in practice. Most commonly, this was because we (or Kahlenberg) identified a district as potentially using an SBSA plan on the basis of a newspaper article or minutes

from a school board meeting that indicated some discussion of the issue of socioeconomic segregation, a proposal to adopt an SBSA plan, or both. When we contacted district officials, however, we often learned that no formal policy had been adopted, or that the use of socioeconomic factors in school assignment had been authorized by a school board but never implemented in practice in the district. In addition, we sometimes found that districts had considered socioeconomic factors in some small way when deciding where to locate a single new school or in determining student assignments for a single school. Because these were not formal policies and affected a very small number of students, we did not consider these formal SBSA plans.

9. Thirty-six of these were districts identified by Kahlenberg; four others (Burlington Community School District, IA; Stamford, CT; Topeka, KS; and Troup County, GA) were identified from other sources (and were later included in Kahlenberg, "Socioeconomic School Integration"). There were also 4 districts among the 116 for which we were not able to determine with certainty whether they used SBSA plans: University Place, WA; Lee County, NC; Rockford, IL; and Hillsborough County, FL. Given that we were not able to identify many additional districts beyond those identified by Kahlenberg, we are relatively confident that our list contains most of the districts in the United States currently using SBSA plans.

10. Throughout this essay, we use the terms "white," "black," and "Asian" to refer to non-Hispanic students of the designated race. We use the term "Hispanic" to refer to Hispanic students of any race. Thus, the categories "white," "black," "Asian," and "Hispanic" are mutually exclusive in our terminology.

11. Reardon, Yun, and Kurlaender, "Implications of Income-Based School Assignment Policies."

12. S. Saporito and D. Sohoni, "Coloring outside the Lines: Racial Segregation in Public Schools and Their Attendance Boundaries," *Sociology of Education* 79 (2006): 81–105; S. Saporito and D. Sohoni, "Mapping Educational Inequality: Concentrations of Poverty among Poor and Minority Students in Public Schools," *Social Forces* 85 (2007): 1227–53.

13. Reardon, Yun, and Kurlaender, "Implications of Income-Based School Assignment Policies."

14. Ibid.

15. Although the CCD contains imputed racial, ethnic, and free or reduced-price lunch enrollment counts for schools with missing data in the years 1987–88 to 1997–98, we count the imputed data as missing, because of concerns about the imputation methods used in the CCD (in many cases, data were imputed for every school in a state in a given year, for example).

16. D. R. James and K. E. Taeuber, "Measures of Segregation," in *Sociological Methodology*, edited by Nancy Tuma (San Francisco: Jossey-Bass, 1985), 1–32; S. F. Reardon and G. Firebaugh, "Measures of Multi-group Segregation," *Sociological Methodology* 32 (2002): 33–67; H. Theil, *Statistical Decomposition Analysis* (Amsterdam: North-Holland, 1972); H. Theil and A. J. Finezza, "A Note on the Measurement of Racial Integration of Schools by Means of Informational Concepts," *Journal of Mathematical Sociology* 1 (1971): 187–94;

B. S. Zoloth, "Alternative Measures of School Segregation," *Land Economics* 52 (1976): 278–98.

17. Specifically, for each of the 23 districts for which we have segregation data before and after the implementation of the SBSA plan, we fit a model of the form $H_t = \beta_o + f(Y_t) + \delta(P_t) + \mathbf{X}_t\mathbf{B} + \varepsilon_t$, where Y_t is a variable measuring time (years) centered on the implementation year of the SBSA policy in the district; f is a polynomial function (usually a cubic, though it depends how many years of data we have available for a given district) of Y; P_t is an indicator of the presence of an SBSA policy in the district in year t; and $\mathbf{X}_t$ is a vector of time-varying district covariates (racial and ethnic composition, proportion eligible for free or reduced-price lunch, logged district enrollment, and number of schools). For each district i, the model for that district yields $\hat{\delta}_i$, an estimate of the change in segregation in the year of the implementation of the SBSA, net of the (cubic) temporal trend and changing district covariates.

18. These models have the form $\hat{\delta}_i = a_o + \mathbf{W}_i\mathbf{\Gamma} + \omega_i$, where $\hat{\delta}_i$ is the estimated effect of the SBSA plan in district i and $\mathbf{W}_i$ is a vector of characteristics of the SBSA plan in district i. We fit these models using weighted least squares, using the inverse of the variance of the estimated $\hat{\delta}_i$'s as weights.

19. S. F. Reardon and J. T. Yun, "Suburban Racial Change and Suburban School Segregation, 1987–1995," *Sociology of Education* 74, no. 2 (2001): 79–101.

20. For example, although one may be tempted to conclude from model 3 that an SBSA plan that used both SES balancing and attendance zones in a district that did not have a prior RBSA plan would decrease segregation of whites and blacks by −0.080 (a large decrease), this conclusion is not warranted because it relies on extrapolation of the model: there are no districts among the 23 that use both SES balancing and attendance zones and only one (McKinney, TX) that uses either of these mechanisms and did not have a prior RBSA plan.

Is Class Working?

Socioeconomic Student Assignment Plans in Wake County, North Carolina, and Cambridge, Massachusetts

Two forces—rapidly changing student demographics and a judicial system largely unreceptive to the implementation of racial desegregation, though not necessarily hostile to its underlying goals[1]—have combined to create a challenging environment for school districts interested in pursuing educational equality through voluntary integration policies. One of the by-products of these challenges has been a shift toward integration by socioeconomic status (SES), or assigning students to schools based on some measure of poverty. As districts around the country seek viable legal strategies to maintain voluntary racial integration plans, the notion that poverty status can be used as a means to desegregate schools is growing in popularity in many communities. It thus becomes increasingly important to examine the impact of SES-based integration plans in school districts already experimenting with the policy.

Supporters of socioeconomic integration suggest that two broad rationales should drive its implementation: (1) SES integration can serve as a proxy for racial integration, especially given the unreceptive legal environment of today's courts, and (2) SES integration will help deconcentrate poverty, which in turn will raise academic achievement.[2] This essay will examine these claims in an effort to better understand the impacts of SES integration in Wake County, North Carolina—a metropolitan school system that includes the city of Raleigh—and Cambridge, Massachusetts. Wake County and Cambridge represent two places where SES diversity policies were pioneered in the early 2000s, though they vary significantly from one another in size, student demographics, and SES integration methods. Both districts also had prior race-based student assignment policies, permitting a closer look at whether SES integration successfully maintains earlier levels of racial desegregation. Further, the two districts have experienced different levels of political support for their SES policies. Given these characteristics, Wake County and Cambridge serve as important examples of the transition from racial integration to SES integration in two widely differing contexts.

The following questions motivated this study:

1. Did the policy change from racial integration to SES integration deconcentrate poverty?
2. Did the shift from using race in student assignment policies to using SES help maintain racial integration?
3. What, if any, political pressures exist under SES student assignment policies?
4. Is SES integration associated with positive trends in student achievement?

The first section of the essay provides a definition of SES integration, along with a brief discussion of how districts measure poverty status. The following portions examine the political context surrounding the Wake County and Cambridge assignment plans, in addition to presenting an analysis of racial and SES enrollment data and student-achievement outcomes. The essay closes with a discussion of implications that might be drawn from SES integration in these two districts.

What Is Socioeconomic Integration?

Many American communities continue to reflect long-standing patterns of segregation by race and poverty.[3] SES-based plans generally attempt to counter-act these trends by distributing students from different income brackets more evenly across school districts. Income can be measured in a variety of ways, including parent education levels (which tend to be highly correlated with income), family income, and eligibility for free or reduced-price lunch (FRL). The ready availability of the last measure prompts many districts operating under SES diversity plans to balance the number of students receiving free or reduced-price lunch in schools systemwide. Yet research shows that FRL data are not always reliable, and that caution should be exercised when basing an SES plan solely on free- and reduced-price lunch statistics.[4]

Data and Methods

This investigation of SES integration in Wake County and Cambridge schools relied on a variety of primary and secondary sources. I analyzed materials from local media outlets, along with prior studies regarding the school districts, in an effort to grasp the historical context of the development of SES integration, as well as the current political climate in Wake County and Cambridge. I also culled school district websites for information regarding the details and development of the socioeconomic student assignment plans. And while demographic figures were available through the district—Wake County Public School System (WCPSS) in particular conducts extensive data collection in this area—this study utilizes enrollment information from the Common Core of Data of the National Center for Educational Statistics (NCES). The NCES collects enrollment data for the federal government from virtually every school district in the country. Finally, state education departments provided data for a comparison of state- and district-level student-achievement data following the implementation of SES diversity plans in Wake County and Cambridge.

SES Integration in Action
Wake County, North Carolina, and Cambridge, Massachusetts

Wake County, North Carolina, began comprehensively desegregating its schools in 1976, the same year a merger plan won approval despite heavy political opposition. For more than thirty years, the Wake County Public School System has included the city of Raleigh and its surrounding suburbs. This arrangement promoted a large-scale racial desegregation plan that included a system of magnet schools, year-round programs, and a 15–45 percent balancing mechanism mandating that African American enrollment at the school-building level should not be below 15 percent or above 45 percent.[5] Today, WCPSS is the largest school system in North Carolina and the 18th-largest in the nation.

Eight hundred miles northward is the Cambridge Public Schools (CPS) district, located just across the Charles River from Boston. The home of Harvard University and the Massachusetts Institute of Technology, with one of the nation's most expensive real estate markets—in addition to a fairly expansive section of subsidized housing—Cambridge boasts an extremely racially and socioeconomically diverse population. According to the NCES Common Core of Data for 2006–7, white children make up just 35 percent of students in the district. Approximately 45 percent of CPS students qualify for free or reduced-price lunch. Cambridge's 14 schools—including only one district high school—seem tiny compared to the 147 school buildings accommodating

Wake County's burgeoning population. CPS's enrollment has been unsteady in the past few years, first with a significant decline in the student population, followed by a recent rise in the number of kindergarteners.[6]

Evolution of SES Diversity Policy in Cambridge and Wake County

CPS operates under a system of controlled choice—a plan allowing parents to rank several schools, with the district making the final assignment decision based on a variety of factors—as part of its efforts to achieve racial desegregation. The plan was modified in 1981 and 1989, in addition to several adjustments in the 1990s.[7] Earlier research on the district found that the controlled choice system resulted in more interracial exposure than previous plans and that student achievement also increased during that time period.[8]

In 2000, however, CPS began another review of controlled choice. The evaluation occurred in the context of newly released research on the benefits of SES integration and an increasing reluctance by the courts (including a local case rejecting racial quotas at an elite Boston magnet school) to look favorably on the use of race in student assignment plans. Following the 2000 review, CPS began considering SES as the primary factor in its system of choice for the 2002–3 school year. Race can still be taken into account if a school is considerably out of balance with racial demographics in the district.[9]

SES integration in Cambridge is based on the districtwide percentage of students receiving free and reduced-price lunch. CPS originally decreed that its schools maintain a population of students eligible for free and reduced-price lunch that fell 15 percentage points above or below the district average. After the first year of implementation, CPS aimed to reduce that range to 10 percentage points around the district average, with the goal of moving to 5 percent.[10]

Also in 2000, after a federal district court ordered schools in Charlotte-Mecklenburg, North Carolina, to begin dismantling their desegregation plan, and amid general judicial concerns regarding race-based student assignment, the Wake County School Board voted to adopt an enrollment cap stipulating that no more than 40 percent of students at any given school in the district should be eligible for free and reduced-price lunch.[11] This core value was complicated by annual assignment of students that wove together many other considerations in deciding where to send students to school. Building capacity, parents' choice of instructional program, stability of school assignments, sibling preferences, proximity of schools to families, efforts to balance the number of English Language Learners (ELLs) at schools, a requirement that no more than 25 percent of students who perform below grade level may attend school together—along with the SES diversity cap—all factored into the Wake County student assignment process.[12]

Opposition to SES Integration

WCPSS has experienced tremendous growth in recent years, doubling its student population since 1985 to over 137,000 students. The rising numbers of students placed considerable pressure on the stability of the SES student assignment plan. While supporters of SES integration in Wake County often suggested that the district's tremendous expansion was a sign that the quality of the school system continued to attract business and development, parental opposition to the diversity plan grew in strength over the past few years.

Since turnover on the Wake school board could profoundly affect the future of the SES diversity policy, uncertainty swirled around every election cycle. And indeed, in October and November 2009, opponents of SES integration filled all of the contested school board seats in what was widely perceived as a resounding defeat for the diversity plan.[13]

The new board members moved quickly to dismantle the SES-based assignment policy, committed to prioritizing assignments closer to students' homes. Due to persistent residential patterns of segregation, many feared that neighborhood schools in Wake would result in the resegregation of students. As a result, the new school board's efforts were met with resistance, with many members of the community rallying in support of SES integration.[14] A series of protests, marches, vigils, sit-ins, and editorials were organized to protest the shift in policy. Yet despite the groundswell of activism, the new board members pushed forward with a neighborhood-based assignment plan.[15] Today, the threat of legal action hangs over the Wake County Board of Education.[16]

As in Wake County, student enrollment patterns in Cambridge have been unstable. The first years of SES integration coincided with a decline in enrollment. In contrast to Wake, however, the school board in Cambridge aggressively pursued strategies to understand and prevent the loss of students, including hiring a private company to conduct a market-based research study of parent attitudes in the district.

In addition to commissioning the survey, the CPS school board increased its parent-outreach efforts, offering brochures, web information, and counseling on the available elementary school options. The school board's efforts occurred just prior to an increase in kindergarten enrollment, and it should be noted that during the past several years the number of wealthy students participating in the system has also increased.[17] This shift, unaccounted for in district enrollment projections—and affecting SES-balance requirements in the district—has resulted in some volatility in the controlled choice plan.

In the spring of 2007, the Cambridge school board voted to increase the acceptable range of students receiving free and reduced-price lunch in kindergarten from 10 to 15 percent—a sharp move away from the original goal of reducing the band to 5 percent. Under these revisions, only two seats were left for incoming students receiving free and reduced-price lunch at three of the most popular elementary schools, boxing low-income students out of schools in high demand. So while more leeway may appease the growing number of advantaged families, it also limits the effectiveness of the SES diversity plan.

Implementation of SES Integration in Wake County and Cambridge

Wake County and Cambridge each relied on eligibility for free- or reduced-price lunch (FRL) in the design of an SES integration policy. As such, examining patterns in FRL eligibility since the implementation of the policies is critical. According to this analysis of NCES Common Core of Data enrollment figures, the percentage of students eligible for FRL in Cambridge fluctuated between the years 2001–7, at times reaching nearly half of the district population. From a high of 49 percent in 2004, the percentage of students receiving free and reduced-price lunch declined in recent years, down to 43 percent in 2006. A somewhat different trend emerges in Wake, where the percentage of students receiving free or reduced-price lunch has steadily increased over the past nine years, from 22.3 percent in 1999 to 28.2 percent in 2007.

In tandem with the increase in the share of students receiving free or reduced-price lunch, compliance with the Wake County SES integration plan waned over the years. Recall that the plan stipulated that no school in WCPSS should enroll more than 40 percent of students receiving free and reduced-price lunches. A breakdown of NCES enrollment data showed that during the first year of implementation, more than 80 percent of Wake County's schools were in compliance with the SES diversity policy. Several years later, roughly three-quarters of schools were enrolling fewer than 40 percent of students receiving free and reduced-price lunch. The uptick in noncompliance with the SES diversity plan may have been the result of the demands of swift population growth, along with the rising number of students in poverty. These two factors placed stress on the SES diversity policy, requiring more extensive reassignment of students to maintain balance.

WCPSS's compliance with the SES integration policy had declined even further by 2007–8. Of the 35 schools that fell outside of Wake County's guidelines, more than 15 reported a majority of students receiving free and reduced-price lunch. In one Wake County school, more than 80 percent of the students received free and reduced-price lunch.

Adherence to SES integration follows a different trajectory in Cambridge, where compliance with the policy has been consistently low. In 2002, CPS was one year into the implementation of SES integration, and calculations using NCES data indicated only three schools (18.8 percent) fell within policy guidelines. By 2004, that number had increased to four schools (roughly 31 percent). In order to abide by the +/– 10 percent rule in 2006–7, no fewer than 33 percent and no more than 53 percent of the students enrolled in a Cambridge school should have been eligible for free and reduced-price lunch. Four years after implementation, CPS still encountered difficulty in carrying out its SES diversity policy. Six schools in 2006 reported percentages of students receiving free and reduced-price lunch that fell outside of the 33–53 percent range.

Like Wake County, CPS has struggled to fully implement its SES diversity plan. And while Cambridge's move to increase the band from +/–10 percent of the district's free and reduced-price lunch population to +/–15 percent will improve compliance (just two schools in 2006–7 would have violated the revised SES policy), it may also dilute the effectiveness of the plan.[18]

Racial and Ethnic Enrollment and Balance in Wake County and Cambridge

According to this analysis of NCES data, white student enrollment in Wake County schools decreased from nearly 65 percent of the total student population in 1999 to 56 percent in 2006. The decline in white students coincided with a dramatic rise in the number of Latino students in the district, which nearly tripled from 3,605 in 1999 to 11,179 in 2006. The percentage of African American students in Wake County remained consistent over the first half of the decade, at roughly 28 percent of the population.

These overall enrollment figures have important implications for how racial balance is measured in the district. The following calculations are based on historical guidelines calling for a +/–15 percent black student enrollment in the district, with an important update recognizing that Latino students are currently underserved by the school system (based on district test scores and graduation rates). Numbers related to the racial balance of Wake County's schools were thus derived using a 15 percent range above and below the district's combined average number of African American and Hispanic students—approximately 30 percent in 1999 and increasing to about 38 percent in 2006.

NCES data shows that, in 1999, one in three schools was not racially balanced under the former desegregation plan. Under this race-based desegregation plan, nearly a quarter of underrepresented students in 1999 attended schools with high concentrations of minority students (e.g., above 45 percent), while just 6 percent went to schools with low concentrations of minorities (below 15 percent).

How has racial balance in Wake County schools been impacted by the SES diversity plan? This analysis suggests that the implementation of SES integration in Wake County schools coincided with deepening racial segregation. Data for the school years 1980–99 was obtained from a secondary source and is based on the historical 15–45 percent rule around the districtwide black student population. During the years of the racial desegregation plan, nearly 91 percent of schools were in compliance in 1990–91, falling to about 65 percent in 1999, the year before SES integration was implemented. This pattern may reflect several court decisions in the 1990s curtailing the reach of desegregation plans, removing pressure on the district to enforce strict adherence to its race-based policy. Compliance with the 15–45 percent rule declined further under SES integration, to around 58 percent in 2006.

Another important way to think about compliance with the previous 15–45 rule is to consider school-level racial balance starting in 1999 as measured by the +/−15 percent calculation around the district's yearly underrepresented minority enrollment percentage (to include Latino students). Racial balance under both measures has steadily declined since the implementation of SES integration. In 2006, roughly two out of five schools in Wake County were no longer considered racially balanced—regardless of the measure used.

Unlike Wake County's striking demographic changes, CPS experienced few shifts in its racial and ethnic makeup over the four years studied. NCES enrollment data indicates that the percentage of African American students rose slightly, from 35.6 percent in 2001 to 37.8 percent in 2006. The white student population declined accordingly, but few other notable changes in racial and ethnic composition occurred. Asian students continued to make up a fairly large share of Cambridge's student population—over 10 percent—and Latino students comprised nearly 15 percent of the student population.

The original desegregation plan in CPS contained guidelines calling for a +/− 10 percent school-level minority population range around the district average of African American students. Based on this policy, Cambridge displays a more prominent version of the WCPSS pattern of noncompliance with racial desegregation in the late 1990s. By 2001, the year prior to the implementation of SES diversity, little more than half of the district's schools were racially balanced. Fast forward to 2006, when the percentage of schools considered racially balanced (around the combined percentage of black and Latino students) actually increased slightly, to 57.1 percent. Yet this statistic obscures the fact that underserved minority students in CPS are attending racially imbalanced schools at higher rates under the new SES diversity plan. The year prior to implementation of SES integration, 12 percent of black and Latino students were attending schools that hovered above the upper racial balance bound (more than 60 percent of school enrollment comprised underrepresented minorities). In 2006, nearly 18 percent were attending such schools. Thus, underrepresented students of color became more likely to attend minority segregated schools under the SES diversity plan.

These numbers indicate an interesting pattern: while the SES plan in Cambridge has corresponded with slightly more racial balance overall (keeping in mind that compliance was low prior to implementation), it is also associated with an increase in more heavily nonwhite schools.

Wake County and Cambridge Student Achievement under SES Diversity Plans

Data from the North Carolina State Department of Education provide the percentages of students by subgroup who passed both the math and reading tests for North Carolina's end-of-grade assessments. Across all years studied, from 2001–8, low-income Wake County students perform just slightly higher on average than their statewide counterparts on these assessments. North Carolina began publicly disaggregating data for low-income students by district and state in the early 2000s, making possible only a comparison of achievement for Wake's FRL-eligible students to their peers statewide *after* SES integration began. However, despite the lack of a statewide benchmark before and after implementation of the SES plan, it should be noted that FRL-eligible students in Wake County have made consistent pass-rate improvements on the statewide assessments over the past 11 years (with the exception of a steep decline for all students following a shift in testing instruments). These gains were documented before SES integration was adopted, but they increased more substantially (relative to other subgroups in the district) after implementation.[19]

With the exception of economically disadvantaged students, all other subgroups, including non-low-income students, white, black, Latino, Asian, American Indian, and multiracial students in Wake County outperform their counterparts statewide. And for the most part, over the past decade students classified as limited English proficient (LEP) have scored better than state averages for their subgroup, though they perform lower than other groups of students in the district.

Standardized test scores, of course, are not the only way to measure student performance. Graduation rates signal a school district's success in shepherding all students through the K–12 system. According to WCPSS, the district's graduation rates are higher than the state average for all racial and ethnic groups with the exception of Hispanic and American Indian students. Low-income WCPSS students, however, graduate high school at a slightly lower rate than the state average. LEP students in Wake County also graduate at lower rates than their counterparts statewide.

Broadly, findings from Wake County suggest that the district's transition to SES integration led to a steady decrease in racial balance at the school level and has not necessarily been associated with higher achievement for low-income students when compared to their statewide peers. However, other subgroups are performing above the state average in WCPSS, and, at the district level, FRL-eligible students have made important gains on the end-of-grade assessments.

In contrast to Wake, patterns indicate CPS has experienced minor success in improving socioeconomic and racial balance within its schools. The divergence extends to student-achievement data, which for CPS looks fairly promising.

Massachusetts State Department of Education results from the district's third-grade reading assessment are moderately high across all subgroups. With the exception of African American students in CPS, all racial and ethnic groups outperform their statewide counterparts in 2007–8. Low-income students in the district, however, scored even with or slightly below other low-income Massachusetts students on the reading and math assessments. A similar, albeit somewhat puzzling situation—with racial or ethnic subgroups outperforming state peers while low-income students fall even or just below the statewide average—also held true in Wake County. However, by eighth grade, nearly all subgroups of students in CPS far exceed state averages in

English language arts. Low-income students in CPS have a Composite Performance Index — an average test score measure for each subgroup — of 87 percent, compared to roughly 79 percent for state low-income students. The results on the mathematics portion of the test are similar, though the difference between district and state percentages is not as striking.

On the whole, these scores provide a snapshot of clear gains for low-income students in CPS. In terms of a before-and-after analysis of SES integration and test scores, it should be noted that achievement results in Massachusetts are difficult to compare longitudinally due to shifting math proficiency standards and the adoption of a composite score indicator.

All students in CPS are likely to graduate, with the district boasting much higher rates than state averages. For example, almost 90 percent of low-income students in CPS graduated in 2008, compared to approximately 65 percent of low-income students in the state. Still, these rates are associated with students educated under a combination of the racial desegregation plan and the SES diversity policy and should be watched closely over the coming years as students graduate who are solely products of the SES plan.

Cambridge Public Schools, then, reveals a complex portrait of a school system striving to implement its controlled choice plan in a changing context. Racial balance has improved by some measures; yet more underserved minority students in the district are attending racially isolated schools under SES integration. And while achievement results from the district are promising, they also indicate that low-income students in the early grades are performing less well than their counterparts statewide.

Discussion

Both Cambridge and Wake provide a nuanced portrait of the design of choice-based SES integration in districts still containing racially and socioeconomically diverse populations. Wake County's structure as a metropolitan school district has helped promote student diversity.[20] The vibrant racial and class diversity of Cambridge Public Schools can be attributed to its small size, geographic location, mixed-income housing, and world-class universities. Within these promising contexts for school racial diversity by way of SES integration, how have the districts fared under two different approaches to implementation?

Enrollment and achievement data from Wake County and Cambridge yielded a variety of thought-provoking findings. Numbers indicate that both districts are struggling to effectively put their SES integration policies into operation, making it impossible to ascertain what racial balance and student achievement might look like with full compliance.

Figures from the partially realized policies suggest, however, that SES integration corresponded with a decline in racial balance in Wake County and decreased levels of balance for black and Latino students in Cambridge. These findings could be explained both by the difficulty Wake County and Cambridge experience in complying with their SES integration policies and their reliance on eligibility for free and reduced-price lunch as a measure of poverty.

How school districts define poverty is a subject that engenders substantial debate. Most experts agree that the United States radically underestimates poverty in general, with the current definition of poverty based on an economist's assessment of the price of food for a family of three in 1960.[21] Compared with the definition of poverty in Europe—half of the average family's income—American estimates are considered extremely low. In terms of schools, students are considered eligible for free and reduced-price lunch if family income falls within a set of guidelines established yearly by the U.S. Department of Agriculture (USDA). For 2007–8, the federal poverty level for a family of three was $17,170. To qualify for reduced-price meals, a family of three would have to fall within 185 percent of the poverty level, with an annual income at or below $31,765. To receive free meals, the same family of three's annual income must be within 130 percent of the federal poverty level, or $26,845.[22] These figures are significant, as they demonstrate the underestimation of poverty both in general and for children in particular.

The inaccuracy of free and reduced-price lunch as a measure is highlighted by the fact that it draws a rather arbitrary line in the sand. What of the children whose families fall within 186 percent of the poverty line? Are they so much better off than the students in the bracket just beneath them who do qualify? The abrupt cutoff results in just two groups of children—those who are eligible to receive free and reduced-price lunch and those who are not.[23] The ineligible group is comprised of students from vastly different socioeconomic classes, from those just above the poverty line to the very wealthy.

A preferable alternative to classifying children as one or the other—rich or poor—would be the use of family-income reports that allow districts to distinguish among a range of student socioeconomic backgrounds. Neighborhood characteristics offer another way to think about poverty. For example, Berkeley Unified School District in California uses Census data (though these data become outdated between Census years) to determine parent income and education levels in a given geographic area, and the district assigns students to schools partly based on that socioeconomic information—along with racial and ethnic background and language and disability status.[24] Such policies provide a more nuanced picture of income and diversity.

Evidence from these two districts also suggests that SES diversity plans are subject to considerable political pressure. Recent political and policy-related changes have been reported in both Cambridge and Wake County—indeed, in the latter, the continuation of the policy looks doubtful (see Richard Kahlenberg's essay in this book). Further research will be vital in both settings to ascertain how racial balance is affected by the modification or abandonment of these plans.

In terms of academic performance, low-income students in both Wake County and Cambridge are performing, on average, slightly lower than their state counterparts—belying prior studies linking poverty deconcentration with improved student achievement. These figures may be due to the partially realized nature of SES integration in each district, in addition to school-level factors that undermine the policy, including ability grouping and tracking. A 2009 study of socioeconomic integration provides support for the notion that tracking is an issue in SES diversity plans. Data from the National Longitudinal Study of Adolescent Health revealed that low-income students were more likely to be enrolled in lower-level math and science courses when they attended schools predominated by middle- and upper-class students.[25]

In the wake of the PICS decision and mounting judicial willingness to grant unitary status, a tendency for districts to disassemble their desegregation plans altogether raises concerns that many school systems around the country will experience rapid resegregation.[26] On the whole, reports from districts using income-based student assignment plans indicate that SES integration works better in some places than in others—depending on the demographic context of the area, political will, the measure and tolerance of student poverty levels, and whether district implementation policies help combat residential segregation.[27] While findings from this study and others indicate that SES integration cannot ensure the level of racial diversity school districts maintained under desegregation orders that directly considered race, it is important to understand that these efforts are far superior to the absence of any alternative plan.

NOTES

1. See Justice Anthony Kennedy's concurring opinion in *Parents Involved in Community Schools v. Seattle School District No. 1*, 551 U.S. 701 (2007).

2. See, generally, R. Kahlenberg, *All Together Now: Creating Middle-Class Schools through Public School Choice* (Washington, DC: Brookings Institution Press, 2001);

R. Kahlenberg, *Rescuing Brown v. Board of Education: Profiles of Twelve School Districts Pursuing Socioeconomic School Integration* (Washington, DC: Century Foundation, 2007); A. Ciolfi and J. Ryan, "Socioeconomic Integration: It's Legal and It Makes Sense," *Education Week*, 14 June 2008.

3. G. Orfield, *Reviving the Goal of an Integrated Society: A 21st Century Challenge* (Los Angeles: Civil Rights Project/Projecto Derechos Civiles at UCLA, 2009); X. Briggs, "Social Capital and Segregation in the United States," in *Desegregating the City: Ghettos, Enclaves, and Inequality*, edited by D. P. Valardy (Albany: SUNY Press, 2005), 245–55; D. Massey, "Origins of Economic Disparities: The Historical Role of Housing Segregation," in *Segregation: The Rising Costs for America*, edited by J. H. Carr and N. K. Kutty (New York: Routledge, 2008), 39–80.

4. Statement Submitted by 553 Social Scientists, in *Parents Involved in Community Schools v. Seattle School District No. 1*, No. 05-908 (2007); S. Reardon, J. T. Yun, and M. Kurlaender, "Implications of Income-Based School Assignment Policies for Racial School Segregation," *Educational Evaluation and Policy Analysis* 28, no. 1 (2006): 49–75.

5. S. Flinspach and K. Banks, "Moving beyond Race: Socioeconomic Diversity as a Race-Neutral Approach to Desegregation in the Wake County Schools," in *School Resegregation: Must the South Turn Back?*, edited by J. Boger and G. Orfield (Chapel Hill: University of North Carolina Press, 2005), 261–80.

6. Cambridge Public Schools, "CPS Enrollment at a Ten Year High," 26 October 2007, http://www.cpsd.us/newsstory.cfm?instance_id=438 (accessed 15 August 2009).

7. Cambridge Public Schools, *Cambridge Controlled Choice Plan* (2001), http://www.cpsd.us/Web/PubInfo/ControlledChoice.pdf (accessed 15 August 2009).

8. C. Rossell and C. Glenn, "The Cambridge Controlled Choice Plan," *Urban Review* 20, no. 2 (1988): 75–94.

9. Cambridge Public Schools, *Cambridge Controlled Choice Plan*.

10. Ibid.

11. Wake County Public School System, *Student Assignment Process* (2009), http://www.wcpss.net/growth-management/student-assign-process.html (accessed 15 August 2009).

12. Wake County Public School System, Wake County School Board Policy 6204.

13. R. Christensen, "Is Decades-Long Effort for Diversity Over?," *Raleigh News and Observer*, 8 October 2009, http://www.newsobserver.com/politics/columnists_blogs/christensen/story/131503.html (accessed 8 October 2009).

14. D. Bowens and A. Owens, "Tensions Rise at Wake School Board Meeting; 19 Arrested," *Raleigh News and Observer*, 20 July 2010, http://www.wral.com/news/education/story/7999211/ (accessed 12 August 2010).

15. "Wake Schools Seek Feedback on New Assignment," *Raleigh News and Observer*, 30 July 2010, http://www.wral.com/news/education/story/8064429/ (accessed 12 August 2010).

16. A. Owens, "Raleigh to Review Wake Student Assignment Policy," *Raleigh News and Observer*, 24 June 2010, http://www.wral.com/news/education/story/7847772/ (accessed 12 August 2010).

17. J. A. O'Leary, "Wealthier Influx Shuffles Classroom Seats," *Boston Globe*, 15 March 2007, http://www.boston.com/news/local/articles/2007/03/18/a_wealthier_influx_shuffles_classroom_seats/ (accessed 16 March 2008).

18. Reardon, Yun, and Kurlaender, "Implications of Income-Based School Assignment Policies."

19. Flinspach and Banks, "Moving beyond Race," 275; North Carolina State Department of Education, District Report Cards at http://www.ncreportcards.org.

20. Flinspach and Banks, "Moving beyond Race."

21. L. Uchitelle, "How to Define Poverty? Let Us Count the Ways," *New York Times*, 26 May 2001, http://www.nytimes.com/2001/05/26/arts/how-to-define-poverty-let-us-count-the-ways.html (accessed 15 August 2009).

22. Numbers were obtained from the Income Eligibility Guidelines, http://www.fns.usda.gov/cnd/Governance/notices/iegs/IEGs07-08.pdf, 3.

23. Statement Submitted by 553 Social Scientists, in *Parents Involved in Community Schools v. Seattle School District No. 1*, No. 05-908, App. (2007), 46. A recent analysis also points toward an important distinction in academic performance between students who qualify for free lunches and those who qualify for reduced-price lunches, suggesting that outcomes and experiences are uneven across different levels of relative student poverty ("Measuring Poverty in Education Policy Research," *School Finance 101*, 25 March 2011, http://schoolfinance101.wordpress.com/2011/03/25/measuring-poverty-in-education-policy-research/ (accessed 1 April 2011).

24. L. Chavez and E. Frankenberg, *Integration Defended: Berkeley Unified's Strategy to Maintain School Diversity* (Los Angeles: Civil Rights Project/Proyecto Derechos Civiles at UCLA, 2009).

25. R. Crosnoe, "Low-Income Students and the Socioeconomic Composition of Public High Schools," *American Sociological Review* 74, no. 5 (2009): 705–30.

26. G. Orfield and C. Lee, *Historic Reversals, Accelerating Resegregation, and the Need for New Integration Strategies* (Los Angeles: Civil Rights Project/Proyecto Derechos Civiles at UCLA, 2007).

27. Statement Submitted by 553 Social Scientists (2006); Reardon, Yun, and Kurlaender, "Implications of Income-Based School Assignment Policies."

SHENEKA WILLIAMS & ERICA FRANKENBERG

Using Geography to Further Racial Integration

In a recent decision regarding the use of voluntary race-conscious school as-signment policies in Seattle, Washington, and Louisville, Kentucky, the U.S. Supreme Court narrowly struck down the practice of using individual stu-dents' race in the school assignment process.[1] The Court's decision was deeply fractured, lengthy, and has led to considerable confusion for school districts that believe maintaining diverse schools is an important part of their educa-tional mission. The plurality opinion, written by Chief Justice John Roberts, prohibited the individual, race-conscious aspect of the districts' student as-signment policies. Louisville's plan was considered such because one of the factors determining whether students' transfers were granted was based on how the students' race or ethnicity would contribute to the racial composi-tion of the schools from which they were leaving and transferring. Roberts re-ferred to such plans as "extreme" because they involved "classifying individual students on the basis of their race and discriminating among them on that basis."[2] While Roberts's plurality opinion suggested that any race-conscious means were legally suspect, Justice Anthony Kennedy left the door slightly ajar by listing some race-conscious and race-neutral methods that he believed were permissible. School districts, Kennedy wrote, should only resort to race-conscious measures after they had "exhausted" all other efforts to desegregate. In sum, the Court agreed with the aims of the school districts but disagreed with means they used to achieve them. While Kennedy's opinion provides critically needed guidance about what integration options remain available to districts, there remains considerable confusion about what his guidance means practically and when race-conscious methods may be legal or when race-neutral measures may be effective.[3]

School districts have long used attendance zones to determine where stu-dents attend schools, regardless of whether the district intended to create di-verse schools or not. For districts seeking diverse schools, attendance bound-aries or zones were drawn around neighborhoods to try to create a deliberate mix of students from different racial or ethnic backgrounds within each zone.

Zoning was endorsed by the Court in its *Swann* decision in 1971 as one way to desegregate schools. In fact, the Court said that districts with deep residential segregation could even draw noncontiguous zones, or those in which two separate areas that are not adjacent to one another are assigned to the same school, in order to desegregate schools.[4]

Louisville's voluntary integration efforts included the use of attendance zones to promote racial diversity and the Court's decision did not affect the legality of such efforts.[5] In fact, Kennedy explicitly endorsed zoning, writing, "School boards may pursue the goal of bringing together students of diverse backgrounds and races through other means, including . . . drawing attendance zones with general recognition of the demographics of neighborhoods."[6] This essay examines the use of "small-scale geography"—the use of geography to join small groups of students for assignment purposes, a measure larger than an individual student but less expansive than geographical zoning—in two districts to pursue diversity in student assignment plans.

Since the decision in *Parents Involved in Community Schools v. Seattle School District No. 1* (PICS, 2007), districts that previously used race as the sole factor in student assignment have redesigned their policies to comply with the Court's decision. While some districts have bypassed the use of race, other districts consider the race or ethnicity of students in addition to other factors, such as parental education, student achievement, and small-scale geography. Such plans, which use variations of geography and population characteristics (e.g., differing combinations of income, race, achievement, and parental education), are implemented in Wake County, North Carolina, and Berkeley, California. We examine how Wake County manages nodes in student assignment, and we investigate how Berkeley utilizes more than 440 planning areas, each of which are four to eight blocks in size, in its integration efforts. While both are geographically based, the two districts differ in how they apply the tools for student assignment purposes.[7] We describe the small-scale use of geography, as employed in both districts' student assignment policies, as an approach for school districts to consider.

Wake County Public School System

The Wake County Public School System (WCPSS) is the 18th-largest district in the nation. With an enrollment of 140,000 students for the 2009–10 school year,[8] Wake County's commitment to diversity has been long-standing. WCPSS was formed in 1976 by a merger between the greater Wake County system, which was majority white, and the Raleigh City Schools, which were predominantly African American. The superintendent at the time, John Murphy, hired a consultant to devise a plan that would ensure desegregation in the district's schools. Although the board struck down the plan, it held on to a useful tool that emanated from the plan—the node. Defined as a group of households in the same geographic area, the node was used as the primary tool for ensuring racial integration.

Wake began considering moving toward a class-based definition of diversity in the late 1990s, when its board reviewed research showing the strong link between family income and achievement.[9] It became official on 10 January 2000, when the Wake County Board of Education officially altered its student assignment policy, shifting from race-based to socioeconomic and performance-based criteria. This move is generally acknowledged as a reaction to a decision by the Fourth Circuit Court of Appeals ending the court-ordered racial desegregation plan in another large, urban North Carolina school district, Charlotte-Mecklenburg. This move also placed Wake as one of the first large school districts to balance the enrollment of students between schools without explicitly considering race. As a result, this shift in policy changed the primary purpose of using the node for student assignment from racial balance to balance that includes socioeconomic status and student achievement. After 2000 geographic nodes were useful in ensuring that (1) no more than 40 percent of a school's student body will be eligible for free or reduced-price lunch and (2) no more than 25 percent of a school's population will read below grade level (averaged over two years).

Geographic Nodes and Student Assignment
Node characteristics provide the basis for student assignment in Wake County schools. There are 1,321 nodes in Wake County, with each node designated to one elementary, one middle, and one high school. The ideal size for a node is 300 students or fewer. This size, according to district officials, makes it manageable to create balance among schools. When a node exceeds 300 students, it is split along existing boundaries such as railroads, major roads, and waterways.

According to interviews with district officials, a database contains child nutrition data, each student's address and node association, and a variety of other information. Wake calculates child nutrition information in the aggregate, that is, the percentage of elementary students in each node who are approved to receive free or reduced-price lunch. WCPSS does not specify percentages above 95 or below 5. This is done to ensure that the participation or nonparticipation of a particular student cannot be determined simply by knowing the node in which the student resides. Additionally, no node is 100 percent low-income or 0 percent low-income.

Wake's use of geographic nodes has brought success in the socioeconomic integration of its schools, but it should be noted that racial isolation has increased in a number of schools.[10]

Berkeley Unified School District

Berkeley Unified School District (BUSD) differs from Wake County in many ways, though the two districts share a commitment to voluntarily implementing integration plans. Berkeley is a much smaller district, with around 9,000 students, and has maintained a steady enrollment since the early part of this decade. By 2008–9, student enrollment had transitioned from a primarily black-white district in the 1960s to one characterized by multiracial diversity: it is now 31 percent white, 26 percent black, 17 percent Latino, and 8 percent Asian (the remaining students identified as more than one race or did not specify). The district has 11 elementary schools, 3 middle schools, and 1 high school.

Like WCPSS, BUSD has a long history of desegregation efforts. Though BUSD has pursued integration for a long time, its use of small geographies to accomplish integration is quite recent. It is a district with deep residential segregation by race, which has been the case for decades. In fact, the district's first major desegregation plan in the 1960s involved extensive cross-district busing, mandatory assignment, and pairing of schools to integrate black students who lived in the western part of the city, while whites lived in the east. In the mid-1990s, faced in part with white students opting out of the district when they were to be bused to schools on the west side, the district switched to a controlled-choice plan. The district was divided into three zones that cut diagonally across the district, with each containing part of the low-income, minority "flats" area in the southwest and the wealthy, white "hills" area in the northeast part of the district. The aim in drawing the zones was to create three sections that had similar school capacities, size of student enrollment, and racial and ethnic composition. The plan gave preference to siblings and residence within the school's zones. BUSD also considered a student's race and ethnicity in determining whether to assign a student to a requested school to ensure that no school deviated substantially from the district's racial and ethnic composition.

The district's commitment to maintaining integrated schools despite neighborhood segregation remained constant as the legal and educational climate shifted. Berkeley's current integration plan was implemented for the 2004–5 school year and is similar to its prior plan but with one notable change: it substitutes the consideration of diversity of a geographic planning area for the consideration of a student's race and ethnicity. The goal of the current integration plan is to diversify schools by parental education, household income, *and* race and ethnicity.[11]

BUSD's plan uses two levels of geography to assign students and pursue its goal of diversity. The district has used planning areas for administrative purposes since 1990. The district is divided into 445 planning areas, which are approximately four to eight blocks in size. This means that an average planning area would have approximately 20 BUSD students. The district provides detailed analysis of different characteristics (family income and adults' educational attainment, etc.) by planning area on its website. The zones that were first used for the controlled-choice plan, for example, aligned along planning area lines. Since the district had been using these for 10 years, the use of planning areas for the purpose of the integration plan essentially just added another use to an existing concept. The district software was already developed and students had been geographically coded to their planning area. The district considers sibling preference first and then gives students who live in the school's zone priority over students who live outside it. For the latter two categories, the student's diversity code (as assigned by planning area) is considered to ensure that each school has a mix of students from each category.

In Berkeley as in Wake County, diversity is conceptualized as including more than just race. BUSD's plan classifies residents according to three characteristics—family income, adults' educational attainment, and racial composition of BUSD students—using BUSD and Census data to assign a diversity code of 1, 2, or 3 to each planning area. Values of "1" indicate low-income households, low educational attainment, and higher proportions of students of color. A diversity-code value of "3" indicates the opposite. Systemwide, the most students live in planning areas with a diversity code of 1 and the fewest in planning areas with a diversity code of 3, though this varies slightly between the three zones. Every student in a particular planning area has the same diversity-code value regardless of the student's own race, family income, or parents' educational attainment. The goal of BUSD's integration policy is to have similar distributions of diversity codes at each school.

In comparison to BUSD schools in 2003–4, the year before the system switched to a student assignment plan using planning areas, elementary

TABLE 12.1. *Deviation from Systemwide Racial and Economic Composition in* BUSD *among Elementary and Middle Schools*

2008–2009

	Asian/ Pacific Islander	Black	Latino	White	Low-income (2007–8)
Composition across all schools	7.6%	18.4%	21.5%	30.4%	48.0%
# Schools whose percentage deviates 10% or more	0	1	2	0	2
# Schools whose percentage deviates 5–10%	1	4	7	1	6

2003–2004

	Asian/ Pacific Islander	Black	Latino	White	Low-income
Composition across all schools	8.1%	29.7%	19.1%	25.6%	60.7%
# Schools whose percentage deviates 10% or more	1	1	3	0	6
# Schools whose percentage deviates 5–10%	1	5	4	6	2

Note: There are 11 elementary schools in BUSD; data from CDE Dataquest Tool and NCES Common Core of Data. American Indians/Alaskan Natives are 0.3% of the district enrollment, and those that gave either multiple responses or no responses at all account for 20.9% of elementary students.

schools in 2008–9 are *more* balanced for students of all racial and ethnic backgrounds (see table 12.1). The current plan seems to be considerably better than the prior one at distributing white students in particular across district elementary schools. The same number of schools (8 of 11) deviate at least 5 percent from the systemwide percentage of low-income elementary students, but most of the schools in 2003–4 deviated to a greater extent than in 2008–9. At least in the years examined, the plan using diversity of students' planning areas seems more successful at creating evenly balanced schools.

Development of Desegregation Efforts

BUSD's desegregation efforts have been challenged under state law several times. In 1996, California voters passed Proposition 209, which forbids governmental preference on the basis of race or ethnicity. In 2003, a conservative legal foundation challenged Berkeley's desegregation plan. While the judge found the district's plan to be constitutional in April 2004, the district had decided before the decision was issued to implement its new plan using planning areas instead of individual race or ethnicity. The lawsuit revived earlier discussion about modifying the student assignment plan, and the new plan was adopted in January 2004, despite the protest by some community members that the use of race was being weakened.

The student assignment plan utilized by BUSD exemplifies a plausible option after the PICS decision. Like Wake County, it uses a geography-based student assignment method, but one that takes account of the racial composition of an area, not the race or ethnicity of individual students. In particular, Berkeley's plan falls within the options listed in Justice Kennedy's opinion because it seeks to advance diversity and reduce racial and socioeconomic isolation throughout the district's elementary schools without considering the race, ethnicity, or socioeconomic status of individual students. In fact, in 2009 the California Supreme Court declined to review a unanimous appellate court decision affirming the legality of the current Berkeley plan with regard to Proposition 209. The unanimous decision held that Berkeley's plan did not violate Proposition 209 because "the challenged policy does not use racial classifications; in fact, it does not consider an individual student's race at all when assigning the student to a school."[12]

Similarities and Differences in Wake's and Berkeley's Plans

Both Wake County schools and the Berkeley school district have been front-runners in using geography to integrate their school districts. Although the ways the districts implement geography differ, their ultimate goal is the same. Wake, for instance, first began using nodes when two segregated county school systems joined to form one integrated system. Nodes, at that time, aided district officials in creating racial balance in the county's schools. Understanding the basic makeup of a node ensured that neither black nor white students were racially isolated in any one school. Currently, nodes maintain balance in Wake schools in terms of social class and achievement of their students.

Berkeley's use of geography in school integration efforts dates back to 1990 and its use of geography in considering diversity to 2004. Geography also provides information about the characteristics of a small group of students—racial composition along with average adult educational attainment and income—that is broader than the individual student. The size of the geographical units and the number of them differ considerably: Berkeley's 445 planning areas include approximately 20 students each, whereas Wake's 1,361 nodes include approximately 300 students each. Wake's nodes often split due to rapid population growth in the district, whereas Berkeley's enrollment has remained relatively constant.

Recommendations for Districts Post-*PICS*

As we examine and consider new directions in the aftermath of *PICS*, it is clear that districts that have assigned students based solely on an individual student's race must seek alternatives. Some districts will choose to not use race at all, while others will use race in combination with other factors.[13] wcpss and busd are two districts that have developed alternatives that are plausible examples for other districts to follow. In both districts, student assignment decisions are contingent on consideration of the characteristics of the node or planning area, and whites or nonwhites alike in each "unit" are treated in the same manner. The districts thus comply with *PICS* while also pursuing integration.

Given the existing high levels of residential segregation, approaches to school integration through geography may seem counterintuitive. These examples, however, suggest that the scale of geography may be an important consideration in devising either race-conscious or race-neutral integration plans that are effective and constitutional. Further, with technological advances in understanding current and future population projections, school districts should have a wealth of information on district characteristics that will allow them to simulate different geographical scenarios to evaluate their effect on diversity and school capacity. In considering different alternatives, districts could consider partnering with local universities to draw on demographic or educational experts: Berkeley's plan was developed, in part, through the suggestions of students from a graduate school seminar.

Berkeley's example demonstrates that this approach can also accommodate family input in the choice of schools. Wake County's plan ensures that students who live very near to one another (i.e., in the same neighborhood) will be assigned to the same school, allowing students to maintain a small cohort moving through the grade levels and providing continuity. In other words, districts can pursue multiple educational goals using this strategy *and* achieve integrated schools that comply with the Court's restrictions.

NOTES

1. *Parents Involved in Community Schools v. Seattle School District No. 1*, 127 S. Ct. 2738 (2007).

2. Id. at 2767.

3. J. Ryan, "The Supreme Court and Voluntary Integration," *Harvard Law Review* 121 (2007): 131–57.

4. *Swann v. Charlotte-Mecklenburg Board of Education*, 402 U.S. 1 (1971).

5. The monitor in San Francisco's desegregation case suggested that the lack of inclusion of geography as a factor in its multifactor diversity index blunted its success. S. Biegel, "Court-Mandated Education Reform: The San Francisco Experience and the Shaping of Educational Policy after *Seattle-Louisville* and *Brian Ho v. SFUSD*," *Stanford Journal of Civil Rights and Civil Liberties* 4 (2008): 159–213.

6. *Parents Involved*, 2007 at 2792.

7. At the time this book went to press, Wake County was in the process of changing its student assignment system, but no new policy had been adopted.

8. http://www.wcpss.net (accessed 25 July 2009).

9. G. Grant, *Hope and Despair in the American City* (Cambridge: Harvard University Press, 2009).

10. See Siegel-Hawley essay.

11. For a more extensive discussion of Berkeley's integration efforts, see L. Chavez and E. Frankenberg, *Integration Defended: Berkeley Unified's Strategy to Maintain School Diversity* (Los Angeles: Civil Rights Project/Proyecto Derechos Civiles at UCLA, 2009).

12. *American Civil Rights Foundation v. Berkeley Unified School District*, Cal. Rptr.3d. WL 678992 (2009), 1.

13. Louisville, Kentucky, implemented a geography-based student assignment system that considers the racial composition, educational attainment, and income of the neighborhoods students live in for elementary schools beginning in 2009–10 for entering first graders.

Magnet Schools, MSAP, and New Opportunities to Promote Diversity

Magnet schools are public schools designed to attract parents and students through specialized curricular themes or instructional methods. Unlike traditional public schools that operate with student enrollment linked to specific neighborhood attendance zones, magnet schools enroll students from a wide array of neighborhoods across a school district in order to produce a racially diverse school population. Enrollment is typically managed through a student lottery. Accepted by federal courts in the 1970s as a tool for desegregation, magnet schools have gained popularity over the past several decades as a viable school choice program in desegregation lawsuits and in voluntary efforts to desegregate school districts. Today, the total number of magnet schools is between 2,800 and 3,000 across 31 states, with an estimated total enrollment of over 2 million students, more than double the number of students enrolled in charter schools.[1]

Federal aid for the development and operation of magnet schools was legislated in 1976 as an amendment to the Emergency School Aid Act and was designed to provide an additional tool (others being redrawn attendance zones and crosstown busing) for districts attempting to desegregate their schools. The Magnet Schools Assistance Program (MSAP) was established in 1984 to explicitly endorse magnet schools as a strategy that districts could invoke to further desegregation aims with the imprimatur to expand parental choice in education.

The legal and policy landscapes have shifted dramatically since the 1980s and early 1990s, when the level of interest and investment in magnet schools as a keystone to districtwide desegregation plans peaked.[2] An array of new policy priorities and legislative purposes attached to MSAP has diluted the founding emphasis of the program on furthering "the elimination, reduction, or prevention of minority group isolation."[3] Today, MSAP grantee obligations encompass broad federal mandates designed to support innovative classroom programs and teacher practices, promote systemic reform, and enable all students to meet challenging academic standards. While these new priorities may be linked to measurable student outcomes and monitored school progress, we argue that the desegregation aims of MSAP stand as scaffolding to support these related academic goals. One thing is clear: these goals must be reclaimed to provide a new pivot point for attaining educational equity, racial diversity, *and* strong student performance.

This essay is designed to amplify a set of new opportunities for educators, school administrators, and scholars to reshape the practical aims and strategic advantages envisioned under MSAP. This essay establishes a framework for policy makers to utilize MSAP to achieve racial and socioeconomic diversity across urban school districts in the aftermath of recent court decisions limiting the use of race in school desegregation plans.[4]

We suggest that magnet schools should continue to play an important role in the policy discourse and priorities linked to desegregation, and that desegregation efforts should not be decoupled from debates around educational equity and excellence. Finally, we argue that MSAP remains a viable and potentially valuable strategy to further desegregation goals, and we outline a set of policy recommendations pegged to this purpose.

Changing Course and Consequence
A Blueprint for New Priorities under MSAP

As a number of scholars have noted recently, the expansion of mandates under MSAP, coupled with the changing demographics of school districts, represent an array of "missed opportunities"[5] that undercut magnet schools as an effective and efficient mechanism for school desegregation. To improve equity and access, policy makers must reform admission and outreach policies that now disenfranchise particular groups, including families who speak a language other than English, low-income families, and educationally disadvantaged students.[6] Free and reliable transportation to all magnet schools, multiple media outlets for information dissemination that reach all socioeconomic and cultural groups, and new admission policies that take account of interdistrict racial and socioeconomic segregation[7] anchor a framework for new MSAP policies that pinpoint school desegregation as the mechanism for social and academic excellence.[8] We describe these new policy directions in the sections that follow.

Interdistrict Workplace Magnet Schools

Over the past two decades, corporate-sponsored elementary schools have been established in dozens of workplaces, including the corporate headquarters of Ryder Trucks and Radisson Hotels and the sprawling campuses of Mt. Sinai Medical Center and Agilent Technologies.[9] These arrangements typically require corporate partners to provide the facility and assume full responsibility for maintaining it; school districts provide the staff and assume the entire responsibility for instruction. Before- and after-school childcare is provided to match the work schedules of the employees with children. These public "schools of choice" give parents employed by the corporation the option to select the workplace as their "neighborhood" school.

Interdistrict workplace magnet schools address the issues of racial isolation that increasingly undercuts the aims of MSAP and magnet school designers. Over the past twenty years, demographic shifts in urban and suburban school districts have shaped a new reality: school segregation is far more intense *between* districts than within them.[10] Workplace magnet schools address these demographic conditions by capturing the racial and socioeconomic diversity found *across* school district lines that coalesces in hospitals, universities, large service and manufacturing businesses, and in downtown "neighborhoods." MSAP could prioritize funding schools-at-the-workplace to underscore the value and vision found in merging educational innovation and social diversity through interdistrict arrangements.

The Downtown Magnet School in Des Moines, Iowa, illustrates this model. The attendance zone for the magnet school is defined by parents' employment status at any downtown Des Moines business. The Downtown School began in 1993 in collaboration with a consortium of downtown businesses rather than a single employer. This K–6 school serves 270 children and reflects the diversity of the downtown employee population and the array of nearby school districts: 28 percent of the children are minority (somewhat lower than the Des Moines district average of 37 percent); 25 percent are eligible for free or reduced-price lunch (the Des Moines district average for all students is 55 percent). Admission is based on a lottery. For the past 10 years, the waiting list for the entering class of five-year-olds has numbered over 100 for 32 available slots.

Workplace magnet schools reflect the new American neighborhoods that group "residents" around their place of employment. One compelling interest in workplace magnet schools as a means to achieve diverse student enrollments lies in the degree to which these schools reflect *integration* among social institutions—families, schools, and workplaces. This social webbing produces schools that are racially and socioeconomically diverse—without the legal questions attached to race-conscious admissions policies. Our research on workplace schools[11] suggests that these schools are comprised of families who share similar values about education but reside in various neighborhoods (many of which are racially and socioeconomically distinct) across a city and its school districts. In selecting a magnet school at the workplace, these parents create the natural conditions for value communities[12] established in some private and Catholic schools. In sum, workplace magnet schools pay rich dividends to all participants—teachers and staff, students and their families—in terms of the enhanced communication, trust, and collegiality.

District Information Dissemination Strategies

Moving the location of magnet schools to the workplace involves rethinking the information dissemination strategies of *all* choice arrangements, pegged to the goal of broad and diverse parent buy-in. MSAP could be amended to strengthen and reward a set of new information dissemination priorities for school districts.

For some parents, school choice and information collection processes remain a social activity; parents utilize social networks linked to neighborhoods, places of worship, and children's schools. New research on the central role of work in parents' lives, however, underscores the urgency of exploring how compression on the work lives of parents is creating new patterns of social networks anchored to the workplace and placing new demands on policy makers engaged in information dissemination processes about school choice. Consider this fact: the proportion of families with children under age 18 in which both parents work outside the home rose to 62 percent, continuing an upward trend in employment patterns among two-parent families.[13]

Our recent research indicates that Latino enrollment in Nashville's magnet schools (less than 2 percent) lags well behind the growing Latino student enrollment in the district (14 percent).[14] We argue that district dissemination strategies (focused upon media outlets and the Internet) and Latino parents' social network patterns explain these trends. Unlike Anglo- and African American parents who use personal (informal) and school (formal) information networks, our data indicate that Latino parents learn about magnet schools on their own. These findings reflect patterns of residential and social isolation for many Latinos in Nashville; most arrived in the city within the past five years and are largely unfamiliar with the school system and choice options. English-language barriers only heighten these other obstacles for the Latino community.

We suggest that all parents, but most pointedly Latino parents, would be better served if school districts collaborated with major and midsize employers (e.g., medical centers, universities, manufacturing plants, hotels and restaurant chains, construction companies) to disseminate information to all employees related to school choice options. Half of all respondents in a survey of employees from Fortune 500 companies identified work as "the place where they had the most friends"; only 16 percent identified their neighborhood; just 6 percent indicated a church or temple.[15] Information at the workplace provides a channel-ready means to expand the networks of information about school choice to Latino parents who might otherwise remain disconnected and disenfranchised. MSAP could be an effective lever to jump-start these new information dissemination arrangements.

Universal Choice Requirements

Elsewhere we have suggested that issues of motivation and incentive shape parents' search for information.[16] Under an *option-demand* magnet program, only the parents with the most motivation and ability—those fleeing underachieving schools who know of alternative programs—search broadly and utilize school- and personal-based networks. We have argued for magnet programs within a universal choice model under which all parents much choose a school, inclusive of neighborhood and alternative or magnet schools (adopted by schools systems in Cambridge, Massachusetts, and Montclair, New Jersey, among others).[17] This approach eliminates the two-step process associated with the option-demand model in which parents first must choose to choose, and then select a particular school. The universal choice model imposes on families an obligation to select a school—whether magnet or neighborhood. The federal MSAP could provide incentives for districts to implement this model.

The power to inform parents would theoretically expand under a universal choice model as information regarding magnet schools would need to appear side-by-side in all of a district's information dissemination plans (rather than a special announcement, application, or brochure that could be ignored). The general problem of awareness is perhaps more salient than the more particularized problem of parent search modes. In sum, many parents simply do not know what "magnet" or "charter" means, and as a consequence they choose *not* to choose. Parents' lack of awareness or understanding of magnet schools may confound policy makers interested in diverse applicant pools. In case studies of lower-income families with children enrolled in inner-city schools in Nashville,[18] the overwhelming majority of parents—almost all of whom were familiar with the term "magnet school"—were nonetheless completely unfamiliar with application procedures or admissions policies; almost all parents interviewed thought that district magnet schools were choice schools available exclusively to academically gifted students (in fact, only 3 of the 12 schools are academically selective). The universal choice approach could broaden the pool of applicants among both white and minority families in districts like Nashville and Charlotte now struggling to produce racial balance in magnet schools under an option-demand model.[19] Evidence from the health care sector documents the productive elements that inform and expand the "culture of choice" under a must-choose model.[20] MSAP provides an appropriate and potentially powerful tool to leverage monetary support for districts that pursue universal choice arrangements designed to produce diverse student enrollments.

MSAP–Public Housing Partnerships: A Call for Coordination, Planning, and Leadership

In 1992, Congress enacted the HOPE VI program to overhaul the nation's public housing policy. Since its enactment in 1992, the U.S. Department of Housing and Urban Development (HUD) has awarded 237 HOPE VI grants to 127 cities, a total of $5.8 billion.[21] HOPE VI provides a critical context to "test" mixed-income public housing policy as a lever for racial and socioeconomic integration that merges public housing reform with desegregation aims. Though a small handful of school districts have partnered with local public housing authorities and developers to establish a new school (sometimes a magnet) or "reform" an existing one to attract a mixed-income population to a neighborhood's HOPE VI project, evidence suggests few changes if any in the sociodemographics of the neighborhood school.[22] Similarly, the HOPE VI mixed-income model has yet to deliver any measurable impact on local schools in terms of socioeconomic or racial diversity, often due to the fact that higher-income HOPE VI residents do not have school-age children.[23] Our proposal underscores the potential leverage gained in these communities through MSAP-supported magnet school grants that target HOPE VI neighborhoods, in a multipronged effort to attract families of diverse racial and socioeconomic backgrounds to the school and, ultimately, to the HOPE VI mixed-income community.

The findings from the review of the research literature and our case studies in Nashville underscore three preconditions that influence the degree of socioeconomic diversity in HOPE VI neighborhoods and neighborhood schools: context, partnerships, and social processes.[24] Our finding related to *context* suggests that the ability to create socioeconomically and racially diverse neighborhoods and schools depends on the degree to which public housing authorities and school leaders tailor strategies to specific community assets. Planners should assess the interest in public housing neighborhoods, school districts, and the community and look for opportunities to create strategic reforms—linked to MSAP-supported magnet schools—that attract new families to the neighborhoods around HOPE VI developments. These MSAP-supported magnet schools could act as the lever to activate local community resources. Utilizing that information, planners should develop *partnerships* that include a range of stakeholders and tap into each organization's area of expertise to maximize available resources.[25] Consistency in leadership is essential; our case studies highlight the finding that partners must understand and commit to *social processes* that will take years to develop and evaluate.[26]

It seems unlikely that one "model" will emerge from research studies on HOPE VI that can be generalized to all communities, but the consensus among community development experts is that these partnerships between public education and public housing have the potential to be more successful in addressing the needs of urban communities plagued with poverty and failing, segregated schools than previous "siloed" efforts, such as full-service schooling. Simultaneously, HOPE VI may hold the potential for creating more racially and socioeconomically diverse school contexts as these communities mature and as new development is incentivized to provoke revitalization beyond the neighborhood blocks defined by public housing. We agree with other scholars who have noted the yet unfulfilled promise of HOPE VI as a partner with high-quality, high-profile, MSAP-supported magnet school programs designed to integrate children within and across district lines to produce racially and socioeconomically diverse school populations.[27] Toward this end, it is vital that HUD and the Obama administration push for greater collaboration and planning between local public housing authorities and local school districts, using HOPE VI reauthorization and new MSAP grants as the lever for renewed focus on racial and socioeconomic integration. This "new localism" justifies continued research and analysis of both established and emerging collaborative efforts that engage a community of neighborhood residents, public housing officials, and education leaders.

Shifting policy contexts related to unitary status raise tough and troubling questions regarding the viability of magnet schools as a tool to create racially and socioeconomically diverse schools. The new legal landscape following the U.S. Supreme Court's decision in *Parents Involved in Community Schools v. Seattle School District No. 1* (2007) elevates these issues, making them all the more pivotal for magnet school educators, policy makers, and parents to consider within the framework of the original purposes and historical mandates connected to diversity aims. In a policy environment dominated by arguments for expanded choice, performance incentives, and school improvement, the purposes of magnet schools will likely be debated, redefined, researched, and most certainly, rigorously tested. Designing magnet schools for diversity requires a set of decisions that are fundamentally different and far more complex than merely opening public school choice options to parents. An expanded role for MSAP as the blueprint for new and specific policy proposals that move magnet school expansion and development to the center of desegregation efforts can kick-start integration.

NOTES

1. E. Frankenberg and G. Siegel-Hawley, *The Forgotten Choice? Rethinking Magnet Schools in a Changing Landscape* (Los Angeles: Civil Rights Project/Proyecto Derechos Civiles at UCLA, 2008); National Center for Education Statistics, *Overview of Public Elementary and Secondary Schools and Districts, Revenues, and Expenditures: School Year 2004–05 and Fiscal Year 2004* (Washington, DC: National Center for Education Statistics).

2. E. Frankenberg and C. Q. Le, "The Post–*Parents Involved* Challenge: Confronting Extralegal Obstacles to Integration," *Ohio State Law Journal* 69 (2008): 1015–72.

3. Public L. No. 80377, 703(2), 98 Stat. 1299 (1984).

4. See Boger essay.

5. Frankenberg and Le, "Post–*Parents Involved* Challenge."

6. C. Smrekar and E. Goldring, *School Choice in Urban America: Magnet Schools and the Pursuit of Equity* (New York: Teachers College Press, 1999).

7. Frankenberg and Siegel-Hawley, *Forgotten Choice?*

8. See DeBray and Frankenberg essay.

9. R. C. Seder, *Satellite Charter Schools: Addressing the School-Facilities Crunch through Public-Private Partnerships*, Policy Study No. 256 (Los Angeles: Reason Public Policy Institute, 1999).

10. E. Frankenberg, C. Lee, and G. Orfield, *A Multiracial Society with Segregated Schools: Are We Losing the Dream?* (Cambridge: Civil Rights Project at Harvard University, 2003).

11. C. Smrekar, "Schools at the Workplace," report to the Spencer Foundation, June 2001.

12. J. Coleman and T. Hoffer, *Public and Private High Schools: The Impact of Community* (New York: Basic Books, 1987).

13. U.S. Department of Labor, *Handbook of Labor Statistics* (Washington, DC: U.S. Bureau of Labor Statistics, 2007).

14. K. Taylor-Haynes, K. Rowley, and E. Goldring, "Magnetic Attraction: Latino Parents' Choice and Magnet Schools," *Urban Education* (in press).

15. B. Murray, "How to Give Working Parents More Time with Their Kids," *U.S. News and World Report*, 5 January 1998.

16. Smrekar and Goldring, *School Choice in Urban America*.

17. Ibid.

18. C. Smrekar, "Beyond the Tipping Point: Issues of Racial Diversity in Magnet Schools Following Unitary Status," *Peabody Journal of Education* 84 (2009): 1–18.

19. R. Mickelson, S. Southworth, and S. Smith, "Resegregation, Achievement and the Chimera of Choice in Post-unitary Charlotte-Mecklenburg Schools," in *From the Courtroom to the Classroom: The Shifting Landscape of School Desegregation*, edited by C. Smrekar and E. Goldring (Cambridge: Harvard Education Press, 2009); Smrekar, "Beyond the Tipping Point."

20. S. Ball, "Education Markets, Choice and Social Class: The Market as a Class Strategy in the UK and the USA," *British Journal of Sociology of Education* 14 (1993): 3–19.

21. U.S. Department of Housing and Urban Development, "FY 2008 HOPE VI Funding Information," http://www.hud.gov/offices/phi/programs/ph/hope6/grants/fy08/index .cfm.

22. M. Abravanel, R. Smith, and E. Cove, *Linking Public Housing Revitalization and Neighborhood School Improvement* (Washington, DC: Urban Institute, 2006), http://www .urban.org/UploadedPDF/411462_public_housing.pdf (accessed 27 May 2008); J. Khadurri et al., *Case Studies Exploring the Potential Relationship between Schools and Neighborhood Revitalization* (Cambridge, MA: Abt Associates, 2003), http://www.abtassociates .com/reports/Schools_and_Neighborhoods.pdf (accessed 5 June 2008).

23. Khadurri et al., *Case Studies*.

24. C. Smrekar, "Public Housing Reform and Neighborhood Schools: How Local Contexts Matter," in *The 108th Yearbook of the National Society for the Study of Education*, edited by R. Crowson and E. Goldring (Hoboken, NJ: Wiley-Blackwell, 2009).

25. Abravanel, Smith, and Cove, *Linking Public Housing Revitalization*; Khadurri et al., *Case Studies*; J. Turnham and J. Khadurri, *Integrating School Reform and Neighborhood Revitalization: Opportunities and Challenges* (Cambridge, MA: Abt Associates, 2004), http:// www.abtassociates.com/reports/SchoolReform_NeighborhoodRevitalization.pdf (accessed 5 June 2008).

26. L. Fenwick, *Putting School and Community on the Map* (Columbia, MD: Enterprise, 2006), http://www.practitionerresources.org/cache/documents/640/64015.pdf (accessed 5 June 2008).

27. P. Tegeler, S. Eaton, and W. Miller, *Bringing Children Together: Magnet Schools and Public Housing Redevelopment* (Cambridge, MA: Institute for Race and Justice, 2009).

PART IV

The Pursuit of School-Level Equity

Resource Allocation Post–*Parents Involved*

Students are resources. In addition to the common pedagogical conception that the varied backgrounds of students represent instructional opportunities for teachers, students themselves contribute to the fiscal dynamics of schools. In some cases, the contribution is direct: poor children, for example, bring with them federal Title I dollars. Special-needs students bring additional resources into schools, depending on individual state funding formulas.

Additionally, recent research indicates that the students in a school can also impact the types of teachers employed there and might—through their peer effects on other students—impact the efficacy of instruction. However, the recent U.S. Supreme Court decision in *Parents Involved in Community Schools v. Seattle School District No. 1* (*PICS*, 2007) limits the ability of educators and policy makers to manipulate school-level student populations by race. The purpose of this essay is to examine the issue of student assignment from a resource allocation perspective and to outline possible policy strategies for educators and policy makers moving into a post-*PICS* environment.

Context: School Resegregation and Resource Allocation

Scholars define policy as a negotiation between competing values.[1] In the field of school finance, these values are often identified as adequacy, efficiency, equity, and liberty.[2] These policy values represent parameters for analysis of education issues from a finance perspective. Within this framework, the field of school finance in particular (and education in general) has seen a shift in attention from issues of equity to issues of efficiency and adequacy.[3] In economic terms, the policy focus in education has shifted from an emphasis on inputs to an emphasis on throughputs and outputs of educational systems. This dynamic has not only been about finances; the shift from equity to adequacy has also affected public concern about the racial composition of schools. Recent education policy has been focused on the qualifications and efficacy of teachers (throughputs) and the diminishment of racial achievement gaps (outputs),

243

rather than on inputs such as funding levels or the racial makeup of schools or classrooms.[4]

As current educational policies emphasize efficient school operations and performance measured by standardized tests over equitable distribution of inputs, one outcome is a resegregation of schools, although few claim that this recent trend toward resegregation bears the overt racism of the de jure past.[5] Court opinions in which districts have petitioned for unitary status hold school-level integration to be an input-focused policy that has therefore become less important than policies which increase students' academic performance and diminish gaps in achievement along the lines of race and socioeconomic status (SES).[6] However, this perspective misses critical connections between school-level student-body composition and its impact on other resource-allocation mechanisms.

Serious questions remain about the effects of resegregation for students in a number of areas. Research on the effects of integrated student populations, while sometimes inconclusive, has overall pointed to the benefits of integrated student populations for student socialization, achievement, and lifetime earnings.[7] More recent research has also examined the converse of this issue by examining the effects of highly segregated or resegregated schools. This research concludes that schools segregated by race or class contribute to hidden fiscal losses and to system inefficiencies. Specifically, although there seems to be less concern about the "inherent" inequality of students attending resegregated schools, researchers and policy makers should remain concerned about relationships between segregation and two key determinants of educational productivity: teacher qualifications and peer effects. The sections that follow will discuss these issues in turn.

Teacher Qualifications

Teacher salaries and benefits are major drivers of educational costs. Education is human resource–intensive, with teacher salaries and benefits accounting for 81 percent of current educational expenditures nationally.[8] In some manner, then, equal access to educational resources implies equal access to teacher qualifications. There has been significant debate about what characteristics identify a high-quality teacher. While it is true that characteristics other than those identified by state-level salary schedules may indicate teacher quality, this essay focuses on those characteristics that are rewarded by state pay scales, since it is the presence or absence of these qualities (years of experience, additional graduate-level degrees) that drive fiscal inequities across schools.

Due to the rigidity of the single salary schedule prevalent across numerous school districts, higher concentrations of less experienced teachers actually represent a financial loss to the school.[9] Consider the difference in salary pool between a school staffed predominantly by experienced teachers with master's degrees compared to a school staffed predominantly by first-year teachers with bachelor's degrees. While it is true that principals never actually "see" the money invested in teacher salaries and benefits, since it is paid directly to the teacher by the district, these salary disparities represent funds that are being differentially allocated across schools.

Additionally, schools with high turnover are more likely to have teachers with zero to three years of experience. While average years of teacher experience has a limited impact on teacher effectiveness as measured by student achievement, teachers with zero to three years of experience are demonstrably less effective than their more experienced peers. Therefore, schools with higher percentages of highly inexperienced teachers are less likely to effectively educate students.[10]

Further, research on teacher labor markets indicates that school-level student-body composition affects teacher decisions about where to work, resulting in increased teacher mobility at high-poverty schools,[11] increased teacher mobility or turnover at racially isolated minority schools,[12] decreased teacher quality in high-poverty, high-minority schools,[13] and increased pupil/teacher ratios in these schools.[14] The traditional correlation between income and race in U.S. schools indicates that many high-poverty schools are also racially isolated minority schools.

Therefore, student assignment policies that allow for high concentrations of poor and minority students may also find teachers in such schools to be both less prepared and less experienced than their peers across the district, resulting in both fiscal inequities and diminished teacher productivity.[15]

Peer Effects

Peer effects occur when classmates and schoolmates exert an influence on individual student learning. Recent research on peer effects has focused on issues of integration and segregation of schools, a well as more recent interest in the specific role peers play in school-level measurements of performance and achievement. Benefits of integration include short-term achievement gains as well as long-term increases in economic productivity.[16] Other research suggests that these long-run benefits are particularly important for minority youth.[17] More directly, research indicates that the economic and ethnic diversity of classrooms can exert a powerful influence on the academic performance of minority students as measured by standardized test scores.[18]

The converse of these findings is that students who attend schools with high proportions of poor and minority children may be negatively affected in terms of academic achievement and long-term economic productivity. From an efficiency and adequacy perspective, then, integrating students by race, socioeconomic background, or both may have positive academic consequences. Unfortunately, the ability to assign students based on race has been weakened by the *PICS* decision. Although a close parsing of Justice Anthony Kennedy's concurring opinion may yield room for legal maneuvering on the issue of race-based student assignment, the implication of *PICS* is that more districts will move toward neighborhood-based student assignment plans and away from assignment plans built around ideas of creating, maintaining, or promoting racial integration. The next section of this essay outlines three broad areas for policy action that educators and policy makers may wish to consider if they seek to maintain fiscal equity of resources in a post-*PICS* environment.

Addressing Resource Inequity in Resegregating Schools

Educators interested in promoting equitable resource distributions in districts have three policy levers at their disposal. Crudely put, they can move students, they can move dollars, or they can move teachers. Each of these approaches has the potential to alter teacher quality or peer effects in public schools. Efforts to distribute dollars and teachers in some manner tacitly acknowledge the creation of racially isolated schools and their potentially deleterious peer effects on student learning. However, not all of these approaches have been shown to work equally well. Each has advantages and disadvantages relative to the others as well as to doing nothing. The sections that follow address the pros and cons of each of these approaches.

Alternative to Race-Based Assignment: Moving Students

The *PICS* decision, while not preventing the use of race completely, calls into question important aspects of race-based student assignment policies. Some districts, facing similar limitations at state and local levels, have experimented with other methods for assigning students in order to maintain racial balance, socioeconomic balance, or both. They have done so by focusing assignment criteria on students' academic performance or (more often) socioeconomic background.[19] The overall finding about these SES plans is that the decision to assign students by SES leads, overall, to slight increases in racial segregation.[20] Case studies of the school system in Wake County, North Carolina, indicate that external pressures of growth and lack of community support lead to only partial implementation of these polices over time.[21] Further analysis of resource deployment across Wake schools during implementation of the SES-based student assignment policy, which was in effect between 2000 and 2010, indicates that relationships exist between school-level concentrations of poor and minority students, on the one hand, and teacher resources such as the percentage of teachers certified by the National Board for Professional Teaching Standards and teacher turnover, but that relationships between school-level populations of poor and minority students and teachers with advanced degrees or highly inexperienced teachers seem to have faded.[22] Taken together, assignment plans based on characteristics such as student economic background or performance try to manage the issue of teacher allocation by creating school environments that provide equal attractiveness to teachers across school districts. The success of policy implementation, then, would be the greatest determinant of whether teachers sorted themselves in ways that perpetuated fiscal inequalities based on student race and class characteristics. These policies also seek to create more integrated schools in order to combat the negative consequences of peer effects. Success of implementation, then, would be indicated by school-level student composition and academic performance over time.

Another method of moving students is to use magnet schools to draw middle-class students into high-poverty schools. However, magnet schools often receive additional funding due to their magnet status. Since they are not systematic in nature, the creation of magnets creates a zero-sum game from the perspective of teacher and peer allocation, leaving magnet schools insufficient to address districtwide resegregation of schools.

Compensatory Spending: Moving Money

Instead of determining alternative student assignment parameters that do not take race into account, other districts have allowed neighborhood-based school resegregation while providing schools with additional compensatory funding. Under these policies, leaders acknowledge the potentially deleterious consequences of creating high-minority and high-poverty schools and attempt to blunt these effects through proactive school-level strategies of resource allocation. In a sense, the strategic plan of leaders in these districts is to balance the known negative effects of creating concentrations of poor and minority students through peer effects with compensatory spending to provide additional school resources and reduce pupil/teacher ratios. With community support, for example, educators in Nashville created different school types to serve schools in low-income neighborhoods and provided additional resources in the form of reduced pupil-teacher ratios for resegregating schools. Studies indicate that, while these efforts were partially effective, schools in low-income neighborhoods still suffered from a lack of physical neighborhood resources such as parks and libraries, and that the overall staffing patterns at resegregated schools consisted of higher proportions of less experienced, less credentialed teachers.[23] While school-level patterns of resource allocation seemed to have no overall effect on student academic performance—that is, additional funding was not able to overcome the effect of school-level segregation—the social wealth of a school's neighborhood did have a positive effect, thereby reinforcing the notion that not all schools share the same level of community resources.[24]

This balance between resegregation and compensatory spending also raises issues of efficiency. For example, the school system in Charlotte–Mecklenburg County, North Carolina, has used a similar funding approach after a court case in 1999 prohibited the use of race-based student assignment. The schools in Charlotte are often contrasted with those in Wake County—since Wake pursued an SES-based student assignment plan over the same time period. The use of this compensatory spending model in Charlotte resulted over time in academic growth by cohorts equal to or better than the more balanced Wake County schools. However, these results seem to have come at a higher cost. Between 1998 and 2006, Charlotte-Mecklenburg schools spent, on average, $451.50 more per pupil in instructional expenditures than did their Wake County counterparts. Of this per-pupil amount, $369.07 came through general state revenue and $48.42 was locally generated.[25]

Finally, the goal of moving money, rather than students, is found in a set of policies developed around weighted student funding. The motivation behind weighted student funding is that dollars should go directly to schools based on pupil needs. To the extent that principals have flexibility in using these funds, weighted student funding may be a powerful link between student needs and school-level resources. Early studies indicate that these formulas still direct funds to principals based on an average salary per teacher rather than acknowledging actual teacher costs at the school level. Additionally, in theory, principals of low-performing schools would still face the difficulty of recruiting high-quality teachers; they would benefit, however, from having additional funds to spend on reducing class size, providing professional development, or other activities to boost student achievement.[26] Theoretically, the additional funding needed to overcome the consequences of peer effects could be factored into student weights, as could other school- and classroom-level composition factors.

The Root of the Problem: Finding Ways to Move Teachers

Since teacher salaries and benefits are the main resources allocated across schools, a final approach to solving the issue of resource disparities in resegregating schools is to disrupt the internal labor market by giving teachers incentives to relocate to schools with high concentrations of poor and minority students. One option, discredited in practice, is simply to use the power of the district to assign teachers to schools, thereby controlling the qualifications and characteristics of teachers at high-needs schools. Experiments with this approach the 1980s and 1990s showed such policies to be highly unpopular.[27]

Another option, more widely embraced, is to give teachers incentives to locate at more difficult schools by altering their salary structures. Under these plans, districts provide compensation bonuses to teachers to teach at low-performing or challenging schools. Research indicates that, while bonuses may not draw teachers into the profession, they may serve as magnets to draw teachers to lower-performing, higher-needs schools, increasing the likelihood of a teacher's doing so by up to 28 percent.[28] Other approaches to these incentive plans include only paying bonuses to nationally certified teachers who plan to work in low-performing schools (as is done in Georgia) or similar nonpecuniary compensation plans.

Performance-Based Pay and Race to the Top

A final wrinkle to these policies is renewed interest in performance-based pay. While there is widespread agreement that paying teachers for the aggregated performance levels of their students on standardized assessments is unfair because of the nonrandom distribution of students' ability levels across schools and classrooms, new research has begun to examine the efficacy of using value-added models to assess teacher quality.[29] Though there are a variety of methods for determining teacher value added, the main idea behind this approach is to only hold teachers accountable for the amount of learning that takes place in a given school year, thereby eliminating or minimizing the inherent differences that students bring into the classroom. This approach focuses on the pace of performance instead of on the absolute level of performance. As such, it is conceptually a fairer use of test data in order to determine teacher performance.

As conceived, such an approach would highlight the worth of individual teachers regardless of the racial, class, or learning backgrounds of their students. If teachers were paid salary steps or bonuses based on these effectiveness ratings, the premium might be enough to shift teachers toward schools that presented the greatest potential for learning rather than the greatest pre-existing learning. Such a shift could redistribute teacher-salary resources in better proportion to student needs. For example, a recent article in the *Los Angeles Times* used teacher value-added data to examine where effective teachers were located and reported that high-quality teachers were more or less randomly employed across grade levels and geographic regions of the district as well as across experience and degrees held by teachers.[30] Payment attached to this performance would reallocate significant amounts of teacher-salary dollars within districts.

It is clear that the Obama administration's Department of Education has seen the potential in these types of policy shifts. Guidelines for the department's Race to the Top grant program—an executively administered program run through the secretary of education and not vetted by Congress—requires statewide reforms to teacher-evaluation and compensation systems. While such changes have drawn fire from teachers' unions and scholars and in some cases have prevented statewide support for the reforms outlined in states' applications to Race to the Top, it is clear that compensation tied to such performance metrics would have potentially important implications for the distribution of salary funds to schools with the highest proportions of poor and minority students. If this proves to be a workable model, the ability to influence student growth more directly may draw teachers to lower-performing schools in the hopes that value-added performance bonuses may be easier to obtain.

The reliability of such approaches is uncertain, however. Experimental work in Tennessee uses a teacher value–added assessment measure as the basis for a performance bonus rather than class-averaged performance levels and found that the opportunity for large bonuses did not impact teacher behavior or student learning.[31] In addition, scholars have pointed to the wide variability in the value–added results themselves, as well as instability in the scales and item rankings used in such value-added efforts.[32] Therefore, although the process of using performance gains to compensate teachers is sound and would serve to address current fiscal inequities present within traditional teacher-salary schedules, the mechanics for successfully carrying out such policies lag significantly.

Conclusion

Desegregation, no longer one of the primary policy goals for educators and policy makers across the country, is now viewed as one goal pursued among many. The primary purpose of student assignment policies is no longer solely the desegregation of schools but rather desegregation in the service of increasing the efficient delivery of instructional services, the attainment of academic standards, and the diminution of persistent achievement gaps based on students' race and socioeconomic status.

This essay has outlined three broad strategies for addressing resource allocation questions in light of this new dynamic. Put simply, policies can address the movement of students, the movement of dollars through compensatory spending, or the movement of teachers within the system. Emerging research suggests that two factors—the characteristics of a student's classroom peers and the characteristics and qualifications of a student's classroom teacher— affect student learning in resegregated or resegregating schools. Although much of the research on the impact of racial integration levels is older, and despite the fact that school-level policies may not address classroom-level segregation,[33] each of these approaches holds some promise for districts.

Generally, while compensatory spending models have been able to distribute resources more equitably in districts with resegregated schools, they have not been able to affect the dynamic of teacher self-sorting. Alternate student assignment plans have met with some success, but they seem to be more politically difficult to implement. Finally, policies that address teacher pay as a way to incentivize teaching at low-performing schools show promise but are also relatively untested.

Naturally, educators can choose to address the issue of school resegregation with multiple polices, and each of these approaches will necessarily be altered by the local context in which they are developed and implemented. Nevertheless, these broad strategies for addressing resource allocation in districts constrained from using race-based policies to foster integrated schools may provide a measure of equity within the larger policy context that emphasizes efficiency and adequacy.

NOTES

1. See, e.g., T. A. Birkland, *An Introduction to the Policy Process* (Armonk, NY: M. E. Sharpe, 2005).

2. See A. Rolle and E. A. Houck, "Introduction to the Peabody Journal of Education's

Special Issue on the Future of School Finance Research," *Peabody Journal of Education* 79, no. 3 (2004): 1. Others have defined *adequacy* as a subset of the concept of equity, see H. F. Ladd, J. S. Hansen, and National Research Council (U.S.), Committee on Education Finance, *Making Money Matter* (Washington, DC: National Academies Press, 1999).

3. For perspectives on efficiency, see L. V. Hedges, R. D. Laine, and R. Greenwald, "An Exchange: Part I: Does Money Matter? A Meta-analysis of Studies of the Effects of Differential School Inputs on Student Outcomes," *Educational Researcher* 23, no. 3 (1994): 5–14; and E. A. Hanushek, "Money Might Matter Somewhere: A Response to Hedges, Laine, and Greenwald," *Educational Researcher* 23, no. 4 (1994): 5–8; see also other perspectives on this issue in Gary Burtless, ed., *Does Money Matter? The Effect of School Resources on Student Achievement and Adult Success* (Washington, DC: Brookings Institution Press, 1996). For perspectives on adequacy and the shift, see W. H. Clune, "The Shift from Equity to Adequacy in School Finance," *Educational Policy* 8, no. 4 (1994): 376–94.

4. See Hawley and Irving essay.

5. G. Orfield, E. D. Frankenberg, and C. Lee, "The Resurgence of School Segregation," *Educational Leadership* 60, no. 4 (2003): 16–20; G. Orfield, *Schools More Separate: Consequences of a Decade of Resegregation* (Cambridge: Civil Rights Project at Harvard University, 2001).

6. See, e.g., *Mills v. Freeman*, Court of Appeals, 11th Circuit, 188 F.3d. 727 (1996); *Capacchione v. Charlotte-Mecklenburg*, 57 F. Supp. 2d 228 (1999); *Keyes v. Denver School District No. 1*, U.S. Court of Appeals, 10th Circuit, No. 95-1487 (1995); *Kelly v. Metropolitan Board of Education*, 436 F.2d. 856 (1998); *Board of Education v. Superior Court*, 61 Cal. App. 4th 411 (February 1998).

7. A. S. Wells and R. L. Crain, "Perpetuation Theory and the Long-Term Effects of School Desegregation," *Review of Educational Research* 64, no. 4 (1994): 531–55.

8. U.S. Department of Education, National Center for Education Statistics, Common Core of Data (CCD), "National Public Education Financial Survey," 1989–90 through 2005–6.

9. M. Roza and P. T. Hill, "How Within-District Spending Inequities Help Some Schools to Fail," *Brookings Papers on Education Policy* 2004 (2004): 201–18.

10. C. T. Clotfelter, H. F. Ladd, and J. Vigdor, "Who Teaches Whom? Race and the Distribution of Novice Teachers," *Economics of Education Review* 24, no. 4 (2005): 377–92. See also R. G. Croninger et al., "Teacher Qualifications and Early Learning: Effects of Certification, Degree, and Experience on First-Grade Student Achievement," *Economics of Education Review* 26, no. 3 (2007): 312–24.

11. R. M. Ingersoll, "Teacher Turnover and Teacher Shortages: An Organizational Analysis," *American Educational Research Journal* 38, no. 3 (2001): 499–534.

12. B. Scafidi, D. L. Sjoquist, and T. R. Stinebrickner, "Race, Poverty, and Teacher Mobility," *Economics of Education Review* 26, no. 2 (2007): 145–59.

13. H. Lankford, S. Loeb, and J. Wyckoff, "Teacher Sorting and the Plight of Urban Schools: A Descriptive Analysis," *Educational Evaluation and Policy Analysis* 24, no. 1 (2002): 37–62.

14. L. Picus, "Estimating the Determinants of Pupil/Teacher Ratio: Evidence from the Schools and Staffing Survey," *Educational Considerations*, no. 21 (1994): 44–55.

15. R. Rubenstein et al., "From Districts to Schools: The Distribution of Resources across Schools in Big City School Districts," *Economics of Education Review* 26, no. 5 (2007): 532–45.

16. Wells and Crain, "Perpetuation Theory."

17. W. L. Trent, "Outcomes of School Desegregation: Findings from Longitudinal Research," *Journal of Negro Education* 66, no. 3 (1997): 255–57.

18. V. E. Lee and A. S. Bryk, "A Multilevel Model of the Social Distribution of High School Achievement," *Sociology of Education* 62, no. 3 (1989): 172–92; C. M. Hoxby, "How Does the Makeup of a Classroom Influence Achievement?," *Education Next* 2, no. 2 (2002): 56–63; E. A. Hanushek, J. F. Kain, and S. G. Rivkin, "Disruption versus Tiebout Improvement: The Costs and Benefits of Switching Schools," *Journal of Public Economics* 88, no. 9–10 (2004): 1721–46; R. W. Rumberger and G. J. Palardy, "Does Segregation Still Matter? The Impact of Student Composition on Academic Achievement in High School," *Teachers College Record* 107, no. 9 (2005): 1999–2045.

19. See Kahlenberg and Siegel-Hawley essays for further discussion of these plans.

20. See Reardon and Rhodes essay for a further discussion of this finding.

21. See Siegel-Hawley essay for a further discussion of Wake County's plan. See also S. M. Williams and E. A. Houck, "'To Turn Back Would Be a Huge Mistake': Race, Class, and Student Assignment in Wake County Public Schools," paper presented at the "National Conference on the Future of Race-Based Assignment in the South," Chapel Hill, NC, April 2009.

22. Wake County data, author's own calculations; T. Keung Hui, "Wake School Board Begins Review of Diversity Policy," *Raleigh News and Observer*, 11 February 2010.

23. E. Goldring et al., "Schooling Closer to Home: Desegregation Policy and Neighborhood Contexts," *American Journal of Education* 112, no. 3 (2006): 335–62; see also E. A. Houck, "Teacher Quality and School Resegregation: A Resource Allocation Case Study," *Leadership and Policy in Schools* (in press).

24. C. C. Klein, "Intradistrict Public School Funding Equity, Community Resources, and Performance in Nashville, Tennessee," *Journal of Education Finance* 34, no. 1 (2008): 1–14.

25. Public Education Research Institute, "Academic Progress: How Do Charlotte-Mecklenburg Students Compare to Wake County Students?," Queens University, Charlotte, NC, 2009, http://www.queens.edu/Documents/Cato/Public%20Education%20Research%20Institute/WakeCounty_and_CMS_Analysis.pdf (accessed 21 March 2011); author's calculations. Data source: National Center for Education Statistics, Common Core of Data, School District Finance Survey Form (Form-F-33), FY 1999–2006, v.1a.

26. L. S. Shambaugh, J. Chambers, and D. DeLancy, "Implementation of the Weighted Student Formula Policy in San Francisco: A Descriptive Study of an Equity-Driven, Student-Based Planning and Budgeting Policy," *Issues and Answers* 61 (August 2008), http://ies.ed.gov/ncee/edlabs/regions/west/pdf/REL_2008061_sum.pdf (accessed 21 March 2011).

27. C. Hendrie, "Legal Issues Complicate Efforts to Integrate School Staffs," *Education Week*, 24 June 1998.

28. E. Liu, S. M. Johnson, and H. G. Peske, "New Teachers and the Massachusetts Signing Bonus: The Limits of Inducements," *Educational Evaluation and Policy Analysis* 26, no. 3 (2004): 217–36; J. L. Steele, R. J. Murnane, and J. B. Willett, *Do Financial Incentives Help Low-Performing Schools Attract and Keep Academically Talented Teachers? Evidence from California* (Cambridge, MA: National Bureau of Economic Research, March 2009), RePEc, http://ideas.repec.org/p/nbr/nberwo/14780.html (accessed 21 March 2011).

29. W. L. Sanders and S. P. Horn, "The Tennessee Value-Added Assessment System (TVAAS): Mixed-Model Methodology in Educational Assessment," *Journal of Personnel Evaluation in Education* 8, no. 3 (1994): 299–311; D. Ballou, W. Sanders, and P. Wright, "Controlling for Student Background in Value-Added Assessment of Teachers," *Journal of Educational and Behavioral Statistics* 29, no. 1 (2004): 37–65; Y. M. Thum, "Measuring Progress toward a Goal," *Sociological Methods and Research* 32, no. 2 (2003): 153–207; Matthew G. Springer, *Performance Incentives: Their Growing Impact on American K-12 Education* (Washington, DC: Brookings Institution Press, 2009).

30. "Who's Teaching L.A.'s Kids?," *Los Angeles Times*, 14 August 2010, http://articles .latimes.com/2010/aug/14/local/la-me-teachers-value-20100815 (accessed 14 August 2010).

31. Matthew G. Springer et al., *Teacher Pay for Performance: Experimental Evidence from the Project on Incentives in Teaching*, working paper from the National Center on Performance Incentives, http://www.performanceincentives.org/data/files/gallery/Content Gallery/POINT_REPORT_9.21.10.pdf (accessed 21 March 2011).

32. A. Amrein-Beardsley, "Methodological Concerns about the Education Value-Added Assessment System," *Educational Researcher* 37, no. 2 (2008): 65–75; Ballou, D., "Test Scaling and Value-Added Measurement," *Education Finance and Policy* 4, no. 4 (2009): 351–83; D. F. McCaffrey et al., "The Intertemporal Variability of Teacher Effect Estimates," *Education Finance and Policy* 4, no. 4 (2009): 572–606.

33. R. A. Mickelson, "Subverting *Swann*: First- and Second-Generation Segregation in the Charlotte-Mecklenburg Schools," *American Educational Research Journal* 38, no. 2 (2001): 215–52.

WILLIS D. HAWLEY & JACQUELINE JORDAN IRVINE

Improving Teaching and Learning
in Integrated Schools

Effective teachers in racially and ethnically integrated schools, by definition, must be able to facilitate the learning of students who likely are culturally, linguistically, and socioeconomically diverse. In many cases, this diversity comes with substantial differences in students' academic achievement. Indeed, one of the most intractable problems in integrated schools is the test score gap, the difference between the scores of African American, Latino, and Native American students as compared to most white and Asian students.

Although certain psychological, economic, political, and sociological perspectives explain the underachievement of students of color, convincing data show that the quality of teaching is the single most important variable in what and how students learn in school.[1] We know, both instinctively and empirically, that what matters most are highly proficient and caring teachers who are responsive to the diverse needs of their students. However, more than 40 percent of teachers say that their classes are so diverse that they can't teach them effectively. And a national panel of prominent researchers and educators convened to identify strategies for school improvement concluded that increasing the ability of teachers to work with diverse students is one of the most important priorities.[2]

This essay outlines (1) some of the beliefs and practices that all too commonly characterize and undermine the teaching of racially and ethnically diverse students, (2) what teachers need to know and be able to do to meet the learning needs of diverse students, and (3) strategies for enhancing the preparation of teachers and their continuing professional development. It is important to note that none of the proposals made in this essay will have a negative affect on the learning of students of any race or ethnicity. Or, to put it another way, teachers who have the expertise discussed below will be effective with all students.

In discussions of effective teaching in racially and ethnically diverse schools, it is not uncommon to hear educators—and policy makers—say that good teaching is good teaching. It is certainly true that research has identified the characteristics of effective teaching and that teachers who have such expertise are likely to be more effective in teaching all students than teachers who lack these skills. But it also true that there are teachers' dispositions and proficiencies that are particularly important to maximizing student learning in racially and ethnically diverse classrooms.[3]

What Teachers Need to Know and Be Able to Do in Integrated Schools

Common Teacher Beliefs and Behaviors That Undermine Student Learning

Researchers have identified several dispositions and practices that teachers commonly exhibit that undermine their effectiveness and that are especially common impediments to the learning of racially and ethnically diverse students. Among these are

- biases and stereotypes;
- misconceptions, misunderstanding, and misinformation;
- oversimplified pedagogy (e.g., teaching to "learning styles," overgeneralization of cultural differences);
- limits on learning imposed by family and community conditions (e.g., beliefs about a "culture of poverty");
- the desirability of "color blindness";
- low expectations rooted in beliefs about inherent ability;
- inappropriate "ability" grouping;
- misdiagnosis of students' learning needs;
- pedagogical practices that favor some learners over others;
- instructional management embedded in majority-culture assumptions; and
- practices that confuse language facility and academic capability.

It is not possible within the scope of this essay to elaborate on each of these beliefs and behaviors and to identify ways to change them. Instead, we focus here on a set of practices called culturally responsive pedagogy (CRP). CRP is not all that teachers need to know and be able to do, but it encompasses many of the fundamentals of what teachers need to do to facilitate the learning of racially and ethnically diverse students.[4] But before turning to that discussion we need to make two observations that will serve as context.

UNDERSTANDING THE MEANING OF CULTURE

As William Julius Wilson says, in order to understand the influence of "culture," group norms, values, and attitudes toward family and work should be considered. But, Wilson argues, we need also to consider "cultural repertoires (habits, styles and skills) and micro-level processes of meaning making and decision making—that is, the ways groups, communities, and societies develop an understanding of how the world works and make decisions based on that understanding."[5] Racial discrimination and segregation in the United States have profoundly affected the development of the cultures that students bring with them to school, a reality that is especially relevant to student learning in integrated schools.

WE ARE MORE THAN OUR CULTURES

Although it is clear that culture, particularly ethnicity, is a powerful force that influences teacher-student relationships and student learning, students of color are not mere products of their culture. Consequently, culture affects individuals in different ways and not all members of the same cultural group behave in identical ways or identify with their culture to the same degree. Identification with one's cultural group is influenced by assimilation, family values, gender, geographic region, membership and identification with other groups, and social class.

Culturally Responsive Instructional Practice

As we noted earlier, teachers who practice culturally responsive pedagogy have more professional expertise than effective teachers who do not have these skills. These teachers understand that all students, regardless of race or ethnicity, bring their culturally influenced cognition, behavior, and dispositions with them to school. They also recognize that the cultural experiences of some students of color can be different from and conflict with the culture of their school educators. Cultural variables become evident in classrooms in the ways teachers deliver instruction—through verbal and nonverbal language. There might, for example, be differences in ethnic students' mastery of English, pronunciation, vocabulary, phonology (rhythm, tempo, or pitch). There also might be differences in assumptions regarding what is spoken and left unspoken, whether one interrupts, defers to others, or asks direct or indirect questions. Teachers need to understand how semantics, accents, dialect, and discussion modes manifest themselves when they communicate with their diverse students. Similarly, nonverbal communications in integrated classrooms are important in the delivery of instruction. These nonverbal issues can raise questions about the cultural meanings of interpersonal space, eye contact, body language, touching, and gestures.[6]

Culturally responsive instruction requires teachers to have a thorough and deep understanding of the subjects they teach so they can represent and deliver content in various ways that will help different students interpret knowledge, store and retrieve it, and make sense of the world they live in. Many students fail in schools not because their teachers do not know their subject matter content, but because their teachers cannot make the connections between the content and their students' existing mental schemes, prior knowledge, learning preferences, and cultural perspectives.[7]

Culturally responsive teachers know how to employ multiple representations of knowledge that use students' everyday lived experiences to motivate and assist them in connecting new knowledge to home, community, and global settings. Multiple representations of subject-matter knowledge involve finding pertinent examples, comparing and contrasting, bridging the gap between the known (students' personal cultural knowledge) and the unknown (materials and concepts to be mastered).

Culturally responsive teachers know how to make connections between school and community knowledge in ways that involve students' families. Likewise, these culturally relevant teaching practices inform teachers' assessment practices. Effective teachers use a variety of formative and summative assessment tools including their own tests and observations as well as standardized tests.

Caring Interpersonal Relationships
An Essential Requisite of Culturally Responsive Pedagogy

Teaching occurs within a social context and involves the development and maintenance of personal, caring relationships. False dichotomies often are drawn between teachers who are proficient instructionally and those who manifest caring relationships with their students. In fact, instructionally effective teachers are caring teachers, and diverse students in particular benefit from these types of teachers. For example, evidence suggests that African American students tend to be more dependent on teachers than their other-race peers and tend to perform poorly in school when they do not like their teachers or feel that their teachers do not care for them.[8] Unlike some of the research on effective teaching, studies of culturally relevant pedagogy emphasize the importance of personal relationships between students and their teachers. In one study of four integrated schools, researchers concluded that, consistent with the results of other inquiries, the most consistent and powerful finding related to school achievement for diverse students was the presence of caring teachers. Students of color said that they liked school and did their best when they thought that teachers cared about them. Students indicated that caring teachers trusted and respected them, recognized them as individuals, set limits, provided structure, had high expectations, pushed them to achieve, and advocated for them in school.[9] It is easy to see, from this perspective, why students of color who trust their teachers and believe that their teachers want them to succeed would be likely to accept challenges to perform at higher levels and to otherwise exhibit positive behaviors in school.

Facilitating Teacher Learning

There are, of course, substantial differences in how teachers are prepared to teach and how best to enhance their professional development. Essential to the effectiveness of both, however, is the importance of involving teachers in authentic learning contexts. This means that the content of what is learned and modes of facilitating learning need to be combined in the same lessons; as much as possible, teachers need to learn in the context of problem-solving that they are likely to experience in their classrooms.

Teacher Preparation

There are two fundamental strategies for preparing teachers to be successful in racially and ethnically diverse schools. The first of these is to embed lessons related to teaching diverse students, such as those discussed above, in courses on teaching content (e.g., courses on the teaching of reading or mathematics). Too often courses on "diversity" or "multicultural education" are stand-alone courses that focus on awareness of and sensitivity to cultural differences, usually with a heavy dose of the invidious consequences of racial discrimination. However important these lessons are, they usually do not transfer to instructional practice and the development of academically productive relationships with students.

The second fundamental of preparation for teaching in racially and ethnically diverse schools is that clinical (i.e., practical) experiences should take place in racially and ethnically diverse schools and communities where teacher candidates can learn from exceptional, culturally responsive teachers. Moreover, this on-the-ground experience should extend beyond the school so that prospective teachers can learn how to interact with families and learn about how their students live day-to-day and the learning resources they bring with them to school.[10]

Continuing Professional Development

No matter how good their preparation programs have been, beginning teachers have much to learn. Indeed, without adequate professional support, novice teachers often narrow their repertoire of competencies and focus on less sophisticated and less effective instructional strategies. This is particularly true of novice teachers in schools serving diverse students where the challenges of teaching are substantial.

Ensuring that beginning teachers have a quality induction experience would seem to be a no-brainer. Why, then, don't more teachers have better induction experiences? The answer to this question may be that effective induction programs make substantial demands on both financial and human resources. While no one program will fit the needs or resources of all districts, scholars who have studied induction have identified several characteristics of the most effective programs.[11] Among the most productive of these are

- mentoring by senior colleagues who are trained and compensated for this role and who, in turn, are supported by a school-based team;
- time provided for professional development targeted on needs for improvement that are identified by continuing evaluation of the novice's performance;
- teaching assignments that minimize different preparations and that match the content the teacher has been prepared to teach;
- placement in schools where exceptional teaching can be witnessed and studied; and
- continuation for a second year, usually at a much reduced level of investment, with program elements tailored to the developmental progress of each novice.

While much professional learning takes place informally, especially in well-functioning professional learning communities, formal professional-development activities are important. Effective professional development requires not only the appropriate content, including the priorities identified in this essay, but also learning experiences that are designed productively. There are many characteristics of effective professional development. The most important of these meet the four "design principles" for structured professional development activities.[12] First, learning should be undertaken in the context of collaborative problem-solving linked to analyses of student performance. Second, professional development should provide experiential opportunities to gain an understanding of and reflect on the research and theory underlying the knowledge and skills being learned. Third, the way teachers' learning is facilitated should mirror the instructional approaches they are expected to master and allow them to experience the consequences of newly learned capabilities. Fourth, professional development should be continuous and ongoing, involving follow-up and support for further learning, including support from sources external to the school that can provide necessary resources and new perspectives.

Despite strong evidence that the quality of teaching students experience is the most powerful influence on how and what they learn in any school, and especially in racially and ethnically diverse schools, colleges of education and school districts could do a much better job than they do now in readying teachers to meet the needs of all students.

The preparation of teachers could be enhanced if standards for preparing teachers to work with racially and ethnically diverse students were clearer and examples of effective practice were available. While accreditation of teacher-preparation programs is productively shifting from process to evidence of what prospective teachers know and are able to do, ways of measuring teacher proficiency need to be developed that focus attention on higher-order student learning and that are appropriate for novice teachers. Moreover, preparation programs cannot improve without knowing how to revise the curriculum and pedagogy especially important in preparing teachers to facilitate the learning of diverse students. There is now no source of such support for improvement. The American Association of Colleges of Teacher Education, the National Council for the Accreditation of Teacher Education, or both might undertake this challenge. This seems a worthy investment of funding that could be reallocated from existing federal programs.

Enhancing the professional expertise of teachers in ways discussed in this essay is the responsibility of school districts. Currently, investments in the professional development of teachers are too often irrelevant and ineffective. Paying teachers to earn graduate credits without linking such learning to specific district and teacher needs makes no sense and provides no incentive for colleges of education to change what they do and how they do it. State and federal money for professional development in districts should be tied to plans for addressing specific student needs that are defined by evidence on student learning. Analyses of student learning should be based on data disaggregated not by broad demographic categories, as is currently required by federal law, but by subcategories of students' racial and ethnic differences. For example, Asians and Pacific Islanders, a common category of students, include students from very different cultural backgrounds. Often students of Chinese heritage achieve at higher levels than students with Cambodian backgrounds. And, of course, following the progress of individual students is the best way to use evidence of student learning.

Too often districtwide programs miss the mark in dealing with variation in teachers' and students' learning needs. Most investments in professional enhancement should be consistent with the design principles outlined in this essay. In particular, professional development aimed at facilitating the learning of diverse students needs to be part of a comprehensive and ongoing school-improvement strategy for every district. The federal government's investments in technical assistance make little impact on teacher proficiency and would certainly be more productive if investments were not strewn among many different and uncoordinated funding programs and delivery systems.

Any new initiative to enhance the expertise of either teacher candidates or teachers must compete with how resources and time are currently invested. Knowing that current investments are not as effective as they need to be does not, it itself, lead to change. Evidence that specific strategies for teacher preparation or professional development enhance the learning of racially and ethnically diverse students would motivate efforts to improve. This essay has made use of the existing research, but much more is needed. The only reasonable source of funding for such research is the federal government, but there has been virtually no research funded that focuses on the teaching of racially and ethnically diverse students. Given talk about racially identified achievement gaps, it is difficult to explain the absence of interest in explanations related to the race or ethnicity of students. Perhaps it is the belief that such research would be politically risky. Perhaps those responsible for federal funding fear acknowledging the possibility that the effects of racial discrimination persist. It is also likely, however, that the widespread belief that good teaching is good teaching, regardless of students' race or ethnicity (an important reason why colleges of education and school districts do not give adequate attention to improving the teaching of diverse students), affects the decisions about research priorities.

NOTES

1. D. Goldhaber and E. Anthony, *Teacher Quality and Student Achievement*, New York: ERIC Clearinghouse on Urban Education, ERIC # ED477271 (New York: Teachers College, Columbia University, 2003); L. Darling-Hammond, *Teacher Quality and Student Achievement: A Review of State Policy Evidence* (Seattle: Center for the Study of Teaching and Policy, University of Washington, 1999).

2. *The MetLife Survey of the American Teacher: Past, Present and Future* (New York: Metropolitan Life Insurance Company, 2008); Forum Conveners, *Democracy at Risk: The Need for a New Federal Policy in Education* (Amesville, OH: Forum on Education and Democracy, April 2008).

3. G. Gay, *Culturally Responsive Teaching: Theory, Research, and Practice*, 2nd ed. (New York: Teachers College Press, 2010); T. C. Howard and G. R. Aleman, "Teacher Capacity for Diverse Learners," in *Handbook of Research on Teacher Education*, edited by M. Cochran-Smith, S. Feiman-Nemser, and D. J. McIntyre (New York: Routledge & ATE, 2008), 157–74.

4. J. J. Irvine and B. Armento, *Culturally Responsive Teaching* (Boston: McGraw-Hill, 2001), 3–17; G. Ladson-Billings, *The Dreamkeepers: Successful Teachers of African American Children* (San Francisco: Jossey-Bass, 1994), 102–26. For extensive descriptions of strategies for teaching racially and ethnically diverse students, see the resources of the Teaching Diverse Students Initiative at http://www.tolerance.org/tdsi.

5. W. J. Wilson, "More than Just Race: Being Black and Poor in the Inner City," *Poverty and Race* 18, no. 3 (2009): 1.

6. E. T. Hall, *The Hidden Dimension* (New York: Doubleday, 1966); W. Longstreet, *Aspects of Ethnicity: Understanding Differences in Pluralistic Classrooms* (New York: Teachers College Press, 1978); D. M. Gollnick and P. C. Chinn, *Multicultural Education in a Pluralistic Society* (Upper Saddle River, NJ: Pearson, Merrill, Prentice-Hall, 2006), 285–87.

7. A. R. Gere et al., "A Visibility Project: Learning to See How Preservice Teachers Take Up Culturally Responsive Pedagogy," *American Educational Research Journal* 46, no. 3 (2009): 816–52; R. J. Sternberg, "Who Are the Bright Children? The Cultural Context of Being and Acting Intelligent," *Educational Researcher* 36, no. 3 (2007): 148–55.

8. J. Vasquez, "Contexts of Learning for Minority Students," *Education Forum* 52, no. 3 (1988): 243–53; R. Sizemore, "Do Black and White Students Look for the Same Characteristics in Teachers?," *Journal of Negro Education* 50, no. 1 (1981): 48–53; S. Johnson and P. Sukai, "The Memorable Teacher: Implications for Teacher Selection," *Journal of Negro Education* 55, no. 3 (1986): 280.

9. Institute for Education in Transformation, *Voices from the Inside* (Claremont, CA: Claremont Graduate School, 1992): 19.

10. For reviews of research on preparing teachers to teach racially and ethnically diverse students, see J. Banks et al., "Teaching Diverse Learners," in *Preparing Teachers for a Changing World*, edited by L. Darling-Hammond and J. Bransford (San Francisco: Jossey-Bass, 2005), 232–74; E. Hollins and M. T. Guzman, "Research on Preparing Teachers for Diverse Populations," in *Studying Teacher Education*, edited by M. Cochran-Smith and K. M. Zeichner (Mahwah, NJ: L. Erlbaum, 2005), 477–548.

11. For a review of research on the characteristics of induction programs for beginning teachers, see K. Fulton, I. Yoon, and C. Lee, *Induction into Learning Communities* (Washington, DC: National Commission on Teaching and America's Future, 2005).

12. W. D. Hawley and L. Valli, "Design Principles for Learner-Centered Professional Development," in *The Keys to Effective Schools: Educational Reform as Continuous Improvement*, 2nd ed., edited by W. D. Hawley and D. Rollie (Thousand Oaks, CA: Corwin, 2007), 117–37.

Latinos, Language, and Segregation
Options for a More Integrated Future

Latinos are both the largest ethnic minority in the United States and the most segregated group in their schools. The Latino pubic school population nearly doubled in the United States between 1987 and 2007, from 11 percent to 21 percent of all students.[1] Since 1987, it has grown more rapidly than any other group. In fact, during this period, the percentage of public school students who were black declined from 17 percent to 15 percent nationwide.[2] Thus, while the problem of school segregation has traditionally been cast as an issue of black and white, today Latinos are actually more likely than blacks to attend segregated schools. In 2005–6, approximately 78 percent of Latinos attended predominantly (50 to 100 percent) minority schools, while about 73 percent of black students attended similarly segregated schools.[3] Nationwide, Latinos are slightly more likely than blacks (39.5 percent vs. 38.3 percent) to attend hypersegregated schools, those that are 90 to 100 percent nonwhite, but in the West, Latinos are much more likely to attend such schools. In the large central cities in the West, more than 60 percent of Latino students are in hypersegregated schools; 47 percent of black students attend these schools.[4] In addition to school district and housing policies, western segregation is also linked to the exploding growth of the Latino population in that area of the country. The majority of new kindergarteners beginning school in Texas and California are now Latino students. In Texas, 14 percent of K–12 students were African American compared to 47 percent Latino in 2008,[5] and in California, a little more than 7 percent of students were African American compared to 49 percent Latino in 2009.[6] This fact results not only in the segregation of Latino students into minority schools in these states but often in their isolation in schools that are almost all Latino.

The rapid growth of the Latino population brings particular urgency to the problem of increasing school segregation. Racial and ethnic segregation of both African American and Latino students tends to be associated with high socioeconomic segregation as well.[7] Studies demonstrate that concentrated poverty is associated with everything from less optimal physical development to families' inability to stay in the same neighborhood long enough for schools to have powerful educational effects.[8] Concentrated poverty in schools is also closely related to students' and their parents' diminished social capital—knowledge of how important institutions work and access to persons with the ability to advocate on one's behalf within these institutions. Black and Latino communities are too frequently powerless to change the circumstances of their neighborhoods or their schools because of this lack of the social capital generated in middle-class communities through equal-status interaction with knowledgeable members of the society.

Latino Students and Triple Segregation

Isolation of Latino students into schools that are largely Latino can carry an additional disadvantage; Latinos are often triply segregated—by ethnicity, poverty, and language. One recent national study found that only 5,000 schools in the United States educated 70 percent of all English Language Learners (ELLS).[9] Likewise, in California in 2005, more than half of all elementary-age English Language Learners attended just 21 percent of the state's elementary schools, where they comprised more than 50 percent of the students on campus.[10] Isolation by language presents a particularly thorny problem: it is difficult to learn the language of the land if one is exposed to few models of native English speakers and has few friends or neighbors who speak the language well. In a 2006 article, Bernard Gifford and Guadalupe Valdés reported that their "analysis of the hypersegregation of Hispanic students, and particularly Spanish-speaking ELLS, suggests that little or no attention has been given to the consequences of linguistic isolation for a population whose future depends on the acquisition of English. . . . For ELLS, interaction with ordinary English-speaking peers is essential to their English language development and consequently to their acquisition of academic English."[11]

A recent study by Marcelo Suárez-Orozco, Carola Suárez-Orozco, and Irina Todorova found that the best predictor of whether an immigrant student will gain a firm mastery of English is whether he or she has a good friend who is a native English speaker. Without such natural language support, it can be very challenging to learn the language, especially at the level of academic English that is required to do well in school.[12]

The schools that serve linguistically isolated Latino students also tend to be much weaker in their ability to deliver a quality education than other schools. They are more likely to be in urban centers, with larger enrollments and larger class sizes. They have higher incidences of student poverty, health problems, and tardiness, as well as difficulty filling teacher vacancies.[13] They are more likely to rely on unqualified teachers and have lower levels of parent involvement. As the concentration of ELL students increases in schools, the percentage of fully credentialed teachers, qualified to serve them, decreases. In an article I wrote with colleagues from UC-Davis and UC–Santa Barbara, we found a very similar profile for schools that served high percentages of English Language Learners in California.[14] We concluded that ELL students received a demonstrably inferior education when compared even to other poor children along seven different dimensions: they (1) had lower-quality facilities, (2) were likely to be taught by inexperienced and uncredentialed teachers, (3) had more inadequate learning materials, (4) had teachers whose weaker professional development prepared them poorly for instructing these students, (5) had less instructional time and adult-student contact, (6) were assessed with invalid tests, and (7) tended to be more segregated than other poor children. Research has shown that in many of these schools it is impossible for ELL (or any other) students to take the courses necessary to prepare for college; the required courses are simply not offered or not offered in sufficient quantity for all students to have access.[15] Such schools foreclose options for ELL students no matter how talented or hardworking they are.

The U.S. Supreme Court recognized the right of Latino students to desegregation remedies in deciding *Keyes v. School District No. 1* (1973, Denver), but this right was never seriously enforced, in good part because the Department of Justice and the Office for Civil Rights were in the hands of administrations opposed to desegregation. With judicial appointments made during those administrations, the Supreme Court began to authorize the dismantling of existing desegregation orders in *Board of Education of Oklahoma City Public Schools v. Dowell* (1991) before Latino issues had ever been addressed in the older desegregation cases. Thus Latinos were never able to take advantage of the courts as an avenue to redress their growing segregation.

Who Are English Learners and What Do They Need?

While Latino students are often characterized as being Spanish-only speakers, with the lack of English cast as the primary impediment to their higher achievement, in fact only about half of Latino students begin school as English Language Learners (i.e., lacking sufficient knowledge of English to learn in it without special intervention).[16] The other half speaks enough English to be considered fluent in English. But this can be misleading. Some of these students were formerly English Language Learners and have been reclassified as "fluent English speakers" based on a variety of assessments or other criteria. They may or may not be fluent readers and writers of the language. Many of these English-speaking students come from homes and communities in which Spanish is still a dominant language and levels of education in English are low. For example, among students of Mexican origin, at least 40 percent have parents who have not completed a high school education, often much less, and less than 15 percent come from homes in which parents have a college education.[17] Therefore, the academic form of the language is not widely used in these children's homes and communities. Idioms that are widely used in English-speaking communities may not be heard where these children grow up, and the concepts embedded in middle-class English discourse may be foreign to children from Spanish-speaking backgrounds.

Recently language policies in schools across the United States have leaned toward immersing non-English speakers in English-only instruction as in "a cold bath," with the mistaken impression that simply forcing students to learn in the new language, often in linguistically segregated settings, will result in more rapid acquisition of English and hence better school performance.[18] The research, however, suggests otherwise. Forcing students to learn in a language they do not yet understand results in neither more rapid acquisition of English nor better achievement outcomes for most of these students. It does, however, appear to result in greater school-dropout rates and, among young people who do stay in school, in achievement levels vastly below those of their native-English-speaking peers.[19] Hence, the solution to educating Latino students from Spanish-speaking backgrounds to attain high levels of English as well as to grade-level competency in other school subjects is neither easy nor quickly accomplished. It requires consistent, high-quality instruction, exposure to good English models in naturalistic settings, and instruction in other subjects that both meets high standards and is intelligible to the students. Most models of instruction for English Language Learners do not meet all of these characteristics; some provide intensive English instruction but at the expense of intelligible content instruction; others provide some primary language instruction in basic subjects but do not incorporate opportunities for acquisition of English in naturalistic settings. In fact, in an intensive study of one Northern California school district, we documented the extremely limited opportunities that many ELLs, even in very high-performing schools, have to actually use the language they are attempting to acquire. As few as two to three minutes a day were actually spent producing oral or written English in the classroom.

Most instruction provided no opportunity for anything other than passive involvement of the students.[20]

Language as a Consideration in Student School Assignment

With the U.S. Supreme Court decision in *Parents Involved in Community Schools v. Seattle School District No. 1* (*PICS*, 2007) — which incorporated cases from Louisville, Kentucky, and Seattle, Washington — the Court signaled that while it believed that school integration served an important social good, it would not sanction any methods devised by school districts to accomplish this goal that involved school assignment based on an individual student's race. This has placed many districts wishing to break down the racial isolation of their students in a quandary. The Court, however, did not say that language difference could not be used as a basis for reassigning students to more integrated schools. Latino students who speak primarily Spanish are an obvious category of students who could profit from assignment to a less linguistically isolated school. Less obvious might be the reassignment of African American or other subgroups of students who speak a nonstandard variant of English and who could profit from the experience of being educated alongside students who speak mainstream academic English. The Civil Rights Project/Proyecto Derechos Civiles in cooperation with the NAACP Legal Defense and Educational Fund published a manual in 2008 to help districts achieve racial balance in their schools under the restrictions imposed by the *PICS* decision. One recommendation was to consider language as a variable in student assignment. It remains to be seen if districts will use this rationale in their emerging desegregation plans.

Dual-Language Education: One Answer to Triple Isolation?

In spite of some statewide and local policies that seek to limit the instruction of ELLS to English-only, there is a rapidly growing movement toward creating dual-language programs. Sometimes these are programs within schools, sometimes they are freestanding schools that provide both ELLS and English-only speakers the opportunity to learn together and to become competent in more than one language. The Center for Applied Linguistics (CAL) maintains an online directory of such programs.[21] Nationally, these programs have grown rapidly, from just 1 in 1962 and fewer than 10 in the 1970s to 368 in 2010. The increase is particularly steep beginning in the 1990s, despite a simultaneous decline in teaching ELLS in their primary language.[22] This would appear to be paradoxical, but below I discuss the unique context and impulse behind these programs. The number reported by CAL, however, underestimates the actual number of such programs nationwide, as the directory is a voluntary effort that only lists programs that happen to report in. For example, while CAL listed 110 programs for California in 2007, the California Department of Education reported more than 200 programs in that state. It is probable, however, that the *growth* in programs reported by CAL is reliable, as similar increases are reported in California and other states.[23]

Dual-immersion, dual-language, or two-way dual-immersion programs (all terms used to describe the programs) educate monolingual English speakers and another non-English-speaking group simultaneously in both target languages with the goal of producing strongly bilingual and biliterate individuals. The programs are built on the premise that such programs can create classroom environments in which both minority and majority students enjoy equal social status. The fact that both languages and cultures are valued equally and play critical roles in the curriculum tends to yield positive student attitudes toward the culture and language of the "other."[24] The classic work of Gordon Allport and Elizabeth Cohen underpins the assumptions of this model—that children will learn from each other and learn to like each other if they are exposed to learning situations in which they have sustained, basically positive contact on an equal social footing.[25] Allport famously found that racial integration in public housing yielded the best results when blacks and whites were in sustained contact, had similar economic status, and social interactions occurred as a function of daily living.[26] Elizabeth Cohen (with Rachel Lotan) has been able to demonstrate that academically heterogeneous groups of students can learn effectively together when status is equalized in the classroom, obviating the perceived need to group students by ability levels.[27] Dual-language programs thus ideally incorporate many of the conditions considered requisite for positive intergroup outcomes: language status is equalized, minority students have a trait that is valued by others (knowledge of a second language), and the students are grouped together for instruction with consistent, naturally occurring contact.

While the potential for helping to desegregate schools and to improve intergroup relations is a powerful incentive for establishing dual-language programs in themselves, there are many other potential advantages to pursuing such educational strategies. From a cognitive perspective, children who develop healthy degrees of bilingualism tend to exhibit greater ability to focus on and use language productively.[28] This skill, called "metalinguistic awareness," has been associated with improved comprehension outcomes. Such children also may develop what is termed "cognitive flexibility," which leads to more creative or innovative ways of approaching learning.

Clearly, however, speaking more than one language, especially when the second language is widely used in the world, has economic as well as cognitive and social advantages. Multilingual people are sought after in many public- and private-sector jobs. One of the fastest growing programs nationally is the International Baccalaureate (IB), which has been adopted at more than a thousand schools in the United States and nearly 3,000 worldwide, serving three-quarters of a million students.[29] The IB is a highly rigorous international curriculum that requires competency in two languages but does not privilege any particular language. Therefore students can enter the program as immigrants, with academic skills developed in their native language, and continue on toward an IB diploma as they acquire the language of their new country. While the program is especially well suited to students who have been in dual-language programs or come to the United States with a good schooling background from their country of origin, it has caught fire with educated parents who seek an internationally competitive education for their own children. The IB provides another opportunity for ELLs and English speakers to study and learn alongside each other in an academically rigorous setting. As the IB takes hold in more communities around the United States, it can be expected that parents' desire to have their children learn in two languages, with commensurate pressure on education policy makers to make this available, will continue to grow.

It is no accident that some of the longest-running and best-known dual-language programs have grown up in communities with access to colleges and universities as well as exceptionally well-educated parents who support the programs. This has certainly been the case in Sonoma, Culver City, and Davis, California; in Cambridge, Massachusetts; and in Washington, D.C. All incorporated university faculty to help design, document, and monitor the programs as well as large numbers of parent volunteers who dedicated countless hours to advocating for the programs and raising funds to make them possible. In most cases these have been middle-class, well-traveled, English-speaking parents who saw the advantages for their children to be competent in more than one language and who were also often prompted by liberal impulses to provide a better education for immigrant and language-minority students in their communities. Such knowledgeable and powerful parents have been able to establish and sustain these programs where less powerful, non-

English-speaking parents have lacked the ability to do so on their own.[30] These well-established programs typically have long waiting lists of students who seek to enroll.[31]

April Linton and Rebecca Franklin describe the cases of a number of dual-language programs that have been started since the passage of voter initiatives to ban or severely limit the use of any language other than English for the instruction of ELL students in California and Massachusetts.[32] Examining dual-language programs in these states, Linton and Franklin find that the banning of such programs has paradoxically contributed to their growth. They quote some educators as believing that the ban removed the stigma of such programs as remedial and provided the opening for parents and educators to design and establish programs that moved away from the old "transitional" models, which focused solely on English Language Learners with the goal of moving them into English as quickly as possible, and toward fully dual-language models with the goal of competence in two languages. As the word gets out that the programs accept both English speakers and ELLs and seek to develop full competence in both languages, parents line up to enroll their children. Of course, to establish these programs in the face of anti-bilingual political pressures has required persistence, determination, and sometimes establishing the schools as magnets or charters to avoid bureaucratic impediments, but the programs have been increasing in popularity and number.[33]

Fred Genesee and I examined the extent to which such dual-language programs in Canada and the United States tend to produce more positive intergroup interactions between language-minority and language-majority students, and the degree to which they increase the likelihood of majority- and minority-group students seeking each other out as friends.[34] This study found considerable evidence for both outcomes, as well as an increased appreciation on the part of the language-majority students for the value of knowing both the culture and the language of the minority group. However, effects were not always sustained over years, and the effects were not universally strong in either the Canadian or the U.S. instances. We attributed this to the uneven implementation of strategies to equalize students' status. As Guadalupe Valdés has cautioned, programs must work against powerful social forces that give the advantage to majority students and families in any school setting, dual-language or otherwise.[35]

Dual-language programs by their very nature tend to produce, if not always equal status, at least greater ethnic and linguistic integration than either English-language-development or English-as-a-second-language programs that group students for instruction according to their language deficits as opposed to their language assets. Dual-language programs can be constructed of students from the same ethnic group but with different first languages. This reduces linguistic isolation but not necessarily either economic or ethnic segregation. However, in a study of 248 dual-immersion programs, Elizabeth Howard and Julie Sugarman found that 54 percent of these programs had no majority ethnic group. They thus hold the potential to significantly increase ethnic and racial diversity in schools.[36] One particularly hopeful sign is the appearance of programs that bring black and Latino students together to learn side by side in two languages.

There is no national or even state or local directory of programs that enroll primarily African Americans alongside Latino students, but at least a few such schools now operate in the Los Angeles area, where the overwhelming majority of students are either Latino or African American. Little is known about the long-term outcomes for students in these schools, but anecdotal reports suggest that they allow two groups that are sometimes at odds in neighboring schools to interact more positively as they share a goal of biliteracy and learn side by side.[37]

Family cohesion and better social adaptation are other outcomes that have been found in students who maintain contact with parental language and culture. One study of sixth, seventh, and eighth graders found that Mexican American students who had maintained competence in their native language and continued to speak Spanish to their parents showed a significant increase in family cohesion at mid-adolescence compared to Mexican American students who were more acculturated and spoke English to their parents.[38] A study of native-born and foreign-born Mexican American and white adolescents concluded that the foreign-born students who maintained language and cultural links to family were more motivated to do well in school and exhibited fewer behavior problems at school.[39] Bilingual development has also been linked to improved family cohesion and self-esteem. Alejandro Portes and Lingxin Hao have attempted to explain these relationships as resulting from "family solidarity and personality adjustment, reflecting cultural continuity and mutual understanding across generations, [although] limited bilingualism and English monolingualism would have the opposite effects."[40] There is also some evidence that where the home language is valued and utilized in instruction, students' self-esteem and confidence are positively affected.[41]

Toward a More Racially and Linguistically Balanced Society

Speaking a language other than standard American English in the United States has too often been constructed as a liability and blamed for the academic underachievement of Latino (and other) students. However, as Richard Ruiz has pointed out, speaking a language other than English can be viewed as a problem or it can be viewed an asset.[42] The fact that schools have chosen to view it as a problem has led to policies that are counterproductive to high achievement. Some researchers have long argued that casting other languages as an asset for the student and the nation would result in a very different educational experience for these students—one that could be additive and enriching rather than deficit-oriented and segregating. In a time when schools seeking to desegregate their student bodies are challenged with so many restrictions in attempting to accomplish this goal, language difference may play a critical role in this process. It may be an asset not only to the students who speak nonstandard variants of English and languages other than English but to the students who are currently cheated of the experience of learning with them and from them. Language difference—and the students who embody this characteristic—may be the key to a more enriching education for all students. Policymakers must have the courage to construct language difference as an asset that can provide students access to an integrated education rather than as a problem that consigns them to weak programs in weak schools where the possibility of going to college, or even joining the economic mainstream, is too often foreclosed.

NOTES

1. National Center for Education Statistics, "The Condition of Education, 2009," *Racial/Ethnic Enrollment in Public Schools: Indicator 7* (Washington, DC: U.S. Department of Education, National Center for Education Statistics, 2009).

2. Texas Education Agency (TEA), "Enrollment in Texas Public Schools, 2007–08," table 4: "Enrollment by Ethnicity, Texas Public Schools, 1997–98 through 2007–08" (Austin: Division of Accountability Research, Department of Assessment, Accountability, and Data Quality, Texas Education Agency, 2009), http://ritter.tea.state.tx.us/research/pdfs/enrollment_2007-08.pdf (accessed 9 September 2009).

3. G. Orfield and E. Frankenberg, *The Last Have Become First: Rural and Small Town America Lead the Way on Desegregation* (Los Angeles: Civil Rights Project/Proyecto Derechos Civiles at UCLA, 2008).

4. Ibid.

5. TEA, "Enrollment in Texas Public Schools."

6. California Department of Education, "Student Enrollment by Ethnicity," *Data-Quest*, http://dq.cde.ca.gov/dataquest/EnrollEthState.asp?Level=State&TheYear=2008-09 &cChoice=EnrollEth1&p=2 (accessed 10 September 2009).

7. G. Orfield and C. Lee, *Why Segregation Matters: Poverty and Educational Inequality* (Cambridge: Civil Rights Project at Harvard University, 2005), http://www.civilrights project.ucla.edu/research/diversity/diversity_gen.php (accessed 10 September 2009).

8. R. Ream, *Uprooting Children: Mobility, Social Capital, and Mexican American Underachievement* (New York: LBF, 2005); R. Rothstein, *Class and Schools: Using Social, Economic, and Educational Reform to Close the Black-White Achievement Gap* (New York: Teachers College Press, 2004).

9. C. Cosentino de Cohen, N. Deterding, and B. C. Clewell, *Who's Left Behind? Immigrant Children in High and Low LEP Schools* (Washington, DC: Urban Institute, 2005).

10. R. Rumberger, P. Gándara, and B. Merino, "Where California's English Learners Attend School and Why It Matters," *LMRI Newsletter* (University of California Linguistic Minority Research Institute, Santa Barbara) 15, no. 2 (2006): 1–2.

11. B. R. Gifford and G. Valdés, "The Linguistic Isolation of Hispanic Students in California's Public Schools: The Challenge of Reintegration," *Annual Yearbook of the National Society for the Study of Education* 5 (2006): 147.

12. M. Suárez-Orozco, C. Suárez-Orozco, and E. Todorova, *Learning a New Land: Immigrant Students in American Society* (Cambridge: Harvard University Press, 2008).

13. Cosentino de Cohen, Deterding, and Clewell, *Who's Left Behind?*

14. P. Gándara et al., "English Learners in California Schools: Unequal Resources, Unequal Outcomes," *Educational Policy Analysis Archives*, http://.epaa.asu.edu/epaa/v11n36/ (accessed 21 September 2009).

15. Individuals with Disabilities Education Act, *Educational Opportunity Report: Latinos* (Los Angeles: Institute for Democracy, Education and Access, UCLA, 2007), http://www.idea.gseis.ucla.edu/publications/eor07/latino_report/index.html (accessed 12 May 2009).

16. J. Batalova, M. Fix, and J. Murray, *Measures of Change: The Demography and Literacy of Adolescent English Learners*, Report to the Carnegie Corporation of New York (Washington, DC: Migration Policy Institute, 2007).

17. P. Gándara and F. Contreras, *The Latino Education Crisis: The Consequences of Failed Social Policies* (Cambridge: Harvard University Press, 2009).

18. A. Zehler et al., *Descriptive Study of Services to LEP Students and LEP Students with Disabilities*, vol. 1 (Washington, DC: U.S. Department of Education, Office of English Language Acquisition, Language Enhancement, and Academic Achievement of Limited English Proficient Students, 2003). Zehler and colleagues show that between 1992 and 2002 the percentage of ELL students who received language services entirely in English increased from 33.7 percent to 47.9 percent nationwide.

19. P. Gándara and M. Hopkins, eds., *Forbidden Language: English Learners and Restrictive Language Policies* (New York: Teachers College Press, 2010).

20. In an unpublished study conducted in 2005 in Northern California's Davis Unified

School District—a highly regarded, award-winning district—researchers found that the average amount of time that elementary students spent over a four-hour period actually producing oral English in the classroom was three minutes; for secondary students, it was less than two minutes.

21. See http://www.cal.org/twi/directory/growth.gif.

22. Zehler et al., *Descriptive Study of Services to LEP Students.*

23. J. Lambert, *Two-Way Bilingual Immersion Programs: State Perspective Administrators Workshop* (Sacramento: California Department of Education, PowerPoint available from author, 2007).

24. F. Genesee and P. Gándara, "Bilingual Education Programs: A Cross-National Perspective," *Journal of Social Issues* 55 (1999): 665–85.

25. G. Allport, *The Nature of Prejudice* (New York: Anchor, 1958); E. Cohen and R. Lotan, "Producing Equal-Status Interaction in the Heterogeneous Classroom," *American Educational Research Journal* 32 (1995): 99–120.

26. Genesee and Gándara, "Bilingual Education Programs."

27. Cohen and Lotan, "Producing Equal-Status Interaction."

28. E. Bialystock, *Bilingualism in Development: Language, Literacy, and Cognition* (New York: Cambridge University Press, 2001); R. M. Diaz and C. Klinger, "Towards an Explanatory Model of the Interaction between Bilingualism and Cognitive Development," in *Language Processing in Bilingual Children,* edited by E. Bialystock (New York: Cambridge University Press, 1991), 140–85; S. J. Galambos and K. Hakuta, "Subject-Specific and Task-Specific Characteristics of Metalinguistic Awareness in Bilingual Children," *Applied Psycholinguistics* 9 (1988): 141–62.

29. See http://www.ibo.org.

30. B. R. Gifford and G. Valdés, "The Linguistic Isolation of Hispanic Students in California's Public Schools: The Challenge of Reintegration," *Annual Yearbook of the National Society for the Study of Education* 5 (2006): 125–54.

31. See, e.g., Bill Hoban, "Flowery Recognized for Dual Immersion," *Sonoma News* (25 May 2009), http://www.sonomanews.com/articles/2009/05/25/news/doc4a1b06b137 fc0572968714.prt (accessed 12 September 2009).

32. A. Linton and R. Franklin, "Bilingualism for the Children: Dual Language Programs and Restrictive Language Policies," in *Forbidden Language: English Learners and Restrictive Language Policies,* edited by P. Gándara and M. Hopkins (New York: Teachers College Press, 2010), 199–217.

33. Ibid.

34. Genesee and Gándara, "Bilingual Education Programs."

35. G. Valdés, "Dual-Language Immersion Programs: A Cautionary Note Concerning the Education of Language-Minority Students," *Harvard Educational Review* 67, no. 3 (1997): 391–429.

36. E. R. Howard and J. Sugarman, "Two-Way Immersion Programs, Features and Statistics," *ERIC Digest* (EDO-FL-01-01) (Washington, DC: ERIC Clearinghouse on Language and Linguistics, 2001).

37. M. Brooks, personal communication, 20 November 2007.

38. J. C. Baer and M. F. Schmitz, "Ethnic Differences in Trajectories of Family Cohesion for Mexican American and Non-Hispanic White Adolescents," *Journal of Youth and Adolescence* 36 (2007): 583–92.

39. M. Suárez-Orozco and C. Suárez-Orozco, *Trans-formations: Immigration, Family Life, and Motivation among Latino Adolescents* (Palo Alto, CA: Stanford University Press, 1995).

40. A. Portes and L. Hao, "The Price of Uniformity: Language, Family and Personality Adjustment in the Immigrant Second Generation," *Ethnic and Racial Studies* 25 (2002): 893.

41. J. W. Lee, "The Effect of Ethnic Identity and Bilingual Confidence on Chinese Youth's Self-Esteem," *Alberta Journal of Educational Research* 54, no. 1 (2008): 83–96.

42. R. Ruiz, "Orientations in Language Planning," *Journal for the National Association of Bilingual Education* 8 (1984): 15–34.

PART V

Integrated Means toward Integrated Ends:

Broadening Social Policies

ELIZABETH DEBRAY & ERICA FRANKENBERG

Federal Legislation to Promote Metropolitan Approaches to Educational and Housing Opportunity

In this essay, we outline a proposal for new federal legislation to create a pilot grant program in selected southern metropolitan areas designed to promote voluntary approaches to expanding access to integrated education and housing. We argue that metropolitanwide solutions are critical to ameliorating school segregation, and we propose a regional combination of housing subsidies and interdistrict school transfers. Drawing on the findings from two housing-relocation programs, the Gautreaux Assisted Housing Program (a court-ordered program referred to as Gautreaux hereafter) and the Moving to Opportunity program (authorized by federal legislation), as well as the experiences of existing school-transfer programs, we describe the duration, scope, and cost of this proposed program, explain how the housing subsidies and school transfers would work together to promote opportunity, and provide suggestions for program design, incentives, administration, and evaluation.[1]

The Need for a Federal Program Promoting Metropolitan Integration of Housing and Education

Housing and educational opportunities are inextricably intertwined. As the suburbs have drawn tax revenue and political clout away from inner-city cores, urban students' access to higher-performing schools has become further limited.[2] Ever since the Supreme Court majority in *Milliken v. Bradley* (1974) overlooked evidence of metrowide housing discrimination in the Detroit area, however, federal courts have treated housing segregation as natural.[3] In *Milliken*, the Supreme Court turned away from its prior position in the 1971 *Swann* decision, which both authorized cross-district busing and recognized the relationship between the location of schools and residential choice. Reflecting the Court's most recent stance, however, Justice Anthony Kennedy argued in *Freeman v. Pitts* (1992) that "where resegregation is a product not of state action but of private choices, it does not have constitutional implications. It is beyond the authority and beyond the practical ability of the federal courts to try to counteract these kinds of continuous and massive demographic shifts."[4] The Supreme Court rulings in this and other school desegregation decisions during the 1990s relaxed the requirements that districts had to meet to prove they had eliminated all vestiges of segregation, in part due to judicial acceptance of housing decisions perpetuating segregation as private actions. In this climate of federal courts' retreating from recognizing an enforceable link between school and residential segregation, we argue that it is nonetheless a vital public policy issue—perhaps even more vital after the Court's decision in *Parents Involved in Community Schools v. Seattle School District No. 1* (PICS, 2007)—and that it is time for federal legislation to use new policy tools to address the link.

Social science research on neighborhood effects supports the benefits of low-poverty relative to high-poverty neighborhoods on various dimensions of children's and adolescents' well-being.[5] These include benefits in mental health,[6] peer-group influence and educational achievement,[7] and safety.[8] This literature also highlights inner-city residents' higher poverty rates, unemployment, and spatial isolation from the mainstream economy.[9] In December 2008, the National Commission on Fair Housing and Equal Opportunity reported that hearings across the country had revealed that housing discrimination and racial and ethnic segregation remained alive and well and are "spreading steadily into growing sectors of suburbia."[10] The commission's report recommended regional coordination to develop plans and measurable goals for fair housing, including Section 8 (the formal name for housing choice vouchers, designed to assist families in relocating from high-poverty to lower-poverty neighborhoods) and public housing.[11]

Further, in addition to coordinating housing and educational desegregation initiatives, any such initiative should extend beyond the boundary lines of school districts; indeed, research demonstrates the strong contribution of between-district segregation to overall segregation at the metropolitan level.[12] One reason why the South has had the lowest segregation for black students until recently is the extent of countywide districts, which often encompass city and suburban areas. Since the early 1990s, however, municipalities have formed nearly 1,000 new school districts; where such fragmentation exists, declines in intradistrict segregation are offset by increasing interdistrict segregation, which particularly threatens integration in the South, where countywide districts are most widespread.[13] Approximately 70 percent of school segregation in metropolitan statistical areas (MSAs) was a result of segregation between districts.[14] Even though many governmental services are administered regionally, only a handful of cross-district programs aim to desegregate across fragmented metropolitan areas.

There is relevant precedent for federal legislation to help communities alleviate school segregation. The Emergency School Aid Act (ESAA) of 1972 is the main example of a targeted federal program that sought to foster school integration across metropolitan areas. Until its abolition by the Reagan administration in 1981, the ESAA funded "training, intervention programs, new curricula development, magnet schools for voluntary desegregation, and large-scale research on ways to improve race relations."[15] While we recognize that our proposed program would be implemented in a very different sociopolitical context—one in which school desegregation is not being mandated by the courts in the vast majority of metropolitan areas—we believe that the need for congressional attention is just as pressing and as relevant as it was 35 years ago. Indeed, new research about the importance of integration and new demographic realities in an age of global interconnectedness suggests that the need for these programs is even greater now than it was a generation ago.

Housing: The Advantages of Building on Gautreaux's Record

The Moving to Opportunity program (MTO) and the Gautreaux program in Chicago are the two major federal initiatives from which lessons may be drawn about housing relocation and poverty deconcentration. MTO, enacted during the Clinton administration as an economic desegregation initiative, was scaled back from a two-year effort to a one-year demonstration program and served 1,425 families across five cities.[16] The Gautreaux program, which resulted from the U.S. Supreme Court's decision in *Hills v. Gautreaux* (1972), allowed public-housing residents to receive Section 8 housing certificates and move to privately owned apartments in the suburbs.[17] Families were counseled to move to low-poverty, low-minority suburban areas. Approximately 7,100 families participated in Gautreaux between 1976 and 1998.

A significant difference between the two programs is that in assigning families to suburban housing, Gautreaux relocated families to specific addresses, while MTO merely specified census tracts, allowing the families to find an apartment within the tract. Perhaps as a result of this flexibility, among MTO movers to low-poverty areas, one-third relocated to areas where a majority of residents were black.[18] By contrast, of the total number of Gautreaux families who moved, only 24.2 percent moved into tracts that had a black majority.[19] This difference is due to the Gautreaux program's design of serving low-income black families—all of whom qualified for public housing—who received Section 8 vouchers to move to private apartments in Chicago or in its middle- and upper-income white suburbs.[20] The court agreement specified that not more than 25 percent of participating families could locate in any portion of the city of Chicago or in minority areas. After 1991, there were no placements within the city.[21] Of Gautreaux families, only 4.7 percent moved into tracts of greater than 50 percent poverty.[22]

We advocate for a Gautreaux-style design to this pilot program for three reasons: (1) the social and educational outcomes for families suburban relocation are strongest, especially for children; (2) Gautreaux was relatively modest in scope, serving a maximum of several hundred families a year in one metropolitan area, making it more acceptable to suburban officials;[23] and (3) the program was explicitly designed to support racial desegregation of housing.

In their surveys of how mothers who participated in Gautreaux characterized suburban schools, Leonard Rubinowitz and James Rosenbaum found greater parental satisfaction with the suburban schools relative to the urban schools their children had previously attended. The reasons the mothers gave included curricular and extracurricular activities, smaller class sizes, and school environment, safety, and discipline.[24] Rubinowitz and Rosenbaum also compared high school completion rates and secondary school attendance for the suburban movers versus the city movers.[25] They found that of those over the age of 17 who were interviewed for the study, almost seven times as many suburban movers went to four-year colleges as did those who moved within the city.[26] The Gautreaux mothers' most significant complaint in the surveys was their children's special education placement in their new schools, which many attributed to racism, cultural differences, or both.[27]

There were other benefits of the program, notably employment: a study of children found that by the time they were young adults, suburban movers were far more likely to be employed in jobs with better pay and benefits than were city movers,[28] while a study of mothers found that employment rates were higher for suburban movers, with effects particularly large for adults who had been unemployed prior to the move.[29] While it is true that the transition to the suburbs was by no means easy for most families, research by Rosenbaum, Stephanie DeLuca, and Tammy Tuck suggests that "even without encouragement, suburban neighbors are often receptive and more accepting over time."[30] These authors further conclude, based on interviews with Gautreaux mothers who moved to the suburbs, that social capital accrued to these families through "reciprocity obligations,"[31] and that they recognized the benefits of that accrual.

Interdistrict Schooling Program

While a number of options provide for interdistrict transfers, including open enrollment and the No Child Left Behind Act (NCLB), we argue that these options are less effective means of increasing metropolitan integration than programs with the explicit aim of integration across boundary lines, extensive outreach, and provision of free transportation to enable all families to access these schools.

Because the federal courts have progressively become less of a venue for promoting voluntary school integration, we and others argue that there is a role for congressionally mandated federal policies to do so.[32] As Jennifer Jellison Holme and Amy Stuart Wells wrote in a recent essay, "Research on interdistrict open enrollment choice policies and interdistrict desegregation plans illustrate that the design of these policies matters a great deal. Thus, we argue that the federal government, which, until NCLB, had never used its powers to mandate school choice, has the unique ability to create equity-minded choice programs that break through existing school district boundary limits."[33]

Another argument in calling for a renewed federal role in promoting interdistrict school transfers is that the public school choice provisions of NCLB have proven too weak an intervention to affect opportunity. While some civil rights advocates had initially hoped that the new provisions for public school transfer in NCLB were a possible venue for poor and minority students to escape low-performing inner-city schools,[34] NCLB choice has not accomplished this goal. One of the reasons is that while the U.S. Department of Education has adopted language encouraging school districts to form interdistrict transfer agreements, there are no financial or legal incentives to do so. Another reason is that in most districts, better-performing schools do not have the capacity to accept transfers, and often the schools offered for receipt of transfers are demographically similar to those attending the school from which students seek to transfer.[35] While NCLB's provisions have been heralded for mandating "gap closing," it is now apparent that that vision will not be realized in racially and ethnically segregated schools.[36] As we mentioned earlier, there is ample evidence of a strong inverse correlation between the poverty level of students' neighborhoods and the performance of their schools.

While there are revisions that could improve the existing NCLB choice provision,[37] it is a far too limited mechanism to address the interrelated issues of housing, fragmentation of local governments, and the lack of incentives for urban-suburban transfer programs. We argue that a coordinated federal pilot program, jointly administered by the Department of Housing and Urban Development (HUD) and the Department of Education, would be far more effective in building real educational opportunity than NCLB's transfer provisions. Further, our proposed program, which would diversify suburban schools, has the added advantage of incorporating knowledge about the benefits of attending integrated schools for students from all backgrounds.[38]

We advocate for a program modeled after the interdistrict desegregation programs because of the findings about the outcomes for participating students. Recent research on these programs is somewhat limited. Further, there are methodological challenges to understanding the cause of any changed student outcomes. A review of the research on these programs described four categories of findings demonstrating the programs' success:[39] (1) racial attitudes of city and suburban students; (2) academic achievement and exposure to an enriched, high-quality curriculum for urban students; (3) improved long-term outcomes such as graduation, college matriculation, and job attainment;[40] and (4) the popularity of the interdistrict programs.[41]

Policy Implementation Considerations

Our considerations about the implementation of housing policy are drawn from the Gautreaux program. For instance, Gautreaux suggested how difficult it was to secure suburban landlords' participation and to assure families' access to affordable housing units.[42] Our considerations about schools are drawn from the experiences of eight currently operating interdistrict transfer programs designed to voluntarily integrate students. These programs differ in origins, duration, and implementation details. Three programs began as remedies to federal court desegregation cases, three were part of state desegregation remedies (though one program had been in existence prior to the state court case), and two began voluntarily. Holme and Wells's review of the eight programs identifies critical state supports necessary to the programs' success as including access for city students wishing to transfer to the suburbs, outreach to notify families that they are eligible for the program, and convenient, free transportation to their suburban school.[43]

Joint Housing and Education Considerations
FAMILY ELIGIBILITY AND OUTREACH
In metropolitan areas where a court order governs either housing or educational racial desegregation, race-based designations of students' and families' eligibility would be both legal and desirable. In those participating metropolitan areas where there is no such court order to support a race-based classifi-

cation, priority should be given to those families living in neighborhoods with a high concentration of poverty, high levels of residential racial and ethnic segregation, and low levels of educational attainment.[44] Participating metros would also need to ensure that where there is more demand for than supply of suburban housing or school slots, the programs are utilized by all groups at the approximate rate of their racial or ethnic representation in the city (or school system) as a whole.[45] It is likely that each metro would need to devise its own mix of socioeconomic characteristics (either neighborhood or individual) in order to identify families and students in low-opportunity areas.[46]

The Gautreaux program could not meet the demand of interested and eligible families for a number of reasons. The available rental housing that existed in predominantly white neighborhoods did not always suffice for large families needing at least three bedrooms, the rents for available housing were above the value of HUD vouchers, or the landlords accepted few or no program participants.[47] As a result, of the 1,700 families eligible, on average, each year, approximately 325 actually moved, just less than 20 percent.[48] The failure to receive an offer of a place to live was thus the main constraint accounting for the relatively low move rate.[49] Gautreaux used real estate staff to locate appropriate housing units; and there were also limited numbers of counselors available to show participants the housing units, critical for successful lease-up when the units were distant and families needed reassurance.[50]

Most interdistrict transfer programs have involved outreach to eligible families. Outreach, in fact, has been part of many school choice programs that are designed to create diverse schools to make sure that families of all racial and ethnic backgrounds are aware of their educational options. In St. Louis, for example, there were ongoing outreach efforts to eligible city residents via U.S. mail to inform them of the program and of the suburban options.[51] Holme and Wells conclude that "evidence from these eight programs suggests that some form of outreach, recruitment and coordination of the cross-district transfer process makes that process much easier for families and students and assures that more children have access to suburban schools."[52] In Minneapolis, federal grant money helped support extensive outreach activities,[53] while the new Hartford settlement agreement included money for parent-information centers to do outreach for the city-suburban and regional magnet programs.[54]

STRONG REGIONAL COALITION AND ADMINISTERING AGENCY

Because one of the major goals of the pilot is to ensure strong regional collaboration beyond the borders of individual townships and school districts, administrative authority should be given to regional alliances or coalitions that have the political capacity to work with both city and suburban governments. These alliances should be able to provide extensive education across a metro area to prospective recipients about the purpose and operation of, and eligibility for, these voluntary programs, as well as intensive counseling to participants. The Twin Cities' Metropolitan Council, the Puget Sound Regional Council, and the Southern California Association of Governments are examples of metropolitan planning organizations that have successfully addressed land-use, growth-management, and transportation issues. Most interdistrict school programs have a regional administering agency that places students in suburban districts and helps with adjustment for families, faculty professional development, and other duties.[55]

One of the vital conditions of aid should be that participating communities or towns agree not to splinter from the participating metropolitan area or regional or county school district during the implementation of the program.[56]

NEED FOR SUBURBAN BUY-IN

A vital criterion for approving regional planning commissions in the pilot program should be a requirement that they examine issues of racial and ethnic transition and stability. It is particularly important for planners of a housing relocation program not to view the suburbs as a monolithic entity but to consider that some suburbs are more ready than others to accept families relocating from inner cities. Myron Orfield has outlined a "new suburban typology" differentiating types of suburban communities from a cluster analysis of suburban municipalities in the 25 largest MSAs; these differences in community characteristics could impact a suburban jurisdiction's ability to maintain stable neighborhoods and not to transition to poor and minority schools and neighborhoods.

If not monitored carefully, the city-suburban school-transfer program also has the possibility of accelerating suburban segregation. In Hartford, several inner-ring suburban districts do not participate in the transfer program because their minority percentage is above the "cap" for compliance with reducing racial and ethnic isolation. This has also been the case in Minneapolis, where falling enrollments among inner-ring suburban districts have made participation in their city-suburban choice program more desirable. Two suburban districts that accepted city students were more racially and ethnically segregated because of the influx of urban minority students.[57]

Access to suburban districts may take the form of school-level requirements or financial incentives for suburban districts to accept urban transfer students.[58] All eight programs in Holme and Wells's study provide funding that goes to suburban schools that accept transfer students and provide transportation for students to the suburban districts. Holme and Wells also conclude that over the longer term, it is necessary for political leaders to frame the transfer program as an expansion of educational opportunities for the most disadvantaged students.[59] Pointing out that, in many cases, the programs do not actually cost extra money, as it merely per-pupil funding that follows the student, may also help to build public support.[60]

The administering regional agencies, anticipating suburban resistance in particular communities, should communicate proactively with suburban residents about the program's benefits—that new construction of affordable housing is not part of the program, that housing-relocation participants in particular will be dispersed across different kinds of suburbs to avoid further segregation, that suburban school systems will receive adequate funding for accepting student transfers, and that there are important benefits for suburban residents that will result from neighborhood and school integration.

EFFECTIVE, INTENSIVE COUNSELING

An independent analysis of Section 8 prepared for HUD found that landlord outreach was the only metropolitan Public Housing Authority policy or procedure associated at a statistically significant level with voucher recipient families' successful lease-up;[61] research on the MTO program also documented the critical relationship between families' successful relocation to the suburbs and the availability of effective counseling, including vocational training and education referral and help with child care.[62] The housing relocation program should have incentives for landlords to participate willingly because the Gautreaux experience demonstrated that it was difficult to get landlords in white, middle-class neighborhoods to otherwise accept urban transfers. Incentives might include targeting middle-class communities where the demand for rental units is not too tight and local councils' efforts to reduce landlords' costs and risks, such as screening tenants' credit.[63] Section 8 subsidies can provide landlords stable revenue; in the case of Gautreaux, this was a major incentive for landlords who did participate, as that revenue stream was guaranteed for five years, with the likelihood of two additional five-year extensions.[64]

Counseling students and families who participate in city-suburban transfer programs is similarly an important aspect of their adjustment.[65] In Hartford, staff members rode the buses during the earlier iteration of Project Choice.

Suburban METCO districts were, until recently, required to use some of their funding to hire a coordinator to assist families and students as they transition to the district. These efforts also included training opportunities for schools.

School districts receiving city students must agree to participate in teacher training focused on issues of diversity and commit to trying to expand the number of teachers of color. As a result of both the school and housing desegregation components of this pilot program—as well as already existent suburban demographic change—there would be an influx of diverse students into what might be largely homogenous schools. Teachers in largely white schools report little training about teaching in diverse classrooms.[66] A study of Hartford's city-suburban transfer program found negligible numbers of teachers of color in suburban districts receiving Hartford minority students.[67] Recognizing this, some programs have made training for teachers a component of the overall program design.

To summarize, three factors—family participation, suburban buy-in, and effective counseling—should be emphasized in the guidelines for services that ought to be specified in a new federal pilot program.

Considerations Specific to Housing

PORTABILITY AND REGIONAL ADMINISTRATION OF PROGRAMS

Assuming the pilot program is authorized to work in tandem with Section 8, there are decisions to be made about the regional administration of the program. While families currently have the right to move to any community where an agency administers a voucher program, in the past, "the administrative geography of the [Section 8] voucher program—its balkanized operation in most metropolitan areas—[has] create[d] substantial barriers to families moving from poorer and more racially concentrated areas to areas with greater opportunities."[68] However, HUD is working on administrative changes to streamline portability of Section 8 housing vouchers, improve Public Housing Authority accountability for racial and economic integration in the voucher program, and increase voucher rents in higher-cost areas.[69]

DEFINITIONS OF LOW-POVERTY OR LOW-MINORITY AREAS TO WHICH FAMILIES WOULD BE REQUIRED TO RELOCATE

The program should follow newly revised HUD rules, called the Section 8 Management Assessment Program, to avoid poverty concentration in the use of Section 8 vouchers.[70] The Gautreaux program's goal of dispersal across metropolitan areas is optimal; our recommendation is that families be prohibited from moving to neighborhoods with greater than 10 percent poverty.

In order to minimize the chances for racial resegregation in suburban reloca-
tions, we propose that participating families move into Census block groups
of no greater than 30 percent African American and Hispanic residents.

Considerations Specific to Schools

Before considering the components of interdistrict transfer, we first posit that
a coherent federal policy for metropolitan school desegregation should include targeted funding for interdistrict magnet programs within the Magnet Schools Assistance Program (MSAP), since at present there are no such
incentives.[71]

TRANSPORTATION

All existing interdistrict desegregation programs provide free transportation
for participating students, which we consider an essential part of our proposal.
Transportation is funded by each state, although states do so through several
different mechanisms: in some instances, the state directly provides transportation, in other places, districts are reimbursed. Transportation is both a
major cost in the implementation of interdistrict programs and has been cited
as a reason participating students leave the transfer program.[72] An evaluation
of the Minneapolis interdistrict program reported that only one-third of participants reported that they would choose the same school without free transportation.[73]

There are trade-offs between the length and cost of transportation. In Hartford, for instance, despite the fact that transportation costs were $3.7 million
in 2006–7, bus rides lasted as long as two hours and were cited as a reason the
interdistrict choice program fell far short of its target number of participating
students by the end of the first settlement agreement.[74] In addition to minimizing attrition, a district also must enable participation in extracurricular
activities by providing multiple transportation options, including a late bus.
This allows urban transfer students to fully participate in the life of the school
community, particularly since they might be either low-income, minority, or
both (unlike the majority of suburban residents). This is particularly important as there might be unfamiliarity or stigma attached to crossing boundary
lines for urban parents, who might also lack the access to cars and the flexible
work schedules necessary to transport their children. To minimize transportation costs, participating suburban districts should take a minimum number of
students. In addition, administering agencies could link certain areas of the
city with neighboring suburban districts to make travel more efficient.

The school-transfer program would be designed to correct for many of the ineffective design features of the No Child Left Behind Act, which provides no meaningful incentives for cross-district transfer agreements. Subgroup accountability sanctions that ordinarily apply under NCLB (such as for corrective action, or requiring parental choice) would be waived for suburban schools accepting students from central cities for a three-year "safe haven" period. This is critical due to the fact that the transition from urban to suburban schools often results in an initial negative effect on students' achievement scores, which subsequently exceed those of city peers as they remain in suburban schools for longer periods.[75]

Summing Up the Cost of the Proposed Pilot

Duration and Scope

We recommend an initial authorized funding period of five consecutive years. In the program's first three years, the housing relocation voucher component should be funded to serve up to 800 new families a year across four metropolitan areas per year (or approximately 200 new families per metro area per year) and up to 1,200 new families (300 new per metro area) in years four and five, for a total of 4,800 families in five years.

The voluntary school-transfer program should serve approximately 6,000 eligible students total per year by year five (or approximately 1,500 students per metro area). Using the Minneapolis city-suburban desegregation program as a model,[76] we envision the program beginning with 500 students per MSA in year one, with an additional 250 students per year until year five. Each student would be guaranteed space in the program until graduation. In addition to adding 250 additional students per year, the program would also need to replace students who leave the program via graduation or attrition. Space should be made available for students at all grade levels, although there would likely be more interest among earlier grades.

Assuming an average of two school-age children per family relocating to the suburbs, by the end of the pilot program, each MSA would have 3,900 students who moved from urban to suburban schools through the housing and educational components (plus any students who participated in the city-suburban transfer program and graduated).

Cost: Housing Program

The total costs of housing vouchers would depend on several factors, including regional differences in cost of living, supply of housing stock, and the extent to which turnover in Section 8 might offset new vouchers. The main consideration is that turnover in Section 8 is extremely low—participants keep the vouchers for around three years on average; turnover in most MSAs is between 1 and 2 percent of all vouchers each year.[77]

To demonstrate how costs differ among MSAs, we calculated an average cost per year for four different-sized southern MSAs based on HUD data from 2007, estimating the annual cost for serving 1,200 families over five years for each MSA, as well as the extent to which a 2 percent turnover in Section 8 vouchers for 2007 would offset the cost of the pilot.[78]

Assuming counseling costs of $3,000 per new family voucher per year, we estimated total counseling costs across all MSAs at $6 million.[79] We further calculated administrative costs of $800 per new family voucher per year, or a total cost of $1.6 million for all MSAs. Thus, the total cost of running the program in these four MSAs is estimated at $31,960,000; much of this cost could be offset by Section 8.

Cost: School-Transfer Program

We make several assumptions in estimating the cost of the school-transfer program. First, we presume that the state's per-pupil funding allocation for each urban student (including any compensatory spending that urban students may get) will follow the student to the suburban district. Thus, the additional costs for the program are compensation for the sending urban district and for transportation. Not all existing programs include funding for urban districts, but we believe this is important to mitigate the financial impact of students leaving the urban districts. We assume a per-pupil expenditure (PPE) of $9,666 in a state, and we thus allocate half of the PPE to the urban district, or $4,833 per participating student. We also budget $2,000 per student for transportation, although this can vary in efficiency and cost based on the proximity and density of participating suburban districts, and the number of students per receiving school, among other factors. It is possible that some of the transportation costs would be offset by the busing of students within urban districts' boundaries, which is already taking place.

Assuming full capacity as gradually scaled up to 1,500 students by year five, the program would cost $27.5 million per MSA for five years in student costs. Based on estimates of other interdistrict programs, we estimate that it would cost an additional $1 million per MSA per year to administer the program, provide counseling for families and students, and to provide training and other educational resources for participating suburban districts. The complete cost for the program is thus $34,165,000 per MSA or $136.66 million total for all four identified MSAs for five years.

Consideration: Continuity of Funding beyond Initial Five Years
The most likely option for funding the school-transfer program is the state. In two of the places where interdistrict programs began voluntarily—Boston and Rochester, New York—state laws were passed that authorize funding for each program. A number of interdistrict desegregation programs have also continued beyond their initial court-ordered time period, and these costs have been borne by the state.[80] A review of the eight interdistrict programs noted that, in fact, "over time in many of these places state legislators . . . have become more supportive of these programs, even if the federal courts have become less so."[81] For the housing component, it is likely that a combination of state and federal Section 8 funds could absorb administrative and counseling costs after year five.

Federal Program Authorization, Administration, and Evaluation

We believe that there are at least two different ways such a program could be enacted. The simplest is likely for the pilot program to be inserted in both HUD and Department of Education appropriations bills and then to be administered jointly by the two departments. A model for this kind of joint administration would be the School-to-Work Opportunities Act of 1994, which was overseen by officials in the Departments of Labor and Education.

The less desirable alternative is for the city-suburban school-transfer demonstration to become part of the Elementary and Secondary Education Act reauthorization while the suburban housing relocation program is created as part of the Housing and Community Development Act (or as a subpart of SEVRA), as was the case with Moving to Opportunity. We described above the policy disadvantages of tying school transfers solely to NCLB because of its current accountability model for identifying schools for public school transfers and its lack of incentives for interdistrict transfers. A better alternative for metropolitan school desegregation would be the inclusion of targeted funds for interdistrict magnets within MSAP.

The chief considerations in creating the housing relocation program should be maximizing both the number of vouchers available per MSA and regional portability. As we mentioned earlier, both the Sustainable Communities and Choice Neighborhoods Initiatives under development with HUD and the Department of Transportation are potential vehicles for the promotion of voucher mobility. In our view, the development and funding of the separate components—housing and education—in two or more different pieces of legislation renders it not only more difficult to mandate a common and consistent evaluation but more difficult to administer with coherent directives to the local administering agencies.

In a separate article, we have included a more thorough discussion of what indicators should be included in evaluating both the housing and education components of the pilot.[82] It will suffice here to state that important components of an independent evaluation are a baseline participant survey, which would include factors such as why families chose to participate, their expectations about either housing or school moves, and their views of their living conditions,[83] as well as demographic information about income, race or ethnicity, background, neighborhood characteristics and experiences before the move. The evaluation of the different sites for both the housing and education components will need to allow for a period of "exposure" of family members to the new environment and thus should allow for measurement of locational effects in years one through five.

We discuss the political considerations surrounding the enactment of the pilot program from both the federal education and housing perspectives in a separate article.[84]

The end of court-ordered desegregation in many areas of the country and the Supreme Court's PICS decision barring local school boards' adoption of race-conscious student assignment policies both signal that this is a favorable moment for Congress to open other constitutional avenues for metropolitan areas that seek to prevent a return to racially isolated schools. As Nancy Denton has written, "By treating [housing and school desegregation] as separate we make it impossible to solve either, while still feeling that we are making an effort."[85] Even though the current economic climate does not encourage creative thinking about this kind of policy priority, we believe it is now more, not less, urgent that the groundwork be laid for students' opportunities.

NOTES

A longer version of this essay was published as Elizabeth DeBray-Pelot and Erica Frankenberg, "Federal Legislation to Promote Metropolitan Approaches to Educational and Housing Opportunity," *Georgetown Journal on Poverty Law and Policy* 17 (2010): 265–86. We thank Gary Orfield, James Rosenbaum, Phil Tegeler, and Mary Cunningham for suggestions and input on drafts of this essay. Micah Kubik and Leah Staub of the Center for Budget Policies and Priorities provided calculations of metrowide Section 8 voucher expenditures. Wendy Dubner also provided research assistance.

1. There have been earlier proposals to expand housing mobility programs. See A. Polikoff, *Waiting for Gautreaux: A Story of Segregation, Housing, and the Black Ghetto* (Evanston, IL: Northwestern University Press, 2006); and J. Goering, "Comments on Future Research and Housing Policy," in *Choosing a Better Life? Evaluating the Moving to Opportunity Social Experiment*, edited by J. Goering and J. Feins (Washington, DC: Urban Institute Press, 2003), 383–408.

2. A. Blackwell and J. Bell, "Equitable Development for a Stronger Nation: Lessons from the Field," in *The Geography of Opportunity*, edited by X. Briggs (Washington, DC: Brookings Institution, 2005), 290.

3. G. Orfield and S. Eaton, *Dismantling Desegregation: The Quiet Reversal of Brown v. Board of Education* (New York: New Press, 1996), 296. See also Orfield essay.

4. *Freeman v. Pitts*, 503 U.S. 467 (1992), 495.

5. J. Brooks-Gunn et al., "Do Neighborhoods Influence Child and Adolescent Development?," *American Journal of Sociology* 99 (1993): 353–95.

6. T. Leventhal and J. Brooks-Gunn, "Moving to Opportunity: An Experimental Study of Neighborhood Effects on Mental Health," *American Journal of Public Health* 93, no. 9 (2003): 1576–82.

7. A. Wells and R. Crain, *Stepping Over the Color Line* (New Haven, CT: Yale University Press, 1997); J. Ainsworth, "Why Does It Take a Village? The Mediation of Neighborhood Effects on Educational Achievement," *Social Forces* 81, no. 1 (2002) 117–52; C. Jencks and S. Mayer, "The Social Consequences of Growing Up in a Poor Neighborhood," in *Inner-City Poverty in the United States*, edited by L. Linn and M. McGeary (Washington, DC: National Academy Press, 1990), 111–86; S. Schellenberg, "Concentration of Poverty and the Ongoing Need for Title I," in *Hard Work for Good Schools: Facts Not Fads in Title I Reform*, edited by G. Orfield and E. DeBray (Cambridge: Civil Rights Project at Harvard University, 1999), 130–46.

8. J. Rosenbaum, S. DeLuca, and T. Tuck, "New Capabilities in New Places: Low-Income Black Families in Suburbia," in *The Geography of Opportunity*, edited by X. Briggs (Washington, DC: Brookings Institution, 2005), 150–75.

9. W. J. Wilson, *The Truly Disadvantaged* (Chicago: University of Chicago Press, 1987); P. Dimond, "Empowering Families to Vote with Their Feet," in *Reflections on Regionalism*, edited by B. Katz (Washington, DC: Brookings Institution, 2000), 249–71; K. Ihlanfeldt, "The Geography of Economic and Social Opportunity in Metropolitan Areas," in *Governance and Opportunity in Metropolitan America* (Washington, DC: National Academy Press, 1999), 213–52.

10. National Commission on Fair Housing and Equal Opportunity, *The Future of Fair Housing* (Washington, DC: NCFHEO, 2008), http://www.civilrights.org/publications/reports/fairhousing.html (accessed 2 February 2009).

11. Ibid.

12. C. Clotfelter, *After Brown: The Rise and Retreat of School Desegregation* (Princeton, NJ: Princeton University Press, 2004); S. Reardon and J. Yun, "Integrating Neighborhoods, Segregating Schools: The Retreat from School Desegregation in the South, 1990–2000," *North Carolina Law Review* 81, no. 4 (2003): 1563–96.

13. E. Frankenberg, "Splintering School Districts: Understanding the Link between Segregation and Fragmentation," *Law and Social Inquiry* 34, no. 4 (2009): 869–909.

14. Clotfelter, *After Brown*, 73.

15. G. Orfield, "Prologue: Lessons Forgotten," in *Lessons in Integration: Realizing the Promise of Racial Diversity in American Schools*, edited by E. Frankenberg and G. Orfield (Charlottesville: University of Virginia Press, 2007), 3.

16. J. Goering, "Political Origins and Opposition," in *Choosing a Better Life: Evaluating the Moving to Opportunity Social Experiment* (2005), 135. Placement of families ended after this time, but services and research on the program continued. MTO was an experimental program during the 1990s whereby low-income families were randomly assigned to one of three groups: an open-choice Section 8 group (the comparison group); a group moving to a low-poverty area, often into mixed-income suburban rental housing (experimental group); or the control group that remained in public housing in high-poverty areas. The regions selected by HUD for participation were Chicago, Boston, Los Angeles, New York, and Baltimore.

17. L. Rubinowitz and J. Rosenbaum, *Crossing the Class and Color Lines: From Public Housing to White Suburbia* (Chicago: University of Chicago Press, 2000), 40, 2.

18. Rosenbaum, DeLuca, and Tuck, "New Capabilities," 157.

19. S. DeLuca and J. Rosenbaum, "If Low-Income Blacks Are Given a Chance to Live in White Neighborhoods, Will They Stay? Examining Mobility Patterns in a Quasi-experimental Program with Administrative Data," *Housing Policy Debate* 14, no. 3 (2003): 320.

20. Rosenbaum, DeLuca, and Tuck, "New Capabilities," 156.

21. Rubinowitz and Rosenbaum, *Crossing the Class and Color Lines*, 68.

22. DeLuca and Rosenbaum, "If Low-Income Blacks," 320.

23. Rubinowitz and Rosenbaum, *Crossing the Class and Color Lines*.

24. Ibid., 130–35.

25. From 1976 to 1991, Gautreaux participants were allowed to move within the city of Chicago and were compared to those relocating to the suburbs. City movers were 30 percent of the sample.

26. Rubinowitz and Rosenbaum, *Crossing the Class and Color Lines*, 165.

27. Ibid., 141. The authors note that there are several possible explanations for the frequency of special education placements, including the suburban schools' higher academic standards and norms.

28. J. Rosenbaum, "Changing the Geography of Opportunity by Expanding Residential Choice: Lessons from the Gautreaux Program," *Housing Policy Debate* 6, no. 1 (2002): 231–69.

29. J. Rosenbaum, "Residential Mobility: Effects on Education, Employment, and

Racial Interaction," in *Legal and Social Changes in Racial Integration in the U.S.*, edited by J. Boger and J. Wegner (Chapel Hill: University of North Carolina Press, 1997), 231–70.

30. Rosenbaum, DeLuca, and Tuck, "New Capabilities," 171.

31. Ibid., 169.

32. Some have called for states to mandate metrowide desegregation through boundary decisions and sharing of resources, measures that would remain legally permissible after PICS. See M. C. Hobday, G. Finn, and M. Orfield, "A Missed Opportunity: Minnesota's Failed Experiment with Choice-Based Integration," *William Mitchell Law Review* 35, no. 936 (2009): 936–76.

33. J. Holme and A. Wells, "School Choice beyond District Borders: Lessons for the Reauthorization of NCLB — From Interdistrict Desegregation and Open Enrollment Plans," in *Improving on No Child Left Behind: Getting Education Reform Back on Track*, edited by R. Kahlenberg (New York: Century Foundation, 2008), 198.

34. See W. Taylor, "Title I as an Instrument for Achieving Desegregation and Equal Educational Opportunity," *North Carolina Law Review* 81, no. 4 (2003): 1751–69.

35. G. Sunderman, J. Kim, and G. Orfield, "Does NCLB Provide Meaningful Choices for Students?," in *NCLB Meets School Realities: Lessons from the Field* (Thousand Oaks, CA: Sage, 2005), 39–56; Holme and Wells, "School Choice."

36. J. Lee, "Can Reducing School Segregation Close the Achievement Gap?," in *Lessons in Integration*, edited by E. Frankenberg and G. Orfield (Charlottesville: University of Virginia Press, 2007), 74–97; S. Dillon, "'No Child' Law Is Not Closing Racial Achievement Gap," *New York Times*, 29 April 2009, http://www.nytimes.com/2009/04/29/education/29scores.html?_r=1 (accessed 29 April 2009); see also the Nation's Report Card report(s) at http://nationsreportcard.gov/.

37. See Sunderman, Kim, and Orfield, "Does NCLB Provide Meaningful Choices?"

38. Wells and Crain, *Stepping Over the Color Line*; more generally, see R. L. Linn and K. G. Welner, eds., *Race-Conscious Policies for Assigning Students to Schools: Social Science Research and the Supreme Court Cases* (Washington, DC: National Academy of Education, 2007).

39. Holme and Wells, "School Choice."

40. R. Crain et al., "Finding Niches: Desegregated Students Sixteen Years Later," in *Final Report on the Educational Outcomes of Project Concern, Hartford, Connecticut* (New York: Institute for Urban and Minority Education, Teachers College, Columbia University, ERIC Document Reproduction Service No. ED 396 035, 1992); R. Crain and J. Strauss, *School Desegregation and Black Occupational Attainments: Results from a Long-Term Experiment* (Baltimore: Center for Social Organization of Schools, Johns Hopkins University, 1985).

41. S. E. Eaton, *The Other Boston Busing Story: What's Won and Lost across the Boundary Line* (New Haven, CT: Yale University Press, 2001); E. Frankenberg, *Improving and Expanding Project Choice* (Washington, DC: Poverty Race and Research Action Council, 2007).

42. Rubinowitz and Rosenbaum, *Crossing the Class and Color Lines*, 7.

43. Holme and Wells, "School Choice," 159.

44. For both the housing and school pilot programs, Section 8 waiting lists, low-income housing rosters, or both are likely sources to be targeted for outreach.

45. Using differing eligibility criteria, Minneapolis and Hartford have both had white city students use the interdistrict transfer program. See, e.g., Holme and Wells, "School Choice."

46. See j. powell et al., *K–12 Diversity: Strategies for Diverse and Successful Schools* (Columbus: Kirwan Institute, Ohio State University, 2007).

47. Rubinowitz and Rosenbaum, *Crossing the Class and Color Lines*, 189.

48. Ibid., 67. Another 300 families applied each year but were not deemed eligible for the program.

49. See DeLuca and Rosenbaum, "If Low-Income Blacks," 312.

50. J. Rosenbaum, personal communication, 2 March 2009.

51. Frankenberg, *Improving and Expanding Project Choice*, 35; Holme and Wells, "School Choice," 172.

52. Holme and Wells, "School Choice," 172.

53. Ibid., 173–74.

54. Press release, NAACP Legal Defense and Education Fund, "LDF Announces Settlement Agreement in Hartford School Desegregation Case," 9 April 2008, http://www .naacpldf.org/content.aspx?article_1265.

55. Such duties include providing after-school tutorial programs, SAT prep courses, exam school prep, and student aid workshops. Frankenberg, *Improving and Expanding Project Choice*, 32.

56. Frankenberg, "Splintering School Districts."

57. M. Orfield, "Choice, Equal Protection, and Metropolitan Integration: The Hope of the Minneapolis Desegregation Settlement," *Law and Inequality* 24, no. 2 (2006): 269–352.

58. Some programs also compensate urban districts that face declining enrollment and therefore state funding.

59. Holme and Wells, "School Choice," 167.

60. Ibid., 169–70.

61. M. Finkel and L. Buron, *Study on Section 8 Voucher Success Rates*, vol. 1, *Quantitative Study of Success Rates in Metropolitan Areas* (Cambridge, MA: Abt Associates, 2001).

62. Cited in M. Shroder, "Locational Constraint, Housing Counseling, and Successful Lease-Up," in *Choosing a Better Life? Evaluating the Moving to Opportunity Social Experiment*, edited by J. Goering and J. Feins (Washington, DC: Urban Institute Press, 2003), 69.

63. Rubinowitz and Rosenbaum, *Crossing the Class and Color Lines*, 59–60.

64. Ibid., 59.

65. Of course, these services would be equally helpful for students participating in the housing relocation program. For one such example, see http://www.prrac.org/pdf/ ConnectingFamilies.pdf.

66. E. Frankenberg with G. Siegel-Hawley, *Are Teachers Prepared for America's Diverse*

Schools? Teachers Describe Their Preparation, Resources and Practices for Racially Diverse Schools (Los Angeles: Civil Rights Project/Proyecto Derechos Civiles at UCLA, 2008). See E. Hollins and M. E. Torres-Guzman, "The Preparation of Candidates for Teaching Diverse Student Populations," in *Studying Teacher Education: The Report of AERA Panel on Research and Teacher Education* (Washington, DC: American Educational Research Association, 2005), 477–548.

67. Frankenberg, *Improving and Expanding Project Choice.*

68. Barbara Sard, *CTR on Budget and Policy Priorities—How to Promote Housing Integration and Choice through the Section 8 Voucher Program: Testimony before the National Commission on Fair Housing and Equal Opportunity.*

69. See http://www.dot.gov/affairs/3209.htm (Sustainable Communities) and C. Bellantoni, "'Choice' Neighborhoods to Combat Poverty Cycle," *Washington Times*, 12 May 2009, http://www.washingtontimes.com (accessed 26 August 2009).

70. J. Goering, "Political Origins and Opposition: Comments on Future Research and Housing Policy," in *Choosing a Better Life: Evaluating the Moving to Opportunity Social Experiment*, edited by J. Goering and J. Feins (Washington, DC: Urban Institute Press, 2003), 394–95.

71. E. Frankenberg and C. Q. Le, "The Post–*Parents Involved* Challenge: Confronting Extra-legal Obstacles to Integration," *Ohio State Law Journal* 69 (2008): 1060. See also Smrekar and Goldring essay.

72. Frankenberg, *Improving and Expanding Project Choice.*

73. Aspen Associates, *Minnesota Voluntary Public School Choice, 2005-2006*, report prepared for the Minnesota Department of Education, January 2007.

74. Frankenberg, *Improving and Expanding Project Choice.*

75. Wells and Crain, *Stepping Over the Color Line*; Frankenberg, *Improving and Expanding Project Choice.*

76. The Choice Is Yours program began with 472 students in 2001–2 and had educated 1,977 students by 2006–7.

77. M. Cunningham, personal communication, 6 February 2009.

78. For more information on how we derived these cost estimates, see DeBray-Pelot and Frankenberg, "Federal Legislation." Annual turnover in Section 8 refers to the number of families who do not hold on to their rental vouchers from the previous year.

79. Estimates for associated counseling and administrative costs are from Poverty and Race Research Action Council, *A National Opportunity Voucher Program: A Bridge to Quality, Integrated Education for Low-Income Children* (Washington, DC: PRRAC), http://www.prrac.org/pdf/opportunityvouchers.pdf.

80. Holme and Wells, "School Choice."

81. Ibid., 171.

82. DeBray-Pelot and Frankenberg, "Federal Legislation."

83. Many of these ideas were drawn from Judith Feins's writing about the MTO program in J. D. Feins, "A Cross-Site Analysis of MTO's Locational Impacts," in *Choosing a Better*

Life? Evaluating the Moving to Opportunity Experiment, edited by J. Goering and J. Feins (Washington, DC: Urban Institute Press, 2003), 81–114.

84. DeBray-Pelot and Frankenberg, "Federal Legislation."

85. N. Denton, "The Persistence of Segregation: Links between Residential Segregation and School Segregation," in *In Pursuit of a Dream Deferred: Linking Housing and Education Policy*, edited by j. a. powell, G. Kearney, and V. Kay (New York: Peter Lang, 2001), 89–119.

Linking Housing and School Integration to Growth Management

School desegregation efforts are presently being dismantled. Where they are occurring, they are unlikely to be related to housing desegregation efforts. To the extent that white suburbs are today building affordable housing, this is much more likely to be occurring under growth management law than civil rights law. It is time to renew the civil rights commitment to integration in housing and schools and to link those efforts both to one another and to a growing movement toward growth management or "Smart Growth."

In the early 1970s, federal antisegregation policies for schools and housing tentatively began to move forward together. It seemed possible that these efforts might be bolstered by a "quiet revolution" occurring in state growth management as several states—now almost half the states—have adopted some form of growth management statute. At least three court decisions in this period outline this hopeful moment: (1) *Shannon v. HUD* (1970), a decision outlining the civil rights siting rules for federally subsidized housing; (2) *Keyes v. School District No. 1* (1973), the first city school desegregation case outside the South; and (3) *South Burlington County NAACP v. Mount Laurel* (1975), a state court case interpreting the housing obligation of cities and suburbs in a metropolitan area under New Jersey's general welfare clause. These cases have not been overruled, and they could still serve as a judicial or legislative framework for more racially integrated metropolitan schools and neighborhoods.

Federal Court Victories in the 1970s

In *Shannon v. HUD*, the third circuit declared that building government-sponsored affordable housing in segregated or unstably integrated neighborhoods was prohibited prima facie.[1] The suit was brought by multiracial plaintiffs in a neighborhood of Philadelphia where integration remained fragile. The plaintiffs wanted to remain integrated and believed that building a significant housing project in their neighborhood would cause it to tip or re-segregate. The court agreed, declaring that it was the responsibility of HUD and recipients of federal funds to prioritize the placement of such housing in neighborhoods with strong elementary schools, racially stable housing markets, lots of jobs, and strong, well-financed local governments.[2] The rules that implemented *Shannon* restated these principles but provided loopholes that have been too frequently exploited by central cities and housing developers eager to build low-income housing in segregated or unstably integrated neighborhoods.[3]

In *Keyes v. School District No. 1*, the U.S. Supreme Court declared that housing and school segregation were "reciprocally" related and that school and housing desegregation should be harmonious in order to create stable school and housing integration.[4] Next *Keyes* created a constitutional presumption of segregative intent based on factors[5] that were almost always present in racially segregated school districts.[6] Moreover, it found that a constitutional violation in one part of a local district would support a court-ordered district-wide remedy to judicially redraw the attendance boundaries that had been created by the local school board.[7] While antisegregation advocates found the decision imperfect in many ways, the ubiquitous nature of *Keyes* violations would dramatically, if temporarily, increase racial integration in school districts across the country.

Mount Laurel
Developing Affordable Housing in Suburban Growth

Keyes and *Shannon* interpreted federal law and were national decisions. However, the 1975 decision of the New Jersey Supreme Court in *Southern Burlington County NAACP v. Mount Laurel*, viewed in concert with a sudden wave of state growth management laws in a 10 or more states (and a general welfare clause in nearly every state constitution), almost instantly had doctrinal implications that were national in significance.[8] While its plaintiffs also brought federal civil rights claims, *Mount Laurel*'s importance lies in delineation of the limits of the police powers delegated to local governments with land-use planning powers for zoning in light of the meaning of the state general welfare clause from whence these powers come. While *Mount Laurel*'s remedy was solely class-based, and hence disappointing with respect to race-based integration, it is a tour de force through the minefield of an intricate American system of highly fragmented local government and land-use planning laws, rules, presumptions, and practices. In this hazardous terrain, as will be outlined below, many efforts toward stable metropolitan racial integration have perished.

Several implications of *Mount Laurel* for stable racial integration in housing and schools should be noted. *Mount Laurel* declared that every city, town, or suburb (any local unit of government with land-use planning powers) in a metropolitan region has a constitutional obligation under the state's general welfare clause to provide for its fair share of the region's need for affordable housing—even for housing the very poor.[9] The court found that only communities that had their regional fair share of affordable housing could use zoning powers to exclude it.[10] The power to zone, which had been controversial until the U.S. Supreme Court's decision in *Village of Euclid v. Ambler Realty Co.* (1926), derives from the state constitutional provision to support the general welfare.[11] It is not a plenary power but rather limited by the federal constitution's due process and takings clauses. The New Jersey Supreme court held that if a city had not met its fair share, its grant of zoning power from the state was not sufficient to allow it to exclude affordable housing, and that the power to undertake such exclusion was not delegated, could not be delegated, and hence did not and could not exist.[12] Moreover, each city that had not met its fair share, because of its status as a creature of state law, had a responsibility to use its zoning powers to reduce barriers in its zoning codes, development agreement, and development practices and to adopt inclusionary land-use and housing strategies to meet its fair share and to maintain its fair share as affordable.[13]

Easier said than done, as you might imagine. Though the decision was impressive doctrinally, how do you implement such a thing politically? The New Jersey Supreme Court prodded, and was prodded by, a roiling legislature and wily executive branch for a decade until it refined its decision and caused the passage of the New Jersey Fair Housing Act of 1985.[14] In so doing the court, legislature, and executive—in a fascinating, difficult, and instructive interplay—refined their fair-share analysis and decided that all exclusionary suburbs were not created equal.[15] In a very *Shannon*-like manner, the Court decided—with the concurrence of the other two branches of government—that suburbs with substantial property wealth, lots of entry-level jobs, and good schools should have higher goals than less prosperous suburbs.[16] In so doing, it created a classification system of suburbs and firmly declared that the wealthy prosperous ones should do more and go first.[17] This was not only good policy but sowed the seeds of a new legislative politics of integration. This refinement helped keep older towns and suburbs that were already integrated from resegregating (under the pressure of un-redressed housing discrimination by realtors, banks, and individuals). Meanwhile, the suburbs that had done something but not enough saw that the court and legislature was giving them credit for what they had done and concentrating its civil rights and antiexclusionary fire on opening up the really exclusive affluent suburbs—suburbs that local teachers and policemen could not afford to live in. Many of the older towns and suburbs, which had done their fair share and were hence exempt from *Mount Laurel*'s commands, thought this both eminently fair and, even more important, in the long-term interest of keeping themselves stably integrated. These principles and politics of suburban classification, credit for fair share, and "worst go first" also were involved in the passage by the Commonwealth of Massachusetts of its anti–snob zoning law.[18] They later would help the pro–fair share Minnesota legislative caucus build political support to pass two very strong metropolitan housing integration bills that were vetoed and a more moderate compromise bill that was signed in 1995.[19]

In another downside for integration, the Mount Laurel political and legislative compromise allowed the wealthy suburbs to buy out of half of their obligation and pay the poor cities and suburbs to build low-income housing in their own segregated neighborhood. This provision of the 1985 act was called the regional contribution agreement (RCA).[20] A very clever tactic of the executive branch, it divided *Mount Laurel*'s legislative supporters in the cities and older suburbs.[21] One group believed that the RCA represented a "sellout" to segregationists.[22] Another group in poor cities and suburbs preferred the money in their budget now to integration in the future for their poorest citizens.[23] Civil rights lawyers said that municipalities' use of RCAs violated *Mount Laurel* and the Fair Housing Act.[24] The Supreme Court's budget was held up in the legislature until the courts allowed RCAs to continue. RCA-like tactics are used over and over again in the settlement of court-ordered integration cases to divide the forces of integration. They will be used again if civil rights forces ever gain momentum.

Finally, because *Mount Laurel*'s remedies were based on class rather than race, poor whites (and all too often seniors) managed to live disproportionately in the new affordable housing created in the wealthier suburbs of New Jersey.[25] This is a clear shortcoming of the colorblind *Mount Laurel* approach. It does not seem to have integrated white neighborhoods very well, much less majority-white schools.

And yet the story is not over. It is also important to note that after twenty years, the RCA provision was repealed in 2008 by a coalition of central cities and older suburbs.[26] Now the wealthy suburbs have to undertake to do their full fair share. Further, after twenty years there are thousands of units of affordable housing in communities where there might have otherwise only been single family homes. If this affordable housing were affirmatively marketed to all races—and there is presently evidence that it is not—and if owners or rental agents were prevented by more thoroughgoing civil rights enforcement from discriminating against people of color, this affordable housing might be occupied by a more diverse population in the future.[27] Perhaps most important, *Mount Laurel* and concepts of regional fair share and inclusionary zoning have been very influential throughout the country; almost two dozen states (and hundreds of local governments) have passed growth management acts, inclusionary housing provisions, or both. In places like Montgomery County, Maryland; Portland, Oregon; San Diego, California; and Minnesota's Twin Cities, *Mount Laurel*–like land-use planning provisions, coupled with better than average fair-housing placement of federally subsidized units, and some scattered fair-housing enforcement, have created very significant opportunity for low-income black, Latino, and Asian students to attend high-opportunity schools in the whitest part of suburbia. None of these places are racially integrated utopias, but all show promise and all have lessons to teach.[28]

The *Mount Laurel* decision had begun to articulate a metropolitan local government strategy for housing, with a categorization of suburbs, credit for service, and "worst go first." It was nascent and complicated, and because its remedy was not race-based, it became compartmentalized more into local government and land-use planning circles than in the civil rights arena. Yet the tools it articulated are critical in navigating the complex local government framework and are also necessary in gaining the political support of the older, less affluent suburbs.

It is clearer than ever that opening up the more affluent suburbs is essential to the stable, long-term integration that now exists and is growing in the older suburbs. Too often in ongoing court-ordered school desegregation, a poor black school would be joined to a fragile white school that was already in danger of white flight and resegregation, while the truly affluent suburban municipalities stood outside and above the fray. The interplay of *Keyes* and *Milliken v. Bradley* (1974) caused this recur over and over, like an overloaded truck careening down a highway without a driver. This helped the forces of reaction.

The Political Impediments to the Full Judicial
Enforcement of School Desegregation

On the school education front, the high point of Supreme Court decisions would be *Keyes*.[29] Hubert Humphrey, one of the most outspoken of antisegregationists, was narrowly defeated by Richard Nixon in 1968. Nixon, heretofore a racial moderate, increasingly saw civil rights through the lens of a "southern strategy" framed through the political campaigns of Barry Goldwater and George Wallace. These political leaders built power on the growing resentment in white working-class neighborhoods adjacent to the ghettoes of large cities.[30]

While civil rights strategists had won decisive judicial and legislative victories, the coalitions they had formed were fragile ideologically and politically. They were brilliant victories against unbelievably long odds that won enormous change with a very small infrastructure of support. After the death of Martin Luther King Jr., political divisions deepened in the Democratic Party and within the civil rights movement. No stable, broad-based political coalition remained, ready for the coming backlash or counterattack. No unifying leader held the power to shape strategy and keep coalition partners together. And the foot soldiers of civil rights were fractured between integrationists and those who preferred resources now in poor, segregated communities.

The forces of segregation had been stunned by the progress of civil rights forces in the 1960s. Now they were back on their feet and had a more subtle and effective southern strategy, as well as the political and economic resources to sustain it. Part of the southern strategy was Nixon's promise to appoint "strict constructionist" judges to the federal courts. In practice, this meant that no judges in favor of court-ordered integration would survive the vetting process for appointment. Moreover, while civil rights forces defeated Nixon's first two antiintegration appointments to the Supreme Court, they could not prevent the selection of judges secretly committed to dismantling desegregation who did not have a paper record. New Supreme Court justices began to dismantle school desegregation. There was not yet any housing desegregation to dismantle. A year after *Keyes*, *Milliken v. Bradley* would, by requiring a separate suburban constitutional violation, effectively halt the progress of racial school integration at the borders of cities and their suburbs.[31] While such a showing was made in Louisville,[32] Indianapolis,[33] and Wilmington, Delaware,[34] most civil rights lawyers did not even try to meet the heightened standard. Government and philanthropic funds to bring these cases, never fulsome, dried up;

and the integrationist perspective seemingly shared by multiracial civil rights communities shattered in the face of fatigue, racial separatism, and RCA-like inducement from government and philanthropy to support racially segregated community-development strategies. Integration was increasingly presumed to be too hard, too unrealistic.

Understanding *Milliken* in light of *Shannon* and *Mount Laurel*, and the general principles of law of local government in the United States, are critical to envisioning the way forward. Nearly 70 years before *Milliken*, in *Hunter v. Pittsburgh* (1907), the Supreme Court had declared in no uncertain terms that all local governments were mere administrative conveniences of their states and that vis-à-vis the federal constitution they had no separate and protectable constitutional identity.[35] There was nothing in their charters, debt agreements, or contracts that could for an instant stop the state from abolishing them or reconstituting them at will. They were only the state, and nothing but the state. The clear implication of *Hunter* is that vis-à-vis the U.S. Constitution, if these local governments violated the Constitution, the state violated the Constitution.

The Court's language in *Hunter* bears repeating in light of what the Court would decide in *Milliken* in 1974: "The State . . . at its pleasure may modify or withdraw all [local government], may take without compensation [local government] property, hold it itself, or vest it in other agencies, expand or contract the territorial area, unite the whole or a part of it with another municipality, repeal the charter and destroy the corporation. All this may be done, conditionally or unconditionally, with or without the consent of the citizens, or even against their protest."[36]

With *Keyes* in 1973, the Court had redrawn attendance boundaries within a school district once a violation was found in any part of the district. No principle based on federalism limited the Court's remedial power to redraw the school's attendance boundary once a constitutional violation was found.[37] In 1974, without overruling *Keyes* (much less even mentioning *Hunter*), *Milliken* added a completely new principle to local government law that stands in stark contrast to everything before it.[38] While federalism allowed the redrawing of boundaries *within* an instrumentality of the state—an entity that heretofore has never before been anything but the state—the Court now held that now things are different. Suddenly, the Court found that the state's creation of a boundary *between* districts constituted a barrier to its remedial power not present with respect to the state-created boundary *within* a district.[39] It found that one state-created boundary (the attendance area) is judicially permeable and less important than another state-created boundary (the school district area).[40] It seemed suddenly to overrule *Hunter*, or at least to imply that school districts are something other than creatures of state laws—that they have some cognizable separate status based on rights to local democracy implicit in the Constitution. The Court never says this explicitly, nor does it ever again expand this principle to any other area of local government law. It never cites *Hunter* or explains itself. This sort of distinction is one that raw politics could shape based on expediency. But even polarized legislatures have trouble so cavalierly running roughshod over an established hierarchy of authority—such a long-established way of doing business—like *Hunter*.

The 5-4 *Milliken* decision is held together politically, if not doctrinally, by Justice Potter Stewart's somewhat cryptic concurrence, which suggested that if he could only figure out why housing was segregated in Detroit, he might have gone the other way.[41] While the plaintiff proved such discrimination to the satisfaction of the district court, the Supreme Court considered only the school segregation claims case on appeal. Two years later, in *Hills v. Gautreaux* (1976), a housing integration case, the same Justice Stewart formed part of a 5-4 majority that supported a metropolitan remedy for housing segregation, in significant part because of the metropolitan jurisdiction of HUD and the extraterritorial jurisdiction of the Chicago Public Housing Authority in the Cook County suburbs.[42] The Court found this result to be consistent with the federal Fair Housing Act and *Milliken*, and to be in the interest of building an integrated society.[43] For years civil rights lawyers tried to figure out how to pull this together and considered jurisdiction. The cases suggest the necessity of a metropolitan substate government of some kind to sustain the remedial jurisdiction of a federal court.

After *Gautreaux*, no significant housing integration cases came before the Court. Moreover, in school integration cases, the Court increasingly declared that housing segregation was unrelated to school integration, and that housing segregation it was itself the product of private discrimination for which the government was not culpable.[44] We should be glad that all of these later pronouncements are dicta, or not formally part of the Court's holding. We should fear that these dicta will slide into precedent.

The Failure of Integrative Federal Housing Policy at the Metropolitan Level

HUD rules promulgated in 1974 under the authority of the federal Fair Housing Act (and *Shannon*) prioritize good schools, jobs, and strong, stable neighborhoods and services as the criteria for the placement of affordable housing, but sadly the rule creates so many exceptions that this principle was seldom effectively used to integrate schools.[45] *United States v. Yonkers* (1994) tried to remedy housing and school segregation together. It especially tried to use housing policy in integrating Yonkers schools. Sadly the case was brought in an older, potentially resegregating older suburb. The areas of the remedy were not large enough in a metropolitan sense for the integration to be effective or sustainable.[46] It was easy for whites to avoid Yonkers. *Walker v. HUD* (2001) in Texas has tried to prioritize the remedial placement of housing under the courts' decree in areas with good schools.[47] *Thompson v. HUD* (2006) in Baltimore also hopes to do this.[48]

Policy for siting of HUD-subsidized housing, although conflictual and ambivalent, was at least in principle regulated by civil rights rules and tried to prioritize school integration, albeit imperfectly. These direct-subsidy programs were dramatically diminished, however, by Nixon and then by the Reagan administration. Direct subsidies were replaced in 1986 by a low-income-housing tax credit program administered by the U.S. Department of the Treasury without clear rules for integrating the siting of housing.[49] Today 90 percent of federal housing subsidies, as well as a program that has built more federally subsidized housing than all other forms of federal housing subsidies combined, is administered without civil rights fair-housing rules, much less regard to school integration. If this was not bad enough, Representative Charles Rangel from Harlem successfully added an amendment to the tax-credit law that quietly created a statutory funding preference encouraging the construction of tax-credit units in neighborhoods where more than 20 percent of people live below the poverty line—neighborhoods that almost by definition had completely segregated public schools.[50]

Building Metrowide Coalitions for Smart, Integrative Growth

So how do we revitalize the integration of housing and schools and reconnect these efforts? We have to end the anti-integration litmus test that has been applied to federal judges. We need to strengthen HUD siting rules and clarify the need to prioritize school integration in siting low-income housing. We have to repeal Representative Rangel's prosegregation incentive from the tax-credit statute and clearly subject this program to stronger siting rules. Philanthropy and government need to support civil rights advocates who believe in integration, or at least stop supporting the forces whose vision is of a continuously racially segregated society. All this needs to be embedded in a more racially proactive framework that echoes *Mount Laurel* and is urged on and sustained by state courts and, more important, by state legislatures.

In this light, if we want an integrated society we have to build coalitions in state legislatures and the Congress between central cities and older, fully developed suburbs. Both central cities and these suburbs are being obviously hurt by housing and school segregation. The representatives of both types of places need to realize that there must be an effective metropolitan system of school and housing integration if they are to maintain stable, long-term racial integration. In this light, we need to open up the new suburbs where opportunity is most abundant and stably integrate these housing markets. We have to build democratically accountable metropolitan-level frameworks, agencies, and local governments with authority because they are more just, efficient, and economically and environmentally sustainable; because, as illustrated by the interplay between *Milliken* and *Gautreaux*, once they are in place, no state-created subregional boundaries will limit the remedial jurisdiction of a court that is bound and willing to enforce civil rights law.

NOTES

1. *Shannon v. HUD*, 436 F.2d 809 (3rd Cir. 1970).

2. Ibid.

3. See 24 CFR 941.202.

4. *Keyes v. School District No. 1*, 413 U.S. 189 (1973).

5. Factors such as unusual school attendance–boundary shapes, school capital programs that underutilized high-minority schools and expanded the facilities of whites' schools, and optional transfer policies that let whites out of integrated school assignments.

6. *Keyes v. School District No. 1*, 413 U.S. at 201.

7. Ibid. at 213.

8. *Southern Burlington Township NAACP v. Mt. Laurel*, 67 N.J. 151 (1975).

9. Ibid., 176–91.

10. Ibid., 198.

11. *Village of Euclid v. Ambler Realty Co.*, 272 U.S. 365 (1926).

12. *Southern Burlington Township NAACP v. Mt. Laurel*, 67 N.J. 151, 176–91 (1975).

13. Ibid., 190–91.

14. See *South Burlington County NAACP v. Mount Laurel*, 67 N.J. 151 (1975) and *South Burlington County NAACP v. Mount Laurel*, 92 N.J. 158 (1983); New Jersey Fair Housing Act, N.J. Stat. Ann. 52:27D-301 et seq. (1985).

15. *South Burlington County NAACP v. Mount Laurel*, 92 N.J. 158 (1983); see also D. L.

Kirp, J. Dwyer, and L. Rosenthal, *Our Town: Race, Housing and the Soul of Suburbia* (New Brunswick, NJ: Rutgers University Press, 1995); C. M. Haar, *Suburbs under Siege: Race, Space, and Audacious Judges* (Princeton, NJ: Princeton University Press, 1996).

16. Kirp, Dwyer, and Rosenthal, *Our Town*; Haar, *Suburbs under Siege.*

17. Ibid.

18. Comprehensive Permit Act, Mass. Gen. Laws. ch. 40 B, §§ 20–23 (1969).

19. Livable Communities Act, Minn. Stat 473.254 § 5(9); Myron Orfield, *Metropolitics: A Regional Agenda for Community and Stability* (Washington, DC: Brookings Institution Press, 1997).

20. New Jersey Fair Housing Act, N.J. Stat. Ann. 52:27D-311 (c) (1985).

21. P. Field, J. Gilbert, and M. Wheeler, "Trading the Poor: Intermunicipal Housing Negotiation in New Jersey," *Harvard Negotiation Law Review* 2, no. 1 (1997): 1–33.

22. K. D. Walsh, "RCAs Contrary to the Goals of Regional Equity," *Cascade* 58 (Federal Reserve Bank of New Jersey, Summer 2005), http://www.philadelphiafed.org/community-development/publications/cascade/58/06_rcas-contrary-to-equity-goals.cfm.

23. See, e.g., "Beck, O'Scanlon and Casagrande Call for Reinstatement of Regional Contribution Agreements to Meet COAH Obligations," press release (26 June 2009), http://www.senatenj.com/index.php/district12/beck-oscanlon-and-casagrande-call-for-reinstatement-of-regional-contribution-agreements-to-meet-coah-obligations/3411 (accessed 18 September 2009).

24. In "Re: Approval of Amended Second-Round Plan, Regional Contribution Agreement, and Mediation Report of Galloway Township," N.J. Super. Ct. App. Div. NO. A-1227-06T1 (7 July 2008).

25. N. B. Wish and S. Eisdorfer, "Mount Laurel Housing Symposium: The Impact of Mount Laurel Initiatives: An Analysis of the Characteristics of Applicants and Occupants," 27 *Seton Hall Law Review* 1268 (1997): 1268–1333.

26. Assemb. R. 500, 213th Leg. (N.J. 1998) (enacted).

27. Wish and Eisdorfer, "Mount Laurel Housing Symposium."

28. M. Orfield, "Land Use and Housing Policies to Reduce Concentrated Poverty and Racial Segregation," *Fordham Urban Law Journal* 33 (2006): 101–59.

29. *Keyes v. School District No. 1*, 413 U.S. 189, 191 (1972).

30. Ronald Reagan had employed a similar strategy in California.

31. *Milliken v. Bradley*, 418 U.S. 717 (1974).

32. *Newburg Area Council, Inc. v. Board of Education of Jefferson County*, 510 F.2d 1358 (5th Cir. 1974).

33. *United States v. Board of School Commissioners*, 503 F.2d 86 (7th Cir. 1974).

34. *Buchanan v. Evans*, 423 U.S. 963 (1975).

35. *Hunter v. Pittsburgh*, 207 U.S. 161 (1907).

36. Ibid., at 178.

37. *Keyes v. School District No. 1*, 413 U.S. at 213.

38. *Milliken v. Bradley*, 418 U.S. 717 (1974).

39. Ibid.

40. Ibid.

41. *Milliken v. Bradley*, 418 U.S. 717, 754 (J. Stewart, concurring).

42. *Hills v. Gautreaux*, 425 U.S. 284 (1976).

43. Ibid.

44. See, e.g., *Dowell v. Board of Education*, 778 F.Supp. 1144 (W. D. Oak. 1991); and *Bell v. Board of Education* 683 F.2d 963 (6th Cir. 1982).

45. 24 C.F.R. 570 (1974).

46. *United States v. Yonkers*, 29 F.3d 40 (2nd Cir. 1994).

47. *Walker v. HUD*, 2001 WL 1148109 (N.D. Texas 2001).

48. Plaintiffs' Proposed Remedial Order, *Thompson v. HUD*, No. MJG-95-309 (31 May 2006).

49. 26 C.F.R. § 1.342-9 (1986).

50. See "In Re: Adoption of the 2003 Low Income Housing Tax Credit Allocation Plan," 848 A. 2d 1 (N.J. 2004); and M. Orfield, "Racial Integration and Community Revitalization: Applying the Fair Housing Act to the Low Income Housing Tax Credit," special issue of *Vanderbilt Law Review* 58 (2005).

Conclusion
Returning to First Principles

Working on civil rights usually means sailing against the wind. The wind has been blowing harshly toward the shoals of resegregation for nearly two decades. The social scientists and legal scholars writing in this book tell us that there will be grave consequences if that continues, and that there are ways to reverse course and head back toward the goal of an integrated society. They say this in a period in which segregation has been steadily growing in all parts of the country.

Segregation and inequality are basic parts of the American story and usually have been silently accepted as normal. Although America was founded with massive racial problems due to slavery and the conquest of Indian peoples, only rarely have there been serious governmental initiatives to change these relationships. Separation and stereotypes have been common, and so has the idea that somehow these problems could be put aside. People of color were often separated from the white majority and allowed a limited sphere in which they could have their own institutions with limited resources and not make claims on whites. For two centuries after the first census the United States had 80 to 90 percent white residents, but we are now in the midst of massive racial transformation that will make us a society with no majority group and with profound inequalities if the existing trends continue. It is too big a problem to keep under the rug indefinitely. There have always been critics of the racial structures of society, but usually they are ignored. Their work, however, sets the stage for the big changes that occasionally come. The last coordinated effort at civil rights reform in the United States came in the late 1960s and rested heavily on the advocacy and research of previous decades. Since that time the proportion of minority students in the United States has soared. Latino students have quadrupled as their ethnic group has become the nation's largest minority. Research shows more clearly than ever that segregation is linked to worse educational outcomes. The importance of education has grown for both individuals and communities as low-skill jobs disappear while income and employment become ever more closely linked to unequal education. And yet many civil rights policies have been abandoned. Reconstruction and the civil rights revolution were each followed by decades of severe political reversals of civil rights policies. Attacking racial change and playing on stereotypes and fears have often been effective strategies for gaining political power. We have been living in a politics framed by reaction to the civil rights revolution, with little support for work on racial equity, for most of the past four decades. There has been a widespread view, often embraced by government, that further civil rights efforts were unnecessary or counterproductive. During most of this period, the people heading the civil rights agencies, those appointed to lifetime court appointments—and, sometimes, those chosen to staff the research agencies—have been opposed to civil rights policies and worked to limit or reverse them.

Facing heavy barriers and with limited resources, many groups in the black and Latino communities have turned back to bootstrap efforts within segregated schools, since it seems futile to ask for systemic changes. During these long periods of reaction, researchers and the legal community often follow, rather than challenge, the political tides as research money and rewards flow to the dominant political issues. However, advocates and scholars with deeper understanding and a longer vision, who are willing to forego the rewards that come to those who embrace the government's agenda, can make a difference in broadening the range of issues and strategies under discussion.

That is what this book does; it is about critically examining and challenging a long, slow drift toward resegregation of American education aided and abetted by a transformed Supreme Court and the five presidential terms in which desegregation was disparaged and promises were made about equalizing schools through accountability systems and competition within a system of accepted segregation. This book features important voices, those of scholars who believe the policies are fundamentally mistaken, that resegregated schools are failing, and that there are alternatives that American educators, policy makers, and advocates must consider.

Alternatives to Desegregation

Often in the post–civil rights era, advocates argue that we should pursue other remedies, that desegregation is too hard, and that society is willing to solve problems in other ways. Looking at this period, however, one finds little evidence that that is true. Since educational achievement is strongly linked to family conditions, a major effort to eliminate poverty, increase social supports, and equalize family resources could have been a real help. In the anti-desegregation era, however, we have instead adopted policies such as very large selective tax and program cuts that have made the society more unequal economically than it has been in generations. For families at the bottom, we have dramatically reduced welfare, sharply cut subsidized housing, and instituted cutbacks in social supports. We do not have the universal day care and preschool most industrialized societies provide and do less than any of our competitor nations in lifting families out of poverty. We rely on schools to solve many societal problems by themselves. The Great Recession has made the problems much worse.

In terms of schooling, there have been three main lines of reform. First, the basic strategy of federal educational policy has been to target funds on high-poverty schools, particularly in early grades.[1] At the state level, a second strategy is to equalize state funding through school-funding lawsuits in most states. And third, the basic strategy of No Child Left Behind and similar state laws is to institute mandated standards and testing backed by sanctions for both individuals and schools and their staffs.

There have been lawsuits about funding in virtually every state, and in about half, the plaintiffs have won court orders to change the funding arrangements. Usually, however, these cases have been about equalizing state funding. Many central cities already had more than the state average in educational revenue, but this was still much less than what is required to deal with the higher operational costs in big cities and the greater educational burdens caused by the concentrations of students with special problems in poor urban neighborhoods. Even where the central city schools were overwhelmingly minority and received far more than many suburban districts, as John Boger notes discussing the Hartford metropolitan area in the first chapter of this book, or in Atlanta, where the city schools spent far more than the suburbs for a decade, there is no evidence that these resources were enough to produce equal opportunity—and they certainly have not produced equal outcomes for urban students.[2]

The standards movement has been central to education reform for almost three decades, but achievement gaps have remained virtually unchanged during this period. The United States is the only industrialized nation that has made no progress on its high school graduation rate since the 1970s.[3]

The last major contribution of Congress to desegregated schools came in 1972 with the enactment of federal desegregation assistance legislation (the Emergency School Aid Act), which was designed to help school districts undergoing desegregation not by paying for busing but by financing training of teachers, human relations programs for students and teachers, curriculum development, creation of magnet schools, and other forms of assistance. The program was completely voluntary, and districts competed very actively for the funds. Substantial research showed that these popular programs helped better both race relations and achievement outcomes at the school level. The programs were terminated arbitrarily as part of a giant package of budget cuts in the first year of the Reagan administration, and Congress has done nothing significant to help interracial schools since that time. In fact, the way the accountability system was set up in the No Child Left Behind Act, an interracial school with the same average score is much more likely to be branded as a failing school than a segregated one-race school.

The truth is that desegregation is hard but separate but equal seems to be impossible. If we ignore the inequalities involved in double and triple segregation and punish the students and the schools for its consequences, it is possible to make very bad conditions even worse.

The Obama Administration: Expanding Choice, Weak Civil Rights Policy
Magnet schools with civil rights policies and "controlled choice" policies were developed to try to use choice in a positive way. Central to these policies were desegregation standards. In other words, the magnet schools had explicit goals for integration, recruitment strategies designed to attain them, and, often, a process of holding seats for the underrepresented group. Controlled choice required that all families rank their top preferences among schools and that assignments be made to the highest preference of the families that was compatible with the schools' reaching their desegregation goals. The idea was that choice was a means to the end of desegregation, a way to use educational attractions to accomplish desegregation. All students would be guaranteed free transportation to the schools they wished to attend and desegregation would be substantial so there would be a critical mass of transfer students—no group of students would feel isolated in a school where they were a tiny minority.

Another, fundamentally different theory, saw choice as an end in itself, as a market-like mechanism that would create pressure on schools and lead to their successful reform. In this theory, absolute individual preference was at the center and there were no significant desegregation policy limits. This ideology gave rise to the in the late 1980s. The basic idea was that schools that were not part of the public school systems would be better. Public funds would be given to private entities to operate schools that would be authorized and judged in terms of a charter issued by the state government or other entity authorized by state law. These schools typically had no substantial civil rights mandate and were not required to have an integration plan or goals or, usually, to provide transportation for students who wanted to come. Some were set up to serve students from particular ethnic groups. As the prior choice experiences had suggested, these schools turned out to be highly segregated, even more segregated than the public school systems. They also turned out to show no convincing evidence of better educational success.

Surprisingly, the reform program of the Obama administration virtually ignored segregation, offered no strategies to deal with the rapid resegregation of many suburban communities, and embraced unrestricted choice, expansion of a highly segregated charter school system, and even more pressure on teachers as its basic educational strategies. It has taken advantage of the desperate fiscal condition of many school districts and state governments in the most serious economic reversal in eighty years to impose these approaches across the country by offering funds provided for economic recovery on a competitive basis to school agencies that adopt its preferred strategies. These strategies include establishing many more charter schools, shutting down low-performing schools and using "turnaround" strategies to reconstitute them, holding teachers more accountable for their students' performance, and increasing the number of nonprofessionals entering teaching from good colleges but without training. None of these techniques rested on evidence that they would make significant differences, and some seemed likely to intensify inequality. The policies as a whole entailed a continuation and intensification of the Reagan-Bush model. The strategy was highly praised by conservatives and strongly opposed by a number of major education and civil rights organizations. With the victory of GOP conservatives in the 2010 congressional elections, these trends may be reinforced and funds reduced substantially.

The charter school emphasis is a perfect example. Uncontrolled school choice, known as "freedom of choice" in the South and "open enrollment" in northern cities, had been found to be very ineffective in integrating southern schools because no whites chose to go to historically nonwhite schools, and a handful of black or Latino students often felt isolated and unwelcome when they transferred to all-white schools. In *Green v. County School Board of New Kent County* (1968), the U.S. Supreme Court ruled that this method was not adequate to comply with *Brown v. Board of Education* (1954). In the open-enrollment plans in big cities, whites often transferred out of integrated or racially changing neighborhoods to white areas, undermining integration and speeding resegregation.

The Obama administration followed the precedent of the three prior administrations in supporting the expansion of charter schools. The charter schools developed strong lobbies at the state and federal levels, and the most educationally successful schools received intense publicity suggesting that they offered the solution to educational inequality. The Obama administration's policy was based in part on Chicago's use of charter schools in the city's reforms, since the new secretary of education had directed the Chicago district[4] and appointed leading charter school advocates to top positions in the U.S. Department of Education.

In terms of desegregation policy, the George W. Bush administration had been strongly committed to ending desegregation orders. Its Office of Civil Rights (OCR) within the Department of Education, in the aftermath of the U.S. Supreme Court's decision in *Parents Involved in Community Schools v. Seattle School District No. 1* (*PICS*, 2007), issued strong guidance to school districts to discourage any efforts for desegregation. Civil rights groups expected the Obama administration to activate the enforcement staffs in the Department of Justice and the OCR to reverse the Bush policy guidance; two and a half years into the administration, no new guidance had been issued. While there was an increase in investigations and some limited enforcement, particularly in a Mississippi case where a school district had been quietly permitting transfers that intensified segregation, and some action to enforce the rights of language-minority students, the basic priorities of the administration were promoting choice and enforcing standards on public schools and their teachers. Some Obama administration officials who came out of civil rights backgrounds and civil rights organizations repeatedly pressed them for more leadership.

The Role of Research

This is not like the period following the end of Reconstruction, when virtually the entire academic world abandoned serious research on the issue for decades and even produced works justifying segregation and theories of racial inferiority. The research in this book argues that the issues of segregation have not gone away and no workable alternative to desegregation has been found. It reflects the views of many scholars and lawyers in the country who want to research and write about this issue, even though nothing positive has been done by national leaders during their adult lifetimes. The situation now is quite different from the Jim Crow era, when the imposition of rigid segregation was passively accepted or approved by almost all whites. There is no consensus in the country, or among the white population, that the schools should return to segregation. Even on the Supreme Court, which is now the leading engine of resegregation, a very close division exists with great decisions being made by a single vote, with a majority affirming a compelling interest in integration even while taking away the tools to achieve it. Surveys show that students in integrated schools, including white students, see them as a benefit, not a burden.

Many educators and policy makers have simply accepted these very close decisions by the Supreme Court as virtually irreversible, and they claim they know how to make schools equal that are almost totally segregated by race and class, with profound multidimensional inequalities. But there are intellectuals studying these trends, fighting in the courts, and warning about the consequences. Passive acceptance is alien to the spirit of the civil rights pioneers who faced a 9-0 Supreme Court and proceeded to invent new constitutional arguments and educate the courts and the nation about the realities of racial inequality that had been so covered up and ignored. Against all odds, they won after a half century of struggle. What we need now is something of that spirit. With divisions much closer and strong intellectual resources in the hands of civil rights supporters and institutions, the possibility of serious resistance to resegregation has appeared, for example, in the struggle over the future of the school district in Wake County, North Carolina, when a proposal to end diversity policies triggered large protests and intervention by business leaders.

In our time, there has been no significant funding for basic research on issues of segregation and racial inequality in U.S. schools. Government and most major funders have turned toward other issues, mostly the Reagan-era focus on tests, accountability, and competition. But a very significant group of researchers and lawyers have kept working on race issues anyway. Any lawyer who has tried a case or read trial decisions knows that the racial structure and segregation of our cities was constructed very deliberately over many years, with all kinds of official involvement, and that it does not heal itself merely with the passage of time. In virtually every federal desegregation case outside the South, the courts have found evidence of continuing violations over generations. Researchers, too, have concerns, because looking deeply into any major data set, they see that there are almost always relationships among the racial and ethnic composition of schools, the opportunities these schools provide, and the life chances and outcomes of their graduates. The Supreme Court may block desegregation, and students in many districts have been sent back to segregated neighborhood schools, but research interest has actually been growing, often with little or no support.

This book is aimed at moving the national discussion to the next stage, describing the rapid resegregation, its consequences, and possible alternatives. Some authors try to move the debate over equalizing segregated schools from the issue of equal dollars per student to more fundamental questions such as possible ways to attract and retain more equal teaching staffs. Others explore the possibilities for using the space between the seemingly contradictory provisions of the Supreme Court's PICS decision to look at ways to use geography rather than race in formulas to assign students to schools of choice. Another suggests that language could be used in ways that would produce more integration for Latinos and good magnet schools. Other policies these researchers explore include breaching the city-suburban dividing lines by building sets of regional magnet schools and facilitating housing desegregation or metropolitan arrangements among school districts. Collectively, this book is about concentrating attention on the challenge and stimulating a vigorous, wide-ranging discussion about what may work.

The Supreme Court has created massive barriers for school districts and communities, erecting a wall between city and suburb, pressing judges to end successful desegregation orders, and making a truly senseless effort to limit voluntary positive policies that were designed and supported by local authorities. Even the current Court majority, however, concedes that segregation is a compelling national problem. Rather than giving up, these researchers are searching for ways to mitigate some of the negative effects and to move on toward testing a variety of approaches and ways to use the law to realize the dream of the *Brown* decision. It is very important that legal researchers and litigators use the expanding base of knowledge about segregation and integration to forge new understandings in the legal community and help lay the basis for the next generation of court decisions and legislative and school board policies.

How Social Movements Begin and What We Need Now

During the 1960s, the era of the Warren Court, many came to view the courts and the law as something that inherently protected the rights of minorities and to rely on the courts and agencies of government to continue on that path. The opponents of civil rights never saw it that way. They began an intense and concerted attack on the courts and the legal rules that had transformed the South. Within a single presidential term, Richard Nixon's first, they were able to replace four of the nine justices and bring the expansion of civil rights law to an end, while turning the Department of Justice from a supporter of civil rights groups to their leading enemy. This focused and disciplined drive eventually changed the meaning of the laws and the Constitution, sometimes turning Warren Court decisions on their head. Desegregation proved to be very resilient, actually increasing throughout the Reagan presidency in spite of strong opposition from the Department of Justice and two decades in which Republicans had all the Supreme Court appointees. But, finally, in the 1990s, mandatory desegregation opponents secured a majority of the Supreme Court and withdrew the courts from enforcing desegregation, opening the way for a return to neighborhood schools that would obviously be segregated. With the appointment of Justice Samuel Alito in 2006, the Court had a majority ready to radically reverse precedents and to prohibit even voluntary efforts to intentionally integrate schools, as was evident in the Louisville-Seattle cases the very next year.

The Obama administration inherited a Court hostile to civil rights and policies discouraging voluntary action toward desegregation issued by the Bush administration, but it made no major policy changes in its first two years. The initiative for change will probably have to come from outside the White House and the Congress, perhaps from some of the new lower court judges and administrators who may make rulings and reframe discussion in ways that open up new possibilities. If this is to happen, the work of social scientists and lawyers showing that there is no good alternative to desegregated schools and that there are feasible ways to desegregate will be very important.

The great expansion of civil rights law was a triumph of a massive social movement, won thanks to major political victories as well as the evidence produced in civil rights trials and studies of segregated institutions and de-segregated possibilities. The reversal of school desegregation and other civil rights changes was the triumph of a conservative political and intellectual movement that persisted long enough to reshape the courts and the law and to reframe the country's social vocabulary and political agenda. If there is to be a major progressive change on this and many other issues, there will have to be a change of ideas and of politics. The election of the nation's first black president, Barack Obama, in 2008, did not assure such change, as was evident in the rapid resurgence of conservative power in Congress. Civil rights groups still face the most hostile Supreme Court in several generations, and it was clear even from his presidential campaign that Obama saw a major risk in being identified as a candidate with a minority agenda rather than as a moderate mainstream Democrat who happened to be of mixed racial background. Though Obama will not appoint anti–civil rights officials or judges, it seems unlikely that his administration will produce anything like the bold initiatives of the Kennedy and Johnson administrations, and the current Supreme Court majority may well outlast his presidency.

New movements often take shape in the depths of defeat, as the conservative movement did in the mid-1960s at the high tide of liberalism. We may be at the beginning of a new movement for integration now after all these years of endless reversals and resegregation. A movement starts when a small group of people ignores the prevailing consensus, argues that the status quo is unacceptable, and insistently calls for change. To believe in integration may be difficult in a time when schools everywhere are resegregating. The reality of desegregated schools is complex and often far from the ideal of perfect equity. Everyone who has experienced it knows that it often falls far short of Martin Luther King Jr.'s dream of the "beloved community" and that making it better requires continuous work.

Believing in a great ideal that often falls short is hard. But to believe in separate but equal requires a much more radical leap of faith — it requires believing in something that never was, something that was tried in thousands of communities for two-thirds of a century and never realized anywhere, something that has been endlessly promised in recent decades and never achieved on any scale. One need only look at the failure of Bill Clinton's promise of racial equality in achievement scores and graduation in his Goals 2000 program and the failure of No Child Left Behind to close the racial achievement gap that was supposed to be gone by 2013–14. The truths pointed out in this book are that segregated schools are profoundly unequal, that we still must deal with the issue of the color line, and that the long-term consequences are ever more serious because so many more of our children are nonwhite and there are so many fewer good jobs that do not require some kind of postsecondary education. In many years of research I have never encountered evidence that there ever were separate but equal schools across any significant community with a substantial minority enrollment, though there were a small number of very successful segregated schools, particularly in the period when the black middle class was segregated and black professionals could rarely get jobs outside of segregated black schools, churches, and other institutions providing services to black clients only. I have often asked those who testify for neighborhood schools in civil rights cases to name a community where this has ever happened in a nation of more than 14,000 school districts. No one has done so.

Where Is the Movement Now?

When we look at this entire book and the statistics of spreading segregation since 1990, we have to ask: Where are we? Perhaps we have reached the bottom of this period of reaction. Many civil right leaders and educators have tried to hold their fingers in the dyke, fighting against resegregation, though they have had limited success. It is a good time now to examine what have we learned from this whole experience. We have learned that there are viable solutions that worked well and that many new ideas exist about how to create positive initiatives. But we also learned that those supporting integration of American society face determined and persistent opposition, and that nothing can be taken for granted. Rights have to be earned, not once, but in every generation. The civil rights groups, attorneys, experts, and educational leaders, and citizens who a century ago supported a much harder struggle against much more implacable enemies, often at serious personal risk, never gave up. This generation can do no less.

After nearly two decades of a Supreme Court committed to rolling back civil rights law, civil rights attorneys have not given up. They are thinking about ways in which loopholes can be found in the PICS decision, writing articles attacking the legal reasoning, and thinking about housing strategies that would produce more stable school integration even without any explicit action by the schools. We are a society in which legal strategies and powerful legal reasoning matter greatly. We need thinking with the boldness and intensity of what brought down the apartheid system of the South, which went from complete segregation in 1954 to being the most integrated region of the country for black students by 1970. Neither the constitutional provisions nor the laws that desegregated the South and many places in the North have been repealed, but they have been largely interpreted away. What has been interpreted away can be interpreted back again, though doubtless under some new legal formulations. The authors of this book make important contributions to this process.

There are many levels at which positive action can be taken. Researchers, journalists, educational leaders, and policy makers at all levels need to take a hard look at what is happening in our schools, both public and charter. They will find a striking relationship between segregation and inequality both in critical elements of opportunity and in outcomes, including the probability of finishing high school and being ready for college. If they look at the supposed successes of segregated schools, they will find they are rare and often do not last. Every effort to raise the performance of segregated schools must be supported even while searching for ways to expand integration. They need to have the courage to ask whether they don't need to implement a serious, coordinated effort to give isolated black and Latino students in highly impoverished schools some real way to get access to the better schools in their community and in other nearby communities. They need to look at schools and communities undergoing racial transition and help create coordinated responses to support stable integration and avoid resegregation where possible. Most important, they need to raise the questions that no one has been talking about and introduce the possibility of positive, mutually beneficial solutions. Teacher organizations should be part of this discussion, since teachers are often blamed for the consequences of segregation and resegregation but rarely given serious help in dealing with them.

Congressional civil rights supporters should do two important things. First, they should challenge the Departments of Education and Justice. There are many highly senior congressmen and congresswomen of color, and members from racially changing suburbs sit on key committees. They and their progressive allies should try to make certain that laws are fully and skillfully enforced and that minimizing segregation is included in the nation's education goals. Second, Congress should restore diversity assistance to school districts to help them adapt to the largest demographic changes in the nation's history, much of which is multiracial. This change is taking place in suburbs that need help in creating successful interracial schools and avoiding the kind of resegregation that afflicted city neighborhoods four decades ago. Such funding should also be available to school districts and universities to increase the supply of teachers of color, whose numbers have lagged very far behind the transformation of school enrollment. A diverse teaching force is critical in many ways; every school must have personnel who can relate to parents who do not speak English, or who worry that their children are not being treated fairly in a school where there are few adults of color. Neither of these issues is about busing— they are about suburban stability in a changing society and about developing teachers from all of our communities.

As the authors would readily admit, more experiments and better research are needed to understand how to make interracial schools work in a complex and changing multiracial society. But much is already known and the only way to learn what is needed is to try things, study how they work, and make that information known. Ideally, knowledge alone would drive policy, but we are resegregating due to a political movement that went directly against what researchers believed to be the most effective policy, took control of our courts, and through them interpreted away the rights of millions of segregated students. Beyond the message in these essays that there are better, feasible ways to go I would add another: We've gone far enough backward into our history of segregated education; we know how that story goes. We have to revive the promise of *Brown*. Readers should think about what role they want to play in that process. This is the second time that very hard-won civil rights have been taken away on a grand scale. Those who understand the costs must act.

NOTES

1. J. McPartland and W. Jordan, "Older Students Also Need Major Federal Compensatory Education Resources," in *Hard Work for Good Schools: Facts Not Fads in Title I Reform*, edited by G. Orfield and E. DeBray (Cambridge: Civil Rights Project at Harvard University, 1999), 104–12.

2. See G. Orfield and C. Ashkinaze, *The Closing Door: Conservative Policy and Black Opportunity* (Chicago: University of Chicago Press, 1991), chap. 5.

3. Yet evidence from the National Assessment of Educational Progress shows that the achievement gap between blacks and whites narrowed when desegregation was most widespread. See J. Vigdor and J. Ludwig, "Segregation and the Black-White Test Score Gap," in *Steady Gains and Stalled Progress: Inequality and the Black-White Test Score Gap*, edited by K. Magnuson and J. Waldfogel (New York: Russell Sage Foundation, 2008), 181–211.

4. Chicago was released from its desegregation order in 2009 over objections from the federal government.

Contributors

Courtney Bell is an associate research scientist at the Educational Testing Service. Previously, she was a faculty member at the University of Connecticut. Bell's research interests include the intersection of policy and practice in the areas of parental choice, teaching policy, teacher learning, and the measurement of teaching.

Robert Bifulco is an associate professor of public administration at Syracuse University's Maxwell School of Citizenship and Public Affairs. His research focuses on measuring school performance, whole-school reform, educational resource disparities, charter schools, the effects of school choice on racial segregation, and the effects of racial segregation on long-term student outcomes.

John Charles Boger is dean and the Wade Edwards Distinguished Professor of Law at the University of North Carolina at Chapel Hill School of Law. A former assistant counsel with the NAACP Legal Defense and Educational Fund, Boger has represented parties and *amici* in various school resource and finance cases in Connecticut and North Carolina.

Casey D. Cobb is an associate professor of education policy and director of the Center for Education Policy Analysis in the University of Connecticut's Neag School of Education. His current research interests include policies on school choice, desegregation, and accountability.

Elizabeth DeBray is an associate professor in the Department of Lifelong Education Administration and Policy in the University of Georgia's College of Education. Her current research interests include federal educational policymaking, national education interest group politics, and response to the U.S. Supreme Court's decision in *Parents Involved in Community Schools v. Seattle School District No. 1* (2007).

Sarah L. Diem is an assistant professor in education at the University of Missouri. Her research interests include the role of race and class in education, particularly how current school-desegregation policies are working to ensure diversity in schools without being legally mandated to do so.

Jacquelyn Duran is a graduate student in the Department of Human Development at Teachers College, Columbia University. Previously, Duran was a schoolteacher in Los Angeles.

Erica Frankenberg is an assistant professor in the Department of Education Policy Studies at the Pennsylvania State University and was formerly a senior research associate at the Civil Rights Project/Proyecto Derechos Civiles at the University of California, Los Angeles. Her research focuses on racial desegregation and inequality in K–12 schools and the connections between school segregation and other metropolitan policies.

Patricia Gándara is a professor of education in the Graduate School of Education and Information Sciences at the University of California, Los Angeles, and codirector of the

Civil Rights Project/Proyecto Derechos Civiles. Gándara's research focuses on educational equity and access for low-income and ethnic-minority students, language policy, and the education of youths of Mexican origin.

Ellen Goldring is a professor of educational policy and leadership at Vanderbilt University. Goldring's research interests include school reform, the role of principals in schools and communities, and the effects of parent participation in education. Her scholarly publications include books on equity in urban school districts with magnet school plans.

Willis D. Hawley is a professor emeritus of education and public affairs at the University of Maryland, where he has served as dean of the College of Education. His most recent research deals with the professional development of teachers, the education of teachers (in the United States and Japan), school restructuring and effectiveness, family influences on the academic performance of Southeast Asian children in the United States, and race relations.

Jennifer Jellison Holme is an assistant professor of educational policy and planning in the Department of Educational Administration at the University of Texas at Austin. Holme researches the politics and implementation of educational policy, with a particular emphasis on the relationship between school reform, equity, and diversity in schools.

Eric A. Houck is an associate professor of educational leadership and policy at the University of North Carolina at Chapel Hill. His research interests include school finance and student assignment policies.

Jacqueline Jordan Irvine is Charles Howard Candler Professor of Urban Education in the Division of Educational Studies at Emory University. Irvine's specialization is in multicultural education and urban teacher education, particularly the education of African American students.

Richard D. Kahlenberg is a senior fellow at the Century Foundation, where he writes about education, equal opportunity, and civil rights. Previously, Kahlenberg was a fellow at the Center for National Policy, a visiting associate professor of constitutional law at George Washington University, and a legislative assistant to Senator Charles S. Robb (D-VA).

Chinh Q. Le is the legal director of the Legal Aid Society of the District of Columbia. Between 2001 and 2006, Le was an assistant counsel at the NAACP Legal Defense and Educational Fund, where he litigated civil rights cases related to school desegregation, educational equity, higher education affirmative action, and voting rights.

Katherine Cumings Mansfield is an assistant professor at Virginia Commonwealth University's School of Education. Mansfield's scholarship focuses on the politics of education and the intersections of gender, race, religion, and class identities on educational and vocational access and achievement.

Gary Orfield is a professor of education, law, political science, and urban planning at the University of California, Los Angeles. He cofounded and directed the Harvard Civil Rights Project and now serves as codirector of the Civil Rights Project/Proyecto Derechos Civiles. Orfield's research interests include the study of civil rights, education policy, urban policy, and minority opportunity.

Myron Orfield is a professor of law at the University of Minnesota, the executive director of the Institute on Race and Poverty, and a nonresident senior fellow at the Brookings Institution in Washington, D.C. He teaches and writes in the fields of civil rights, state and local government, state and local finance, land use, regional governance, and the legislative process.

Douglas D. Ready is an assistant professor at Teachers College, Columbia University. His research examines the influence of policies and practices on educational equity and access. In particular, this work focuses on racial, ethnic, and social class disparities in young children's cognitive development.

Sean F. Reardon is an associate professor of education and sociology at Stanford University. Reardon's research focuses broadly on educational policy and inequality. His primary research examines the relative contribution of family, school, and neighborhood environments to racial, ethnic, and socioeconomic achievement disparities.

Lori Rhodes is a doctoral student in the History of Education Program at Stanford University. Her research focuses on how Latino students in the San Francisco Bay Area in the 1960s and 1970s interacted with the education system, creating multiple, overlapping ethnic and racial identities.

Janelle Scott is an assistant professor in the Graduate School of Education and the Department of African American Studies at the University of California, Berkeley. Scott's academic pursuits center on the racial politics of public education, the politics of school choice, and the role of private-sector actors and elites in shaping urban public education policies.

Genevieve Siegel-Hawley is an assistant professor at Virginia Commonwealth University's School of Education. Her research examines the impact of segregation and resegregation in American schools and explores viable policy options for a truly integrated society.

Megan R. Silander is a PhD student in the Leadership, Policy, and Politics Program at Teachers College, Columbia University, where she also is a research assistant at the Consortium for Policy Research in Education.

Claire Smrekar is an associate professor of public policy and education at Vanderbilt University. Her research focuses on the social context of education and education policy, with specific reference to the intersection of desegregation plans and choice policy on families, schools, and neighborhoods.

Amy Stuart Wells is a professor of sociology and education at Teachers College, Columbia University. Her research interests include the sociology of education and critical qualitative policy analysis. Her primary research interest is educational policy pertaining to the politics of race and culture, including school desegregation, school choice, and detracking in racially mixed schools.

Terrenda White is an EdD candidate in the Department of Sociology and Education at Teachers College, Columbia University. She has worked as a research assistant on projects dealing with changing racial demographics, urban gentrification, and suburban segregation.

Sheneka Williams is an assistant professor in the Department of Lifelong Education, Administration, and Policy in the University of Georgia's College of Education. Her research interests include student assignment policies, school governance, and school and community relations.

Index

Federated regionalism. *See* Regions

Finances, school, 16–17, 23–24, 157, 159, 243; and *Sheff*, 23; and *Leandro*, 24; and Supreme Court, 27 (n. 11)

Flinspach, Susan Leigh, 175

Forman, James, 37

Foundations, nonprofit: Bill and Melinda Gates Foundation, 43; Broad Foundation, 43

Fourteenth Amendment, 2, 13, 169, 187

Franchises, school, 42

Frankenberg, Erica, 4, 5–7

"Freedom of choice" plans. *See* Choice, schoolFree-lunch eligibility (FLE), 60, 134, 143, 154, 161, 168, 170–78 passim, 187–88, 191, 196–98, 209–11, 213–14, 216, 219; in Hartford, 16; and child nutrition, 225. *See also* Virginia: Richmond

Freeman v. Pitts (1992), 76, 78, 168, 188–89, 282

Friedman, Milton, 38

Funding of public education, state, 294, 316; in Hartford, 16–17, 23; fairness in, 17; in Charlotte, 23; of private schools, 42; in Kansas City, 65; in Omaha, 153, 158; per-pupil expenditures, 293

Gallup poll, 56

Gautreaux Assisted Housing Program (Chicago), 7, 67, 94, 281–90 passim; and Moving to Opportunity program, 7, 94, 281–90 passim. See also *Hills v. Gautreaux*

Geography: and diversity, 57, 99, 227; and schools, 94; and SES, 180–81, 229–30, 321. *See also* Nodes; Segregation: residential; Zones

Gifford, Bernard, 266

Gintis, Herbert, 37

Globalism, 19

Goldring, Ellen, 6

Governments, local and state, 308; role of, 75

Graduation rates, 55, 83, 177, 316

Grants, 8, 83; and Obama administration, 8; in Connecticut, 15, 28 (n. 11); and Education Cost Sharing (ECS), 28 (n. 11). *See also* Magnet Schools Assistance Program; Race to the Top program; Technical Assistance Program for Student Assignment Plans

Green v. County School Board of New Kent County (1968), 6, 17, 18, 189, 318

Growth management, 302

Grutter v. Bollinger (2003), 7, 57

Hao, Lingxin, 273

Hartford, Connecticut, 5, 14, 15–18, 23, 64–65, 132–33, 138, 142–43, 146, 287–91, 316. *See also* Choice, school: interdistrict plans for

Hawley, Willis, 7

Head Start, 106, 176

Heritage Foundation, 39

Hierarchical linear modeling (HLM), 95, 99

Hills v. Gautreaux (1972), 283, 309, 311

Hispanic Council for Reform and Educational Options (HCREO), 36

Hispanics, 101, 177–78, 197, 201–2. *See also* Latinos

Holder, Eric, 20

Holme, Jennifer Jellison, 285–86, 289

HOPE VI program, 237–38. *See also* Housing

Housing, 58, 66–67, 115, 122, 282, 288, 293, 310; integration in, 66, 122, 289, 307; affordable, 67, 302, 304, 306, 310; and systematic discrimination, 84; in Charlotte, 127–28; and education, 295; direct subsidies for, 310. *See also* HOPE VI program; Segregation: residential; Zoning

Murphy, John, 225. *See also* Wake County, North Carolina

Nashville, Tennessee, 4, 236–37, 347
National Academy of Education (NAE), 5
National Assessment of Educational Progress (NAEP), 5
National Association for the Advancement of Colored People (NAACP), 3; and vouchers, 36, 49 (n. 17); and language, 269
National Board for Professional Teaching Standards, 247
National Center for Education Statistics (NCES), 95, 210, 213–25. *See also* Common Core of Data
National Commission on Fair Housing and Equal Opportunity, 282
National Council for the Accreditation of Teacher Education (NCATE), 261
National Institute of Education (NIE), 67
National Longitudinal Study of Adolescent Health, 220
National School Lunch Program, 21. See also Free-lunch eligibility
"Nation at Risk, A," 39
Neighborhoods: and "home school guarantee" plan, 23; composition of, 57; and low educational opportunity, 59, 103, 115, 171, 179, 219
New Jersey Fair Housing Act of 1985, 304
New School Ventures Fund, 43
Nixon, Richard, 310, 321; and southern strategy, 307
No Child Left Behind (NCLB), 15, 42–43, 61, 64, 81, 285–86, 292, 294, 316–17, 323
Nodes (neighborhood zones), 172, 225–26, 229. *See also* Wake County, North Carolina
Norms, peer, 92
North Carolina Supreme Court, 24; and *Leandro*, 24

Obama, Barack, 20, 84, 85, 128–29; and Race to the Top program, 24, 43; and Investing in Innovation program, 43; and charter schools, 46, 318; and Domestic Policy Council, 85
Obama administration, 8, 24, 43, 45–46, 80, 82, 85, 128, 218–19, 238, 250, 317–19, 322, 328
O'Connor, Sandra Day, 7
Office of Civil Rights (OCR). *See* U.S. Department of Education: Office of Civil Rights
Office of Urban Affairs, 85
Omaha, Nebraska, 151–62 passim
Omaha World Herald, 154–56, 158
Open Choice program, 142–44, 147. *See also* Hartford, Connecticut
Orfield, Gary, 18
Orozco, Carola Suarez, 266
Orozco, Marcelo Suarez, 266
Outcomes, student, 201, 233; and schools, 8, 94, 175, 177, 197; and segregation, 314
Outputs: of educational systems, 33, 243

Pacific Legal Foundation, 169
Parents, 126, 171
Parents Involved in Community Schools (PICS), 1–4, 6, 53, 57–58, 64, 77, 117, 131, 147, 167, 170, 179, 181, 187, 189, 220, 223–24, 229–30, 238, 243, 245, 269, 282, 295, 319, 321, 325
Pedagogy. *See* Culturally Responsive Pedagogy
Peers: and norms, 92; and quality, 93, 145; peer environments, 97, 147; peer effects, 244–47
Performance, student, 15–17, 21. *See also* Achievement, student
Plessy v. Ferguson (1896), 13, 40
Policy: formation of, 3, 34, 316; race-conscious, 13; definition of, 243
Portes, Alejandro, 273

118, 129; and SES, 24, 106; and school choice, 33; and charter schools, 33, 44; in San Francisco, 59; and workforce, 123; and West, 265. *See also* Geography

Separate-but-equal doctrine, 13, 40, 323

Shannon v. HUD (1970), 302–3, 308

Sheff v. O'Neill, 4, 17–18, 23–24, 132–33, 142–43, 146–47. *See also* Wake County, North Carolina

Small-scale geography, 6, 224, 226. *See also* Berkeley Unified School District; Wake County, North Carolina

Smrekar, Claire, 6

Snider, William, 39

Social composition, 92

Socioeconomic status (SES), 3, 6, 59–60, 63, 65, 96, 155, 174, 208–9, 216, 287; in Connecticut, 15; and student performance, 17, 97–99; and voluntary integration, 22, 151, 153, 167–71 passim, 178, 208–9, 211, 219; and segregation, 24; and race, 91, 161, 169, 175, 187; and income equality, 125; and family data, 179–81; and geography, 180, 229; and socioeconomic status–based student assignment (SBSA), 187–99, 201–4, 205 (n. 8), 212, 215, 225; and racial balance, 218–19, 225

Sohoni, Deeneesh, 191

Sotomayor, Sonia, 2, 3, 20, 30 (n. 44), 54, 118, 120, 124

South, 321; and school districts, 17, 30 (n. 44), 54, 65, 118, 120, 124, 282; and "freedom of choice," 37, 318; and charter schools, 44–46; and "twoness" (or double consciousness), 115, 122, 125; and racial apartheid, 115–16, 123, 324

South Burlington County NAACP v. Mount Laurel (1975), 302–6, 308, 311; and regional contribution agreements (RCAs), 305

Standards, educational, 145, 148–49

(nn. 6–8); and standards movement, 33, 39, 168, 316

Statistical methods, 33, 39, 94, 96, 316; and unmeasured attributes, 103, 196; and regression analysis, 137, 139, 141, 145

Stewart, Potter, 309

Stone, Deborah, 19

Strict constructionists, 4, 6, 19, 33, 53–58 passim. See also *Parents Involved in Community Schools*

Student assignment plans: and local school boards, 2; interdistrict, 2, 17, 32–33, 41, 64, 132, 138, 143–44, 152; using SES, 6, 17, 21–22, 173, 176, 215; using race (or RBSA), 6, 20–21, 33, 36, 40, 57–58, 61, 63, 80, 106, 117, 167–69, 174, 181, 187, 192–93, 197–99, 201–4, 211, 215, 223, 225–26, 246; and small-scale geography, 6, 224, 299, 239; resegregative, 14; race-neutral, 14, 21, 58, 65, 69, 131, 147, 161, 167, 171, 176, 181, 223; in Connecticut, 17, 132; in Wake County, 21–22, 36; multifactor diversity index, 49, 228; neighborhood-based, 212–23, 246; and planning areas, 229–30; language-based, 269. *See also* Desegregation; Integration; Socioeconomic status; *Tuttle v. Arlington County School Board*

Suburbs, 33, 41, 47, 64, 137, 139, 144, 152, 161, 284, 292, 304–6

Supreme Court, U.S., 168–69, 267, 281–82; role of, 13, 315, 319–20, 322, 324; and educational opportunity, 18, 20, 117; split, 20, 40, 75; rejection of racial classification, 106, 308. *See also* Courts, federal

Sustainable Communities and Choice Neighborhoods Initiatives, 295

Swann v. Charlotte-Mecklenburg Board of Education (1971), 17, 20–22, 65, 117, 151, 223

Swanstrom, Todd, 153

War on Poverty, 114

Warren, Earl, 19, 26, 321

Washington v. Davis (1976), 14, 16; and discriminatory purpose, 27 (n. 5)

Weir, Margaret, 153, 155, 160

Wells, Amy Stuart, 285–86, 289

White flight, 36, 41, 63

Williams, Polly, 45–46

Wilson, William Julius, 257

Wolman, Harold, 153

Workplace schools, 234; and survey of Fortune 500 companies, 236

Yun, John, 187–88, 192

Zelman v. Simmons-Harris (2002), 41. *See also* Cleveland voucher plan

Zones: and attendance, 58, 77, 144, 191, 193, 197, 223–24, 232; and neighborhoods, 171, 178–79; and workplace, 234. *See also* Emergency School Aid Act of 1972; Neighborhoods

Zoning, 58, 128, 303–4; and student assignment plans, 58, 224, 226; and limited powers of local governments, 303; Massachusetts anti-snob zoning law, 305; inclusionary, 306. See also *Southern Burlington County NAACP v. Mount Laurel*